Wasted by Lakers
Knicks Gain 111-108 Overtime Victory After Trailing by 14

West: 'One of the Toughest Losses I Can Remember'

Graberkewitz' Bat Helps Osteen End Phillies' Streak, 6-1

MESSERSMITH'S RECOVERY SHOT IN ARM FOR ANGELS

SIEBERT THUMBED IN BEANBALL FIGHT

a Good Race

TRACES RISE OF PRO FOOTBALL

SPORTS

Lakers Repeat Their Title Feat

L.A. Wins for Fifth Time in the '80s

Mike Downey

Lakers Are Worthy of Another One

For Thomas, It's Painful Way to Go

Victorious McEnroe Wins Them Over

Leary Beats Braves, 2-1, on 4-Hit Complete Game

Lakers Win...

Forget Critics, He Is Simply Big Champion From Now On

O'Neal, Bryant Lead Surge at the Finish to Beat Pacers

Los Altos Retains Magic, Rallies for 22-15 Victory

It's Bruins vs. the Irish

SPORTS

Lakers Leave Boston Hanging in Rafters

111-100 Victory Ends Decades of Frustration

PURE KAREEM
With the Big Fella Churning, It Was Easy for Lakers to Rise to the Top

Dodgers Make 5 More Errors, Making It Easy for Atlanta, 10-3

Struggling Angels Score a Run; Romanick, Moore Make It Good

SPORTS

Magic's Hook Reels In Celtics, 107-106

His Basket With :02 to Play Gives Lakers 3-1 Advantage

Scott Ostler

Magic Takes It Into His Own Hands

Magic 1-Ups Bird Again in Ongoing Game of 1-on-1

1987 NBA PLAYOFFS

Leary Is Off to New Start in 5-3 Win

Angels' 6-5 Win Is Anything but Pretty

Mike Downey

Is Three Enough Charm for Baylor?

SPORTS

Lakers' Fifth Title Is a Feat of Magic

Johnson Sparks Third-Period Romp That Carries L.A. to 106-93 Win

JIM MURRAY

At Showtime, They Played Real Defense

SCOTT OSTLER

Magic Handcuffs Celtics, and Mystique Disappears

Hendrick Helps Sutton Get Win No. 313, 12-0

All the Dodger Stadium Cheering Is for Lakers

The Lakers

L.A. Gets Overtime...

McKinney Still Listed as Serious but Improved

GAFFED IN THE GARDEN

UCLA Meets Beleaguered ASU in the Also-Ran Bowl

A WHIPPERSNAPPER CO...
Bruce Allen, 23, Is 'Older and Wiser'...

Los Angeles Times
SPORTS

81!
Bryant's record night is stunning but not shocking — he's been working up to this

MARK HEISLER

He's No. 2

NFL PLAYOFFS : CONFERENCE CHAMPIONSHIPS

They're the Big Two in Detroit

BILL PLASCHKE

Big Ben Is Ready for Prime Time

NATIONAL EDITION
SPORTS

Threedom Rings

NBA Finals: Lakers win third consecutive championship over the New Jersey Nets

J.A. ADANDE

Not Much Zen but a Lot of Wins

102ND U.S. OPEN CHAMPIONSHIP

PUBLIC ENEMY
No one is sure what to expect from Bethpage Black, a difficult course made tougher this week

School Transfer Requests Soaring

Los Angeles Times
SPORTS
Friday, May 14, 2004

NBA PLAYOFFS / LAKERS 74, SAN ANTONIO 73

The Fisher Fling

Guard answers Duncan's miracle shot with his own at the buzzer for a 3-2 edge

BILL PLASCHKE

Four Nervous Ticks Add Up to a Laker Moment for All Time

J.A. ADANDE

Spotlight Finally Comes His Way, and He Delivers in the Clutch

Lakers Almost Let a Big One Get Away, but Now They're Back in Control

LOS ANG...
SPO...

NBA PLAYOFFS

Horry Is I...
His latest clutch three-pointer at...

BILL PLASCHKE

Looking for Luck in All Right Places

They'll Settle Things Later

Tough Outing for Nomo

Dodgers Lose More Than Merely a Game

50 AMAZING YEARS

IN THE CITY OF ANGELS

LOS ANGELES LAKERS

50 AMAZING YEARS

IN THE CITY OF ANGELS

FOREWORD BY PHIL JACKSON

PHOTOS FROM GETTY IMAGES
STORIES BY THE LOS ANGELES TIMES SPORTS STAFF

Editor	Narda Zacchino
Design Director	Tom Trapnell
Senior Editors	Dick Rogers
	Karen Chaderjian
Assistant Editor	Gary Metzker
Photo Editors	Jason Sundberg, Getty Images
	Mike Zacchino
Contributor	Scott Ostler
Researchers	Kassandra Zuanich
	Chloe Zuanich
	Shahien Nasiripour
	Rich Pestorich
	Christopher Weills
	Taylor Green

SPECIAL THANKS

Getty Images — Eric Rachlis, *Director, Research, Rights & Clearance*; Kenwood Yow, *Research Manager*
Los Angeles Times — Sean Patrick Reily, *Director, Editorial Business and Planning*
Los Angeles Lakers — Jeanie Buss, *Executive Vice President, Business Operations*; Linda Rambis, *Manager, Special Projects*; Gayle Waller, *Assistant to Phil Jackson*

With appreciation to Dr. Jerry Buss and his children: Johnny, Jimmy, Jeanie, Janie, Joey, and Jesse.

Time Capsule Press LLC
P.O. Box 4395 San Leandro, California 94579
www.timecapsulepress.com

TIME CAPSULE PRESS

President and CEO	Dickson Louie
Publisher and Editor	Narda Zacchino

CONTENTS

FOREWORD: LAKERS' DESTINY

BY PHIL JACKSON

In opening comments over the public-address system at Staples Center, our announcer, Lawrence Tanter, says: "The franchise with the most wins in the history of the NBA." That says it all. A personal note: when I was a high school freshman in North Dakota, one of my classmates did his class speech on his trip to watch the Minneapolis Lakers. It was the 1959-60 school year, and he was a loyal Lakers fan who opposed the Lakers' move to Los Angeles. It was the first time I was aware the Lakers were moving. Now half a century has passed, the Lakers are the heartthrob of Los Angeles, and I've been the lucky one to be chosen to coach this team, now longer than any other coach. A person only has to travel with this team to appreciate the legacy framed by the past five decades of superior basketball. We are supported by the most avid sports fans that any team in any sport has anywhere in the world. This book is dedicated to you.

Almost fifty years ago the Lakers' franchise in Minneapolis was looking to revitalize the team, copying baseball's move to the West Coast. Jet travel was available and ownership changed hands, and as in baseball, two NBA franchises made the move. Before that, Minneapolis was the farthest west any team had ventured. For almost all of the 1960s, the Lakers were denied a chance to win a championship by the Boston Celtics, which won eleven NBA titles around the great center Bill Russell. Fred Schaus was the coach of those L.A. teams, dominated by two of the league's most prolific scorers, Jerry West and Elgin Baylor. It must have been frustrating as each time those Lakers came up with a great season, the Celtics were there to deny them the championship.

One year was a particularly bitter season, 1968-69.

During that summer the Lakers had traded three quality ballplayers for Wilt Chamberlain, the greatest scorer the game had ever seen. Wilt, Baylor, and West presented a package of scorers unrivaled in basketball. Their combined career averages totaled 84.5 points. However, the Boston gremlin showed his colors again. In Game 7, a Don Nelson shot with 1:17 left hit the rim but dropped in to secure a win. The beautiful Forum in Inglewood was packed with fans and the rafters were filled with balloons as Jack Kent Cooke's team came out to fulfill its destiny, only to have many things go wrong. Wilt Chamberlain, who had never fouled out of a NBA game, was in foul trouble. He had to sit for a pivotal part

Kobe Bryant and Phil Jackson bring home the Lakers' 15th title and 10th in Los Angeles in 2009.
Pages 6-7: Photo illustration of NBA trophies representing the Los Angeles Lakers' 10 championships.

of the fourth quarter, and the Celtics were able to wrap up a miraculous playoff run 108-106 for another NBA championship. Those balloons have always been an image those Lakers disdained.

The 1970s dawned and the Lakers lost another chance to break that spell with the Knicks, who won their first championship. That historic year, 1970, witnessed Willis Reed's heroic return to the floor for a Game 7. Willis had been hobbled by an injury in Game 5 and missed Game 6 but got to the floor and gimped around for enough minutes to deny the Lakers another ring. It was as if they were doomed. Bill Sharman, a former USC and Boston Celtics player, was brought in to coach these talented Lakers and they finally succeeded in 1971-72, after winning a record-shattering 33 games in a row. They went up against another New York Knicks team, but this one had lost Willis Reed to knee surgery, and the Lakers won the Finals in five games.

I was a member of those Knicks teams, although I was injured for the first Knicks championship year, and they were quick and very disciplined. Their coach ran a version of the famous triangle offense credited to my assistant, Tex Winter, a teammate of Sharman at USC. The 1971-72 Lakers had a starting five of Wilt, Jerry West, Happy Hairston, Gail Goodrich, and rookie Jim McMillian, who replaced an injured and retired Elgin Baylor. That year was memorable in more ways than one. It must be noted that Elgin missed out on a championship run after those years the Lakers came up short. I should mention other members of that team: Keith Erickson, Pat Riley, Flynn Robinson, Leroy Ellis, John Trapp, and a rookie who has coached with me for seventeen years, Jim Cleamons.

We met up again the next year for another Finals, and this time age was in the Knicks' favor as they beat an injury-prone Lakers team on its last legs. Wilt was nursing a bum knee and Happy Hairston was injured and missed the playoffs. Sharman instituted a new practice in the league, the shoot-around. Bill tells the story that it was purely by accident that he started having the team go over to the arenas during the late morning to shoot the ball and walk through the game strategy. It was something to get Wilt—the Stilt—motivated. It worked and everybody had to copy the Lakers. Bill was a great coach, who had his career shortened by damage to his vocal chords that left him literally speechless in a job that required not only a strong voice but a voice that could be heard above the din of 18,000 fans.

In the mid-1970s, the Lakers were able to secure Kareem Abdul-Jabbar through the astute maneuvering of Sharman, who was about to become general manager. Kareem's presence brought another era of Lakers dominance to the NBA. Jerry West had a stint as head coach and would remain in management for another twenty-some years.

In 1979, Dr. Jerry Buss finally worked out a deal to buy the Lakers from Jack Kent Cooke after a couple of years of working on it. Dr. Buss showed that he was going to be a hands-on owner and stipulated that the Lakers draft Magic Johnson, then a sophomore at the NCAA champion Michigan State. "Showtime" basketball became the motto of this team that raced up and down the NBA court for the decade of the 1980s.

FITTING IN MAGIC

Magic's first year in the NBA was like his name, magic. He brought an enthusiasm to the game that hadn't ever been seen. His joy for basketball was infectious. The 1980 Finals were against the Philadelphia 76ers, with a juggernaut of talent headed by Ju-

1980: Magic leads Lakers' celebration rally outside the Forum (above) and connects with fans while riding in ticker-tape parade in Los Angeles (right).

lius Erving in the Spectrum. Kareem Abdul-Jabbar was rendered inactive for that Game 6 because of a sprained ankle, and Magic played center and scored 42 points, had 15 rebounds, and seven assists, virtually dismantling the Sixers. What a year! That team had a most unusual coaching situation. In preseason, new coach Jack McKinney had a head injury from a biking accident that left him incapable of coaching. An assistant coach, Paul Westhead, did a remarkable job taking that team to a championship. One-plus seasons later the Lakers released Paul and replaced him with Pat Riley, who became the driving leader of the Lakers for the rest of the decade.

Early in the 1981-82 season, the Lakers had struggled to win and find a way to integrate Magic's role as a 6-foot-9 point guard. The remedy was to replace Paul Westhead with a co-coaching choice of Jerry West and Pat Riley. Pat was doing radio broadcasting for the Lakers but did not have coaching experience and Jerry West was working with Bill Sharman as a consultant—remember he had coached the Lakers in the mid-1970s. The Lakers had a press conference and Jerry Buss got up, told the press that the decision had been made to have co-coaches and introduced Jerry West. Jerry got in front of the media and announced that Pat Riley would be the sole head coach. When Chick Hearn, the Lakers' legendary announcer, would tell the story, he would turn to the person next to him and say: "Joe Q Public, if you were standing next to Jerry West he would have handed *you* the job." But things seem to happen for a reason, and Pat assumed the head coaching job with Bill Bertka as his assistant coach and did a remarkable job, winning four more championships in that decade.

There was almost a storybook nature to the great fortune of player after player coming to the Lakers during that decade to replenish age with youth and with older players filling out bench

roles. The first group had Norm Nixon and Jamaal Wilkes help-ing to carry the scoring load with Kareem and Magic, with power players like Mark Landsberger and Kurt Rambis doing the grunt work on defense and the boards. Then the Lakers got the first pick in the draft—James Worthy—a prolific scorer on the block and on the break, and in a trade for Norm Nixon got rookie Byron Scott to refuel their renowned Showtime Break and become a shoot-ing guard next to Magic. The defensive-minded Michael Cooper draping his body around Larry Bird was another image from that era. Older players at the twilight of their careers came to help win those championships, including Bob McAdoo and Mychal Thomp-son, who were most capable of coming off the bench and getting double-figure points.

One cannot mention the 1980s Lakers run without reminding our fans of the great matchups with the Celtics. History wasn't on Boston's side in these series as the Lakers won all but one of their significant battles. The legend of Bird-Magic played out bigger than life and created a lot of NBA fans. The series to remember was in 1985 when L.A. finally broke the jinx and won the title on Boston's floor. The sight of Magic sweeping across the lane for the perfect game-winning hook shot in 1987, the takedown of Kurt Rambis by Kevin McHale in 1984 that put an end to the myth that the Lakers were soft, and the unwarranted treatment of Jack Nicholson by the Boston fans have made those series indelible in the memory of the Laker Nation and given that rivalry a spark that will continue for another twenty years.

In the 1990s, Lakers fans suffered through Magic's sudden ca-reer-ending medical condition and multiple coaching changes, but in 1996 Jerry Buss and Jerry West engineered the sweet move of getting Shaquille O'Neal and Kobe Bryant in off-season deals that paved the way for a new era of great basketball for L.A. It took a

couple of years to season Kobe and acclimate Shaq. I was fortunate to be in a sabbatical year and therefore available to coach when they were ready and able to challenge for an NBA championship.

NEW CENTURY, NEW CHAMPIONS

The century changed, and the Lakers were back on top. Shaq was the MVP, and Kobe, who missed almost the first month of the season, teamed up with him for a dramatic Western Conference Finals win against the Portland Trail Blazers. Even though Kobe had a seriously sprained ankle in the second game of the NBA Fi-nals, the Lakers were capable of beating the Indiana Pacers for the 2000 title. Staples Center had been christened, and another era of dominant Lakers teams emerged. The nucleus of that team other than Shaq/Kobe was Derek Fisher, Robert Horry, Rick Fox, Brian Shaw, Ron Harper, Glen Rice, and a returning A.C. Green.

Lakers fans will never forget the fourth-quarter comeback in Game 7 of the Portland series that gave this Lakers rendition the grit to win three championships in succession, a remarkable feat. With the Lakers down fifteen points just after the start of the fourth quarter, Portland had an attitude that said "We can't be beat." They were wearing out Shaq and our guards on high screen rolls. I called a timeout almost immediately and told the "big fella" that this was the time to get out on screen-roll defense and help the guards stop their man. He did, and we went on a run that overcame the lead. Brian Shaw was instrumental, engineering plays on both offense and defense, but the play everyone remembers is Kobe's pass to Shaq at the rim that turned the tide.

The next season saw the most remarkable finish any team has had in the playoffs since Moses Malone predicted the Sixers would go "Fo, Fo, and Fo" [three four-game sweeps in the playoffs]. His 76ers did take the title in '83, but they lost one of the twelve games needed to win the title. In the 2001 playoffs, we swept through the first three series and ended up losing one overtime game in the Finals to those very same Sixers. This team ended the season with eleven consecutive wins. Couple that with wins in fifteen of sixteen playoff games against the best teams in the NBA, and one would have to admit that this was the most dominant team in modern basketball.

THREE-PEATING IS MOST DIFFICULT

The following season was trying. Everyone was gunning for our crown, but no one was as capable as the Sacramento Kings that year. They had been trouble for us in our first championship year and had added talent. The rivalry had grown to almost grudge level. Their tandem of Vlade Divac, a former Laker, and Chris Webber gave them two great passers and leaders. Mike Bibby was added the year before and had become a real scoring threat. They had three-point shooting European players in Peja Stojakovic and Hedo Turkoglu, with a defensive two-guard, Doug Christie. They had achieved the best Western Conference regular-season record and were no longer intimidated by the Lakers.

After splitting the first set of games in Sacramento, we lost our first game in L.A. The fourth game was a miraculous win. Playing catch-up most of the game, we had a chance to win in the final seconds. Kobe went to the hoop and a ball batted by Divac ended up in Robert Horry's hands with the clock running out. He made the three-point shot, big shot Robert. It gave us life and tied the series at two games all. Each team won on its home court, although both games were disputed at the end. In the fifth game, in Sacramento, referee Jack Nies gave the ball to the Kings in a disputed call. Mike Bibby came off a Webber pick and hit a shot for the lead we couldn't match. In Game 6, the Kings lost both Divac and their backup center, Scot Pollard, to fouls. At the end of the game in a pressing situation Kobe broke through a grasping Bibby, bloodied his nose and was not called for a foul. Tit for Tat!

So Game 7 was going to be a knockdown, drag-out affair. This team was one of the best-focused groups I've had—comparable to the Bulls teams of the 1990s. The pregame situation called for a brunch and a videotape of past games. When I got down to the ballroom at our hotel, the team was already waiting to start our meeting. This team was one where I used a technique called mindfulness, a meditation. They were ready to sit and meditate to get clarity and unity for their effort that afternoon. The game required just that type of focus, and they had it. It was won in overtime. All our players contributed, but the one who stood out that day was Rick Fox. One of the tri-captains, he dogged Stojakovic and had some critical offensive efforts for that three-peating Lakers team. One final note: Fox and Christie still exhibited residual feelings in the next season's exhibition game, were thrown out of the game, and continued the action in a Staples Center hallway. Oh, and Christie's wife got into the fray too. What a rivalry.

In the 2002 Finals, we beat the New Jersey Nets, led by Jason Kidd, in four games. They were game, but no match for Shaq or Kobe. It made this group of Lakers distinguished for winning three championships. People don't understand the level of commitment it takes to grind out a season and then manufacture a title through four playoff series. The players are drained. One championship run is almost like another season in terms of wear on a player's body. Injuries mount and the sheer mental exhaustion is terrific.

We had little left for 2002-03, especially when Shaq missed the first twelve games of the season due to toe surgery. Mitch Kupchak

1982: Lakers' victory parade travels on Broadway in Los Angeles.

had talked with me about how to renew our roster with younger players or older veterans. The five core players during this run turned out to be Shaq, Kobe, Rob Horry, Rick Fox, and Derek Fisher. Gone were Harper, A.C., Glen Rice, and other veterans who had helped us win those first championships. Winning a fourth was not going to happen this season.

We had another chance to win in 2003-04. In the off-season we made deals to acquire Gary Payton and Karl Malone. It was the year that Kobe had to travel back and forth to Colorado for his upcoming trial. We started out winning big, but a knee injury to Karl in December cut short our run for another championship. We played most of the season without Karl, and lost him again in the Finals against the Detroit Pistons. The most memorable moment of that season has to be the remarkable finish in Game 5 vs. the San Antonio Spurs. We had a knockdown, drag-out game that kept turning on each possession. We got the final possession with 0.4 seconds left. Robert Horry had gone to the Spurs that season and knew almost every play we ran for a final shot. We each called a timeout after the teams lined up, and I knew Robert would be hedging toward Kobe. We ran a line and broke the players out and Gary picked out Derek Fisher, who turned and shot in one motion for the victory. Sweet win.

Should we consider the next year of the Lakers' history a glitch? A year without the playoffs—a year that everyone wondered: "How did this happen?" Shaq was gone and the team had seven, eight new members. I was on a hiatus or what I've called a sabbatical. It was late January 2005 when I was in Australia that Jeanie [Buss] called and said: "Come back." There was no chance I was missing out on New Zealand. Biking around the South Island with my brothers or missing the vacation time in Tahiti—actually Bora Bora—an island so nice they named it twice. In fact, I wasn't all that sure I still had

1985: Magic (above) wants to hear from the crowd at the Forum. 1987: Pat Riley (right) stands near the front of a family-filled float in the championship parade.

my chops to coach the Lakers.

I came back and watched March Madness and realized that I really still loved the game. I got to see the Lakers' final game vs. the Portland Trail Blazers, which ended in an overtime loss. It was a tough year for Kobe and Lamar Odom, who came from Miami in the Shaq trade. They played less than half the season together because both had injuries that limited their playing time. First I had to call Kobe and see if he felt we could still work together, and then we went out to get some players that could operate in the triangle system. The Lakers had finished out of the mix and were in the lottery. Jeanie [Buss, Executive VP] flew out to New York and sat in for the pick. We got the tenth pick. [Executive VP] Jimmy Buss wanted me to consider a 17-year-old high school player, Andrew Bynum. I sat with Drew and talked about the responsibility of being a first-round draft pick. The transition to professional athlete is akin to growing up from a boy to a man. He and we would have to hurry that maturation if we were going to win. He became the tenth pick in June, the highest pick the Lakers have had since Eddie Jones in 1994.

AFTER THE "SABBATICAL"

There were a lot of Kobe/Phil dynamics in the run-up to the beginning of the next season, but we both were professional and believed that we could work it out. Kobe had two great seasons, leading the NBA in scoring, and one year scored 81 points vs. Toronto, which set a Lakers record. We had two tough runs in the playoffs against the Suns after average seasons. After 2007, we knew there had to be changes for the team to get back in the top echelon. Kobe became disenchanted with the chances for the NBA Finals and challenged management to trade him. He met with Dr. Buss in Spain during the summer and got a promise from Jerry

that the Lakers would listen to trade offers. The next three months were filled with pressure on management. We were into the last week before the 2007-08 season began without the issue resolved. The cards were on the table, and there wasn't a reasonable offer the Lakers could accept. Dr. Buss said that it was as if he had a rare diamond in his hand and everybody bargaining could offer only semiprecious stones. Kobe took a day or two, swallowed the news, and came into the season as ready to play as anyone could expect after that disappointment. The one thing he had heard was that we were going to improve the talent of our ball team.

We journeyed along the early season of 2007-08 and were happy with Andrew's progress as a player. An early deal was made to get Trevor Ariza for Brian Cook and Maurice Evans. Trevor made an impression on us right away, and I began inserting him in the starting lineup. But injuries would haunt us in January. First Andrew landed on Lamar's foot, injured his patella and damaged the structure of his knee. Then Trevor came up with a fractured foot. We went out on a nine-game trip in late January concerned about surviving this road test to keep pace with the conference leaders. Two games into the trip we traded our rookie Javaris Crittenton and Kwame Brown for Pau Gasol of the Memphis Grizzlies. We had talked about Pau for a year as there had been rumors that he was available. After Drew's injury we needed some help to keep pace. Little did we know how much help we would get from the perfect player for our team.

The trip was a brimming success as we went 7-2, and we then tore through the rest of the year to finish first in the conference. The playoffs seemed to fall before us and we beat Denver in four games and handled Utah in six. The two teams we were worried about went to a seventh game in New Orleans, with San Antonio coming away with the winning combination in the seventh game. That night the

Spurs boarded their jet to come to L.A. for the Western Conference Finals and found the contract with their carrier ran out at midnight and they had to sleep on the plane. It seemed to be our good fortune and their malady as we won the first two games, split on their home court and finished the series on our court in five games.

In the other conference, the Celtics, who were expected to run away with the title, were confronted in their first two series with seven-game sets and with six games in the Eastern Conference Finals. I was leery of the Celtics because their combination of players had us in matchups that didn't favor us. Kevin Garnett was playing exceptional ball, Paul Pierce was their go-to guy in the stretch, and Ray Allen punched that three-point shot better than anyone else we've ever seen. It was their defense that bothered us the most, because they had been able to contain Kobe and keep our system stymied.

Defense turned out to be their winning card, and it was our lack of defense that undid us in Game 4, when we lost a big lead in the second half. It was our only home court loss during that playoff, and it hurt. We extended the series to six games, but that game was a victory march for them from the second quarter on. They celebrated in the second half and the chants of "Beat L.A." had never seemed so loud or obnoxious to me.

Our exit from the locker room took forever and it was 1 a.m. before we even got the bus to get away from their home court. The Celtics' celebration was happening just feet from our bus, and to top that off, we had to drive through the streets of the Back Bay and the motorcycle brigade escorting us drew more attention than it provided protection. Our bus was mobbed by drunken revelers trying to tip the vehicle over and guys jumping on the bumper in front yelling "F--k L.A.—you losers!" The driver had no recourse but to stop the bus and wait until the crowd got tired of taunting us. It was something we did not forget.

The 2008-09 season started and ended as great as a coach could hope for. We started fast and finished strong. Again we suffered a knee injury to Bynum, in almost the same week against the same team as the year before. However, we remained strong and Lamar jumped into the starting lineup, and we continued playing great ball without missing a beat. That injury to Drew happened in Memphis in the second game of a six-game road trip. We continued to New York and Kobe had a blowout game vs. the Knicks, scoring 61 points, and then we went on to Boston to beat the Celtics in overtime, checking their twelve-game winning streak, and finished up in Cleveland, defeating the Cavaliers for their first loss on their home court. It gave the Lakers a sense of being the best.

The season ended with a 65-17 record, the best in the West, but one game off the pace of the Cavaliers. We were pleased, but I told the guys that we would have to improve as a team both defensively and offensively if we were going to be champs. We did! Series after series this team improved its game at both ends of the court and found ways to win the close ones. Utah fell first in five games. During that series my longtime mentor and assistant coach, Tex Winter, suffered a stroke. He was not able to return to Los Angeles to consult or insult (his term) us for the rest of the playoffs. Next we hit a hot Houston team that challenged us to play better basketball. We went to a seventh game with the Rockets and we won big. We came away knowing this had made us more focused and more intense. Little Aaron Brooks went through our defense like a dart and Ron Artest was a thorn in our side. Yao Ming got hurt in the third of those games and the change in their lineup really changed the way they played, which bothered us. No one will forget the fact that Fish was suspended after Game 2 for a shiver he gave Luis

2000, 2001, 2002: Shaquille O'Neal celebrates the title and his Finals' MVP award in 2001 (above), achievements that were duplicated the year before and the year after.

Scola. We'd split our first two games and without Derek in Game 3 we won in Houston, with Jordan Farmar starting and playing a solid game for us. Shannon Brown and Jordan both played a backup role in that series that was crucial for our success.

ON THE WAY TO A 10TH TITLE

The Western Conference Finals vs. the Denver Nuggets was difficult. They came into the series having blasted through their first two opponents, New Orleans and Dallas, in ten games. They were full of confidence, and we had to raise the level of our game to match. We won Game 1. Denver had a chance before Trevor Ariza stole an inbounds pass and sealed the victory for us, but we lost Game 2. On to Denver, tied 1-1 and needing a victory on their court. Game 3 almost ended like Game 1 with Trevor again stealing the ball and racing down court to seal the road victory. They won Game 4 to tie the series, and we came back to L.A. The Lakers seemed to grow in understanding the process needed to get through this. We won successive games to close the series and get to the Finals for our second year in a row.

We all posed for the conference trophy presentation knowing this was not our goal, just a process or stopping point toward winning it all. The East playoffs had been full of dramatic series. The Chicago Bulls challenged the Boston Celtics, who won in seven games. The Philadelphia 76ers had stretched the Orlando Magic in one bracket while in the other bracket the Cleveland Cavaliers had romped through the first two series without a loss. They looked unstoppable. However, the Magic had the answer for the Cavs' success. They absorbed great games by LeBron James and concentrated on shutting down the other contributors from Cleveland. Orlando won in six games, disappointing the pundits and many others by nixing the matchup between James and Bryant.

1988: Magic Johnson and Pat Riley (above) embrace after back-to-back titles. 2009: Phil Jackson (right) is at the center of a champagne shower.

We were very aware of the Magic. We had beaten the Celtics and the Cavs both games during the season, but the Magic had won both times against us. We respected their game and their personnel. Game 1 was all Lakers, but Game 2 the Magic pushed us to the limits. We scored late to tie the game and with just 0.6 seconds on the clock the Orlando team found their guard Courtney Lee open for a layup, which he missed, thankfully.

We won in overtime and headed off for three games in Orlando up two games to zip. Orlando came out in Game 3 and shot better than any other team ever in a Finals game. They were just on fire. Even with them playing terrific ball we had a chance to win late in the game, but they came up with a good defensive play to put us back on our heels. Before Game 4 we had pressed our guys to get focused on the task at hand. Their screen-roll game was difficult to defend, with big Dwight Howard picking our defenders and rolling down the lane and their three-point shooters lining up for a kill. Derek stood before the team prior to going out on the court and reminded them how hard we had worked this year and now was the time. It was the game we desperately wanted to win.

It's strange how things work out. Derek didn't seem able to buy a shot the first half as we fell behind by twelve points at halftime. In the second half we surged back into the game only to have them push back. In the last minute, down by five points, we were able to get back into the game with remarkable plays. One we scored, and next Howard missed two foul shots to give us a chance to tie the game. We took a timeout and went from the backcourt with just nine seconds to play. With the Lakers down by three points I thought they would foul us and give us two foul shots to avoid a three-point shot, so I told Kobe to move the ball ahead if they came to foul him. He did. It went from Kobe to Trevor to Fish, who drib-

bled over halfcourt and hit a three-pointer. His first three-point make of the game. Overtime. He followed that shot with a killer three-pointer in the extra period to give us security and a win that put us up, three games to one. We were in the driver's seat.

Game 5 was a great team game. We broke the game open in the second period with a 16-0 run and although the Magic got back to within five points in the second half they never seemed quite able to challenge us that night. Kobe was terrific and was rightly chosen as the MVP of the Finals, and I've never seen him so happy.

The Lakers were once again at the top of the league with their 15th championship and had won four titles in the decade. My own personal pleasure was winning the 10th title as a coach. My kids handed me a cap with a big Roman numeral X to put on during the presentation of the trophy. My agent, Todd Musburger, had made up this bright gold cap, which had the initials PJ on the back and the years of those championships—nice touch. We celebrated our success, which was particularly great for Kobe and Derek, who had been through good times and bad.

Championship celebrations take on different formats; one time we had our ceremony at the L.A. Department of Water and Power headquarters because City Hall was under renovation. We had taken buses down Figueroa and celebrated at Staples in front of about 250,000 people, but that parking lot was now Nokia Theatre and L.A. LIVE. The best was this year's event at the Coliseum in front of 90,000 fans.

The court was placed on a platform ten feet high at one end of that massive field. We told the fans how it felt and why we had won. At the end, Kobe, after thanking the fans, had the team form a circle and put our hands together and asked the teeming crowd to join us in what we said before every game: "Ring!" The circle will be unbroken—these young men had found a bond that solidified them for life.

Relocated, renamed, and restocked, the Minneapolis Lakers (né Detroit Gems), shown in 1949, were the champions of the NBL and then the NBA. From left, Don Forman, Herman Schaefer, Don Carlson, Don Smith, Tony Jaros, John Jorgensen, Earl Gardner, Arnie Ferrin, Jack Dwan, Jim Pollard, and George Mikan.

Boston Celtics guard Bill Sharman, who would become Los Angeles Lakers coach and general manager, draws attention of Minneapolis Lakers center George Mikan in this game in 1955.

Pages 16-17: In 2000, Los Angelenos poured out for the champion Lakers, surrounding Staples Center after a twelve-year wait.

PROLOGUE: IN THE BEGINNING

BY SCOTT OSTLER

A humbler beginning for a sports franchise would be hard to imagine.

The 1947-48 Minneapolis Lakers were warmed-up leftovers, a reincarnation of the Detroit Gems, who went 4-40 the previous season in the National Basketball League. One quiet night in Detroit, the Gems' paid attendance was six.

In Minneapolis, Sid Hartman, who wrote sports for the *Minneapolis Star Tribune* and also delivered the newspaper, dreamed of running a sports team. Hartman convinced two wealthy local businessmen that pro basketball would be a marvelous gift to their community. They ponied up $15,000 and bought the tarnished Gems.

Instant dynasty—just add water, in the form of Minnesota's 10,000 lakes.

Relocated, renamed, and restocked, the Lakers rose above their lowly roots, winning an NBL championship that first season, and NBA titles in five of the next six seasons.

Hartman was paid $75 a week to run the Lakers from behind the scenes while keeping his day job. Sid, 27, was a triple-threat man—he made the news, wrote it, then flung it onto front porches. Fate smiled on the Lakers early that first season. George Mikan, basketball's reigning superstar, was playing in a new league that folded almost immediately. The NBL held a dispersal draft and the Lakers, thanks to the Gems' ineptitude, had the first pick. They took Mikan, but he was being courted by other leagues.

Mikan flew to Minneapolis. Contract talks stalled and Mikan had a plane to catch. Hartman drove Mikan to the airport, but "accidentally" took a wrong turn, causing him to miss his flight. He stayed overnight and signed with the Lakers the next day.

Mikan, 6 feet 10 and 245 pounds, had been a klutz in high school, and he wore eyeglasses as thick as the Minneapolis phone book. But big George developed himself into a masterful low-post scorer and was quietly ferocious. Bud Grant, a Lakers teammate who later coached the Minnesota Vikings, called Mikan "the greatest competitor I've ever seen or been around in professional sports."

Big No. 99 always got top billing, but the Lakers truly were an ensemble. In '47 Hartman signed star AAU forward Jim Pollard, the Kangaroo Kid. Two seasons later, the Lakers drafted guard Slater (Dugie) Martin and forward Vern Mikkelsen. Those core four Lakers would wind up in the Naismith Memorial Basketball Hall of Fame, along with their young coach, John Kundla.

Pro basketball then was a game that today's NBA fans would scarcely recognize. Dunking was considered unsportsmanlike. There were no assistant coaches. The lane was six feet wide, and the Lakers' home court was several feet narrower than regulation. The 24-second clock didn't exist until 1954.

NBA gyms usually filled with cigarette smoke, and when Syracuse fans learned that the smoke bothered Mikan, they perfumed their arena by puffing cigars en masse.

The league's complexion was lily white until integration in 1950, and for several more years the owners quietly maintained unwritten racial quotas, fearing loss of fans if black players came to dominate.

Outside of league play, the Lakers and the Harlem Globetrotters formed an intense rivalry. Beginning in 1948, the two teams played seven exhibition games over five seasons. The Lakers hoped to validate their claim as the No. 1 pro team, while the Globbies, who made their money clowning, wanted respect for their serious basketball skills. The games drew huge crowds and national interest. The Globetrotters won the first two games, the Lakers took the next five. Game 3 of the series was the Lakers' first-ever televised game.

The mighty Mikan retired after the '53-54 season, only 29 years old but worn down and (he felt) underpaid. Pollard retired a year later. The dynasty had run its course. Home attendance plummeted and in '57 the Lakers were sold to Bob Short, a local trucking magnate.

The Lakers' league-worst record in '57-58 gave them the No. 1 draft pick and they selected Seattle's Elgin Baylor. The 6-5 forward immediately became the league's first black offensive force, introducing the creative inner-city style to the NBA.

Despite Baylor's heroics, the team continued losing money. Short decided a move to Los Angeles was the best hope to save the franchise. An omen, perhaps, that their Midwest era was over: One January night in 1960, the Lakers were flying through a storm when their DC-3 lost its electricity and navigation aids. In the dark, the pilot made an emergency landing in an Iowa cornfield. As the relieved players jumped off the plane, they were greeted by the town's undertaker.

Three months later the NBA owners hastily approved the Lakers' move to Los Angeles, hoping the team would establish a foothold on the West Coast before the upstart ABL could plant its flag.

The Lakers packed up their uniforms and trophies and headed west, leaving behind thirteen seasons of Minnesota memories.

The bitter Lakers-Celtics rivalry intensified with the Lakers' first game in Los Angeles—an exhibition matchup on October 9, 1960. Above, in the 1966 NBA Finals at the Los Angeles Memorial Sports Arena, Elgin Baylor elevates for a shot around the Celtics' Bill Russell. The Lakers went to a Game 7 before losing the Finals.

CHAPTER ONE

Welcome to the City of Angels

Seasons 1960-61 through 1965-66

WERE THE LAKERS eager to move from Minneapolis in 1960? Guard Hot Rod Hundley and forward Rudy LaRusso, inspired as gold-rush 49ers, hopped in their cars and raced across country to Hollywood. They stopped in Las Vegas long enough to play one hand of blackjack, win $400, and celebrate by jumping fully dressed into a hotel pool. Then they sped across the desert, arriving in Los Angeles as the sun was rising over a new era of pro basketball.

The Lakers represented the future of the NBA.

The new Los Angeles Memorial Sports Arena was the league's first modern venue—goodbye gyms and armories. Elgin Baylor was one of the NBA's first African American superstars, and he and rookie Jerry West forged a dynamic new style in a league that had been known more for busted teeth than broken scoring records. Under first-year Coach Fred Schaus, the Lakers were one of the first sports teams on which blacks and whites roomed together on the road.

It was the birth of Showtime. Doris Day sat courtside. James Garner and Pat Boone were regulars. At a playoff game relocated to the Shrine Auditorium, home of the Academy Awards, a Detroit Pistons player tumbled into the orchestra pit. Broadcaster Chick Hearn, the only man who could talk as fast as the Lakers played, had new fans glued to their radios.

Along with the instant L.A. style, there emerged a collective heart and soul. In a land with no lakes, the Lakers were home.

—Scott Ostler

Remember Those Early Lakers Days?

Prompted by the Lakers' long-awaited NBA championship victory over the Boston Celtics on June 9, 1985, the daughter of former general manager Lou Mohs wrote a letter recalling when her father brought the Lakers from Minneapolis to Los Angeles twenty-five years earlier.

By JIM MURRAY
June 28, 1985

The letter opened a window on a memory.

Dear Mr. Murray, it began.

In reflecting on yesterday's stupendous Lakers' victory, I felt compelled to write you "in remembrance of things past," of my father, Lou Mohs, and for the sake of my mother, Alice, who is alive with such memories of the Lakers' early days.

I remember so well coming out to Los Angeles with the Minneapolis Lakers . . . Bob Short, the owner, had sent my Dad out with the team and a debt of $300,000 with the order, "Call me for anything but money."

That very first year was lean. My Mom recalls, quite happily, how our family bought the first basketballs, how Mom washed the team jerseys at home, how we all sat up late at night after home games, counting ticket stubs, how the young players, out before their families arrived, would come over for home cooking.

The team in the early '60s was a family nucleus with all the wives and children gathering for holiday parties while the team was on the road. At each home game, everyone involved sat in one corner area of the old Sports Arena and silently prayed, not necessarily for the team but watching the counter mark for each fan's arrival. Once it had marked 4,000, we knew we had made it into the black for the game—and sometimes that was a struggle.

But with marvelous players, the likes of Baylor and West, and with LaRusso, Selvy, Hawkins, Felix, Hundley, Schaus, along

LOS ANGELES TO GET NBA FRANCHISE IN '61

Los Angeles Times, January 23, 1960

PHILADELPHIA, Jan. 22 (AP)—Los Angeles will be granted a franchise in the National Basketball Assn. possibly next season but definitely in 1961-62, the Associated Press learned today.

Although league officials denied such a move was discussed, it was brought up informally in meeting yesterday.

Los Angeles will be given a new franchise outright or one of the other franchises will be transferred to the West Coast city, probably to the Los Angeles Jets, a group headed by Vito J. Guarino, stepfather of Len Corbosiero, sports film executive.

A source close to the situation told the Associated Press two owners are blocking expansion to Los Angeles. He declined to name them, however.

The source said also that Ben Kerner, owner of the St. Louis Hawks, who is on the NBA expansion committee, had promised to go to bat for the Los Angeles Jets.

Kerner was quoted also as saying "With Jets flying on a regular schedule coast to coast there is no reason they (Los Angeles) shouldn't be in the league right now."

The Minneapolis Lakers' franchise might be moved to Los Angeles since the club had not been drawing too well recently. But Lakers owner Bob Short asserted today: "I'm not here to move my franchise. I'm not bankrupt and I want to stay in Minneapolis. But if I can't make a go of it then I'll have to consider a move."

NBA Eyes Warrior-Laker Game as New L.A. Test

Los Angeles Times, January 31, 1960

It appears that the National Basketball Assn. desires another Los Angeles plebiscite in regard to granting or moving another franchise to this area.

The NBA owners will witness with more than cursory interest the attendance figure for tomorrow night's league game between the Philadelphia Warriors and the Minneapolis Lakers at Sports Arena.

At a recent meeting the NBA tossed cold water on Los Angeles' aspirations for a franchise this year although rumors were prevalent that Minneapolis might move here by the 1960-61 season.

Response Ignored

The fact that the St. Louis Hawks - Philadelphia Warriors' game drew in excess of 12,000 fans at the Sports Arena last Sept. 30 while competing with the Dodger-Brave play-off game was apparently overlooked by the NBA moguls.

Los Angeles has been given the friendly stall by NBA president Maurice Podoloff since 1954. At that time Podoloff was quoted as saying:

"The NBA is keenly interested in extending its operation to the West Coast in the next few years. Los Angeles—third largest city in the nation—is missing one of the top thrills in all sports through lack of adequate facilities to house big league,

professional basketball."

Los Angeles has the facilities now in the 13,500 (approximate basketball capacity) Sports Arena, but what is the definition of a "few years."

Anyway, tomorrow night's game is a wonderful attraction, pitting the 7-ft. Wilt (The Stilt) Chamberlain of the Warriors against Minneapolis' slick sophomore, Elgin Baylor.

The Warriors and Lakers clash in San Francisco this afternoon in a league encounter. Both clubs are expected to arrive here late tonight.

Proceeds from tomorrow night's game will benefit the Salesian Fathers' youth activity program on the East Side. —MAL FLORENCE

NBA Officials Delay Lakers Shift to L.A.

Los Angeles Times, February 26, 1960

PHILADELPHIA, Feb. 25 (UPI) — Directors of the National Basketball Assn. today discussed but delayed a decision on a proposal by the Minneapolis Lakers to shift their franchise to another city.

Lakers' president Bob Short sought to move to Los Angeles, but Pittsburgh and Baltimore also have cropped up as potential transfer sites.

Short said his request to move was not turned down and that he was told to "explore all possibilities" and return to the next meeting

of the NBA, which most likely will be held during the April 11 draft session in New York. Short has been losing money at Minneapolis the last three seasons.

Chicago Out in '60

The directors agreed that there will be no team operating out of Chicago for the 1960-61 season. Max Winter, who holds the franchise, said through David Trager, his representative, that it would be unwise to start operations in Chicago next season "in view of all conditions now prevailing." One of the conditions was believed to involve available dates.

LAKERS' SHIFT TO L.A. OKAYED

BY MAL FLORENCE

Los Angeles has gone "big league" again with the announcement that the Minneapolis Lakers have been granted approval by the National Basketball Assn. to move their franchise here next season.

The Rams established residence here in 1946, the Dodgers went into business in 1958 and now the Lakers.

When Minneapolis owner Robert E. Short came to terms with the Coliseum Commission Tuesday on rental and playing dates, the official announcement was almost a foregone conclusion.

The OK came from New York where the NBA board of governors unanimously approved the shift

yesterday "providing a satisfactory schedule can be drawn."

The board slated meetings in New York May 9 and May 16 to consider schedule problems.

However, Short and Maurice Podoloff, president of the NBA, were confident that a schedule would be worked out to the satisfaction of the other seven teams in the league.

Short turned over to the league more than 70 available home dates of which 28 will be in the 14,500-capacity Sports Arena and a few at the Los Angeles State gym (5,200).

The Lakers also plan to play some "home" games in San Francisco next season in order that rival teams

Please Turn to Pg. 5, Col. 4

LAKERS' L.A. SHIFT OK'D

Continued from First Page

can play a two-game series on each western swing.

Since the Lakers have exclusive use of the Sports Arena, it is believed that the Los Angeles Jets, recently granted a franchise in the new American Basketball League, will not compete against the Los Angeles entry of the NBA.

Lakers Here Before

Whether the ABL will ever begin operation without Los Angeles as a "key" city remains to be seen.

The Coliseum Commission threw its support behind the Lakers when it telegramed the NBA urging the group to support the move.

Los Angeles fans had the opportunity of seeing the Lakers play three league games in the Sports Arena last season. Elgin Baylor, Hot Rod Hundley and Co drew 22,307 customers for the three contests.

Short said that if a similar average can be maintained next season it will be sufficient to support the Lakers who have been losing money steadily in Minneapolis.

In Baylor, the former Seattle U All-American, the Lakers boast one of the greatest stars in the game. Elgin is a magnificent shooter, play-

maker and rebounder. He holds the NBA single game scoring record of 64 points

Hundley, the colorful ex-West Virginia collegian, became a favorite here with his driving, slashing type of play. Tom Hawkins (Notre Dame), Rudy LaRusso (Dartmouth) and Frank Selvy (Furman) were also favorites.

West Drafted

In addition the Lakers have drafted Jerry West, a two-time All-American at West Virginia. West played here in the Los Angeles Basketball Classic last December.

However, the Lakers have lacked that big man and have had to give way to opponents on the boards. This accounts for Minneapolis league showing in recent years.

The Lakers finished third in the Western Division last season and second in 1959 beating St. Louis in a playoff series the latter year before bowing to Boston in the championship final.

Dominated League

Between 1948-1955 the Lakers dominated the NBA winning six world titles. Those were the days of the great George Mikan, Jim Pollard (the present coach) and Vern Mikkelsen.

Minneapolis drew its nick-

name from the many lakes that abound in Minnesota Does the Laker tag fit in Los Angeles? Only time will tell

Laker Move Natural, Regrettable—Mikan

MINNEAPOLIS, April 27 (AP)—George Mikan, one of the stars who built the Lakers to greatness in Minneapolis, said tonight the move of the professional basketball team to Los Angeles "feels like part of us is leaving."

Mikan, now an attorney here, agreed with Laker coach Jim Pollard that the move is a natural in view of Los Angeles' reputation as a growing population center and a good sports town.

Pollard, who said he hasn't discussed a coaching contract with the Lakers management in connection with the move, said he thinks the players will enjoy it.

"It's a good sports town. They've proved it in baseball and football," Pollard said. He said the youthful team is probably at the best stage to make a move since not many have close ties with Minneapolis.

SHIFTS TO L.A. — Elgin Baylor is outstanding player for Minneapolis Lakers who will move here this year. Shift was unanimously approved by NBA.

Los Angeles Times,
April 28, 1960

Lakers Open Drills Today

Sixteen players, eight of them returning veterans, are expected to report to new coach Fred Schaus today when the Los Angeles Lakers open basketball drills this afternoon at Pepperdine College.

Heading the list of returnees will be Elgin Baylor, one of the National Basketball Assn.'s outstanding performers.

Other veterans who will report for the twice-daily practice sessions are Rudy LaRusso, Tom Hawkins, Hot Rod Hundley, Frank Selvy, Bob Leonard, Ray Felix and Jim Krebs.

Among the new candidates will be John Werhas and Jim Hanna, former SC stars; Sterling Forbes, Pepperdine; Bobby Goodall, Tulsa; Barry Brown, Stanford, and Howard Joliff, Ohio U.

Los Angeles Times,
September 12, 1960

---

with the voice of Chick Hearn, L.A. soon learned to love the Lakers.

With the memory of so many almost-wons against the Celtics... it was with such pleasure to see this year's team blow away the ghost of the past. Do you remember those days?

—*Martha Mohs Higgins*

Dear Martha:

Do I remember those years?! Better than last year...

I hate to brag, Martha, but I was one of the only writers west of the Pecos writing on pro basketball in those days. I know I was the only columnist. Even in New York, the citadel of basketball, the journalistic heavyweights like Red Smith, Jimmy Cannon, and Dick Young pretty much ignored basketball.

In order to draw in those days, pro basketball had to schedule doubleheaders with the Harlem Globetrotters. I remember, I went to the Sports Arena one Sunday afternoon in the first few months I was writing a column, and the Lakers were playing a playoff game against the St. Louis Hawks—and the "crowd" on the Sports Arena counter was 2,400. They get that to watch them practice today.

Your Dad told me Wilt Chamberlain was making $15,000 a year in those seasons, and that was also what they paid Jerry West.

You bet, I remember Lou Mohs and Fred Schaus and Hot Rod and Elg and all the guys. I learned more basketball in one trip with those guys than I have since. The game kind of passed me by when they stopped having three-to-make-two,

and something called the "loose ball foul" came into being. We didn't have any fancy-schmancy rules about "loose ball fouls." You got a foul, you went to the line in those days.

We used to go on trips in quaking, asthmatic old planes, one of which had plowed up a cornfield in a blizzard with the Lakers one night, and often, the little two-engine wheezer would be occupied by both Lakers and Knicks en route to a doubleheader in Syracuse or Kankakee...

I like to think we all kind of washed jerseys for the Lakers in those days, Martha. But you and I and Chick Hearn and Jerry West and Elgin are the only ones around who remember it. Thanks for bringing it up.

—*Sincerely, Jim Murray*

1960-61

L.A. Warms to Lakers in Exhibition Debut

Season Record

W36–L43 (.456)
Division: 2nd
West Finals

Coach

Fred Schaus

Players

Elgin Baylor

Jerry West

Rudy LaRusso

Hot Rod Hundley

Frank Selvy

Tom Hawkins

Jim Krebs

Ray Felix

Slick Leonard

Howie Jolliff

Gary Alcorn

Ron Johnson

There was great anticipation among the respectable crowd of 7,000 that turned out for the exhibition debut of the new Los Angeles Lakers on October 9, 1960, at the Los Angeles Memorial Sports Arena. The team included Elgin Baylor, one of the country's best players, who earned All-NBA First-Team and Western Division All-Star Team honors the previous season. Despite impressive performances by Baylor and rookie Jerry West, the team lost, 106-101, to their rivals, the Boston Celtics.

By MEL ZIKES
October 10, 1960

The Lakers lost their first home exhibition game in their new Los Angeles uniforms, but it looks as though Southern California basketball fans have some new heroes.

Boston's Celtics were the villains, beating the Lakers, 106-101, before 7,507 people in the Sports Arena, but it didn't take Southland fans long to decide the Lakers belonged.

The fans were rather cool in the early going, seemingly withholding their feelings until they got a look at Los Angeles' newfound National Basketball Assn. entry.

About halfway through the second quarter the fans warmed up, cheering the Lakers for good plays, giving the Celts a hard time on occasions and sometimes even giving the officials a hard time.

Hot Rod Hundley, aggressive Elgin Baylor and Jumping Jerry West of the Lakers found a home real fast. Bill Russell, Bob Cousy and Jim Loscutoff of the Celtics proved too much for the Lakers to handle. However, the young Lakers showed promise of being one of the NBA powers in the coming season.

Russell tallied 15 points and Cousy added 17, both of them coming through in the crucial moments. Loscutoff, long the "Mack the Knife" in the rough going for the Celts, broke up all kinds of L.A. plays under the baskets before fouling out early in the last quarter.

Baylor, everyone's All-American while playing at Seattle U, again was the Lakers' big man as he took team- and game-scoring laurels with 30 points.

The clowning Hundley established himself. The Hot Rod wasn't at his scoring best, but his playmaking kept the Celts loose and his ball-handling furnished delighted moments to the fans.

West, the rookie who came to Los Angeles from West Virginia by way of the Olympic Games, is in far better condition than most of the rest of the pros and showed he will be in line for rookie-of-the-year laurels this season.

His 16-point effort was second only to Baylor for the Lakers, and he proved a leaping demon on the defensive boards as well.

The game could have gone either way until the waning moments when the overeager Lakers, most notably West and Hundley, were caught fouling, and the Celtics scored seven of their last nine points via free throws.

POSTSCRIPT

The first season in Los Angeles had its upbeat moments for the Lakers, who rose in the playoffs after finishing 15 games behind the first-place St. Louis Hawks in the Western Division standings. The Lakers defeated Detroit in the first round, then pushed the Hawks to the limit in the Western Division Finals before losing in Game 7. The Lakers even had a chance to seal that series in Game 6 at the Sports Arena, but lost in overtime, 114-113, on March 29, 1961.

Tom Hawkins (20), at right, floats back for a shot as the Hawks' Larry Foust (14) tries to cut him off during Game 6 of the Western Division Finals.

Baylor Raises the NBA Standard Again With 71 Points

A wire-service account of Elgin Baylor's record-setting game made clear that even the New York Knickerbockers fans in Madison Square Garden appreciated the performance of the Lakers' star.

From THE ASSOCIATED PRESS
November 15, 1960

NEW YORK—Elgin Baylor set an NBA single-game scoring record Tuesday night with 71 points as the Lakers defeated the New York Knickerbockers, 123-108.

In the first game of a doubleheader at Madison Square Garden, the Detroit Pistons edged the Boston Celtics in overtime, 115-114. The Celtics blew a 20-point lead in the game.

Baylor's total broke the NBA record of 64 points he had set against Boston on Nov. 8, 1959, at Minneapolis. Against the Knickerbockers, he scored 34 points in the first half for a Garden record. His 15 field goals in that first half were also a record.

The 6-foot-5 star with a remarkable wrist, which enabled him to give the ball a corkscrew twist on his shots, had the crowd in an uproar throughout the second half. Every time the Lakers would get the ball there would be a chant: "Give it to Baylor." When he was taken out of the game with 28 seconds remaining, he was given a standing ovation by the 10,132 fans.

The Knicks made a game of it in the first half despite Baylor's heroics. They tied the score twice early in the second period and even took an eight-point lead late in the quarter.

Baylor scored on 28 of 48 shots and 15 of 19 free throws in compiling his record total. The 28 field goals is also a NBA record. It eclipsed the mark of 27, set by Joe Fulks of the Philadelphia Warriors on Feb. 10, 1949, against Indianapolis.

Detroit and Los Angeles will clash in Los Angeles on national TV next Saturday morning.

POSTSCRIPT

In an interview with Art Ryon for the *Los Angeles Times* the day after his record-breaking game, Baylor said he did not feel "particularly hot" before the game, but "During the warm up, I didn't miss a shot. That has happened before, but this time, it just continued during the game."

Elgin Baylor, shown in 1960, had a 55-point game in the 1958-59 season and a 64-point game in 1959-60 before his record game at Madison Square Garden.

He talked about his disappointment in the low fan turnout at the Los Angeles Sports Arena and, perhaps thinking about the cheering he received the night before from York fans, observed that "You'd be surprised what a big crowd of local rooters can do for a team."

1960-61 Season Highlights

The Lakers move to Los Angeles after 12 seasons and five championships in Minneapolis. The team is coming off a 25-50 season in which it had lost in the Western Division Finals.

Before becoming the first player drafted by the Los Angeles Lakers, West Virginia's Jerry West wins a gold medal as a member of the U.S. basketball team in the 1960 Rome Olympics.

With the clock showing 54 seconds left, Elgin Baylor scores a basket for his 68th and 69th points during his 71-point performance against the Knickerbockers.

Elgin Baylor averages an all-time franchise-high 34.8 points (for an injury-free season), ranking second overall in the NBA.

Baylor also leads the team in rebounding (19.8 average) and assists (5.1). He is selected to the All-NBA First Team.

Chick Hearn, who came to Los Angeles in 1956, broadcasts the fifth game of the Western Division Finals, launching his 42-year career as the Lakers' play-by-play announcer.

The Lakers lose their first three regular-season games before recording their first victory, 120-118, over the New York Knickerbockers at the Sports Arena.

1961-62

Blood on the Floor

Season Record

W54-L26 (.675)
Division: 1st
NBA Finals

Coach

Fred Schaus

Players

Elgin Baylor

Jerry West

Rudy LaRusso

Frank Selvy

Jim Krebs

Tom Hawkins

Hot Rod Hundley

Ray Felix

Howie Jolliff

Wayne Yates

Bob McNeill

Bobby Smith

The Lakers-Celtics rivalry doesn't always play itself out under the basket, outside the key, or in a championship series. Sometimes it feels more like the Friday night fights.

By JIM MURRAY
February 20, 1962

The game was barely a minute old when a funny thing happened to Rudy LaRusso on his way to the basket. He dropped the ball.

The next thing he knew, Boston's Bob Cousy, one of the least clumsy men in the league, was trying to help him pick it up. For once, Cousy was all thumbs—and some of them Rudy seemed to think were trying to find his eye. Rudy promptly called up his own reserves—elbows. The ball lay forgotten as he used them to probe for cavities in Cousy's mouth and, finding none, to try to induce a few.

That's when Cousy struck a fighting stance and the Celtics-Lakers basketball game Sunday changed from a bare-knees ballet to a bare-knuckle brawl. Fans who had just tuned in Chick Hearn's broadcast thought they had stumbled on the Golden Gloves by mistake.

Cousy threw a left that indicated he has a lot of work to do before he's ready for Floyd Patterson, and LaRusso, seeing he could probably handle Cousy with one hand, thoughtfully picked up the ball with the other and started a jab. After all, he did not want the Celtics running up 14 points while he outpointed Cousy.

That's when Tom Heinsohn made his bid for a concussion. He shot across the door, suddenly remembering he had been assigned LaRusso in the game, and he sneaked over a crazy right that caught the Lakers forward behind the ear. It was not a good punch and not a good idea. As the old Confucian saying goes, "If you shoot at a king, be sure you kill him."

Heinsohn only made LaRusso—and the Lakers—mad. There was still 10:06 of the first period

to be played when—in a melee under the Lakers' basket—the whistle blew and the dust cleared and Heinsohn was sprawled face-down on the floor. The Celts didn't know it then, but their star shooter had been TKO'd.

He got up gamely and staggered back to a congress of flying elbows. LaRusso accidentally slammed him into the iron pipes under the basket. I say "accidentally" because Rudy really intended to knock him out onto Santa Barbara Avenue but the pipes broke his fall. By the end of the period, Heinsohn's left eye had been almost closed, and he looked as if he had just gone seven rounds with a good left-hooker. By the middle of the second period he was sitting on the bench with an ice pack on his jaw. By halftime, he was in Daniel Freeman Hospital. It was a good thing. The way things were going, by the end of the game he could have been in Forest Lawn. If he had jumped into Elgin Baylor once more, the city's undertakers would have started scouring for their extra-large stock in caskets.

The Celts' coach, Arnold (Red) Auerbach . . . got in the act by pouncing on an errant photographer and dribbling him out of bounds. It was the first old-fashioned two-handed dribble I have seen in a long time. The thing that bugged Red was that the photographer was minding his own business and if there's one thing Auerbach can't stand when he's losing a basketball game, it's someone who's standing there, minding his own business . . .

I have seen Pro Bowl games that were tamer. Basketball normally is an athletic contest where the trainer brings a Band-Aid and some dental floss. It is supposed to be as polite as bird-watching. They even play it in wheelchairs, which is lucky because, if the Celts and Lakers don't lay those elbows down, they may find that's the way they'll have to play it.

The grudge between the Lakers and the Celtics is as genuine as a husband-and-wife fight.

"They're arrogant," Lakers Coach Fred Schaus says bitterly. "Why, when he's introduced, Bill Russell *walks* on court . . . They think they're the New York Yankees and Notre Dame rolled up into one."

The heat of the Lakers-Celtics rivalry in the 1962 Finals has continued through the years. Tempers have flared in many seasons, including the 1984 Finals (left) when Larry Bird and Kareem Abdul-Jabbar faced off.

In the dressing room, the Celts' Auerbach has his teeth bared too. A man who has been pelted with eggs in St. Louis, with fines by the league, he has the unique achievement of making L.A. basketball fans finally behave like basketball fans. For the first time since the Lakers came to town, the Sports Arena looked like a crowd at the Roman Colosseum who had come to root for the lions. They pasted Auerbach with peanuts and epithets, blew horns in his ears, and hooted Heinsohn all the way to the hospital as he staggered out, clutching ice to his swollen jaw.

There's nothing like a little blood on the floor to bring out people in the worst way—and vice versa. It's not the way Dr. Naismith intended it—or Dr. Schweitzer either. But that prototype of the sports fan—Nero—would have loved it. So would Mickey Spillane.

Baylor Gets 61 points as Lakers Beat Celtics in Game 5 of Finals

Other players got more assists and more rebounds, but no one approached Elgin Baylor's 61 points in Game 5 of the Finals, one of five NBA playoff records he shattered in this game. Even the fans in Boston saluted his achievement. It gave the Lakers an edge in the series, but they would eventually fall to the Celtics in a Game 7 overtime.

By MEL ZIKES
April 15, 1962

BOSTON—It took a record performance for the Los Angeles Lakers to beat the Celtics here Saturday night, 126-121, and Elgin Baylor was up to it.

Boston fans, 13,909 of them, normally not the friendliest in the world when it comes to visiting teams, were singing the praises of Baylor after he poured in 61 points in this "crucial" fifth game of the NBA Finals.

That 61 points wiped out Bob Pettit's four-year standard of 50 points set here in Boston Garden when his St. Louis Hawks were beating the Celtics in the sixth and final game of the 1958 championships.

Baylor's effort could mean the crown for Los Angeles.

The Saturday win gave the Lakers a 3-2 lead in the best-of-seven series.

Now the scene switches across country to the Los Angeles Sports Arena for the sixth game Monday night.

The seventh game, if necessary, will be back in Boston Wednesday night.

"We'll win it now. We've got 'em back home now. When we get home Sunday night we're moving the whole team into a hotel, going into hiding. This way we're sure of being rested," said smiling Lakers Coach Fred Schaus after the game.

The Lakers' dressing room was bedlam after the victory.

But a few minutes before there were no smiles.

The Lakers, with Baylor and Jerry West furnishing the momentum, tied the score at 112-112 on West's jumper with 5:51 left in the game.

The next 4 minutes 39 seconds saw the score tied twice and the lead change hands three times before Baylor's 15-foot jump shot put the Lakers out front for the last time with 1:22 left.

West ended up the Lakers' second-leading scorer with 26 points.

Tommy Heinsohn led the Celtics with 30. Sam Jones and Bill Russell each had 26 points.

Russell led all rebounders with 20. This is the department in which Baylor, in addition to his points, makes the big difference when he is rested.

Even with Baylor pulling in 22 rebounds and Rudy LaRusso 12, the Lakers could not beat Boston in rebounding, ending up on the short end of a 74-67 count.

Boston's incomparable Bob Cousy paced everyone in assists with 10. The Lakers had only 14 in all, five of those by Frank Selvy.

Big Jim Krebs, doing about as good a job on Russell as can be expected of anyone, continued his hustling, inspiring play for the fired-up Lakers.

Baylor, rebounding like a demon and scoring on unbelievable off-balance shots, was the dominant figure in the first half, even though the Lakers were trailing at intermission, 68-66.

Elgin scored 18 points in the first quarter, at the end of which the Lakers led for the first time in the game, 31-30. He added another 15 points in the second quarter to give him 33 for the half. All that and he was playing with one eye on the officials—he drew his third foul late in the opening quarter.

Heinsohn's 18 points represented the Celtics' top production in the first half.

Boston hit 50% from the court in the first half; the Lakers 41%.

Baylor shattered four other NBA playoff records:

—46 field goals attempted, game (Pettit, former record, 34)

—25 field goals attempted, one half (Pettit, 20)

—22 field goals made, game (Pettit, 19)

—33 points scored, one half (Pettit and Joe Fulks, 29).

The Lakers also tied the mark of 40 free throws by one team, set by Boston vs. St. Louis in 1958.

Despite Baylor's 13 points in the third quarter, which brought him to 41, the Celtics still held a 99-93 lead at the end of the stanza.

West came to life in the last quarter, joining Baylor on the firing line as Zeke scored half of his 26 points. Baylor potted 15 in the fourth quarter, his 13th putting them ahead for good, 118-117, and he added two free throws right after that with 54 seconds remaining.

Sam Jones thrilled the home crowd with two jumpers in the final seconds.

1961-62 Season Highlights

The Lakers win their first Western Division championship in Los Angeles in their second season since moving from Minneapolis.

Elgin Baylor, Jerry West (44, at left), and Frank Selvy (next page) are chosen for the All-Star Game. Rudy LaRusso is also selected but doesn't play because he's injured.

Elgin Baylor, shown here in Game 1 of the 1962 Finals, averaged 38.6 points per game in the playoffs that year, slightly more than he did in the regular season, but it wasn't enough.

Baylor averages 38.3 points a game, but plays in only 48 regular-season games because of military service. West averages 30.8 points.

Wilt Chamberlain's 78 points against the Lakers on December 8, 1961, makes a list of Chick Hearn's most memorable games.

The Lakers lose to the Boston Celtics in Game 7 of the NBA Finals, 110-107, in overtime.

1962-63

No Place Like Home – Lakers Triumph

Season Record

W53-L27 (.663)
Division: 1st
NBA Finals

Coach

Fred Schaus

Players

Elgin Baylor

Jerry West

Dick Barnett

Rudy LaRusso

Frank Selvy

Jim Krebs

Leroy Ellis

Hot Rod Hundley

Gene Wiley

Ron Horn

Howie Jolliff

The fans did their vocal best to give the Lakers a home-court advantage in Game 7 of the Western Division Finals against the St. Louis Hawks. Did it make a difference? Well, let's just say it didn't hurt. The more they cheered, the more the team gave them something to cheer about. This victory sent the Lakers into their second consecutive NBA Finals matchup against the Boston Celtics. The rivalry was intense, even then. As the Lakers prepared to depart for Boston, the Los Angeles Times observed that "there is much bitterness between the clubs and it even extends to the coaches . . . The Lakers feel the Celtics have ruled long enough, while the Celtics consider the Lakers upstarts." Unfortunately for L.A. fans, the Lakers came up short for the second straight year. In 1962 the team forced Boston into a seventh-game overtime contest. The Celtics ultimately squeezed out a 110-107 victory. In 1963 the Lakers managed just two wins.

By DAN HAFNER
April 12, 1963

The Lakers, with midnight about to strike them out of the National Basketball Assn. playoffs, cut loose with a vengeance Thursday night and sent the St. Louis Hawks flying into oblivion. Elgin Baylor, Jerry West and their hustling teammates delighted 14,864 screaming Sports Arena fans by saving their best performance for last as they ran out this lengthy Western Division Finals with a well-deserved 115-100 victory.

A sparkling defense, which included ball-hawking that has been missing for many weeks, all-out hustle and enough sharpshooting to turn back every Hawks threat, sent Fred Schaus' crew into the NBA Finals against the Boston Celtics. This is the battle pro basketball fans have been looking for since the season opened, and it'll get underway in Boston Sunday night.

The major difference in Thursday's game was that Los Angeles had its one-two punch of Baylor and West, but St. Louis didn't.

Although Bob Pettit played his usual brilliant game, scoring 31 points, Cliff Hagan, the 6-foot-4 veteran who prolonged the seven-game series with his spectacular play, managed only two points.

Schaus opened with Baylor on Hagan and the Lakers' ace, who still found time to score 31 points, held the hot-shooting Hawk to two points.

With Rudy LaRusso doing a workmanlike job on Pettit, this defense made it possible for the Lakers to take charge of the game.

They went in front after six minutes of seesaw action and never looked back. When the Hawks tried to make a run in the third period, first West, playing his best game since being hurt, then Baylor bombed them out of all chance.

An action-packed first half in which both sides played brilliantly in stages wound up with the Lakers on top, 57-50.

It seemed like old times with LaRusso playing one of his finest games and Dick Barnett, not exactly impressive in some of the other games, coming through with a 13-point second period that kept Los Angeles in command.

Pettit, who never rested a minute in the Hawks' all-out effort to score an upset, carried the big load, scoring 18 of the St. Louis points.

Baylor, who held Hagan to a single field goal for 14 minutes, also found time to lead the Lakers in scoring with 15.

Both teams hit their first shots, and for the first torrid six minutes were even. But right after the halfway point, LaRusso came through with six points and L.A. forged in front.

West and Frank Selvy chipped in with points to make it 30-24 at the end of the first quarter.

In the second period, the Hawks moved within two points several times. But once Barnett made up his mind to start firing his sensational jumper, the Lakers were back on the beam.

They went 11 in front at one point, but Pettit fooled Ellis for a couple of baskets to cut the margin at intermission to seven.

Rudy LaRusso, shown here against St. Louis during the regular season, found his touch against the Hawks in the Western Division Finals, averaging 13.3 points and 10.7 rebounds

Lakers' Frustration in Finals Continues

Another fine season, winning their second consecutive division title, and another loss to the Celtics in the Finals. It's bad enough that the Celtics walked all over the Lakers. So powerful was the rival that not even an injury to the relentless Bob Cousy was enough to give the Lakers a leg up. By game's end, the other shoe dropped.

By JIM MURRAY
April 26, 1963

At approximately 10 minutes before 10 p.m. on the floor of the Los Angeles Sports Arena, a massive shoe was poised in the air in the vicinity of the L.A. Lakers basketball match. It hovered for a brief second or two then crashed to the floor with a foundation-stunning impact as if the U.S.S. Missouri had run aground again . . .

The Stomper, Lakers Coach Fred Schaus, permitted himself the luxury of a small but fervent oath. After 80 games of the season, 13 playoff games, endless miles of the implacable boredom of DC-3 charter flights, long struggles up runways with 100 pounds of luggage, botched-up reservations at 4 o'clock in the morning in Fort Wayne and rain running down your neck from a leak in a Chicago dressing room, the Boston Celtics, to the possible surprise of a Kurdistan sheepherder and a guy who has been at sea for two years, had again won the basketball championship of the whole world.

Schaus tried to concentrate on the few remaining minutes of the lost cause, but it was a miasma of three-point fouls, jump balls, confusion and heartache. The Celts had the game so safely won that Tom Sanders stopped fouling Elgin Baylor for the time being, and Bill Russell politely stepped aside and let the Lakers make a layup or two to bring down the point spread . . .

Freddy Schaus would rather beat the Celtics than be president, but it begins to appear as if he might as well aspire to climb the Matterhorn in high heels. This is not a team, it's a dynasty.

There was a brief moment of hope when Bob Cousy sank to the floor midway in the fourth quarter, clutching his ankle and writhing in pain, and there was some chance you might get someone in there who considered it just a game and not a holy war . . .

The Celts won because they had Cousy playing with demonical fury. They also had Russell, the only man I know who seems to grow two more sets of arms when he gets back under his own basket. Russell is the world's best basketball player, but he could have been history's greatest pickpocket if his mother hadn't instilled a proper set of values. Any man who can separate a man from a basketball in full view of 15,521 spectators, including two referees and a man from the State Department, and not even draw a one-shot foul could stand on dry land and pick the pocket of a man at sea. I swear Russell could scratch his knee with one hand, screw in a light bulb with another and sign an autograph at the same time. He could get an elephant out of a circus tent without causing an alarm.

In the last analysis, though, you beat the Lakers by holding Elgin Baylor under 40 points, and Baylor was held under 30 by a boy who hero-worships him so much he has to spend the first five minutes trying to keep from asking for his autograph . . .

"Elgin Baylor has always been my idol as a cornerman," polite, quiet Tom Sanders, who answers to the inelegant name of "Satch," was saying softly as he screwed in his contact lenses to go out and trade elbows with his idol.

In the game that followed, he acted more as if Elgin owed him money. Satch Sanders stayed so close to Elg, they looked like two guys trying to get on the same bike. They would have needed only a table for one in a restaurant . . . Satch was all over Elg like a lovesick grizzly, so much so that Schaus finally moved his star to the backcourt which is like making Red Grange a linebacker. Satch's eyes aren't too good so he took no chances with Elg. He made sure he could feel him. He knows every bump on Elg's back. He should; he put a few of them there.

They're giving a parade and a banquet for Bob Cousy somewhere in Worcester some time this weekend. But somebody, somewhere in that end of the country should stake Tom Sanders to a trolley ride and a bowl of chili, at least. You see, if he didn't have this high regard for Elg Baylor, they might be throwing the party at this end of the country and it would be Red Auerbach's mouth that would have to be washed out with soap instead of champagne.

1962-63 Season Highlights

Jerry West ranks sixth in NBA scoring average with 27.1 points per game.

Elgin Baylor (22) ranks second in NBA scoring average (34.0), fifth in total assists (386) and fifth in rebounding average (14.3).

Rudy LaRusso, Baylor, and West play in the All-Star Game at the Sports Arena.

Elgin Baylor (22) powers to the hoop as the Celtics' Bill Russell holds his
ground in the deciding Game 6 of the 1963 Finals at the Sports Arena.

1963-64

Lakers Win in Final Second of Playoff Matchup

Season Record

W42-L38 (.525)
Division: 3rd
West Semis

Coach

Fred Schaus

Players

Jerry West

Elgin Baylor

Dick Barnett

Rudy LaRusso

Leroy Ellis

Frank Selvy

Don Nelson

Jim Krebs

Gene Wiley

Jim King

Hub Reed

Mel Gibson

Jerry West earned the nickname "Mr. Clutch" for his ability to make a shot in a pivotal situation, but in Game 3 of the 1964 playoffs against the St. Louis Hawks, it was Elgin Baylor who kept the Lakers alive. With one second left on the clock, the game tied, and the Hawks leading the best-of-five series, two games to none, Baylor sent the ball up and through the hoop, driving the fans into a wild frenzy.

By DAN HAFNER
March 26, 1964

Although 11,728 highly partisan fans died a thousand deaths, the Lakers, on Elgin Baylor's 22-foot jump shot in the final second, stayed alive in the Western Division semifinal playoffs Wednesday night by scoring a 107-105 victory over the fighting St. Louis Hawks.

The fantastic finish, which sent the clubs into a fourth game to be played at the Sports Arena Saturday night, came after an unbelievable last 39 seconds in which the Lakers not only blew a three-point lead, but, in an amazingly charitable act, gave the Hawks a chance to go to the front.

When it was all over, the fans refused to leave. For several minutes they just stood around stamped their feet and screamed.

"This might be just what we needed," said Coach Fred Schaus, who saw his club assume an 11-point margin with less than five minutes to play, then almost blow it all. "There have been many times this season when we have lost them just like this."

Then, facetiously, he added: "Those were two nice plays we made just before the finish."

The embattled Lakers head man was referring to the gruesome five seconds after Zelmo Beaty managed to hit only one of three free throws to cut the lead to 105-103.

Dick Barnett tossed in to Leroy Ellis after the charity toss. Ellis flipped the ball to St. Louis' Mike Farmer and he banked it in. That tied it, but the worst was yet to come.

Ellis took the ball out and there were 34 seconds remaining. As Schaus commented later, the center should never pass the ball in bounds against a press, but he did.

Barnett grabbed the toss in, but stepped on the line and St. Louis had the ball. . . . Chico Vaughn, who hit a 35-footer during the Hawks' amazing rush, took the shot, it was partly deflected and the hustling Baylor grabbed the free ball.

With 11 seconds left Los Angeles took time out. The Lakers' plan was to get Baylor on a one-on-one situation. They did, but Baylor couldn't get free. He jumped back and flipped his jumper, which swished through just before bedlam broke loose.

It was the climax to a magnificent Baylor performance in which he scored 23 points, grabbed off 16 rebounds and made 11 assists.

But the other half of the Lakers' one-two punch, Jerry West, made it possible with one of the finest shooting performances of his career.

After hearing for several days how well Richie Guerin had handled him while the Hawks were winning the first two battles, Zeke from Cabin Creek went on a rampage, winding up with 39 points.

Barnett, inserted as a starter to pep up the attack, did just that, pouring in 24 points and was especially sharp in the last period when the Lakers zoomed to their 11-point edge.

The Lakers, running for their lives, opened [the game] strong, and with Barnett and West on target, soared to a 16-point lead in nine minutes.

But give the Hawks credit. They are a tremendous team. Although Cliff Hagan was unable to keep away from Baylor and Rudy LaRusso was keeping Bob Pettit in check, the Hawks fought back into contention.

Ten back at intermission, they were only five back at the three-quarter mark and battling tenaciously.

Barnett's sharpshooting made it an 11-point margin with exactly 4:56 left on the clock.

Then the real fun began.

Elgin Baylor, shown here winding through the Celtics in October of 1963, demonstrated his ability to make big shots in Game 3 of the Western Division Semifinals against the St. Louis Hawks.

It's Over for Lakers in First Round

There was little for fans to crow about in the 1963-64 season. The Lakers led the NBA in free-throw percentage (.766) and managed to win forty-two games against thirty-eight losses, enough to get them into the playoffs. But the season came to a disappointing close in the Western Division Semifinals when the St. Louis Hawks dispatched the Lakers handily at the end of a five-game series.

By DAN HAFNER
March 31, 1964

ST. LOUIS—The explosion that rocked Kiel Auditorium Monday night sent the sizzling St Louis Hawks on a rocket to San Francisco.

The battling Hawks, bouncing back from two losses in Los Angeles, went on a pair of tremendous scoring sprees to put 9,574 partisans in an uproar as they knocked off the Lakers, 121-108, in the final game of the best-of-five series.

Little Lenny Wilkens triggered the explosions and once more stole the Lakers blind with a performance that earned a standing ovation from the throng when he departed the Western Division semifinal playoff game.

The 6-foot-1 backcourt star set a personal all-time high of 30 points, and he and his mates made the fact that Elgin Baylor became the leading scorer in playoff history a matter of little solace to the downhearted Lakers.

A season that began miserably when Baylor's ailing knees turned out to be of a serious nature wound up that way when the Hawks put on one of the finest shooting performances this observer has ever seen.

A run of eight straight right after the start of the game—the first two by that man, Wilkens—put the Lakers in an early hole, but it was a burst of fastbreak buckets in the middle of the third quarter that really did in the Lakers.

Although Jerry West ran into foul trouble and was rendered useless on defense for the last one-third of the game, Coach Fred Schaus refused to alibi.

"They just outplayed us," he said quietly. "Especially, they outshot us."

Indeed, the Hawks excelled in all departments. They shot exactly 50%, took over complete control of the backboards in the second half and had far more assists because of a blistering fastbreak.

Baylor poured in 28 points and now, in six years of playoff play, has 2,146 points, five more than George Mikan, the old Minneapolis Laker. But Bob Pettit, brilliant on the boards and able to score just enough to prevent the Lakers from going on a spree, will soon pass him.

The Hawks open a best-of-seven series in San Francisco Wednesday night, and the 6-9 veteran needs only 101 points to take over the lead.

While the Hawks won all the glory, Frank (Pops) Selvy closed out his pro career with a fine effort. Selvy's quick hands and hustle helped the Lakers pull out of an early slump, but when he tried to do the same thing in the third period, the Hawks were too much in command.

The eight straight field goals helped St. Louis build a 30-21 lead in the first 10 minutes, and the Hawks stretched it to 11 soon after the second period opened.

But Selvy, Rudy LaRusso and West, who was phenomenal in the first half, put the Lakers on "go," and they caught up before the second quarter was half over.

At halftime the clubs were all even, but little did the Lakers suspect that Wilkens, who suffered a painful, though not serious, foot injury in the third session, was going to go on another spree.

The little man did, though, and when he, Cliff Hagan and Pettit were through with their second hot hand, the Hawks had a 12-point lead with three minutes to play in the quarter.

That same threesome stretched the lead to 17 soon after the final period started. Baylor and West had one surge left, cutting the lead to eight with 6:45 to play, but the Hawks had something left, and they quickly wheeled into command for their big celebration.

POSTSCRIPT

There was one bright spot in the Lakers' 1963-64 season. The high-scoring duo of Jerry West and Elgin Baylor was named as first-team NBA All-Stars. It was a small measure of satisfaction for Lakers fans. Although their team didn't make it to the championships, the local heroes did make the first team while Tom Heinsohn, Bill Russell, and John Havlicek of the rival Celtics were voted to the second team. The Celtics got the last laugh, though: Boston beat the San Francisco Warriors, four games to one, in the NBA Finals. The Lakers, meanwhile, had to content themselves with looking forward to the NBA draft and preparing for the next season.

1963-64 Season Highlights

Jerry West (right) ranks third (28.7 points per game) and Elgin Baylor ranks sixth (25.4) in NBA scoring average.

Baylor (22) and West are named to the All-NBA First Team.

Jerry West (44) does his best to disrupt Tom "Satch" Sanders (16) as Darrall Imhoff (14) and Rudy LaRusso box out the Celtics' Bill Russell, but all the Lakers' gritty work early in the regular season went for naught in the playoffs.

The Lakers pick Walt Hazzard (42), the college basketball player of the year from UCLA, in the first round of the 1964 draft. He later changes his name to Mahdi Abdul-Rahman.

Regular-season home attendance at the Sports Arena is 322,331, an average of 8,954. It is the last season the Lakers will average fewer than 10,000 in attendance.

The Lakers lead the NBA in free-throw percentage (76.6%).

1964-65

It's Up to Elg

Season Record

W49-L31 (.613)
Division: 1st
NBA Finals

Coach

Fred Schaus

Players

Jerry West

Elgin Baylor

Rudy LaRusso

Dick Barnett

Leroy Ellis

Jim King

Gene Wiley

Darrall Imhoff

Walt Hazzard

Don Nelson

Cotton Nash

Bill McGill

Jerry Grote

The Lakers were formidable with Jerry West and Elgin Baylor on the court together. When West was injured and needed surgery midseason, Baylor proved to doubting critics that he could carry the day without his high-scoring teammate. Later, in the Western Division Finals, it would be Baylor who was out with a serious knee injury, and West would lead the team to victory. In the end, though, one without the other wouldn't be enough to defeat the Boston Celtics in the '65 NBA Finals.

By Jim Murray
January 17, 1965

CINCINNATI—"Good morning," sang out the girl on the hotel switchboard. "It is 5:45 a.m. and the temperature is 11 degrees."

She neglects to mention it is also snowing, but, at that hour of the morning, you are grateful for any information you can get. Like, what town you are in, for instance.

In the lobby, the sleepy athletes gather. The Los Angeles Lakers have had, at most, only four hours sleep. But this is the way the NBA is.

The game the night before was a scrimmage and the team's only backcourt all-star player sports a nose like a plum. It has been broken for the third time in his career by a vagrant elbow thrown up by the enemy player, Ray Scott, of the Detroit Pistons. Jerry West has to stay in Detroit for an operation, but he is up with the gang because you cannot sleep with a broken nose. You can hardly even breathe.

He plays for two quarters with a broken nose because it looks like just another bloody nose. Except Jerry West's uniform is more red than blue when the horn sounds. He spends the traditional midnight "supper" hour in an emergency hospital with the coach, Fred Schaus, who has logged many an hour in the league's emergency hospital. He is a den mother of a troop, which is always walking in the poison ivy, stepping on snakes or going into water over their heads.

"Yep, it's broken," the all-night doctor, a guy who

lost in the draw for that unenviable position, announces as cheerfully as if he just discovered how to cure cancer. Anyone who ever passed hygiene in high school can see that. Jerry West's nose is on a collision course with his left ear. It has more dents in it than a car driven by a guy in a black leather jacket.

The Lakers crackle to life in the lobby at the sight of Jerry. "Hey, Gene Fullmer," Dick Barnett observes delightedly. "Carmen," shouts his roommate, Elgin Baylor. "Carmen Basilio, who won, baby?"

Elgin is consoling. "Cheer up, baby," he soothes. "You might come out of the operation pretty."

The Lakers are now a one-lung team. Jerry West is staying in Detroit for an operation that will let him breathe without doing it through his ears. The season, for the moment, is up to Elgin Baylor.

Elgin Baylor is a basketball player—and horse player—who announces in the car on the way to the airport, "I will give Jerry my nose any day for his knees. I need two good knees. My nose can take care of itself."

He is also fiercely resentful of press stories that he is doing a day-to-day impersonation—that this is not Elgin Baylor at all, but Sammy Davis Jr. or Larry Storch, copying the mannerisms of Elgin Baylor without the talent of Elgin Baylor.

Elgin fights the notion. "Listen," he says, through set teeth. "I am playing better basketball than I have ever been playing. You have to watch action at both ends of the court. You have to look for statistics that no sportswriter ever looks for."

"OK," promises Elg. "Tonight, I show you."

"Tonight" is Detroit. This is a team of happy-go-lucky freelance artists who came out of the dressing room shooting. They have nothing to lose.

Elgin Baylor plays as if Arnold Toynbee were scorekeeper. He makes a second, third and fourth effort under the basket. He almost personally beats Detroit, 104-100. He puts up 38 points, steals 30 more from Detroit via rebounds, offensive and defensive.

"For one game," a Detroit official confides, "El-

gin Baylor can still be the best they ever put on the floor. For 80 games, I don't know."

Elgin Baylor doesn't believe it. He has carried this team before. A man never really believes he can't run up the stairs as fast at 50 as he did at 20. Age brings wisdom but age brings illusion, too. The funny part of it is, the things you now know how to do are the things time robs you of the ability to do.

Elgin Baylor has been many times blessed. But the march of time is in black-and-white. On Nov. 15, 1960, Elgin Baylor threw 71 points through the basket. He was on a team that would throw a party if anyone else on it managed 10.

The record book is his worst enemy, not the press. From a high-point game of 71 in 1960, Elgin Baylor declined to 63 in 1961, to 52 in 1962 and way down in the fine print of 40 points in 1964. His average has declined from the high 40s to the low 20s.

Elgin fights it. Like the hitter who can't get around on the fastball anymore, or the quarterback who can't find anyone open, he feels that the skills of the mind will replace the skills of the body. But the facts of the matter are that it works in brain surgery more often than it works in athletics. When you can't get around on the fastball any more, no one throws you curveballs.

With Jerry West in a nose guard—or a hospital— Elgin Baylor will need a 71-point night. Anything less, and he will have to be explaining how clever he was under the defensive basket.

He may be alone as Horatius at the bridge, Churchill at Dunkirk or the first man on the moon. But Elgin Baylor thinks he has the secret of this game, and even though there are not 71 points opposite his name, there may be more opposite the Lakers' name. And, if this is, as it has to be, the object of the game, a 38-point Elgin Baylor may be better than the 71-point one. One guy who thinks so is Elgin Baylor—who may know better than anybody.

Jerry West skies above a crowd of Celtics' stars during Game 4 of the 1965 NBA Finals at the Sports Arena. The Lakers dropped this game, 112-99, and lost the best-of-seven series, 4-1.

Cooke Buys Lakers for $5,175,000

By the time Jack Kent Cooke came along, the Lakers had already won three Western Division championships in their first five seasons in Los Angeles. Cooke wasn't satisfied as part-owner of the Washington Redskins football team, according to Dan Hafner. He wanted a piece of pro basketball—the "most exciting game there is." The $5,175,000 price tag was eye-popping at the time, but even more startling was that team owner Bob Short, who led a group that paid $150,000 for the team eight years earlier, wanted to be paid in cash. Twelve bank vice presidents rolled the cash on carts through an underground tunnel from one New York bank to another, and on September 16, 1965, Cooke announced the deal was done.

By DAN HAFNER
September 17, 1965

Jack Kent Cooke disclosed Thursday that he paid $5,175,000 for the Lakers. The sale of the professional basketball team by Bob Short was confirmed at a press conference at the Beverly Hilton Hotel.

"I worked long and hard to swing this deal," said the Canada-born Cooke, who is now a Los Angeles resident. "It's a high price, but I think the Lakers are worth it.

"I own 25% of the Washington Redskins, but I really feel that pro basketball is the most exciting game there is and that I now have the most exciting team."

Cooke, who said he was the sole owner of the team—subject to the approval of the National Basketball Assn. owners, which is a mere formality—had this to say on other matters:

On changing of staffs—"There will not be a hair turned."

On General Manager Lou Mohs—"He is a fine general manager and one of the best judges of talent there is."

On Coach Fred Schaus—"He has proved his ability. Why should I interfere with anyone so capable?"

On Elgin Baylor—"Why would anybody bother to go to the Royal Ballet when they can see him? He's poetry in motion. That's corn. I mean he's Shakespeare in motion."

"I could only wish for Fred Schaus another miracle in the form of another Baylor because that's what Elgin Baylor is, a miracle."

On Jerry West—"He's such a great player and then to find that he is a clean-cut gentleman too."

On Short—"He doesn't believe in logic. That's why I had to pay $5,175,000 for the Lakers when experts valued them at a little under $4,500,000."

Purchase of the Lakers for the highest price ever paid for a pro basketball team (the world champion Boston Celtics recently sold for $3 million) climaxes a 10-year bid for a major sports franchise by Cooke.

Cooke, who became a U.S. citizen by a special act of Congress five years ago, bought the Toronto baseball team of the International League in 1952 and the next year was selected by the Sporting News as "minor league executive of the year."

He made an unsuccessful bid for the Detroit Tigers in 1955, then helped Branch Rickey and William Shea organize the Continental League in 1958. The league was short-lived, but it forced the major leagues to expand to 10 teams. Cooke was shut out once more.

In 1960 Cooke bought a quarter share of the Redskins, but his desire to purchase his own team was not diminished.

He made several unsuccessful bids for

1964-65 Season Highlights The Lakers win third Western Division championship, as rookie Walt Hazzard (right) slowly works into the lineup, playing in 66 games.

Elgin Baylor (right) is fourth in scoring in the NBA with a 27.1 average. Jerry West is second with an average of 31 points per game.

the Lakers before he and Short came to terms. For Short it marked the end of five extremely profitable years as absentee owner.

When he moved the franchise here before the 1960-61 season, the Lakers, according to Short himself, were $300,000 in debt. It didn't take long to erase the deficit and by the 1962-63 season, the Lakers were making more money than any other team in the league.

While Short was seldom in Los Angeles, Cooke said he intends to take an active interest in the team.

"I'm not going to be just a fan. I want to learn the finer points. Of course, when I do, I may find I don't know anything."

Jack Kent Cooke poses with players (from left) Archie Clark, Walt Hazzard, and Jerry West in October of 1966.

West (right) and Baylor become the first teammates in NBA history to score 2,000-plus points in the same season, as West scores 2,292 and Baylor 2,009.

The Lakers, playing at the Sports Arena (right), continue to be No. 1 in NBA attendance, drawing 392,004 for the regular season.

West and Baylor are named to the All-NBA First Team.

1965-66

Lakers Outlast Hawks for Western Division Title

Season Record

W45-L35 (.563)
Division: 1st
NBA Finals

Coach

Fred Schaus

Players

Jerry West

Elgin Baylor

Rudy LaRusso

Walt Hazzard

Bob Boozer

Leroy Ellis

Gail Goodrich

Jim King

Darrall Imhoff

Gene Wiley

John Fairchild

The St. Louis Hawks pushed their playoff series with the Lakers to the distance five times in seven seasons from 1959-60 to '65-66. The Hawks won three of those. But, in 1966—with the Hawks fielding such greats as Zelmo Beaty, Richie Guerin, Joe Caldwell and future Hall of Famer Lenny Wilkens—the Lakers pulled away after a tightly contested first three quarters and never looked back, winning Game 7 of the Western Division Finals.

By DAN HAFNER
April 16, 1966

The biggest Sports Arena gathering of the year, 15,193 fans, showed up Friday night for the seventh and final playoff battle between the Lakers and St. Louis Hawks, and they saw another sizzler.

Led by Jerry West's 35 points and Elgin Baylor's 33, the Lakers staved off the battling Hawks for a 130-121 victory and the Western Division championship.

The game was a sellout early in the day and the throng really whooped it up as the teams took turns grabbing a good lead and then losing it.

Tragedy almost struck the Lakers before they reached the floor for warmups. The water bucket was left sitting by the edge of the court and Walt Hazzard fell over it. Hazzard bruised his right knee, but after first aid seemed to be all right.

Hazzard made the first two baskets of the game, then was hit in the head and had to have more help from trainer Frank O'Neill.

Walt, obviously out to make amends for two weak games, came right back with a driving layup and Los Angeles had a 12-5 lead. The game was just past the three-minute mark and only Cliff Hagan had scored for the Hawks.

Rudy LaRusso made four points from the line, and West made his first basket to run the count to 16-5. Then the Hawks, just as they have all through

the series, came storming back.

Hagan was the big gun, and the Hawks were running well and scrapping. The Hawks twice scored six points in a row and with 2:04 left they were even. When Joe Caldwell took West inside twice to score with jumpers, the battling visitors had a 28-27 lead at the end of the first quarter.

Baylor went to guard to open the second session, but Caldwell got free and the lead quickly became seven with only 2:15 gone in the period.

West returned and the Lakers started to fight back slowly although Caldwell still was tossing in some fantastic shots.

A Bob Boozer basket tied the count with 5:45 to go, but Caldwell, whose only misses were free throws, made a three-point play and Lenny Wilkens quickly scored to give the Hawks a five-point lead.

With Hawks subs on the floor, Baylor made a steal from Hagan and sailed in to score. It drove the fans into a frenzy. The Lakers tried to respond, but Wilkens made the last basket, and at intermission it was the Hawks in front, 58-57.

West had only 12 points and Baylor eight as Caldwell, playing only about 12 minutes, counted 15 to lead everybody.

Caldwell, a Los Angeles youngster, was fabulous, banging in six of his first seven field-goal attempts, while Hagan had 19 points to also play a prominent role. Cliff hit seven of 11 shots.

Hazzard was the Lakers' leader with 14 points, clicking on six of nine field-goal tries.

The Hawks as a team hit 50% and were getting more easy shots than they should have.

The Hawks, who shot four more free throws than the Lakers, went to the line for their first four points in the second half.

They went to a three-point lead, but West and Baylor were really playing now. The Lakers were running and shooting with abandon.

Baylor made a couple of sensational plays, and he and West each hit Hazzard with passes on the fastbreak. With 7:18 to go in the third quarter Los

Angeles led, 75-70.

The Hawks brought Caldwell in at this spot and when Leroy Ellis missed a couple of free throws, the Hawks caught up, finally taking the lead again when Richie Guerin and Bill Bridges scored to make it 78-77.

Guerin was on a real tear, and he was keeping the Hawks in the battle all by himself. The player-coach had a 15-point period and when the wild third ended the Hawks were even, 91-91, and West had five fouls.

POSTSCRIPT

Because of deadlines, the story ended at the third quarter. The next day Dan Hafner reconstructed the exciting close of the game, focusing on Baylor and West.

"Elgin was just under 50% while West, posting a 34.8 average, clicked on 52.1% of his shots. The fabulous one-two punch was at its best in the final quarter Friday night. They had 27 points in the last 10½ minutes as the Lakers rallied from four points down to win."

Jerry West uses his vintage style to stay a step ahead of the Hawks' Lenny Wilkens in the Western Division Finals. West's form was the model for the NBA logo.

Celtics Totter, but Lakers Fall in Finals

A loss is a loss, but it is particularly painful when it comes in a championship game against a fierce rival. Think Packers-Bears in football, Yankees-Red Sox in baseball. In basketball it's the Lakers and Boston Celtics. After a 1965-66 regular season in which the Lakers led the NBA in scoring, it all came down to Game 7 of the NBA championships.

By DAN HAFNER
April 29, 1966

BOSTON—The bells are ringing and the champagne is flowing. The Boston Celtics, sports' greatest empire, tottered, but did not fall.

Bill Russell, taking advantage of the coldest-shooting night the Lakers have had in a long time, rallied his weary club to a tough defensive game Thursday night that gave it a 95-93 victory and presented retiring Coach Red Auerbach with an unprecedented eighth straight NBA championship.

A screaming mob of 13,000 fans nearly tore down Boston's dirty old Garden celebrating, but the fans had to hold off their party until the final gun.

For the Lakers, a game group throughout this seven-game series, found their shooting eyes with 40 seconds to play, scored four straight baskets and were still battling for a chance to tie it in the last two seconds.

Instead, it was the same old story, Auerbach lit the victory cigar and the Lakers were the runners-up for the fourth time in five years.

The Lakers let Boston run up the first 10 points, and they never could catch up against a rugged defense that harassed them all over the court.

Coach Fred Schaus tried all sorts of combinations, but nobody could hit with any consistency.

Russell spearheaded the defense, pulling down 32 rebounds, and he made the key points every time the Lakers threatened to climb back into the battle. The Bearded Wonder also led his team in scoring with 25 points.

The Lakers' trouble was that they couldn't get more than one guy hot at any time. Elgin Baylor couldn't buy a basket in the first

half and Jerry West, who wound up the leading scorer with 36, had only a few.

Then Baylor got hot in the third, and it was West in the final period, but except for a first-quarter spurt by Leroy Ellis and one by Walt Hazzard, the one-two punch didn't get much help.

The low point of the Lakers' season was reached in the second quarter when they went almost 10 minutes without a field goal. The amazing thing is that they didn't fall more than the 15 points they were behind at intermission.

The Lakers were back in the battle—eight points behind midway through the third—and then they went three more minutes without a field goal, and that was too much!

Boston was shooting its normal game, which is just about the worst in the league. However, when the Lakers hit a lull someone, almost always Russell but once in a while Sam Jones or John Havlicek and at a key spot in the third quarter, Larry Siegfried, would bang in a couple of shots and the Lakers would be back in the hole once again.

Russell, who becomes player-coach next season, was magnificent. In addition to his rebounding and scoring, he blocked a number of shots and he made two of the three baskets the Celtics scored in the last 5½ minutes as the always-trying Lakers cut a 12-point deficit to two in a frantic finish . . .

The Lakers' 38 points at halftime, when they trailed 53-38, were 10 fewer than their lowest total in any previous first half in the series.

1965-66 Season Highlights

For the second consecutive year, the Lakers select their first-round pick from the UCLA Bruins' roster. This time it's left-hander Gail Goodrich (right).

Jerry West averages a career-high 31.3 points a game to rank second in the NBA. He also converts 840 free throws, an all-time NBA single-season record.

Baylor scored nine of his 18 points in less than five minutes of the third quarter, and when the Lakers cut the lead to 65-57 with 7:40 gone in the period, the few Lakers fans on hand took hope.

The score was 76-60 when the last quarter opened, but the Celtics were tired old men. They still had guts, though, and they hung on despite a typical barrage.

Elgin Baylor breezes to the basket, leaving the closest Celtics—Bill Russell (6) and John Havlicek (right)— flat-footed in the 1966 Finals, which ended in the Lakers' 95-93 heartbreaking defeat in Game 7.

Chick Hearn's broadcast of the Lakers' win over Philadelphia on Nov. 21, 1965, starts his streak of 3,338 consecutive games.

West and Rudy LaRusso (right) play in the All-Star Game.

West is named to the All-NBA First Team.

The Lakers lead the NBA in scoring with an average of 119.5 points a game.

Two giants of two Lakers' eras rise in prelude to a generation of champions.
Kareem Abdul-Jabbar would put a hook in the Lakers' NBA-record 33 consecutive
victories, Wilt Chamberlain would be above all as the 1972 Finals' MVP, and
in the end Los Angeles would bring home a winner for the first time.

CHAPTER TWO

Streaking to a Title

Seasons 1966-67 through 1973-74

COSMIC FORCES, it would seem, were conspiring to deny the Lakers an NBA championship in Los Angeles.

Seven times between 1962 and 1970 the Lakers fought into the Finals and lost. They lost Game 7 in L.A. in '69 when the Celtics were enraged by balloons packed into the rafters in anticipation of a Lakers title. The Lakers lost Game 7 in '70 when the Knicks were inspired by the surprise return of injured leader Willis Reed.

Years later, a politician would build a winning presidential campaign on what he called "the audacity of hope." The Lakers made their breakthrough with a slightly different concept: The hope of audacity.

Audacity: Bold or arrogant disregard of normal restraints. See: Jack Kent Cooke and Wilt Chamberlain.

Cooke—brilliant, theatrical, tyrannical, abrasive, and charming—bought the Lakers in 1965 for an audacious $5,175,000, cash. He blew up the old mom-and-pop operation, transporting the Lakers into the future and, in 1967, into the Fabulous Forum.

In 1968 Cooke traded for the NBA's Mr. Audacious, Wilt Chamberlain, creating a volatile mix of superstar egos. It all came together in 1971-72 under master-chemist/coach Bill Sharman, a Celtics legend who ran the Lakers with sensitivity and creativity. Result: A 33-game win streak, and a 4-1 Finals triumph over the Knicks.

There would be setbacks ahead, but the breakthrough had been made. The Lakers now knew how to win it all. The cosmos was on red alert.

—Scott Ostler

1966-67

Hawkins, Clark Help Lift Lakers into Playoffs

Season Record

W36-L45 (.444)
Division: 3rd
West Semis

Coach

Fred Schaus

Players

Jerry West

Elgin Baylor

Rudy LaRusso

Gail Goodrich

Darrall Imhoff

Archie Clark

Walt Hazzard

Mel Counts

Tom Hawkins

Jerry Chambers

Jim Barnes

John Block

Hank Finkel

A rookie and a veteran gave Lakers fans a lot to cheer for in the 1966-67 season. Archie Clark and Tommy Hawkins helped bring the team to the Western Division Semifinals, but the Lakers lost to the Warriors in three straight games.

By DAN HAFNER
March 15, 1967

The Lakers, in a season which began on a sour note and improved only slightly, can give thanks for the unexpected contributions of two players for the fact they managed to reach the playoffs at all.

Weird trades, injuries and numerous other problems confronted Fred Schaus' club along the way, but Tommy Hawkins and rookie Archie Clark, who were not part of the preseason plans, provided the spark that carried the Lakers to third place.

The Lakers, with one eye on the playoffs which begin next week, will wind up their Sports Arena season tonight against the record-setting Philadelphia 76ers, and the two hustlers figure to be much in evidence.

Hawkins, a member of the Lakers when they moved here from Minneapolis, was purchased for a small sum from Cincinnati, while Clark was a third-round draft choice from Minnesota.

The way these two have fit into Schaus' team is the pleasant surprise of the season.

The Lakers have the shortest starting team in a sport that puts special emphasis on height. In order to survive against the giants, the Lakers needed speed, quickness and tough defensive play.

The 6-foot-5 Hawkins and the 6-2 Clark have provided these things, but surprisingly, have made major contributions to the Lakers' offense also.

Hawkins, for instance, has shot at a 48.1% clip from the field, while Clark, a 52% shooter over the last 18 games, has a season mark of 45.2%.

"We knew that Hawkins was a good defensive player," said Schaus as he ran most of the Lakers through a light shooting drill Tuesday at Loyola, "but he has improved tremendously. He and Dick Van Arsdale (of New York) are the only forwards in the league who have been able to even slow down Rick Barry.

"On offense Hawkins is tough to handle in close, and his speed gives us fastbreak opportunities. I think this has been the best year of Hawkins' career. I don't think we would have made the playoffs without him in view of the troubles we have had."

There are many experts who believe that right now Clark is the best rookie in the league. The 24-year-old service veteran has put on a brilliant stretch drive, averaging nearly 18 points a game in the last 18 games.

"Archie was impressive in rookie camp, but I never dreamed he would progress so far so rapidly," said Schaus. "Archie and Jerry West complement each other well. Archie can create situations that make it easier for West to get his shot. Also, the opposition can't afford to let him get open, because he has proved he can shoot too."

There is a possibility West, who has been nursing a pulled hamstring muscle for a week, will return to action tonight. However, none of the veterans is expected to be overworked in the last three games, because Schaus wants them ready to face the San Francisco Warriors in the playoff opener Tuesday night at Oakland.

POSTSCRIPT

As valuable as Hawkins and Clark were, they would not remain much longer with the Lakers. Clark would play one more season with the Lakers, averaging 19.9 points and 4.4 assists per game in 1967-68 before becoming one of three Lakers traded to Philadelphia in return for Wilt Chamberlain in 1968.

Hawkins, who retired after the '68-69 season, became a fixture in Los Angeles sports, with his roles ranging from Dodgers executive to a radio and television broadcaster. He also served as master of ceremonies when Elgin Baylor and Jerry West were honored with plaques at the Coliseum in 2009 (see p. 256).

Tom Hawkins, curling a hook shot over Billy Cunningham of the Philadelphia 76ers, provides a welcome lift for the Lakers, leading the team in shooting percentage (48.1%) in 1966-67.

Future Anything but Bright for Lakers

It was no surprise that the Lakers were swept by San Francisco in the Western Conference Semifinals, coming off the L.A. team's worst season (36-45) since arriving in Los Angeles. Injuries to Jerry West, who missed 15 games, and Elgin Baylor, who missed 11, contributed to the poor showing. Next season, the prospects again look dim.

By DAN HAFNER
March 28, 1967

Lakers management and the club's more ardent fans tend to write off the season which ended Sunday in San Francisco as just a hard-luck year, but, in truth, the outlook is bleak.

Just a year ago the Lakers extended the Boston Celtics to the seven-game limit for the world championship, losing the finale by only two points. They were the toast of the coast. In addition to having two of the best players in the sport, Jerry West and Elgin Baylor, the Lakers had more depth than any other team in the league.

New owner Jack Kent Cooke had the most valuable franchise in the National Basketball Assn. But the situation has changed. The Lakers struggled to finish third in the weaker Western Division this year.

They now face the prospect of losing three players in the expansion draft, and another, Jerry Chambers, to the Army. The collegiate crop of seniors is the poorest in many years and, besides, the Lakers do not have a selection until the 17th player. They may not come up with a player who can make the team.

People are wondering how an organization can collapse in such a short time. Here's how:

The Lakers lost two fine players, Bob Boozer and Jimmy King, in the stocking of the new Chicago franchise last spring. At the time, many observers felt it was big mistake to make Boozer, a strong 6-foot-8 forward, available.

The real decline of the Lakers' empire began with the trading of 6-11 Leroy Ellis to Baltimore for Jim Barnes. Ellis not only had improved each year as a center, but he was capable of doing a good job as a forward too . . .

Barnes' inability to provide the needed help at center behind Darrall Imhoff led to another ill-fated swap. In a three-way deal, the Lakers acquired 7-foot Mel Counts and gave up veteran forward Rudy LaRusso. When LaRusso retired, the price the Lakers paid for Counts was LaRusso plus their first-round draft choice.

Supposedly the Lakers were building a young team around West and Baylor, but as it turned out they had to buy veteran Tom Hawkins from Cincinnati to get a team strong enough even to make the playoff.

Of the new talent, only Archie Clark played up to NBA standards. He was a real find and seems destined to become a star . . .

Furthermore, neither Walt Hazzard nor Gail Goodrich, the former UCLA Bruins stars, developed as expected. Undoubtedly, Hazzard will go in the expansion draft, and it is possible that with a new team the talented guard will become a star . . .

Goodrich, a little man in a sport of gi-

ants, only rarely displayed the ability that made him a standout in the playoffs last year.

Imhoff, a fine player the first half of the season, tailed off considerably, perhaps because he played twice as many minutes as he did any other previous year. There were times when Counts played well, but it would appear that Coach Fred Schaus will have to spend considerable time working with him during the off-season. Even then, it does not appear that Counts is the answer to the long Lakers search for an outstanding center.

West, a young veteran, should bounce back from his injury-plagued season to be one of the league's great performers again. Baylor had a big year, but he is now 32 and cannot compete with bigger forwards on the backboards every game.

Next year the Lakers will have seven or eight, at the most, of these players, plus Dennis Hamilton, a 6-8 forward, and John Wetzel, a 6-4 guard, both of whom tried out for the team last fall.

Wetzel who suffered a broken wrist in training camp, is rated a prospect. Hamilton is not a good shooter, but is a good rebounder . . .

As one observer put it, the Lakers could have a better record next year, but it will have to be done with the same old talent . . .

The only hope is to buy a player, preferably a center.

The great ones are not available, but a Luke Jackson, a Willis Reed, a Walt Bellamy, or even a Clyde Lee would be a big start in the right direction. Otherwise it may be a long time before the Lakers again challenge the top teams.

1966-67 Season Highlights

Jerry West misses 15 games and Elgin Baylor (22) misses 11 because of injuries, but they still end the season with scoring averages of 28.7 and 26.6 per game.

Elgin Baylor, Darrall Imhoff (14), and Jerry West play in the All-Star Game.

In 1966-67, the Lakers felt the void of several players who left in the expansion draft or were traded. Among them was Leroy Ellis (left), who was dealt to Baltimore before the season. The 6-foot-10 center-forward returned to L.A. in 1971, and by 1972, he was fully reimmersed in the city, joining Lakers teammate Jim McMillian (right) in a guest appearance on TV's *Columbo* series with Peter Falk (center).

Jerry West (44) and Elgin Baylor are named to All-NBA First Team.

Fred Schaus ends his seven-year coaching stint with a 315-245 regular-season record.

As two views of Jerry West show, the Lakers were in for a uniform change from 1966-67 (left) to 1967-68 (right).

1967-68

Goodrich Finds His Playoff Role — as a 'Coach'

Season Record

W52–L30 (.634)
Division: 2nd
NBA Finals

Coach

Butch
van Breda Kolff

Players

Jerry West

Elgin Baylor

Archie Clark

Gail Goodrich

Mel Counts

Tom Hawkins

Freddie Crawford

Darrall Imhoff

Erwin Mueller

Jim Barnes

John Wetzel

Dennis Hamilton

Cliff Anderson

Coach Bill "Butch" van Breda Kolff's animated and vocal sideline style got lots of attention–sometimes from the officials. In this game in 1968 during the NBA Finals against the Boston Celtics, he had to bring in an understudy to finish the game, which the Lakers won 119-105. But for the fifth time in seven years, L.A. lost the championship series to Boston, 4-2.

By DWIGHT CHAPIN
April 29, 1968

Gail Goodrich stuck his head through the locker room door, his face wreathed in a puckish smile, and asked:

"Any questions?"

The rookie "coach" of the Los Angeles Lakers then ducked back into the safety of the locker room before the barrage could start.

Goodrich, who still looks like a 12-year-old kid despite the fact he's a dozen years older than that and a couple of years out of UCLA, hasn't seen much action or had much attention in the current NBA playoffs. But he got it Sunday night.

It was 8:31 of the third quarter at the Forum and referee Mendy Rudolph's thumb was flailing the air, signaling the second technical foul of the game—and automatic ejection—for Lakers Coach Bill van Breda Kolff.

That's when "Stumpy" Goodrich got his chance.

"Before he left," Goodrich said, "the coach told me what kind of matchups he wanted for the rest of the game. And to stay with his style of play."

All season long, Goodrich has sat next to Van Breda Kolff on the bench. One of his main jobs has been to restrain his voluble boss.

Goodrich's success up to Sunday night was marked chiefly by failure.

Van Breda Kolff, in his first season as a pro coach, has been charged with 28 technical fouls—at $25 a crack—and also got a $250 fine for rapping the NBA's rough style of play.

That's still far short of former Boston Celtics coach Red Auerbach's all-time league mark of

$17,000 but Red had 20 seasons to roll it up. Van Breda Kolff's $950 in one year is an impressive start. Bill has felt all season long, however, that he's been the victim of his reputation. And he said that was what happened Sunday night.

"The first technical, I was just getting up," he said. "I thought I saw Sam Jones or somebody walking with the ball. Rudolph was coming by when I got up and he nailed me."

But it was the second technical that particularly angered Van Breda Kolff.

"The one time I'm trying to be a peacemaker, I even get one," he said.

Van Breda Kolff explained that Lakers forward Tom Hawkins had been bounced to the floor under the basket during game action and Lakers trainer Frank O'Neill started to jump up to assist Hawkins.

But Van Breda Kolff thought O'Neill was rising in anger and he leapt up to get O'Neill back down. That's when Rudolph threw him out.

O'Neill said that Van Breda Kolff's version of the incident was exactly correct. So did Goodrich.

"For once," he wasn't hollering at an official," said Goodrich. "I couldn't believe he'd get called then."

Rudolph, however, said that Van Breda Kolff was ejected for "continuous harassment and overreaction on the bench."

In any event, his early exit gave Goodrich an unaccustomed moment in the spotlight. Goodrich even got into the game for longer than usual after Van Breda Kolff left.

"Well," Goodrich said. "Freddie Crawford and Archie Clark had five fouls . . . you know."

There was still a group of reporters clustered around him when the rest of the players were showered and dressing and teammate Darrall Imhoff came over and advised:

"Hey, coach, don't give away our game plan."

And then Van Breda Kolff yelled from the other side of the room:

"Hey, Gail, what time do you want the guys there for the plane to Boston?"

Elgin Baylor drives to the basket while Jerry West trails the play in Game 1 of the Western Division Finals. The Lakers swept the Warriors (4-0) thanks to a heart-stopping jump shot by Archie Clark in the last 12 seconds of Game 4.

The House That Jack Built

It came to be known as the Fabulous Forum, the home of the Lakers and hockey's Los Angeles Kings, dedicated on Dec. 30, 1967. The Lakers played their first game there the next day, New Year's Eve, defeating San Diego. The building was designed to look like the ancient Colosseum in Rome, with eighty massive white columns supporting the roof. Ushers dressed in togas to reinforce the theme. Even the team got new uniforms, shedding blue and white for purple (Cooke preferred "Forum blue") and gold. It all began as just the improbable dream of an improbably bold sports magnate. Seeing, however, was believing.

By JIM MURRAY
November 30, 1967

The trouble with Jack Kent Cooke is, nobody ever believes him.

Take the time he owned the Toronto Maple Leafs baseball team and Horace Stoneham wanted a relief pitcher for his Giants. Jack was horrified at the man he wanted. "Horace," pleaded Jack, who loved the Giants, "don't take this guy. He's a drunk, a child-molester, and will spend more time in court than he will on the mound."

But Horace knew a fast shuffle when he heard one, and he began shoveling players at Cooke—among them two guys who later became All-Star pitchers, another who became a leading home run hitter for two teams—so fast Jack could not resist. So, Cooke shrugged, and quit arguing. And the pitcher in question never finished an inning, never mind a game, for the Giants, and everybody said, "Boy, is that Cooke a smart

one. Look at the way he slickered old Horace."

Then, Jack said he was going to buy the Lakers for $5 million, give or take a little loose change, and everyone said, "Hah! Where's he gonna get $5 million? It's just a stunt to get his name in the paper." And Jack Kent Cooke gave Bob Short $5 million in cash for the team.

Then, he entered the bidding for an expansion hockey team, and everyone said, "He's over-extending himself. He'll go broke, and they'll never give him the team anyway." So, he got it.

And his landlords at the L.A. Sports Arena got huffy and had done everything they could to push Dan Reeves' rival bid, and they began to get sticky about dates and percentages, and Cooke said, "Knock it off, or I'll go build my own arena."

And everybody laughed and laughed.

So he went out and bought the land. And everybody said, "A grandstand stunt. I hear he's hocked everything, and is $8 million in the hole already. They'll never even sink a steam shovel."

So, the other day I went out to Inglewood, and there, gleaming a brilliant white in the afternoon sun, was Jack Kent Cooke's arena, the Forum, a magnificent structure that looks for all the world like a monster white concrete crown set down in the verdant hills of Prairie Avenue.

If Jack Kent Cooke is going to the poor house, he's going in style.

The arena is, without question, gorgeous. It seems a shame to clutter it up with basketball and hockey. Like Dodger Stadium, it seems to deserve more Brahms, Liszt, Beethoven, ballet, great paintings. It

seems obscene to sweat in it.

Jack is now a full-fledged octopus of sport—with 25% of the Washington Redskins, 60% of the Seattle Totems, and 100% of the Springfield Kings. He named his hockey team "Kings" after a long and arduous search, saying he wanted something "uniquely American and Los Angeles . . ." His choice, of course, prompted a wag to suggest that Jack's nickname for the team was "uniquely American" because the team was named after George the Third.

Jack is especially proud of his Forum location because it is free of "slum suffocation" which overtakes most American arenas as soon as they are built.

Some years ago, Walter O'Malley rejected a Flushing Meadows location for his then-Brooklyn Dodgers because it was hard by a cemetery and a body of water (the Atlantic Ocean), and O'Malley explained, "We're not likely to get any customers from either place."

Jack Kent Cooke is surrounded by a cemetery too, but he's glad of it. "Dead people don't stick guns in the faces of your customers and say 'Your money or your life,' and I know some arenas around this country where the dead bodies around them are still warm."

If he stays out of debtor's prison, Jack's facility will open on Dec. 30.

Maybe Jack is doing it all with credit cards, but I have to say this traveling salesman from Canada has done an awful lot for a guy who started out with an armful of encyclopedias door-to-door, and wound up with a $16-million edifice with nice quiet neighbors. Jack's only worry is that people will start believing him, and take all the fun out of it.

1967-68 Season Highlights

Elgin Baylor leads the Lakers in scoring (26), rebounding (12.2), and assists (4.6).

Bill van Breda Kolff is the Lakers' new head coach

Of all that Jack Kent Cooke brought to Los Angeles, two stood tall amid the city's landscape—the Fabulous Forum in Inglewood and future Hall of Fame center Wilt Chamberlain, who cuts an imposing figure, with his dogs, outside the arena in 1972.

Jerry West is the season's playoff scoring leader, averaging 30.8 points.

Elgin Baylor (22), Archie Clark (21), and Jerry West play in the All-Star Game. They are the top three scorers for the West team.

The Lakers' scoring average of 121.1 points per game is the most in Lakers' history.

1968-69

Big Deal: Three Lakers for Wilt (and Title?)

Season Record

W55-L27 (.671)
Division: 1st
NBA Finals

Coach

Butch
van Breda Kolff

Players

Jerry West

Elgin Baylor

Wilt Chamberlain

Mel Counts

Johnny Egan

Keith Erickson

Bill Hewitt

Tom Hawkins

Freddie Crawford

Cliff Anderson

Jay Carty

In his five years with the Lakers, the incomparable "Big Dipper" helped take the team to the NBA Finals four times. By the time his NBA and Lakers career ended in 1973, he had amassed a lifetime total of 31,419 points and 23,924 rebounds, averaging 30.1 points and 22.9 rebounds per game.

By MAL FLORENCE
July 10, 1968

It has long been a generally accepted view that the Lakers would be the dominating force in professional basketball if they had a center of the stature and strength of Wilt Chamberlain.

Now this assumption will be put to a test.

The Lakers have Chamberlain. It became official early Tuesday morning when it was announced that Los Angeles had traded Archie Clark, Darrall Imhoff and Jerry Chambers to the Philadelphia 76ers for the controversial Chamberlain, the NBA's all-time leading scorer.

Chamberlain, who is in New York City working on former Vice President Richard M. Nixon's presidential campaign, was unavailable for comment. He is expected to be present at a news conference at the Forum Thursday morning.

Now that the Lakers have acquired Chamberlain, another question is posed. Is it possible for a team to have too many stars? The Lakers already have two outstanding players in Elgin Baylor and Jerry West.

Bill van Breda Kolff, the Lakers' coach and an avowed adherent to the team style of basketball instead of the star system, thinks that the "new" Chamberlain will complement Baylor and West.

"I don't know if I would have wanted Wilt three or four years ago," said Van Breda Kolff Tuesday. He was referring to the fact that Wilt, who once scored 100 points in a game (an NBA record) used to operate as a one-man team. In recent years with the 76ers, Van Breda Kolff observed, Chamberlain has become more of a team player.

"Somebody said to me that if we ever had Chamberlain we'd have to have two or three basketballs so he could share with Elg and Jerry," the Lakers' coach facetiously remarked. "That's not true. We should be an even better team with Wilt. He's a good passer and sets those little picks that should give the others an opportunity to score.

"And, remember, Wilt is a 60% field-goal shooter and he doesn't have to shoot as much to get his share of the points."

Van Breda Kolff also reasons that the presence of the 7-foot Chamberlain should also add a couple of years to the NBA "life" of Baylor, who has been called upon to share the rebounding duties with Imhoff in addition to his obvious scoring role.

A few months ago the 33-year-old Baylor candidly admitted that he probably could play in the league for many years to come if the Lakers had a center as physically endowed as Chamberlain or San Francisco's Nate Thurmond.

The Lakers have won the Western Division championship five times since the franchise was moved from Minneapolis in 1960. But, on each occasion, they have been defeated by the Boston Celtics in the NBA championship series.

Now that Los Angeles presumably has a center to offset Bill Russell, it will undoubtedly be a consensus choice to end the Celtics' long reign as world champions . . .

The 31-year-old Chamberlain, who reportedly earned $250,000 last year with the 76ers, has been regarded by some as a problem player. He began his career nine years ago with the old Philadelphia Warriors, then played in San Francisco when the franchise was transferred there and was finally traded to the new Philadelphia team in 1965.

Although he is considered to be the most devastating force in the game, Chamberlain has played on only one world championship team—the 1967 76ers club that momentarily interrupted Boston's string of titles

. . . Chamberlain is reportedly satisfied that he is now a member of the Lakers. His parents live in Los Angeles and he has long regarded the West Coast as his "home." . . .

Wilt Chamberlain, 31 when he joined the Lakers, relaxes on a train trip in the mid-1960s

It's a Bird! a Man! a Car! a Bullet! . . . It's Super Jerry!

Even before Jerry West became the only player from a losing team to be selected the Most Valuable Player of the 1969 NBA Finals, Jim Murray was over the moon about the ability of No. 44.

By JIM MURRAY
April 27, 1969

Jerry West and his Lakers teammates sign autographs at a free benefit workout at the Forum in 1971.

The first time you see Jerry West, you're tempted to ask him how are things in Glocca Morra. The Lakers didn't draft him, they found him under a rainbow. Either that or they left a trail of bread crumbs in the forest and then snapped the cage when he showed up. There are those who swear Jerry arrives for work every day by reindeer. He wears the perpetually startled expression of a guy who just heard a dog talk. He doesn't walk anywhere—he darts. He has the quickest hands and feet ever seen on a guy without a police record. If they put a cap on him sideways and turned him loose on the streets of London, there wouldn't be a wallet in town by nightfall.

He can hang in the air like Mary Poppins . . . He could play Peter Pan without wires. Some night he's going to go up for a jump shot in the first period—and they're going to have to get the fire department to get him down. His nose has been broken so many times, he sneezes through his ears. Cigarette smoke would come out of his nostrils in corkscrew patterns. His septum is so deviated, he's breathing yesterday's air. He goes through life with such a s-w-o-o-s-h . . .

Inch for inch, he's the greatest basketball player in the world. There is no more exciting sight in the world of sports than Jerry West dervishing down court with a basketball, eyes and nose flaring, basketball thumping. His shots are a blur.

He's such a bundle of exploding nervous energy that by the end of the season, they don't need a chest x-ray. They just hold him up to the light. If you put a picture on him, you could send him as a postcard. Jerry wasn't born, he was pressed. A steamroller would miss most of him.

He can hit a golf ball 300 yards (with a two-wood) and be there when it comes down. He would make one of pro football's great defensive backs. He could play the outfield like Willie Mays if they could get him to stand still in one place that long . . .

He is a nine-year veteran in the league, but he always looks like a kid getting his first sight of Disneyland. A guy asked to guard him sometimes feels as if he had spent the night in a revolving door in the dark, but Jerry has never even had a cross word with an opponent . . .

He has arms so long he could drive a car from the back seat. No one has ever caught him asleep. He's as democratic as a panhandler. He chats with anyone. He talks as fast as he runs . . .

He had a brother killed in Korea and has never been able to find a mere game worth complaining about since, not even in late season when he is so exhausted pigeons try to feed him. He even eats fast. He shops so fast he can get a complete wardrobe and take the same elevator back down. He's supposed to be injury-prone, but he has never missed a playoff game. He's so modest, game journalists avoid him after his good nights. "Talk to Jerry and you'll wind up knocking him for an all-time scoring night," a regular once warned.

His play in the opening playoff game against the Celts last week was, to understate it badly, historic. In the presence of a dozen of the game's greatest scorers, one of every four points was thrown in by Jerry West.

"It was such a good game I wish I could have seen it!" glowed Jerry afterward, ignoring the fact he had left smoke coming out of both baskets.

A lot of the Celts assigned to guard Jerry wish they could have seen it too. Like a lot of people, they figure Jerry is a figment of someone's imagination, like the Easter Bunny, Santa Claus, leprechauns and witches. And, as soon as they can find it, they're going to hide his broom.

Lakers' Title Hopes Suspended in Air

Balloons, affixed to the ceiling in anticipation of a celebration, remained there amid a question whether Wilt Chamberlain should have stayed on the bench in the final minutes of Game 7 of the NBA Finals.

By MAL FLORENCE
May 6, 1969

I t seems that the Lakers are not destined to defeat the Boston Celtics in the NBA championship finals.

This was supposed to be the year that the Lakers were going to interrupt the Celtics' domination . . . They had three superstars and the advantage of playing the seventh and deciding title game at home.

But, it wasn't to be as the wise, old Celtics prevailed again, nudging the Lakers, 108-106, Monday night in a foul-marred game . . .

The Lakers gave it the big try after . . . they trailed by 17 points with a little less than 10 minutes remaining.

But Jerry West, limping noticeably at times on his injured left leg, fired his team back into contention. The Lakers, who never led in the game, closed to within one point of the lead (103-102) with 3:07 left.

This, as it turned out, was to be the end of the trail, and the Celtics were NBA champions again, for the 11th time in the past 13 years . . .

Many of the regulars were in foul trouble including Wilt Chamberlain and Bill Russell . . . Chamberlain injured his knee and removed himself from the game in the final five minutes.

It had to be a galling, bitter defeat for West, who suffered a pulled hamstring muscle in the fifth game, but still carried on . . .

He led all scorers with 42 points and totaled 556 for the entire playoffs to easily break the NBA record of 521 established by Rick Barry in 1967 . . .

There are many factors . . . in analyzing the Lakers' defeat. . . . Chamberlain, who

Jerry West finds a clear path to the basket in the 1969 NBA Finals, where he became the only player from a losing team to be selected the series' Most Valuable Player.

has never fouled out of a NBA game, was cited for his fifth personal with 3:39 to play in the third quarter . . .

Or, the Lakers . . . missed 15 straight field goals and were seven for 25 for the period . . .

Or . . . you could conjecture why the Lakers didn't get the ball to West in the last four minutes. He took only one shot (it missed) after scoring 14 of the Lakers' 16 points . . .

However, the third quarter belonged to the Celtics, who . . . were apparently breezing, 97-76, at the outset of the final quarter.

Then, the Lakers began to make their move . . .

In the midst of the Lakers' surge Chamberlain suddenly began to limp. A 20-second injury timeout was called with 5:19 to go and Wilt hobbled to the bench . . .

Chamberlain, though, wanted to get back into the game. This was confirmed by Lakers Coach Butch [Bill] van Breda Kolff.

"I told him that we were doing well enough without him," said Butch . . .

The clincher came . . . with 1:17 remaining when Don Nelson . . . cast off from the foul line.

As luck or fate would have it, the ball hit the front rim, bounced high into the air and then settled into the net to provide the Celtics with a three-point cushion at 105-102 . . .

This was it as the Lakers had run out of time . . .

There were balloons attached to the rafters high above the Forum. They were supposed to be released when the Lakers won.

They might remain in their roost for some time to come.

1969-70

West-Baylor Show Rocks Cow Palace — and Warriors

A decade before the Showtime era, two Lakers were putting on a show of their own. On this night, Jerry West and Elgin Baylor humbly but expertly took down the opposition in a way Bay Area fans could appreciate.

By MAL FLORENCE
February 12, 1970

SAN FRANCISCO—Two veteran pro basketball sluggers, Jerry West and Elgin Baylor, wore down a surprisingly tough opponent Wednesday night at the Cow Palace and, eventually, scored a knockout.

The Jerry-Elgin show was at its devastating best in the final quarter as the Lakers, who trailed throughout most of the game, ran away with a 125-115 victory in the closing minutes.

West and Baylor each scored 43 points and neither superstar could recall when they last went over 40 points in a game as an entry.

It wasn't just the number of the points they scored, but when they got them that was so important.

Elgin dropped in 17 points in the last quarter and Jerry accounted for 12. Moreover, after the Warriors took their last lead at 108-106 with 4:26 remaining, Baylor and West were responsible for all but two points in a withering 10-point blitz.

It was the 10th time West has scored over the 40-point barrier this season and the second for Baylor in a week. But the Lakers, who meet the Western Division-leading Hawks tonight at the Forum, couldn't gain any ground on Atlanta, which defeated San Diego to remain 1½ games ahead of Los Angeles.

A small crowd of 5,362 forgot its partisanship and politely applauded the exploits of the famed cornerman and guard near the end of the game. Class was at work. And in this instance, it told.

Baylor and West both shrugged off their accomplishments.

"It was just one of those nights when we were both shooting well from outside and our teammates sacrificed by getting us the ball," said Baylor, who has now scored 167 points in the last five games for a 33-point average...

Baylor, the 35-year-old Lakers' captain, who has been bothered by a lingering groin injury the entire season, has been charging the past week.

"Sure, it still hurts, but now after playing three games in five nights I know I can play with the injury. In fact, I can play this way forever if it doesn't hurt any more than it does now."

Al Attles, the Warriors' player-coach, who was sidelined with a fractured hand, poked fun at himself.

"Who said he (Baylor) has slowed down?" said Attles. Then he smiled and added, "I said it."

Baylor was 18 of 28 from the field, seven of 10 from the line and had 11 rebounds. West was 17 for 30, nine for nine and had 7 assists.

And, there was little opportunity for a respite. Baylor played 43 minutes while West was on the floor for 47.

They were needed as forward Keith Erickson, who already has a sprained left ankle, turned his right ankle in the second quarter. He played again before halftime, tried to continue in the third quarter, but was finally forced to the dressing room.

The Lakers seemed to be on a treadmill most of the game. They were continually playing from behind and, every time they would draw even with San Francisco, the Warriors would spurt ahead again. The game was tied on 17 occasions.

San Francisco led at halftime, 60-58, eased out by 90-84 at the end of the third quarter and were on top throughout most of final 12 minutes. In fact the Lakers apparently suffered a strategic and psychological blow after assuming a 106-105 lead with 4:29 to play. The much-traveled Dave Gambee collided with Rick Roberson, but official Jack Madden cited the rookie center with a blocking foul. Rick protested and drew a technical. Fritz Williams cashed the technical foul and Gambee converted both of his free throws and the Warriors were two points up... This was their last gasp as Baylor and West, with an assist from Mel Counts, began to bombard the Warriors from every conceivable position on the floor.

Even before Elgin Baylor and Jerry West scored 43 points each in a game against the San Francisco Warriors, the two Lakers did a star turn for Sports Illustrated in 1968. Through SI's first 50 years, the Lakers were on the magazine's cover more than any team other than the New York Yankees.

West's 60-Footer
Wasted by Lakers

Back in his playing days, Bill Sharman landed a 70-foot basket during an NBA All-Star Game. In 1977, Norm Van Lier of the Chicago Bulls scored from 84 feet out. By comparison, Jerry West's soaring toss from beyond midcourt, which the Los Angeles Times reported to be 55 feet, wasn't one for the record books, but it was enough to put fans on the edge of their seats. The NBA's official estimate puts the shot at 60 feet, calling it "perhaps the most famous buzzer-beater of all time."

By MAL FLORENCE
April 30, 1970

Jerry West made a 55-foot shot to send the Lakers' third NBA Finals playoff game against the New York Knicks into overtime Wednesday night at the Forum.

But, despite the breathtaking distance of the shot in the final second of the regulation game, it might as well have been a layup.

The Lakers couldn't capitalize on such an emotional moment and were defeated in overtime, 111-108, by a team that trailed throughout most of the game—by 14 points at halftime.

By winning, the poised New Yorkers, who refuse to be blown hopelessly out of any game, assumed a 2-1 lead in the best-of-seven tournament that resumes here Friday night.

Now, it's the Lakers who must scramble for a split at home before the series returns to New York for the fifth game Monday evening.

The Lakers looked like an aging fighter who had built up an early lead in the first 10 rounds and was gamely hanging on trying to win the decision.

But, the overtime and the game belonged to the balanced Knicks. The outcome was sealed when West missed a jumper with 30 seconds left in the extra period and Dick Barnett converted a 10-foot shot in the final four seconds.

In fact, Jerry couldn't find the magic touch in the five-minute extra period as he went 0 for 5 from the field.

West said he was tired, but he didn't ask Coach Joe Mullaney to take him out of the game. So he remained on the floor for the entire 53 minutes, an iron-man performance matched only by Wilt Chamberlain . . .

It appeared that the Lakers were beaten when steady Dave DeBusschere hit his favorite shot, a 20-footer while being pressured by Happy Hairston with three seconds to play.

But West, realizing the Lakers were out of timeouts, hurried up the court and, before he reached the circle at midcourt, cast off with an arching one-hander. The ball didn't touch the backboard but rattled around the rim and then dropped in.

The capacity crowd of 17,500 roared with delight. The Lakers were still incredibly alive.

But the Knicks never lost command in overtime after West's foul shot tied the score at 108 with 1:46 left.

Willis Reed sank a free throw for a 109-108 lead and fouled out Elgin Baylor in the process. West then missed two shots in the last two minutes before Barnett, who was 0 for 7 in the first half, sank the clinching basket.

It didn't appear that the Lakers could possibly lose the way they were performing in the first half.

From a defensive standpoint, it might have been their best game of the season with 53.7% efficiency from the field. Chamberlain was sweeping the defensive boards, Baylor was rebounding and making clever assists while scoring. Keith Erickson was scrambling and West was scoring.

As a result, they owned a 56-42 lead at the break—their largest advantage—thanks to Erickson's 40-footer just before the halftime buzzer. But the Knicks never lost their cool after shooting only 33.3% in the first 24 minutes. They kept gnawing away at the deficit and were within five points of the lead (73-68) at the close of the third quarter.

The Lakers then spurted and held leads ranging from seven to eight points for almost seven minutes of the last quarter.

Then, Barnett, the former Laker, began to draw the Knicks ever closer with his deft shooting. As a result, New York earned a 96-96 tie with 1:18 to go and gained its first lead (98-97) since early in the first quarter with 50 seconds remaining in the regulation game.

The rest you know . . . DeBusschere's shot, West's bomb from past midcourt and the collapse in overtime.

. . . Baylor had only 13 points but he wasn't looking for his own shots as his 13 assists will attest. He also had 12 rebounds. Erickson was diving for loose balls the entire evening and scored . . .when he had the open shot. And, Hairston hustled at both ends of the court as did Dick Garrett . . . But the Knicks prevailed.

1969-70 Season Highlights

Joe Mullaney (left), with Jack Kent Cooke at his side, becomes the new Lakers coach and leads the team to the Western Division title.

Baylor and West play in the All-Star Game. Baylor (right), who was limited to 54 games by injuries, still averaged 24 points a game.

Jerry West, guarded by former Laker Dick Barnett, had 33 points and 13 assists in a 135-113 victory in Game 6 of the 1970 Finals. But the shot for which West is most remembered came in Game 3, when his 60-footer sent the game into overtime.

Jerry West (left) leads the NBA in scoring with a 31.2-point average.

Wilt Chamberlain plays in only 12 regular-season games after injuring his knee.

1970-71

Wilt Leads Late Charge as Lakers Whip Bulls

Season Record

W48-L34 (.585)
Division: 1st
West Finals

Coach

Joe Mullaney

Players

Jerry West

Wilt Chamberlain

Happy Hairston

Gail Goodrich

Keith Erickson

Jim McMillian

Willie McCarter

Rick Roberson

Fred Hetzel

Pat Riley

John Tresvant

Elgin Baylor

Earnest Killum

Wilt Chamberlain was once again healthy, but injuries kept Elgin Baylor on the sidelines for all but two games this season. Along with Baylor, Jerry West also missed the entire postseason due to injury. The team nonetheless fought its way past the Chicago Bulls in the Western Conference Semifinals to earn a shot at the Bucks in the Western Conference Finals. But that's where the Lakers ran out of steam, losing to Milwaukee, 4-1.

By MAL FLORENCE
April 7, 1971

Wilt Chamberlain sat in the Lakers' dressing room sipping a glass of champagne and extolling his team for accomplishing so much in adversity.

His teammates returned the compliment.

For if any one man was responsible for leading the Lakers to a sudden-death, seventh-game victory Tuesday night over the Chicago Bulls, that man was Chamberlain.

Chamberlain was everywhere as he scored 23 points, grabbed 19 rebounds and made the intimidating blocks in the fourth quarter when the Lakers ran away with the game, 109-98, to win the closely contested Western Conference Semifinal series, four games to three.

A Forum capacity crowd of 17,505 saw the Lakers maintain the home-court mastery in the competitive series. Neither team had lost at home and that turned out to be the difference.

Now, it's on to Milwaukee Friday night for the start of the best-of-seven Western Conference final series against Lew Alcindor's Bucks.

"I don't even want to think about that now," said Wilt, obviously wishing to savor the win over the Bulls a bit longer.

The Lakers are a team with considerable playoff experience and this factor helped them in the clutch minutes of the fourth quarter.

The determining spurt came when the Lakers were clinging to a tenuous, 88-87 lead midway through the period. Then, they went on a seven-point blitz and the Bulls couldn't recover their composure.

Chamberlain was quick to point out that he had plenty of support and this was evidenced by the performances of Happy Hairston, Gail Goodrich, Keith Erickson and Jim McMillian, the other starters.

Hairston, with 22 points and 12 rebounds, and Erickson, who had 14 points, were offensive forces in the waning minutes of the game. Goodrich, who finished with 29, was doing his thing—outside jumpers and drives, while McMillian did a cool job of controlling the ball when the Bulls resorted to an abortive press late in the encounter.

Playoffs are nothing new to the 31-year-old Chamberlain, a 12-year pro, but this team—obviously not the most talented in numbers he's ever been associated with—seems to mean something special to him.

"I commend the Lakers," said Wilt. "There's a team without Jerry West and Elgin Baylor and I don't know if we were expected to win or lose this series, but I've never been associated with a team that accomplished so much under adverse conditions. Even if we don't go any further, we've already achieved a great deal."

Joe Mullaney, the Lakers' coach, admitted that he was surprised that his team [comported] itself so effectively on offense during the past series.

"I didn't know that Keith would come up with so many big shots or that Mac (McMillian) would play with so much confidence or that Gail would increase his scoring average so substantially (17.5 to 30 points a game)."

The Bulls, who had never participated in a [Game 7] in their five-year history (this was the Lakers' ninth seventh game), faltered in the closing minutes after exchanging leads with the Lakers throughout the third and part of the fourth quarter. For example, Bob Weiss, the seemingly unstoppable outside shooting guard, missed his last seven shots in the fourth quarter.

"I think they were a little tight," observed Elgin Baylor, the Lakers' captain.

Wilt Chamberlain plays a keep-away game with Matt Guokas (24) of the Bulls in 1971. During the season, Chamberlain pulled down an NBA-leading 18.2 rebounds per game. Twice, he grabbed 31 boards in a game.

1970-71 Season Highlights

Keith Erickson (right) averages 15.6 points in the playoffs.

Gail Goodrich, back from Phoenix, averages 17.5 points per game.

Jim McMillian (5), who would take over for Elgin Baylor in the next season, is the 13th pick in the first round of the 1970 draft.

1971-72

Baylor Ends Fabulous Career After 13 Years

Season Record

W69-L13 (.841)
Division: 1st
NBA Champion

Coach

Bill Sharman

Players

Gail Goodrich

Jerry West

Jim McMillian

Wilt Chamberlain

Happy Hairston

Flynn Robinson

Pat Riley

Leroy Ellis

John Trapp

Elgin Baylor

Jim Cleamons

Keith Erickson

Elgin Baylor captured the fans' imagination with his arrival in 1960 for the Lakers' first exhibition game in Los Angeles. The game's top scorer with 30 points, Baylor continued to excel until his retirement 11 seasons later. He amassed a lifetime scoring average of more than 27 points and led the Lakers to the NBA Finals eight times.

By MAL FLORENCE
November 5, 1971

Elgin Baylor, one of the greatest basketball players in the history of the game, has retired.

The famed Lakers' captain came to this decision Thursday afternoon after a remarkable 13-year career in the NBA.

The 37-year-old Baylor will remain with the Lakers in a public relations and scouting capacity. He also will be a TV analyst on the college basketball game of the week.

No man has contributed more to the success and popularity of the Lakers since they moved to Los Angeles from Minneapolis in 1960 than Baylor.

As an athlete, the graceful, 6-foot-5 forward had no peer. He was a man of a thousand offensive moves and his hang-in-the-air acrobatics are part of the lore of pro basketball.

"I hoped to end my career after one last, successful season," said Baylor. "Out of fairness to the fans, to the Lakers and to myself, I've always wanted to perform on the court up to the level and up to the standards I have established throughout my career.

"I do not want to prolong my career to the time when I can't maintain those standards."

Baylor has made several comebacks from injuries during his career. But no injury was more serious than the severed Achilles' tendon that enabled him to play in only two games last season.

Yet, when the present season started there was old No. 22 performing at his familiar starting cornerman position. Still, he wasn't at his physical best . . .

"I was depriving Jim McMillian of playing time," said Elgin, "and I know the same would be true when Keith Erickson comes back. I felt the injury was coming around, but I know that time is so valuable to the coach (Bill Sharman) that there is no sense in putting him in a bad position." . . .

Baylor, who carried himself with dignity both on and off the court, will never see his No. 22 jersey worn by another Laker.

Lakers owner Jack Kent Cooke has seen to that, saying, "that is as it should be." . . .

Sharman, who used to play against Baylor when he was a star Boston Celtics guard, expressed his admiration for the man who is probably the all-time NBA forward.

"I've always admired Elgin Baylor and knew him to be a superstar," said Bill. "Now, after coaching and working with him I've also found him to be a super person . . .

Baylor retires as the third-greatest scorer (23,149 points) in NBA history behind Wilt Chamberlain and Oscar Robertson.

More amazing is the fact he's reached this lifetime total while missing 170 games in 13 seasons.

He was also the greatest rebounder for his size in the league. In a domain that belongs to the giants of the game, Baylor was fifth on the all-time rebounding list (11,463). Elgin earned other statistical credits—second ranked in the NBA in field goals attempted and made and No. 5 in free throws converted.

And, it was almost 11 years ago today that Baylor scored 71 points against the New York Knicks at Madison Square Garden—the highest figure ever recorded by an NBA forward . . .

Elgin was almost a perennial all-league selection since his rookie season with the Minneapolis Lakers in 1958-59 when he was rookie of the year. He was also a member of the NBA All-Star Team on [11] occasions.

About the only honor not to accrue to Baylor was playing on an NBA championship team. But he and Jerry West fought the good fight, battling the

Elgin Baylor (22), who floated to a 71-point game and 10 All-NBA First-Team selections in his career, never played the game as if he were run by the clock. "I do not want to prolong my career to the time when I can't maintain those standards," he said.

Boston Celtics' dynasty in some historic title series—many going to the seventh and deciding game ...

Baylor leaves the NBA with a lifetime scoring average of 27.4 points and the legacy that he was a member of a select group—the Russells, Wests, Chamberlains, Robertsons, Cousys—that promoted pro basketball from a barnstorming, second-rate sport to the high level of popularity it now commands.

Elg came to the Lakers as an exciting All-American from the University of Seattle. Bob Short, then the Minneapolis owner, recently reflected on Baylor's worth to the franchise.

"If he had turned me down then, I would have been out of business. The club would have gone bankrupt."

Streak Snapped . . . Abdul-Jabbar, Bucks Stop Lakers at 33

Records might be made to be broken, but the Lakers' 33-game winning streak isn't likely to be shattered any time soon. The Houston Rockets came closest, but their run of wins was stopped at 22 on March 18, 2008, when the Celtics defeated them, 94-74. Although the Bucks broke the Lakers' winning streak, the Lakers got revenge in the Western Conference Finals, beating Milwaukee (4-2) to head into the NBA championship series.

By MAL FLORENCE
January 10, 1972

MILWAUKEE — The win streak is dead at 33.

Kareem Abdul-Jabbar and the Milwaukee Bucks accomplished something that no other NBA team could in more than two months—defeat the Lakers.

And they did it with a flourish Sunday afternoon, running away from the careless Lakers in the fourth quarter for a 120-104 victory before a capacity crowd of 10,746 at Milwaukee Arena and a national television audience.

The streak—the longest in American major league professional team sports—had to end sometime, but the Lakers were disappointed that it expired against NBA champion Milwaukee and the manner in which it did.

"We lost it. Milwaukee didn't win it," said forward Jim McMillian.

There's justification for his attitude because the Lakers slumped as a team. There wasn't any third- or fourth-quarter spurt that has occurred almost automatically since the streak began Nov. 5—only turnovers (24), inaccurate shooting (39.3%) and porous defense.

The Bucks, of course, contributed to the Lakers' defeat. Abdul-Jabbar, maintaining advantageous floor position, couldn't be contained by Wilt Chamberlain and the other Lakers.

The Bucks' graceful 7-footer battered the Lakers' defense with sweeping hooks, short jumpers and intimidating stuff shots.

He finished with 39 points, 20 rebounds and a technical "knockout" over Happy Hairston.

Early in the second quarter Abdul-Jabbar became incensed when fouled by Hairston and threw a right-hand chop—without the ball—that landed flush on Happy's jaw. Hairston remained motionless on the floor for several seconds as Chamberlain gently led Abdul-Jabbar away from the fallen Laker.

"I simply lost my temper," said Abdul-Jabbar, who could have been ejected from the game. However, he only drew a personal foul.

"Sure, I fouled him," said Happy. "Fouls are part of basketball but slugging isn't."

Then, Hairston turned his head so reporters could view the lump that was prominent on the right side of his face.

When asked what kind of foul he committed, Happy snorted: "That's the silliest question I've ever heard. A foul is a foul."

Hairston became entangled with Abdul-Jabbar's legs under the Milwaukee basket when the Bucks' center unloaded on the Lakers' forward.

The Bucks were unloading the entire day, namely Abdul-Jabbar and reserves John Block and Lucius Allen, who divided 35 points. Block, the former USC star, also grabbed some timely rebounds (10). It was one of the 6-foot-9 cornerman's most effective performances as a pro.

There weren't many positive aspects to attribute to the Lakers, however. Jerry West, whose personal win streak ended at 41 games, threw the ball away several times and was only five for 16 from the field (20 points). Oscar Robertson forced Jerry to work hard at both ends of the floor.

The other Lakers shooters were misfiring too. Gail Goodrich was five for 20 (18 points) while McMillian was seven for 19 (18) . . .

The Lakers warmed up a bit in the second half after shooting only 29.5% in the first 24 minutes in which they experienced a miserable, 17-point second quarter . . .

Flynn Robinson came off the bench in the fourth quarter to hit three quick baskets as the Lakers closed to 94-90. Robinson left the floor at this juncture in favor of Goodrich and the Bucks left the Lakers . . .

When it was all over, Lakers Coach Bill Sharman kept the dressing room door locked for 15 minutes. He had written a speech to deliver to his team in case it lost but, game after game, the dog-eared piece of paper remained in Bill's coat pocket.

"Oh, I had a couple of corny things written, but I didn't read them today," said Sharman. "If I had to single out one thing I'd say that the Bucks' aggressive defense was the difference . . . In the long run, I think this defeat will help us. We made some mistakes while we were winning, but it's hard to learn from them when you've won a game."

1971-72 Season Highlights

The '71-72 Lakers are listed by NBA.com as one of the top 10 teams in league history. Their 31-7 road record remains the best road winning percentage (.816).

Bill Sharman (left), in his first year at the Lakers' helm, is named co-NBA Coach of the Year. Pat Riley (right) is a Lakers reserve who is a future Coach of the Year.

Wilt vs. Kareem: The two future Hall of Famers square off in a game that ended the Lakers' 33-game win streak at Milwaukee. The 24-year-old Abdul-Jabbar had 39 points and 20 rebounds. The 35-year-old Chamberlain, limited by four fouls, had 15 points, 12 rebounds, and six blocks. In their rematch in the Western Conference Finals, the Lakers won and Chamberlain went on to become the NBA Finals' MVP.

Jerry West leads the NBA in assists, averaging 9.7 per game, and is honored (left) as MVP of the All-Star Game.

Gail Goodrich is fifth in the NBA in scoring, averaging 25.9 points per game.

In the record streak, the Lakers won their last 14 games of November, 16 of December and the first three of January, beating Milwaukee's mark of 20 set in 1971.

L.A. Goes Wild! Lakers Are World Champs

Not since the Minneapolis Lakers defeated the Syracuse Nationals in 1954 could the Lakers' franchise claim a national championship. Since arriving in Los Angeles, the team went up against the Celtics six times and once against the Knicks in a futile quest. The eighth time, however, was the charm.

By MAL FLORENCE
May 8, 1972

The deliriously happy crowd poured onto the court and hoisted Wilt Chamberlain to its shoulders while Jerry West, laughing and, perhaps, crying a little, barely beat the mob to the dressing room.

The Forum organist played "Happy Days Are Here Again" and why not?

Finally, after 12 years of frustration, the Los Angeles Lakers attained the goal that has eluded them so many times in the past—champions of the National Basketball Assn.

They accomplished it with a withering, fourth-quarter assault Sunday night at the Forum, defeating the determined New York Knicks, 114-100, to win the playoff in five games.

Chamberlain, not expected to play because of a severely sprained right wrist, shrugged off the injury and was a dominating factor in the victory—the Lakers' first in eight appearances in the final series.

The 7-foot-2 center was also voted the Most Valuable Player in the championship round and will get an automobile to add to his fleet.

Wilt got the green light to play after the swelling in his wrist subsided—an injury he suffered during Friday night's game in New York.

He performed with a football-type pad wrapped around his huge right hand.

"It's an unbelievable feeling . . . something I've always wanted to experience,"

said an elated West. "Now, I know what it feels like to be a champion."

The 33-year-old All-Pro all-time guard has received almost every honor imaginable in his career. But a championship was the thing he coveted the most.

Jerry is the only Laker who has been with the team since its inception in Los Angeles and he has been in seven previous championship series, only to taste defeat, sometimes in the fleeting seconds of the seventh game . . .

The win capped an incredible season in which the club won a record 69 games while compiling a 33-game win streak—the longest in major league sports history. And the man who brought it all about is Coach Bill Sharman, who has now won championships in three pro leagues—ABL, ABA and now NBA . . .

"They deserved to win," New York Coach Red Holzman said. "They're a tremendous team."

Dave DeBusschere added: "I thought we played a really good game tonight, but

the Lakers played a better game. They are a tremendous team and they deserve the championship." . . .

The Lakers tried to blow them out with a 10-point blitz at the outset of the game, but the Knicks recovered and even led before the period ended.

This was the trend practically the rest of the game: The Lakers moving out to modest leads and the Knicks catching them. But New York ran out of comebacks in the fourth quarter when Los Angeles went on a decisive 13-2 tear for a 98-65 advantage with a little more than five minutes remaining.

It was all over and this was underscored when Chamberlain and West left the game with 1:37 to play and the fans chanting, "We're No. 1, We're No. 1."

Chamberlain . . . playing injured, was at his best in the clutch.

He scored 24 points and grabbed 29 rebounds and tracked Jerry Lucas and the other Knicks all over the floor.

West, who had been in a shooting slump in the last two playoff series, was making the big plays when it counted— on drives and smooth jumpers. He accounted for 23 points, although his accuracy (10 for 28) was not up to his usual high standards.

Other Lakers made notable contributions, namely:

—Jim McMillian, who was a sharpshooter at the start of the third quarter when the Lakers snapped a 53-53 halftime deadlock. This momentum carried over to the final period. Mac finished with 20 points.

—Gail Goodrich, who broke out of a third-period slump (he was 0 for 8 at one time) and wound up with 25 points.

—Steady Happy Hairston, who snatched 14 rebounds and scored 13 points . . .

Wilt not only was playing with a sprained wrist but a fracture on the same hand sustained several years ago. His left hand also was heavily bandaged to protect a bruise.

Wilt Chamberlain draws a crowd of starry admirers in the 1972 Finals against the Knicks, including (from left) Jerry West, Jerry Lucas, Walt Frazier, Happy Hairston, Phil Jackson, and Bill Bradley.

The fans converged on him after the game and carried the 35-year-old, 285-pound man a few steps before collapsing under the burden. All the while, Wilt held his right arm aloft—more to protect it rather than a victory gesture . . .

Like the Dallas Cowboys, who finally broke their second-place jinx this year and won the Super Bowl, the Lakers can no longer be called next year's champions.

They've arrived.

1972-73

Goodrich Gets 44; Lakers Move On to Finals

Season Record

60-22 (.732)
Division: 1st
NBA Finals

Coach

Bill Sharman

Players

Gail Goodrich

Jerry West

Jim McMillian

Wilt Chamberlain

Bill Bridges

Keith Erickson

Happy Hairston

Pat Riley

Jim Price

Mel Counts

Travis Grant

Bill Turner

Flynn Robinson

Leroy Ellis

John Trapp

Roger Brown

At 6 feet 1 he was short by NBA standards, but Gail "Stumpy" Goodrich stood tall in the Western Conference Finals as the Lakers once again went to the championships. After defeating the Warriors (4-1), the team was pulling for a chance to face the Knicks rather than the Celtics, but as they later learned, sometimes you have to be careful what you wish for.

By MAL FLORENCE
April 26, 1973

Gail Goodrich said he found his rhythm again Wednesday night and it was all in his swinging left hand as he shot the Lakers into the NBA championship series.

Goodrich, who had been in a playoff shooting slump, fired in 44 points—21 in a torrid third quarter—as the Lakers ran away from the Golden State Warriors, 128-118, at the Forum.

By disposing of the Warriors in five games of the Western Conference Finals, the Lakers will defend their NBA championship against either Boston or New York. This is the ninth time in 13 years that Los Angeles has made the final round of the playoffs.

It was accomplished with an opportunistic fast-break and stifling defense reminiscent of last year's record-breaking team. In fact, the Lakers are probably playing their best basketball of the season now. Goodrich and Jerry West combined for 71 points, Wilt Chamberlain had 22 rebounds and Jim McMillian and Keith Erickson shrugged off injuries to contribute ...

The Lakers led 58-50 at halftime and then shot 75% from the field in the third period—a 12-minute session in which Goodrich went wild.

Stumpy made 10 of his first 11 shots in the period, and it seemed he couldn't miss with his bull's-eye jumper. His 10 field goals in the quarter were a playoff record, one more than Elgin Baylor made in 1960. And, his 21 points were one shy of Baylor's playoff mark for a quarter.

"It's just hard to explain when you shoot like that," said Goodrich, who was only 42% against Chicago and 38% against Golden State, but made 10 of 26 from the field Wednesday evening. "I felt a little tired prior to the game and that helped to relax me.

"When I started to hit, the players got me the ball, especially Wilt and Jerry. I can never remember having so many good shots, and I can't ever remember shooting a better percentage (73%)."

Goodrich had 37 points after three quarters and, when he took a brief respite in the final period, he was accorded a standing ovation.

And, another Laker was similarly honored: Happy Hairston, who was in uniform for the first time since he injured his knee last December. Hairston got into the game with 4:13 left and made his only field-goal attempt ...

So, the Lakers must now await the outcome of the Knicks-Celtics series. The Knicks lead, three games to two, with a sixth game scheduled Friday night in New York ...

The Lakers were almost unanimous in preferring to play the Knicks, mainly because they would have the home-court advantage ...

"We seem to play New York better," said Bill Bridges, "but the way we're playing now it probably wouldn't make any difference." ...

Although Goodrich received most of the attention after scoring a career playoff high of 44 points, West was equally effective.

The 34-year-old All-Pro guard had that quick step to the basket and opened up the game with his relentless drives. He finished with 27 points, was eight for 18 from the field, 11 for 11 from the line and had nine assists—padding his record for most playoff assists in NBA history ...

The oldest Laker, the 36-year-old Chamberlain, is ready for the championship series right now.

"Some others may want a rest," he said, "but I don't need one."

With that remark, Wilt asked for another glass of champagne, which was flowing freely in the dressing room. The world champs are now one more tough series away from repeating.

Gail Goodrich, who averaged a team-leading 23.9 points during the regular season, rides a 21-point third quarter to 44 points total during the Western Conference Finals against the Warriors.

1973-74

Lakers Wish Chamberlain Well — in the Courts

In his 14-year NBA career, Wilt Chamberlain filled the record books and the stands. His exploits were legendary; at various times he scored 100 points in a single game (still an NBA record), made 18 consecutive field goals, and grabbed 55 rebounds. After playing with the Philadelphia/San Francisco Warriors, the 76ers, and the Lakers, he left the league in 1973 to be a player/coach with the San Diego Conquistadors in the American Basketball Association. But he owed the Lakers the option year of his contract, and the team sued to prevent him from playing for that year. After one season with San Diego, he retired from basketball.

By CHARLES MAHER
September 27, 1973

You know all about Wilt Chamberlain and coaches. Well, he's finally found one with whom he should be able to work in complete harmony. Himself.

After five years with the Lakers, Chamberlain announced Wednesday he has signed on for three years as player-coach of the San Diego Conquistadors of the American Basketball Assn . . .

His salary was not announced but guesses run as high as $600,000 a year.

Whether he will play his first season here is a matter likely to be settled in the courts. His contract with the Lakers has run out, but they have an option on his services for another season. The question is whether the option clause is legally enforceable.

In a statement, the Los Angeles club said:

"The Lakers feel a sense of loss with the departure of Wilt Chamberlain. We wish him well. The Lakers are proud they have been able to obtain the NBA's great, promising young center, Elmore Smith. We hope Wilt will have every success as a coach in San Diego and certainly appreciate his many contributions to past Laker successes.

"As for his status as a player, the Lakers' legal position, according to club attorney Alan Rothenberg, is quite clear. Chamberlain has a binding contract with the Lakers for the 1973-74 season . . ."

The big man who is the most prolific scorer and rebounder in NBA history has slowed in recent years and has concentrated on defense with the Lakers . . .

In his book (Wilt: Just Like Any Other 7-Foot Black Millionaire Who Lives Next Door), Chamberlain made candid, critical remarks about some of his Lakers teammates. Asked if they were angered, and if this had anything to do with his decision to leave, he said:

"Not at all . . . I don't believe they were terribly upset. In fact, Jerry West conveyed that to me personally." . . .

Chamberlain began his NBA career with the Philadelphia Warriors in 1959, moved with them to San Francisco in 1962, was traded to the Philadelphia 76ers in 1965 and went to the Lakers in a trade in 1968. He played on one championship team in Philadelphia (1966-67) and one in Los Angeles (1971-72) . . .

Chamberlain succeeds K.C. Jones, former Laker assistant coach, who resigned to coach the Capital Bullets.

In Denver, ABA commissioner Mike Storen said that the most important result of Chamberlain's switch will be "increased attendance around the league. He probably is the best-known athlete in the world . . . We hope he'll play for a long while."

. . . Lakers comments:

Happy Hairston: "Wilt and I were a great rebounding team. It will be an adjustment to get used to Elmore."

Bill Bridges: "We'll miss him. He was very intimidating defensively."

Coach Bill Sharman: "I wish Wilt good luck. He had an awful lot to do with our success. We wouldn't have won 69 games in [1971-72] and 60 in [1972-73] without him.

"And his cooperation was outstanding. You hear things about Wilt missing practice. He didn't miss a practice his first year, and we had an understanding last year that if he wanted to miss the morning practices, he would be excused."

Wilt Chamberlain, shown in the 1970s, played his last game for the Lakers in 1973 at age 37. He averaged 30.1 points and 22 .9 rebounds for his career.

Lakers Win Pacific Title, Shoot Into Playoffs

Wilt Chamberlain was gone and Jerry West, 35 and injured, lasted just 31 games. The team turned to new arrivals Elmore Smith and Connie Hawkins to help pick up the slack. It was enough to get them into the Western Conference Semifinals, but that's where their season ended.

By MAL FLORENCE
March 25, 1974

The Lakers won the Pacific Division championship and roared into the playoffs with their most impressive offensive show of the season Sunday night before a capacity crowd of 17,505 at the Forum.

They outscored Buffalo, 150-124, to keep intact their record of making the playoffs every year since the franchise moved here from Minneapolis in 1960.

As it was, they didn't even need to win to clinch the Pacific title and a playoff berth. Obliging Golden State (43-37) lost its fifth straight, bowing to Phoenix to forfeit the championship to Los Angeles (47-34).

The Forum was converted into a shooting gallery as Elmore Smith scored a season-high 37 points; Buffalo's Bob McAdoo got 40; Gail Goodrich and Happy Hairston scored 35 and 29 points and ex-Laker Jim McMillian had 31.

So the Lakers, appearing out of contention last weekend when they were swept by the Warriors, begin the playoffs in Milwaukee Friday night after a final, meaningless regular-season game here against Seattle Tuesday night.

Champagne flowed freely in the Lakers' dressing room and Goodrich was on the phone to owner Jack Kent Cooke in New York, saying, "We're going to bring you a world championship."

McAdoo, the league's leading scorer, drew admiring gasps from the crowd with his machine-gun precision shooting. At one time he had hit 16 of 19 on medium-range jumpers and only one layup.

But this is expected of McAdoo. Smith, averaging 12 points most of the season, has his teammates talking about his sudden emergence as an offensive threat.

Smith has averaged 26 points the past six games and is rebounding and cutting better than at any time in the season.

"Elmore is unbelievable. He's incredible," said Happy Hairston, shaking his head and smiling while holding a glass of champagne...

Smith, a quiet, almost shy athlete, was surrounded by reporters. He seemed uncomfortable with all the attention.

"My role on this team was a defensive player and shot-blocker," said Smith, implying that he wasn't expected to score. "When we weren't scoring against Golden State, I decided to do something. No, I never talked to Coach Bill Sharman about it and he didn't ask me to shoot more."...

Connie Hawkins said that Sharman has been emphasizing offensive movement and that his job is to get the ball high and then pass off to the cutting shooters like Goodrich, Smith and Jim Price.

"And, Elmore is shooting now," said Hawkins. "Earlier in the season he would pass off."

"I'm getting better position," said the Laker center, "and, of course, when you're hitting it helps your confidence."...

Smith is shooting 62.5% from the field the past six games. And he has pulled down 83 rebounds while continuing to lead the NBA in blocked shots, an average of five a game.

As a team, the Lakers shot 56.6% but had a difficult time shaking the Braves until the final quarter. A 15-4 second-quarter tear propelled the Lakers to a 67-59 halftime lead, but they only led by eight points, 106-98, at the outset of the final period.

Then, Goodrich scored 10 straight points. Smith hit from the side, Hawkins and Hairston got layups and Pat Riley banged in a jumper. It was all over at 128-110 with a little more than five minutes remaining.

A few seconds later McAdoo got a standing ovation after fouling out. The same salute was accorded Smith when he left the game with 3:11 to play.

The 150 points was a season high for the Lakers, surpassing the 143 scored here against Baltimore...

The Lakers were picked to finish no better than second in the Pacific Division at the start of the season. Golden State was the consensus favorite.

But the Warriors unaccountably went into a slump the past week and the Lakers wouldn't fold. In winning their fourth straight—and 15 out of 19—they had to dispose of playoff bound teams: New York, Milwaukee, Chicago and Buffalo.

The Lakers won the season series from the Bucks, four games to two, but the playoffs are a different season. Milwaukee (59-23) has the NBA's best record.

"I think they'll be thinking about us," said Hawkins, implying the Bucks have respect for the Lakers. "Can we go all the way? I don't even want to talk about that until the Milwaukee series is over."...

1973-74 Season Highlights

Pat Riley's look might be evolving, but the Lakers are nearly a constant in the Pacific Division, where they win the title again.

Elmore Smith (3) blocks 17 shots against Portland on October 28, 1973, an NBA record. He also averages 12.5 points a game for the Lakers.

Called by NBA.com "a man of remarkable talent who played much of his career in the shadows," future Hall of Famer Connie Hawkins finger-rolls his way to a score in a season when he needed to pick up the slack for the Lakers.

Gail Goodrich leads the Lakers in scoring (25.3) and is named to the All-NBA First Team.

An injury limits Jerry West to 31 regular-season games and one playoff game, but he still is second on the team in scoring, with a 20.3-point average.

West has a team-record 10 steals in a Dec. 7, 1973, game against Seattle.

The Lakers' game changes in 1975, with "The Captain" on board. Kareem Abdul-Jabbar (33), looking for a way out of Milwaukee, welcomes a move to Los Angeles.

Passing the Torch

Seasons 1974-75 through 1978-79

BY 1974, THE CHEMISTRY that produced the first championship for the Lakers in Los Angeles had destabilized. The team was reeling.

Jerry West came to training camp in 1974 in great shape, at age 36 still a prime-time player. But West and Jack Kent Cooke argued over salary, tempers flared, and West abruptly retired.

"It started over money," West said, "but then it became personal."

Wilt Chamberlain also retired, and Bill Sharman found his squad short two all-time superstars, a huge void. Sharman lost his wife to cancer in '74, and frayed vocal chords would force him out of coaching after the '75-76 season.

The Lakers fell hard. In '74-75, for the first time in the 14 seasons they had been in Los Angeles, they missed the playoffs. Help arrived after that season when Cooke and Sharman traded for center Kareem Abdul-Jabbar, the NBA's premier star, but Kareem alone couldn't restore the Lakers to greatness.

The rebuilding continued in '76 when West and Cooke made peace and West returned as coach. Jamaal Wilkes and Norm Nixon arrived in '77, keys to the future.

But oh, that delicate chemistry. Kareem was a sometimes-moody presence. West and Nixon clashed. West and his inner demons clashed. West and Cooke clashed again in '76 when Cooke opted not to pursue Julius "Dr. J" Erving after the ABA disbanded. Cooke and his wife clashed, their divorce necessitating his sale of the Lakers.

The NBA Finals, long the domain of the Lakers, were a distant dream.   —*Scott Ostler*

1974-75

West Leaves 'Em Asking for More

Jerry West was synonymous with great defense and an unerring jump shot. He also was synonymous with the Lakers' franchise. After 14 years with the team, he decided to retire—and this time he meant it. His departure was felt keenly as the team fell to a 30-52 record.

By MAL FLORENCE
October 4, 1974

Season Record

W30-L52 (.366)
Division: 5th
Missed Playoff

Coach

Bill Sharman

Players

Gail Goodrich
Lucius Allen
Elmore Smith
Brian Winters
Happy Hairston
Cazzie Russell
Stu Lantz
Pat Riley
Zelmo Beaty
Connie Hawkins
Corky Calhoun
Kermit Washington
Stan Love
Jim Price
Bill Bridges

The Lakers' Jerry West, considered by many the greatest guard in basketball history, announced his retirement Thursday, saying he no longer can play to the high standards he sets for himself.

Reminded at a press conference that he has "retired" many times in recent years only to play again, West told reporters:

"You knew then I wasn't really going to retire. I'm emotional in many things I do. But this decision wasn't an emotional thing.

"My retirement is firm—very firm. I didn't want to make the decision, but I felt I had to."

West, 36, a pro for 14 years, spoke with a twinge of sadness.

"When you set standards for yourself and you have to sacrifice those standards, you're not honest with yourself," he said. "I didn't want to sacrifice those standards." . . .

His coach, Bill Sharman, General Manager Pete Newell and owner Jack Kent Cooke disagree. They urged their superstar to reconsider—to no avail.

"This is one of the most emotional moments I've ever known," Sharman said. "Jerry is a personal friend. There has never been a guard who could do the things Jerry does.

"He's a superstar on offense and defense and knows what it takes to win games. He said he couldn't perform up to his standards. Well, I still say he's the best guard in the league." . . .

West signed a contract last June that called for him to work for California Sports Inc., the firm that owns the Lakers, once his playing career ended.

West isn't sure what he'll do for the organization.

Someone suggested that he might become Sharman's assistant.

"I can't help Bill coach," West said. "You can't help the best coach in the game."

West didn't rule out the possibility that he might coach someday—but said it would be only in the Los Angeles area.

In arriving at his decision to retire, West said, he considered both mental and physical factors.

"You have to want to play," said the athlete known as Mr. Clutch. "Through all my 14 years in the league, I followed a pregame procedure. I would eat at a certain time, go to bed at a certain time and would think about the other team—even if it was the worst in the league.

"Well, if we were going to play Philadelphia next week, I can't say I'd be in the same mental frame. And physically I couldn't accomplish what I want." . . .

West said he talked about retirement with his wife, Jane, and three sons. "My kids agreed with me," he laughed. "They don't think their dad is the best any more."

But he'll be remembered as the best. The skinny kid from West Virginia—Zeke from Cabin Creek.

In his prime, he was relentless on offense with his almost unstoppable, quick-release jump shot and timely drives. On defense, his darting eyes saw everything on the court and he frustrated rival shooters with his quick hands, or stole the ball from unsuspecting hot-shot dribblers . . .

The honors and statistics were there: 10 years a first-team All-Pro, a perennial All-Star, most prolific scorer for a career or season in the playoffs and most points (63) by a guard in an NBA game. And who could ever forget his remarkable [60-foot] shot against the New York Knicks in a Forum championship game in 1970?

West and the Los Angeles Lakers grew up together.

He joined the team as a rookie in 1960-61 when the franchise moved here from Minneapolis. West, along with Elgin Baylor, brought pro basketball to its prominence here in the '60s.

Oscar Robertson has retired; so has Wilt Chamberlain. Now Mr. Clutch.

"You won't see another like him," Sharman said.

———

POSTSCRIPT

Jerry West cited mental and physical factors for his retirement, but there was more to the story. According to Roland Lazenby, author of *The Show,*

West had believed his salary of $250,000 was the same as Wilt Chamberlain's, as promised by team owner Cooke. But when Chamberlain left for San Diego in 1973, West learned Chamberlain was being paid $400,000. West told Lazenby he felt "deceived" by Cooke. "I have always viewed trust as an important factor, trust in a coach, trust in the people you've got around you. And I lost that trust with Jack Cooke."

Jerry West tells reporters he'll retire, saying: "I didn't want to make the decision, but I felt I had to."

Happy's Unhappy: His Art Is Unappreciated

In this, his last year of play, Happy Hairston set an NBA record with 13 defensive rebounds in one quarter against Philadelphia. Hairston was a member of the Lakers team that set an all-time NBA-winning streak of 33 games in the 1971-72 season.

By JIM MURRAY
February 5, 1974

Although his own best work will never hang in any museum, Harold Nathaniel Hairston, an artist of sorts, knows what Rembrandt Van Rijn felt like when someone came up to him and said, "Is that all you do, paint a picture in half-light, and they give you all that money?"

Or, when they came up to Picasso and said, "Very nice. What Is it?"

Or, they read a Gertrude Stein poem and said, "Was she sober?"

Or, they looked at a Bufano sculpture, "Madonna and Child," and said, "I know it's a shell, but what millimeter is it?"

You see, the nuances of artistic performance elude most people.

What William Faulkner writes is not for everyone. Neither is what Stravinsky composed.

Happy Hairston, you might say, is a collector. He collects basketballs for a living—usually scraping them off the backs of boards or the backs of people. When he gets them, he passes them but to other people.

This is hardly a glamour operation. It's a kind of complicated trash pickup—refuse engineering.

You should get a broom and a shovel. It's a scavenger hunt. People who go to watch rebounds would buy tickets to a paper drive.

There are some people who claim they watch the guards in football, or get a kick out of watching the infield cheat a step in baseball. But, the facts are, most fans, to a man (or a woman), like to see the bomb in football, the home run in baseball and the mid-court basket in basketball.

They reach for the popcorn when someone comes down with a rebound. They know it will be 20 seconds before they see what they came to see—scoring.

It is a public attitude that irritates Hairston more than an elbow in the face. On the subject of rebounding, he becomes Unhappy Hairston.

"I'm not bitter about it," he claims. "On this team, I'm a rebounder. On this team, when we win, they say, 'The offense won it.' When we lose, they say, 'Well, the rebounding lost it. They didn't get the ball in to Jerry.' I have never been an All-Star. Never made that team although I have been in the top 10 in rebounding. If I were in Phoenix or Portland, I'd be definitely an All-Star . . ."

But Happy has always had a job in the chorus because, when he was drafted out of NYU (where teammate Barry Kramer got all the headlines), he was picked on a team (Cincinnati) that had Oscar Robertson. Oscar was the "Big O" and the rest of the team was the "Big Nothing." Nobody noticed who got the ball for Oscar because, if Oscar didn't have it, nothing was going to happen.

Happy got traded to Detroit, a team with nothing but rebounders. Yet, Happy's 959 were second only to Walt Bellamy, and well ahead of Dave DeBusschere.

At L.A., Happy found himself in group photos with Wilt Chamberlain, Elgin Baylor and Jerry West, the kind of pictures editors say, "Left to right, Elgin Baylor, Wilt Chamberlain, and Jerry West. Man to West's right unidentified."

Yet, when Happy tore his knee apart in Chicago in December, the Lakers were a cinch to come up several rebounds short in the championship playoff. And they did.

Happy, on two healthy hinges now after an operation, is careering along at a 660-rebound clip this season, and more than 200 have been under the offensive basket.

The difference between an offensive and defensive rebound is the difference between catching a line drive and a pop fly, the difference between tackling Larry Csonka or Larry Smith, striking out Babe Ruth or striking out your sister Ruth.

Still, Happy feels the fans do not appreciate the heights of artistry inherent in the rebound. He still feels like the oil painter whose patrons prefer calendar nudes, or the operatic tenor who has just hit high C and the guy in the stalls wants to know, "Can you sing 'Melancholy Baby'?"

Or, there's the night he drags down 30 rebounds, and whips 10 outlet passes, and the kid at the door thrusts a book and pen at him and says, "Can you get me Jerry West's autograph?"

1974-75 Season Highlights

Elmore Smith (right) finishes second in the NBA in blocked shots, averaging 2.92 per game.

Cazzie Russell, the Lakers' fourth-leading scorer with a 15.7-point average, is limited to 40 games because of a knee injury.

The Lakers' Happy Hairston looks in his element, working above the talented crowd under the basket during the 1973 NBA Finals.

Gail Goodrich, who averages a team-leading 22.6 points, plays in the All-Star Game.

The Lakers trade Jim Price to Milwaukee for Lucius Allen (40, right) on November 11, 1974.

Allen is the team's second-leading scorer (19.5 points) and finishes eighth in the NBA in steals (2.06).

1975-76

The Buck Stops Here; Abdul-Jabbar's a Laker

Season Record

W40-L42 (.488)
Division: 4th
Missed Playoff

Coach

Bill Sharman

Players

Kareem
Abdul-Jabbar

Gail Goodrich

Lucius Allen

Cazzie Russell

Don Ford

Donnie Freeman

Cornell Warner

Corky Calhoun

Stu Lantz

Kermit
Washington

Jim McDaniels

Cliff Meely

Ron Williams

C.J. Kupec

Pat Riley

John Roche

Walt Wesley

He's been called "The Captain," "The Franchise," and "Captain Hook," but what mattered when Kareem Abdul-Jabbar arrived in Los Angeles is that he was called a Laker.

By Ted Green
June 17, 1975

Last season the Lakers didn't get off the ground. So now they've reached for the sky by sending four players to the Milwaukee Bucks for pro basketball's best center, Kareem Abdul-Jabbar.

The announcement, which ended weeks of speculation, came Monday at an elaborately staged, carnival-like press conference at the Forum.

The trade—center Elmore Smith, guard Brian Winters and Los Angeles' first two choices in the 1975 National Basketball Assn. draft, forward Dave Meyers of UCLA and swingman Junior Bridgeman of Louisville, all for Abdul-Jabbar and another center, Walt Wesley—had been finalized Saturday night.

It materialized principally for two reasons: Abdul-Jabbar, disenchanted with Milwaukee (the town and the team), had requested a trade either to New York (his first choice) or Los Angeles, and the Lakers, in the words of one high-placed NBA source, "were committed to the belief they couldn't win a championship with Elmore Smith."

Another possible reason: The Lakers were embarrassed by their last-place finish in the Pacific Division—and some empty seats at the Forum—and wanted to ensure it wouldn't happen again.

They almost certainly did that much by signing the player who has been called "The Franchise" to a five-year contract. Terms weren't disclosed but the figure might be as high as $500,000 a year . . .

He . . . came to Los Angeles nine years ago from his native New York City and led UCLA to three national collegiate championships (1967-69). And though he wasn't quite that successful in Milwaukee—the Bucks won four division titles but only

one championship (1971) in Abdul-Jabbar's six years there—he was nevertheless the league's most dominant player, one who could demoralize a team by scoring, seemingly, whenever he wanted to. Records and awards have come in bunches: a career scoring average of 30.4 points a game and shooting percentage of 55%, both better than any player, active or retired; Most Valuable Player three times; first team all-pro four times, and much, much more. But the statistic that most impressed the Lakers was this: UCLA won 98% of its games with Abdul-Jabbar. Milwaukee 71%. That's why Lakers owner Jack Kent Cooke may not have been off base when he said Abdul-Jabbar is "the best basketball player in the world and, for all I know, maybe of all time." . . .

As Lakers Coach Bill Sharman said when asked if he thought Los Angeles could win a championship this season: "I certainly hope so . . . the thing is, it puts us in a contending position right away."

Abdul-Jabbar was . . . cool, candid and smiling. At first he said a few obligatory words ("I hope I can live up to the buildup . . . It's nice to be here") and answered questions . . .

"I had to think in terms of having a place to have outside interests, something to relate to," he told a few reporters. "In Milwaukee, all I had was my job. That's all I was there for—work." . . .

Abdul-Jabbar made it clear he would rather have gone to New York.

"I had a strong desire to go home," he said. "It's always been my dream to play for the Knickerbockers. But Mr. Cooke and the Lakers made it clear they wanted me, and they were sincere . . .

In Los Angeles Abdul-Jabbar will be reunited with his good friend and UCLA teammate, Lucius Allen, and another ex-Bruin, Gail Goodrich.

That's probably the backcourt, and with, say, Cazzie Russell and Kermit Washington at forward, the team resembles the Bucks in their good year. A fine backcourt. A shooting forward. A rebounding forward. And Abdul-Jabbar.

"He's such a great all-around player," Sharman said, "he can help us all in all departments."

Kareem Abdul-Jabbar is the center of expectations in June of 1975 as Coach Bill Sharman (left) and owner Jack Kent Cooke join him at a news conference announcing his acquisition.

Cazzie Russell Came to Shoot

Statisticians will tell you there's nothing to the "hot hand" theory that if you land several baskets in a row, you're more likely to sink the next one. But in his twelve NBA seasons, three of them with the Lakers, Cazzie Russell must have made more than a few number-crunchers revisit their formulas.

By JIM MURRAY
December 16, 1975

"When Cazzie is hot, he could score from a locked room."

"Some nights, Cazzie throws in so many points so fast the scoreboard is two baskets behind."

"Cazzie could play in the dark and hit 15 or 16 in spurts."

The greatest scorer in the history of basketball was Wilt Chamberlain. It says so right on p. 262 of the NBA Guide. What it doesn't tell you is who was the fastest scorer in the history of basketball.

Most people, including teammates, coaches and opponents, who are authors of the above quotes, agree that this is Cazzie Russell, who scores points in such swift succession some nights the scoreboard seems to have developed a stutter.

Some people are known as "Mr. Two Points," but Cazzie is "Mr. Two-Two-Two-Two Points." He is not the most prolific scorer in the game in per-minute play.

But the elapsed time between the first basket and the 10th of this Gatling gunner of the Lakers is frequently only a few minutes.

Cazzie is the sixth man on the Lakers. The "sixth man" concept is credited to Red Auerbach of the Celtics, and such celebrated scorers as John Havlicek and Frank Ramsey played part or most of their careers at this demanding position for him.

A sixth man is a specialist who is rushed into the game at the odd moment when the front five seem to have developed lock wrist or basketball elbow and suddenly are one for 12 from the floor or worse. The basket seems to have shrunk or developed a lid...

A sixth man is sent in not to mark time for a teammate in foul trouble. He's not the equivalent of a penalty-killer in hockey. His job is to punch a hole in that basket quickly, so that the temporary logjam of air balls isn't terminal. Cazzie has to get the team out of handcuffs.

Cazzie Russell does this better than anyone since the young Havlicek. His scoring bursts are legendary. His career totals compare favorably with guys who have played three times as many minutes. Cazzie's job is to throw up a whole flock of unanswered points—to open fire. Cazzie is not out there to bunt.

Cazzie Russell (and Bill Bradley) may have revived the career of the 6-foot-5 forward.

Coaches and general managers had figured Elgin Baylor would be the last in the NBA. A scorer who can come off the point and make 10 baskets in a row, as Cazzie has, has revised this thinking.

To opponents, it sometimes seems as if there are three of him.

Released from the bench, Cazzie runs out on the floor like a litter of bobcats let out of a bag. He looks like a one-man cat-and-dog fight. He runs around the floor like he was circling wagons. The guy who guards him gets cross-eyed. Cazzie is in such furious motion that the guy who drew a picture of him for the ad in the paper put the wrong number on him. The way Cazzie runs around, he was lucky it was only one digit off.

Cazzie believes he is able to be such a model of frenetic energy because he treats his body as if it were something that might leave him if he took it for granted.

"I don't eat junk food on the road," he says.

Pizza parlors are safe from him. So are taco stands and all-night diners.

Although the basketball only weighs 22 ounces, Cazzie prepares his body as if he had to throw the 16-pound shot.

Breakfast is frequently a witch's brew of hot tea, honey, herbs, or apple juice and wheat germ. Soups, salads, lean meat and eggs (poached) make up the rest of the day's diet.

Cazzie frequently boards planes with equal piles of vitamins, crossword puzzles and paperback best-sellers.

Cazzie thinks his diet makes him a fast healer.

When he tore a lateral ligament in a low-bridge foul in an exhibition game a year ago, the doctors thought Cazzie would be out a season if not a career. Cazzie came back Jan. 21 and threw in 24 points in 27 minutes. They took him out then because of the fire laws. The basket was beginning to glow.

1975-76 Season Highlights

Kareem Abdul-Jabbar (27.7) leads, but Gail Goodrich (19.5, No. 25 in photo), Lucius Allen (14.7), Cazzie Russell (11.8), and Donnie Freeman (10.8) score in double figures too.

Abdul-Jabbar is the first Los Angeles Laker to be selected as the NBA's most valuable player.

Cazzie Russell (right), stopping to get open against the Celtics' John Havlicek, had a 47.4% shooting touch in his three seasons for the Lakers.

Abdul-Jabbar leads the league in rebounding (16.9 per game) and blocked shots (4.12).

On December 14, 1975, against the Detroit Pistons, Abdul-Jabbar grabs 29 defensive rebounds, an NBA record.

Abdul-Jabbar also leads the league in minutes played— 3,379—which averages to 41.2 per game.

The Lakers have a 31-9 home record but only 9-33 on the road, keeping them out of the playoffs for the second straight season.

1976-77

Lakers Go West for Their Coach

Season Record

W53-L29 (.646)
Division: 1st
West Finals

Coach

Jerry West

Players

Kareem Abdul-Jabbar

Cazzie Russell

Lucius Allen

Earl Tatum

Don Ford

Kermit Washington

Bo Lamar

Don Chaney

Tom Abernethy

C.J. Kupec

Johnny Neumann

Mack Calvin

Marv Roberts

Cornell Warner

Allen Murphy

In three years of coaching, Jerry West achieved a 145-101 record and won a Pacific Division championship. It was just the beginning of his post-playing role with the Lakers. He went on to scout for three years, then, in 1982, became the team's general manager. He is widely considered to be a major architect of the Lakers' dynasty to come.

By TED GREEN
August 20, 1976

Just last Tuesday, Jerry West said Lakers owner Jack Kent Cooke was so angry about some things West had said about the club that, "There's no way I will ever coach that team . . . I assure you my chances are irreparably damaged. I am now totally out of the picture."

Wednesday, West got a telephone call from Cooke. Thursday, he was named coach of the Lakers.

So ended a bewildering and often clandestine summer-long search for Bill Sharman's replacement. It could have been called "follow the bouncing coach" because until Wednesday Cooke apparently had been vacillating between West and Jerry Tarkanian. And they'd been vacillating right back.

In 14 memorable years as a player, West was Cooke's brightest star, but the two had been estranged—and adversaries in a lawsuit—since West's retirement in 1974 . . .

After an hour-long press conference at the Forum—during which West was at times misty-eyed over what he called "probably one of the three most exciting days in my life"—he said he was "very, very surprised" by Cooke's call Wednesday . . .

Tarkanian, the University of Nevada Las Vegas basketball coach, at one point last week said: "I think the job is mine if I want it." And, like West, he did want it, but he told close friends that finally he felt compelled to remain at the school, where the NCAA is investigating allegations of recruiting improprieties.

Tarkanian, one source said, changed his mind so often "he was impossible to keep up with." . . .

West had a $6-million lawsuit against the owner for allegedly not paying him for the 1974 season. Though he retired just before the regular season began, West said he had the money coming because it said so in his contract. Cooke claimed otherwise . . .

The two apparently made their peace because, West said, "I wouldn't be standing here if it wasn't completely solved . . ."

Cooke repeated a familiar theme—his longtime admiration for West—and said he picked him because "he has a very good chance of becoming one of the great coaches in Laker history . . .

When it was quietly announced recently that Sharman would move to a position in the front office, it wasn't clear what it would be. Thursday he was named assistant general manager.

But the man of the hour . . . was Jerry West, who, at a youngish 38, still looks like he could be the big guard the Lakers seem to need so badly . . .

"I spent 26 years of my life (in basketball)," he said. "If you've been around it that long, you never lose that desire to get back to it to the scene of something that was pleasant . . . When you've had the attachment I've had here, you don't forget that . . ."

[H]is eyes filled with tears when he told newsmen that he had called his mother in West Virginia and she said it was among the happiest days of her life . . .

More than anything, last year's Lakers . . . seemed to lack desire as well as first-rate players to complement Kareem [Abdul-Jabbar] . . . West addressed himself to both matters, saying:

"I can assure you of one thing: I will not tolerate lack of effort, not at all. I expect the players to play 100 percent . . . I expect it every game . . ."

And, on personnel: "It's easy to say they had a horrible year . . . but they made tremendous personnel changes. The people we have now, if they're put in the right defensive structure . . . there's no question we can be a winner. And there's nothing more contagious than winning." . . .

West said that while Cooke has final say on trades and such, "I'm gonna be strong in who I like and who I don't . . . And I don't want people with previous reputations as troublemakers. It's very important to build character in an organization."

Jerry West said of
returning to the
Lakers as a coach:
"When you've had
the attachment
I've had here, you
don't forget that."

Unexplained Chemistry Blended as the Lakers Advance

In chemistry, catalysts speed up reactions without themselves being consumed. Basketball has them too. Was it Coach Jerry West who helped the Lakers race to a Pacific Division championship? Or a pair of rookies? Or the veterans? Whatever the answer, the team had chemistry enough to achieve the NBA-best 53-29 season record and beat the Warriors in the Western Conference Semifinals, four games to three, before being swept by the Portland Trail Blazers in the Western Conference Finals.

By TED GREEN
April 15, 1977

On Feb. 18, one week and one game after forward Kermit Washington went down and out for the season with a knee injury, the Lakers were soundly beaten by the Atlanta Hawks. Since it was only their third loss in 28 games at the Forum, Coach Jerry West was his usual composed, carefree self.

Outside the locker room he spotted a friend, took him by the arm, turned to see if anyone was eavesdropping and said:

"Do you think we're good now? How many you figure we'll win the rest of the way? We might get the bleep kicked out of us, the way Atlanta did tonight. You think we'll get far in the playoffs? Hey, we may be dead."

For once, West seemed to have cause for alarm. For 50 games Washington had gotten the Lakers the ball off both backboards—any way he saw fit. He was their best rebounder, their enforcer and the em-

bodiment of Los Angeles' Spirit of 77.

He was also the man who made life in the lane a lot easier for center Kareem Abdul-Jabbar . . . Washington's forearms, elbows, Mr. America biceps, fast fists and exceedingly short fuse tended to discourage forwards from felonious assaults on the center.

With those two as a nucleus, with a team of selfless, eager role-players and with smart coaching, the Lakers to everyone's surprise had the best record in the National Basketball Assn.

Gone along with Washington, it appeared, was the team balance West had regarded as tenuous at best, and the consensus was that it would be a great surprise if the club remained on top to the end of the season . . .

But in early April, when Washington sat in street clothes at courtside taking in his first game in seven weeks, the team somehow still had the best record.

What's more, the Lakers already had clinched their first Pacific Division title since their coach's last hurrah as a player . . .

Rookie forward Tom Abernethy, in Washington's role as sixth man, more than held his own on the boards . . . Rookie swingman Earl Tatum, getting more playing time, gave the team life in his own jukin' and jivin' playground way.

Abdul-Jabbar continued a pace that is almost certain to put a fourth Most Valuable Player trophy in some closet in his house in Bel-Air.

Second-year starting forward Don Ford, after more than a few conversations with West, decided it was time to muss his beach-boy-blond hair by mix-

ing it up inside instead of finessing from afar. Veterans Cazzie Russell, Lucius Allen and Don Chaney were enjoying their professional rebirths too much to let it all slip away.

And the team that is unmistakably Jerry West's, because it hustles and cares and never quits and makes big plays in the fourth quarter, won seven straight in a season-ending stretch and approached the second round of the playoffs with the kind of think-it-but-don't-flaunt-it confidence characteristic of clubs that believe in themselves.

Even West . . . had to call a halt. Instead of talking about his "YMCA pickup team," "$40,000 ballplayers" and "misfits, rejects, castoffs and rookies," he began saying things like: "This team has worked hard. It's smart. It deserves to be where it is." . . .

What the Lakers did have . . . is a chemistry that can be seen but not always explained. There were players who'd been there before . . . There were kids out of college and others new to the league who were happy to have a job . . .

That the Lakers are even being mentioned in the same breath with division titles and playoffs and maybe winning it all is, at the bottom line, a tribute to West . . .

He had the brains and confidence to delegate X's and O's authority to assistant coaches Stan Albeck (offense) and Jack McCloskey (defense), thus freeing himself to teach and urge and motivate and even inspire. "I used to watch that man on TV," Earl Tatum said. "He was cool; I dug him. When he says dive for a loose ball, you don't ask questions. You dive."

1976-77 Season Highlights

Bill Sharman (right) takes over for Pete Newell as Lakers general manager.

Kareem Abdul-Jabbar, guarded by Julius Erving (6), has a team-high 21 points to lead the winning West team in the All-Star Game.

Kareem Abdul-Jabbar and Portland's Bill Walton duel under the boards in Game 4 of the 1977 Western Conference Finals.

Abdul-Jabbar, the league's MVP again, tops the Lakers in points (26.2), rebounds (13.3), blocks (3.2), and field-goal percentage (57.9%).

The Lakers use one of their three first-round picks in the 1977 draft to take Norm Nixon from Duquesne.

The Lakers finish the season a team-record 37-4 at home, including a streak of 21 consecutive victories at the Forum.

Cazzie Russell specialized in rapid-fire offense, averaging 14.5 points in 26.8 minutes a game during his three seasons for the Lakers.

1977-78

One-Punch Knockout

Season Record

45-37 (.549)
Division: 4th
First Round

Coach

Jerry West

Players

Kareem
Abdul-Jabbar

Lou Hudson

Norm Nixon

Adrian Dantley

Jamaal Wilkes

Don Ford

Charlie Scott

Tom Abernethy

James Edwards

Earl Tatum

Kenny Carr

Kermit
Washington

Dave Robisch

Ernie DiGregorio

Brad Davis

Don Chaney

Witnesses remember the sound and the eerie silence that followed. The punch on December 9, 1977, sent Rudy Tomjanovich to the floor in a pool of blood and Kermit Washington into a two-month exile from basketball. "To this day it changed everyone's life, the mistake I made—a mistake in judgment," Washington said later in an NBA documentary. Tomjanovich recovered, returned to the game, coached the Houston Rockets to two NBA championships, and briefly coached the Lakers in 2004-05. Washington founded a nonprofit in Africa, to which the NBA has donated funds, and did some preseason coaching with the Denver Nuggets. After many years of distance, Washington and Tomjanovich renewed their relationship. The Los Angeles Times' Bill Plaschke visited Washington in 2000 to talk about the incident.

By BILL PLASCHKE
May 28, 2000

Just up the road, a universe away, there was a lesson in the heavy eyes that watched the Lakers and Portland Trail Blazers shoving each other around the Rose Garden on Friday...

Careful, the eyes said.

You can throw a punch and be pummeled by it.

The most famous jab in the history of team sports has knocked him through 23 years and three teams and countless stares and rejection.

It has knocked him from a Lakers uniform to a loud sports bar in a drab strip mall in a tiny corner of the Pacific Northwest.

Here, Saturday afternoon, a woman named Francie Tomacci is eating one of his hamburgers.

She is asked if she knows the owner. She does...

"Yeah, he used to play basketball," she says. "Wasn't he the one who hit Tom-jan..."

A couple of tables away, an order pad at his side, Kermit Washington shrugs.

A life of 48 full years seemingly reduced to those two syllables.

Tom-jan.

That's the first part of the difficult-to-pronounce last name of a former Houston Rocket, Rudy Tomjanovich, who was nearly killed by an on-court punch in 1977.

Kermit Washington was the Laker who punched him.

Tomjanovich suffered a fractured skull, broken jaw, broken nose and spinal fluid leakage, but has long since recovered to coach two NBA champions and be named coach of the current Olympic team.

Washington suffered no physical damage but still feels as if he is being flattened.

He is a former all-star who wants to return to the game as a coach, but he says nobody will hire him because of the mere connotation of his name.

He graduated from American University with honors, but says the NBA won't let him help with its stay-in-schools effort because of his name.

Spend an afternoon with him at Le Slam Sports Cafe ... and it is difficult to imagine this soft-spoken man ever hit anybody.

But the minute people find out who he is, they can do nothing but imagine...

"I just don't want to die like this," he says softly. "I just don't want everyone remembering me for something negative."

Since being shipped out of town by the Lakers shortly after the incident at the Forum on Dec. 9, 1977, Washington has tried mightily to be remembered for something else...

He finished his career as an all-star with the Trail Blazers. He was briefly an assistant coach at Stanford. He helped run Pete Newell's famed big man's basketball camp.

He became a Portland-area radio talk show host. He began leading relief efforts to Africa. He bought a sports restaurant.

He says none of it matters...

"Every time there is some violence in the sports world, I know I'll be seeing myself on ESPN again," he says. "The same clip, over and over again. People who never saw me play, all they know is that I punched."

And that is too bad.

Kermit Washington, the subject of an NBA TV documentary, *Redemption*, got a coaching job for one season in 2005 as an assistant with the Asheville, N.C., team in the NBA Development League. The team went on to win the league title.

It has been 23 years, and he has not thrown a punch since.

The most important use for his hands these days is to rub medicine on the bodies of the diseased Africans he has helped during one of his 10 relief missions to war-torn areas. On three of those occasions, he has sold some of his memorabilia to fund an entourage of nearly a dozen doctors and nurses.

"I saw the video of him on TV, and I couldn't believe this was the same person," said Pat Cook, a Portland nurse who accompanied Washington on one of his missions. "He is the most caring, sweetest man. He is like a mother hen . . . "

It has been 23 years, and you look at a replay of a punch that has not lost its chill, and you start to think.

Maybe time does more than heal the wounds. Maybe time creates new ones. Sometimes, maybe, time actually changes the names of the victims . . .

Lakers' Season a Downhill Run

Fights, fines, trades, and a suspension. It was a memorable year, but mostly for the wrong reasons. The Lakers managed a 45-37 record, thanks to a 28-13 run in the second half of the season. But it all came to an end in the first round of the Western Conference playoffs.

By TED GREEN
April 17, 1978

SEATTLE—The Lakers' bizarre 1977-78 season started with a bang when Kareem Abdul-Jabbar broke his hand punching Milwaukee's Kent Benson.

Six months later, it nearly ended with a whimper on the big guy's 31st birthday. The Lakers, playing as if they just had been introduced to each other at training camp, trailed the Seattle SuperSonics by 19 points late in the third quarter of Sunday's third and deciding first-round NBA playoff game.

Only 12 points in the fourth quarter by Dave Robisch saved the Lakers the embarrassment of being blown out on national television in their biggest game of the year. But their season ended anyway, when the SuperSonics repelled a late rally to win, 111-102.

For much of Game 3, the Lakers were embarrassed enough. The young and hungry SuperSonics out-shot, outrebounded, outpassed, out-thought and outhustled them in building a lead that was too big to relinquish, what with a sellout crowd of 14,098 at Seattle Center Coliseum screaming for Wilkens' Wonders.

So, the SuperSonics—44-19 since Coach Lenny Wilkens replaced Bob Hopkins Nov.

30 and 28-3 at home, where they've won 14 straight—head to Portland to meet the defending NBA champions in the Western Conference semifinals.

Lakers Coach Jerry West was heading farther south, back to his new home in Pacific Palisades. There he may wonder why his high strung, low-profile and talented-on-paper team never really meshed, despite a 28-13 record in the second half of the season that served to shorten the Lakers' vacation by one week.

West may also wish that next season, his third as L.A.'s coach, won't take him for the kind of emotional roller-coaster ride this one did.

Recalling the fights, fines, trades, suspension (of Kermit Washington, now with Boston) and difficulty integrating a group of players lumped together largely by owner Jack Kent Cooke's checkbook, West said; "This hasn't been a very pleasant year for me."

Then he said: "Late in the third quarter today, I would have said I was bitterly disappointed. Now I'm disappointed, but for different reasons.

"I'm disappointed because I really feel that this team, executing well, maybe could play against anyone. But talent is only talent when it's written about. A lot of players in this league don't get publicity when it's justified ... like Seattle's.

"You know," West said, "when I took this job, I said I didn't think I'd be around very long. Not because I don't enjoy basketball, but because too much emphasis is placed in the individual in this league. You (players) have to want to do what's best to win. If a coach really cares about what he's doing,

it's impossible to do this job very well."

West didn't criticize anyone directly; he rarely does. But in this case he didn't really have to. It was clear enough that the play of new additions Charlie Scott and Jamaal Wilkes this season had made it seem as if their reputations and salaries were inflated; that two more first-year Lakers, Adrian Dantley and Lou Hudson, sometimes were one-way (offensive) players, and that Abdul-Jabbar often acted as if he were more interested in which band was playing at The Roxy in Hollywood than he was in winning and losing.

Shortly after Sunday's loss, the mood in L.A.'s locker room was hardly subdued. Scott, chattering away, waved a couple of new tennis racquets. Abdul-Jabbar asked if they were graphite and Hudson and Norm Nixon joined them in laughter.

The SuperSonics, of course, had more reason to laugh.

Everyone who's anyone on their team had a hand in eliminating a Lakers team from the first playoff round for only the fourth time in 16 years ...

After Seattle had led, 59-50, at the half, SuperSonics rookie forward Jack Sikma just about singlehandedly did in L.A., with 20 of his 24 points in the second half. Guard Gus Williams scored 16 before halftime and finished with 22. Center Marvin Webster had 20 and 18 rebounds; though Abdul-Jabbar scored 31 points, the 7-1 Webster outplayed him in the second half. Forward Johnny Johnson of the Geritol Squad scored 18. No. 3 guard Fred Brown threw in some long jumpers and scored 14. Guard Dennis Johnson held Hudson to four points on one-for-six shooting. And reserve forward Paul Silas grabbed nine rebounds in 24 minutes.

1977-78 Season Highlights

Norm Nixon sets a Lakers rookie record for assists with 14 against Chicago on November 20, 1977.

Charlie Scott ends up in a revolving door, arriving December 27, 1977, in a trade with Boston and leaving June 26, 1978, in a deal with Denver.

Adrian Dantley (4), acquired in a December trade with Indiana, did most of his work on the offensive end in the 1977-78 season, finishing second in team scoring with a 19.4-point average.

Kareem Abdul-Jabbar leads the team in scoring (25.8 points per game) and in rebounding (12.9).

Abdul-Jabbar misses 20 games after breaking his right hand when he punches Milwaukee Bucks center Kent Benson in the season opener in retaliation for an elbow.

After the Lakers win 28 of their 41 second-half games, they lose in the first round of the playoffs to Seattle, which has home-court advantage.

1978-79

A Hard Guy to Find

Season Record

W47-L35 (.573)
Division: 3rd
West Semis

Coach

Jerry West

Players

Kareem
Abdul-Jabbar

Jamaal Wilkes

Norm Nixon

Adrian Dantley

Lou Hudson

Ron Boone

Kenny Carr

Don Ford

Jim Price

Dave Robisch

Ron Carter

Brad Davis

Michael Cooper

Down the road at Lockheed in Burbank, engineers were developing sophisticated aircraft stealth technology. But over at the Forum, Jamaal Wilkes was demonstrating his own techniques for staying under the radar. So good was he that the four-time NBA champion and three-time All-Star was dubbed "Smooth as Silk." He played with the Lakers from 1977-78 through 1984-85.

By JIM MURRAY
March 25, 1979

The players call him "Silk." You don't really see him, you just hear this rustle as he goes by, like taffeta in candlelight.

He has made a career of not being noticed. He's more like a spy than a participant. He's 6 feet 6 and may weigh 190 right after dinner. If he stood on a basketball, he'd look like an exclamation point. If he turns sideways, he disappears. He's not a player, he's a shadow. You could use him for a sun dial. Or a minute hand.

All his life, he's played in the shadow of someone else. At UCLA, everyone was watching the redhead in the center, Bill Walton. So he quietly became the seventh all-time scorer in UCLA history.

Drafted by the Golden State Warriors, he was the other forward. Rick Barry was throwing in 30 points a game and shooting 90% from the line. So, he became Rookie of the Year and Golden State became world champs, the first championship team Barry had been on in 10 years in the game.

He signed with the Los Angeles Lakers, a team with Kareem Abdul-Jabbar and not much else.

If they made a movie, Ronald Reagan would play his part—the hero's best friend. Tonto. Good ol' Joe. The one who doesn't get the girl.

Good ol' Jamaal Wilkes is accustomed to blending in with the scenery. He goes through life as if he's wanted someplace and fears extradition. On the basketball court, his stock is surreptitiousness. His specialty is making the other guys think the Lakers only put four men on the floor that night.

He doesn't run down court, he just flows. He's a "Where did he come from?" player. You don't play him, you track him. Every so often, the other coach calls time out to see where Wilkes went. He's like the butler in a mystery movie. When the other team gets killed, no one believes he did it because no one saw him do it. But, when the Lakers win, his fingerprints are all over the ball. And he's standing there looking innocent with a "who me?" expression on his face . . .

He even looks harmless. He has these big, gray eyes that always seem to be looking someplace else. He plays basketball as if it were a skill, not a rumble. The game has been given over lately to something called the "power forward," a prehistoric form of man who was taught to bust up a game, not play it . . .

"Silk" doesn't get into this bone-breaking melee. They don't need the three-second violation for him because he doesn't stay anywhere for three seconds, never mind the key. He moves so much so fast, it would be hard to keep him in Rhode Island for three seconds.

His real specialty is the defensive rebound. Wilkes can read the carom like Willie Hoppe. And he can screen out a freight train. Which is a good thing. Because they frequently give him one to screen out. They give him Elvin Hayes and Maurice Lucas to match up against. He doesn't know whether to play them or climb them.

Moving without the ball is an art most people can't master. It's like dancing by yourself or arranging a meeting in the dark. Most guys horde the ball like a bank book. Wilkes runs more without the ball than a defensive halfback. He doesn't attack, he infiltrates . . .

Of course, he's playing out his option. Wilkes doesn't like to stay in one place too long on or off the court, in or out of the key . . .

If the Lakers let him go, they will be making the same mistake the league's forwards do. They will turn around just in time to see him throwing up the championship for someone else, or rebounding a playoff win. There aren't that many forwards around the league that can get eight baskets and 10 rebounds before the other guys realize they showed up.

Quietly, Jamaal Wilkes
was the Lakers'
second-leading scorer
for five consecutive
years, beginning with
the 1978-79 season.

In the Lakers' Version, Nixon Succeeds Ford

This Nixon wasn't about to be kicked around by anyone. Known as a good passer and shooter, Norm Nixon also had larceny in his heart. In this season he tied Eddie Jordan of the New Jersey Nets to lead the league in steals with 201. He also was third in assists (737) and fifth in minutes played (3,145).

By TED GREEN
February 28, 1979

Phil Ford, the Kansas City Kings' polished young guard from North Carolina, is a shoo-in for NBA Rookie of the Year. In some circles, he's even being called a Most Valuable Player candidate for being the prime mover in the Kings' startlingly successful season.

Ford is a good little basketball player, and more than anyone else, he makes Kansas City go. But make no mistake, he is not the only gifted point guard in pro basketball.

The Lakers have one named Norm Nixon, and Tuesday night at the Forum he not only outplayed Ford but virtually beat the Kings by himself in the fourth quarter.

With the Lakers leading by only three points in a tightly fought, entertaining game, Nixon hit four consecutive jump shots—two right in Ford's face—and they provided the turning point as Los Angeles went on to defeat Kansas City, 122-114, in a matchup between division leaders.

The victory over the league's hottest team (Kansas City came in with a 10-2 February record) increased the Lakers' Pacific Division lead to 1½ games over Seattle and 2½ over Phoenix, the furthest L.A. (39-24,

25-6 at home) has been ahead this season.

The Kings, meanwhile, could afford the loss. Now 40-23, second-best record to Washington's 41-19, Kansas City still leads the Midwest Division by six games.

As usual the Kings, who are no fluke, were competitive for a long time, despite the fact the Lakers' front line of Jamaal Wilkes, Kareem Abdul-Jabbar and Adrian Dantley was scoring points almost as fast as the scoreboard operator could push the buttons.

As so many NBA games do, this one had its critical period in the fourth quarter. That's when Nixon took over.

The 6-foot-1, second-year playmaker from Duquesne, who has blossomed this season into one of the league's best guards, first swished a 15-foot baseline jumper at the end of a fastbreak. Score: 108-103.

Then he backed Ford down—one little man "posting" the other—turned, and with his superior jumping ability, hit from 12 feet straight-away: Score: 110-103.

Now Nixon was cookin', and his play reminded of something he'd said a few weeks back, almost matter-of-factly—that he felt he could score with Ford guarding him anytime he wanted. This time he backed Ford down again and hit from just above the free-throw line: Score: 112-103.

Moments later, Nixon swished another medium-range jumper to cap another in a seemingly endless procession of fastbreaks. Score: 114-103. And score a personal victory in the matchup between the NBA's two most "pure" point guards.

Nixon finished with 18 points and nine assists to only six points and six assists for Ford.

Kings Coach Cotton Fitzsimmons gave his star rookie the quick hook after Nixon did his damage. Ford was sent back to the bench after he'd been in the lineup in the fourth quarter for only two minutes.

Needless to say, Nixon and Ford will meet again . . . and Ford will no doubt have his days. In fact, he's already had them against the Lakers; in the two previous games this season he averaged 18 points and 15 assists.

Nixon, too, wasn't the only Laker who had a major role in a game watched by a crowd of 12,909.

Center Abdul-Jabbar played with emotion and dominated the inside: 25 points, 11 rebounds, six assists and eight blocked shots . . .

Forward Jamaal Wilkes, who just has to be one of the most consistent players in the league this season, had 28 points, six rebounds, three assists and three blocks.

Dantley scored 19 points, all in the first half. Forward Kenny Carr again played well coming off the bench, particularly in the fourth quarter when he, instead of Dantley, was in the game . . .

The Lakers, typically, won despite being outrebounded by a whopping 19-3 on the offensive boards. A big reason, just as typically, was their accurate shooting—57.3%.

The Kings are guard-oriented with Ford and second-year shooting machine Otis Birdsong, who also had an off-night with 15 points on six-for-17 shooting. The Kings' front line held its own with Bill Robinzine (20 points, 11 rebounds), Scott Wedman (18 and 8) and center Sam Lacey (15 and 11).

Ultimately, though, Kansas City—whose hub is a point guard—was done in by one.

1978-79 Season Highlights

Jerry West, shown with assistant Stan Albeck (right), quits as coach at the season's end with a 145-101 regular-season record and a 8-14 playoff mark.

Jamaal Wilkes is second on the team in both scoring (18.6 points per game) and rebounding (7.4).

Norm Nixon glides toward the basket in the 1970s. He averaged 16.4 points in six seasons for the Lakers.

Norm Nixon is third in the NBA in assists (9.0 per game) and second in steals (2.45).

Kareem Abdul-Jabbar (bottom row, third from left), who is selected to the West All-Star Team, finishes second in the NBA in rebounding with 12.8 per game.

Michael Cooper is the 60th pick of the 1978 draft. For seven seasons in the 1980s, he would lead the Lakers in three-point shots made.

Earvin "Magic" Johnson's drive time: five championship rings, three-time NBA Finals' Most Valuable Player, three-time NBA MVP, two-time All-Star MVP, and a new era of Lakers basketball.

CHAPTER FOUR

Showtime!

Seasons 1979-80 through 1989-90

IT WAS a dynasty built on a smile.

When Lakers owner Jack Kent Cooke saw photos of effervescent 19-year-old Earvin "Magic" Johnson leading Michigan State to the 1979 NCAA title, Cooke knew how he would spend the No. 1 overall pick in the NBA draft.

Skeptics said the theatrical Cooke was dazzled by an illusion. In the NBA, college hotdogs lose their smiles one tooth at a time.

The Lakers, and the league, were reeling. Attendance was down, the game was trapped in artistic doldrums. In Los Angeles, Kareem Abdul-Jabbar at 32 was a superstar in decline, weary from the weight on his shoulders, his hope for a second championship ring fading.

A spark was needed.

"If there are some crazy basketball fans," Johnson said, "tell 'em to come on out."

They came, they saw, and the Lakers conquered. Eight trips to the NBA Finals in eleven Showtime seasons; five championships.

Cooke signed Magic with the emphatic endorsement of Jerry Buss, who was in the process of buying the team. Buss gave the world Coach Pat Riley and General Manager Jerry West, the Laker Girls, and unique ticket-pricing that allowed Joe Fan to join the high-five party.

Beneath it all, a belief in the kid with the smile. The Lakers were caught in a hotel fire in Philadelphia in '83. Johnson led a group of panicky guests through the smoke to a drop-down escape ladder. Magic looked down and hesitated.

From above came a calm voice: "Go ahead, Earvin. You can do it."

It was Kareem.

—Scott Ostler

There's a New Show in Town

When the Lakers first hit town in 1960, the team was lucky to draw 2,000 fans on some nights. But owner Bob Short soon figured that a town noted for celebrities would respond to a team with a celebrity following. So he started comping movie stars, and the fans followed. Actress-singer Doris Day was a fixture near the corner of the court, where she could distract opposing players and attract starstruck fans. Other Hollywood names came along and attendance jumped to more than 11,000 a game. When Jack Kent Cooke bought the team, however, he did away with the comps. Some stars, like Day, left, but others paid and stayed.

Savvy businessman Jerry Buss bought the team in 1979 and embraced celebrity, entertaining Hollywood's elite in his greatly expanded owner's box and welcoming the flood of stars who came to see the Magic show. Today, NBA.com even maintains an all-time top-10 list of Lakers celebs: Ms. Day, Arsenio Hall, Leonardo DiCaprio, Penny Marshall, Denzel Washington, Andy Garcia, Ice Cube, founding members of the Red Hot Chili Peppers—Anthony Kiedis and Flea—Dyan Cannon, and First Fan Jack Nicholson.

But celebrities weren't enough for this life-in-the-fast-lane owner. As Buss told Los Angeles Times reporter Susan Carpenter, "I thought the game itself was fantastic, but the ambience was really kind of dead. It was quiet and boring, and so I thought what I'd like to do is spice it up with having some dancers." Thus the Laker Girls came into being. More than anything though, it was the Lakers of the '80s—and their star, Magic Johnson—that really made it "Showtime!"

The Laker Girls have become a fan favorite since they began performing in 1979.

Laker Girls Facts

Founded by Jerry Buss when he bought the team in 1979.

Composed originally of former USC and UCLA songleaders.

Evolved into a professional dance squad.

Twenty-two-member squad chosen from more than 500 candidates; must be 18 years old to audition.

Perform routines at least four times per game.

Practice six hours minimum a week; may work up to 40 if Lakers play more than three home games a week.

Paid per event; position is part time. Have included a college professor, financial analyst, elementary and high school teachers, event planner, medical/pharmaceutical salesperson, and mother.

Perform at home games during timeouts and quarter breaks; heavily involved in Southern California community events.

Have represented NBA in Europe, Asia and Australia.

To identify the people pictured on this page, please turn to page 251

1979-80

This Dr. J Has a PhD and Owns the Lakers

Season Record

W60-L22 (.732)
Division: 1st
NBA Champion

Coaches

Jack McKinney
(10-4) and
Paul Westhead
(50-18)

Players

Kareem
Abdul-Jabbar

Jamaal Wilkes

Norm Nixon

Magic Johnson

Jim Chones

Spencer Haywood

Michael Cooper

Mark Landsberger

Don Ford

Brad Holland

Marty Byrnes

Ollie Mack

Ron Boone

Kenny Carr

Butch Lee

The word came in an early morning call to Jerry Buss from sports magnate Jack Kent Cooke. The deal, in the works for many months, was on. Cooke was ready to sell the Lakers, the Kings hockey team, the Forum, and his 13,000-acre ranch. After lengthy negotiations, Buss was ready to buy. At $67.5 million, it was said to be the biggest sale in sports history.

By TED GREEN
May 30, 1979

He likes fast cars, fast women and fast scores in business and does his darndest to indulge in them. He squires Playboy bunnies around in a Rolls-Royce Camargue . . . or Cadillac limousine . . . or a Lincoln (that limo has a TV).

His tastes run from Kahlua to California wines and he has an insatiable sweet tooth. His office looks like Willy Wonka's chocolate factory, stocked with M&Ms, candy bars by the hundreds, jelly beans, lollipops and other sweets.

He lives in Bel-Air in a house with seven bathrooms and six fireplaces, has a Japanese houseboy who cooks midnight suppers, plays tennis on his own court and is host to major league parties.

If he isn't weekending in Palm Springs, recuperating in a plush corner of the hotel he owns, he's apt to be living it up in Las Vegas or New York or nearly anywhere he decides to jet to on a whim.

If all this sounds hedonistic, downright Hefneresque, be advised that Dr. Jerry Buss happens also to be a careful, conservative businessman who's a whiz at other figures—the numerical ones. He has a PhD in physical chemistry (which involves much math) from USC. Is there another owner in the major leagues with a PhD?

Yes, the L.A. real estate man who's in the process of buying the Lakers, the Kings and the Forum from Jack Kent Cooke has two distinct sides: By day he's a calculating tycoon whose every move in his multimillion dollar business is carefully thought out.

Jerry Buss leaves very little to chance. But by night there's very little he won't chance.

The quintessential story of Buss, the sports owner, involves Jimmy Connors, whom Buss was trying to sign for his Strings of World TeamTennis. Connors, a few years back, had just bought a new black Porsche, which he was proudly showing off to his buddy, Ilie Nastase. Just then Buss drove up in a new Maserati, jumped out, dangled the keys in front of Connors and said, "You want it? Just sign."

Connors never signed. But a year later Nastase did, bringing his unique act to L.A. for two seasons. So did Chris Evert Lloyd, who led Buss' team to the WTT title . . .

By first helping form the fledgling tennis league, then just about floating it financially for five years before it [at the time] folded; by romancing Connors and other stars when WTT hardly had any, and by taking a $2-million beating trying to sell the concept . . . Buss gained a reputation as a dreamer.

Somehow, most of his dreams came true. He signed stars, put the Strings on their economic feet, celebrated with his underlings when they won the championship last summer and sipped champagne, knowing all the while that the next time he sipped it might be to celebrate a bigger victory: the purchase of Cooke's mini-empire.

Buss' path to the major leagues was, to say the least, as unconventional as Buss himself. He left home in Kemmerer, Wyo., at 16, took a room above a pool hall, hustled games downstairs for $50 a ball (backed, he says, by his chemistry teacher) and still graduated from high school with honors.

He left college for a year to roam around the rodeo in Cheyenne and still got a doctorate before his 24th birthday.

He left a desk job at a giant aircraft company, complaining he was part of a "herd of very educated cattle" and pooled his savings with a friend, Frank Mariani, to buy one apartment building in LA. in 1958.

A few years later, by the mid-60s, these two eggheads were running a real estate business which blossomed to what Buss says it is worth today—

about $350 million after its bank obligations...

Buss enhances the notion that he is a 46-year-old flake by dressing in old jeans, western shirts and cowboy boots, which he often wears to the office in Santa Monica. There he oversees a business that includes 5,000 apartment units in L.A., 5,000 more in Phoenix, Las Vegas and Sacramento, hotels in Palm Springs and Phoenix, assorted condominiums, plus shopping centers and office buildings in the planning stages. Now, with Tuesday's announcement, there is also Cooke's 13,000-acre ranch in the Sierra.

Actually, Buss is not so much a flake as an iconoclast who prides himself on being pragmatically up-to-date...

Buss, divorced years ago and now happily single, wears his graying hair long and does nearly everything he can to project a swinger's image... Like nearly all the other wealthy men who own teams, Buss is in it for the kicks, for ego, for a place in the sun and for whatever challenge the world of fun and games offers.

"Sports is a world in miniature," he once said. "The ups and downs of life, the frustrations and depressions and elations, all come out in a two-hour, sped-up, emotional experience. I really enjoy it. And the closer you are to it, the more emotional it becomes.

"Owning a team is just a very big experience."

Jerry Buss, who got his doctorate before his 24th birthday, shows off the NBA championship trophy in his first season as owner of the Lakers.

Magic Tells the Captain: Let's Dance

From the first to the last game of the 1979-80 season, rookie Earvin "Magic" Johnson left no doubt the league would forever be different with him in it.

By TED GREEN
May 17, 1980

PHILADELPHIA—The season started with Magic Johnson gleefully hugging Kareem Abdul-Jabbar after the captain tossed in a skyhook at the final buzzer to win the opener in San Diego.

Six months later, the season ended with Magic Johnson gleefully hugging the National Basketball Assn.'s championship trophy." I know your ankle hurts, Kareem," Johnson said, "but why don't you get up and dance, anyway?"

All the Lakers were dancing late Friday night, and pouring champagne on each other and praising Abdul-Jabbar, after they won the 1979-80 championship with a 123-107 victory over the Philadelphia 76ers in Game 6 of the final series.

This was an improbable win, and an improbable end to a season that had an almost dreamlike quality, for it was accomplished without the game's most dominant player. Abdul-Jabbar watched the clincher on TV, having sprained his left ankle the previous game.

So for a few minutes . . . the Lakers' locker room seemed strangely subdued ... But then Butch Lee popped open a bottle of champagne, someone started spraying another, and it wasn't a dream anymore. Before long, Coach Paul Westhead's three-piece, pinstriped suit and perfectly styled hair were drenched in the bubbly, too.

Johnson eventually joined in, but first he said he had something important to say.

"Big fella," he said, "We did it for you." And: "Kareem is the one who got us this far. And he was with us (in spirit) tonight,"

It was a nice gesture from the man of the hour, from the series' Most Valuable Player, from the rookie who scored 42 points and proved that he is not only a man for all positions but for all leagues. From an NCAA title a year ago last March to an NBA title in May, it could only be Magic.

Westhead (and all the Lakers) didn't know who to talk about first, the center who wasn't here or the incredible kid who filled his shoes for the night of nights. "Kareem shared in this. He knows it. And we know it," Westhead said.

Then: "You know, when we got to the airport yesterday (Thursday) and we knew Kareem wasn't coming to Philly, I told you guys that Magic was going to play center. So several reporters asked Magic about it and he said, 'Oh yeah, that's nice.'

"Then he goes in and sits in the man's seat (Row J, Seat 1. Abdul-Jabbar's customary seat on all team flights), Then he turns around and gives me this little grin. The next thing I expected was for him to pull a blanket over his head, the way Kareem always does."

The Lakers' coach then said of Abdul-Jabbar: "When we came into the locker room after the fifth game (a 108-103 win at the Forum, a win featuring 40 points for Abdul-Jabbar, who scored 14 in the fourth quarter on a painfully sprained ankle), Kareem said. 'One more. We gotta get one more.' . . . Westhead said. "Those were the last words I heard Kareem utter before he went off to be X-rayed. Obvi-

ously, the players were listening."

They apparently listened well because the Lakers blew away a somewhat befuddled 76ers team with a nonstop running game. When the running stopped, forward Jamaal Wilkes, with 37 points, had also scored a career high, as did Johnson. And Johnson scored points with those who refused to believe he is already among the game's top players. If only because he is just 20 years old.

Johnson played low-post center, high-post center, power forward, small forward, point guard, shooting guard. He drove on big guys and shot over smaller ones. He took it to Darryl Dawkins and Julius Erving, He killed Caldwell Jones on the boards. He made those no-look passes through traffic to get his teammates layups. He stole passes. He made like Abdul-Jabbar and threw in a little hook. He almost threw in a much longer one, from beyond midcourt, just before the halftime buzzer. The miracle was it didn't go in.

That wasn't Magic, brothers. Just talent. To think the Lakers won his draft rights with the flip of a coin. "Magic is no rookie," Wilkes said. "He's never played like one. He's a winner, a champion, something very, very special."

"Magic was born to play and born to win," said rookie guard Brad Holland, who finally got a chance to contribute and did, handsomely. "It's hard to picture Magic Johnson losing."

Just then, Johnson, posing for cameramen, kissed the gold championship trophy. It, too, got soaked with champagne and kissed by another rookie—rookie owner Jerry Buss—who made the rounds joyfully congratulating everybody.

1979-80 Season Highlights

Magic Johnson (shown in his hometown of Lansing, Mich.) comes to L.A. and the Showtime era opens. Attendance jumps from 482,611 the previous season to 582,882.

Paul Westhead (right) takes over as the Lakers coach, with Pat Riley his assistant, after Jack McKinney suffers a life-threatening injury 14 games into the season.

Kareem Abdul-Jabbar dunks for two of his 40 points in Game 5 of the 1980 Finals despite Julius Erving's in-your-face defense. Abdul-Jabbar was later injured and missed Game 6.

It's Magic! The Rookie Produces Finals Win

In 1979, the New Orleans Jazz and the Chicago Bulls, last-place teams in their divisions, tossed a coin to see which would open the draft. The Bulls called "heads." The coin came up "tails." But the Jazz (which later moved to Utah) owed its pick to Los Angeles to compensate for signing Lakers free agent Gail Goodrich. Thus Magic Johnson joined the likes of Kareem Abdul-Jabbar and Jamaal Wilkes; the Lakers won 60 regular-season games, and the championship returned to Los Angeles for the first time since 1972.

By SCOTT OSTLER
May 17, 1980

PHILADELPHIA—When they erect the statue of Magic Johnson in some prominent location in Los Angeles, as they surely will soon, chiseled on the pedestal will be Magic's favorite saying:

"It's winnin' time."

That's what time it was Friday night in the Spectrum when Magic, a 20-year-old rookie, led the Lakers to one of the true upsets in National Basketball Assn. playoff history, a 123-107 win over the Philadelphia 76ers.

With center Kareem Abdul-Jabbar watching the game from the comfort of his living room 3,000 miles away, his sprained left ankle propped up on a coffee table, the Lakers won the championship of the NBA, four games to two.

Magic, who literally laughed at the added pressure when Abdul-Jabbar was scratched, started at center and scored 42 points, grabbed 15 rebounds and handed out seven assists. He made 14 of 23 field-goal attempts and 14 of 14 free throws.

The Lakers outplayed the 76ers from the start but with five minutes left, Philadelphia pulled within two points, 103-101.

As 18,276 Spectrum fans sat back and waited for reality to take over from fantasy, the Lakers outscored the 76ers, 20-6. Magic had 11 of those 20 points.

When Jamaal Wilkes threw down a dunk to give the Lakers a 12-point lead with 50 seconds left, Abdul-Jabbar must have spiked his TV to his living room carpet in jubilation.

It is the Lakers' first NBA championship since 1972, a perfect anniversary present for the team's 20th season. In those 20 years, the team has been in the Finals 10 times, and won twice.

Johnson was voted the Most Valuable Player in the series, Abdul-Jabbar's monumental contributions in the first five games notwithstanding.

Magic had help.

Who can believe . . .

— Quiet Jamaal Wilkes, a non-All-Star, outplaying Julius (Dr. J) Erving? Wilkes scored 37 points, the most he's had since high school. Erving had 27 points.

— Brad Holland, Lakers rookie, outscoring teammate Norm Nixon, 8 to 4? Until Friday night, Holland was the Human Victory Cigar, entering games only when the outcome was decided. He scored six straight points near the end of the first half.

— The Lakers—without Abdul-Jabbar, remember—outrebounding the 76ers, 52-36 (17-7 on the offensive boards)? It's called desire. Wilkes, Jim Chones and Mark (the Shark) Landsberger had 10 rebounds each. No 76er had 10.

— Jim Chones, the reluctant stand-in for Abdul-Jabbar, outplaying Darryl (Chocolate Thunder) Dawkins? Chones had 11 points and 10 rebounds; Dawkins 14 points and four rebounds . . .

Also helping pick up the slack for Abdul-Jabbar and the off-key Nixon (whose dislocated left ring finger was taped and painful) was Mike Cooper, who scored 16 points.

Two of Cooper's points came on free throws early in the fourth quarter after Dawkins slammed him to the floor on a hit that would have brought tears of pride to the eyes of Jack Tatum.

Cooper finished the game, and has been cleared to attend the team's victory rally today at noon . . . There will be a ticker tape

parade Monday at 11:30 a.m. in downtown L.A.

With Abdul-Jabbar out after his injury in the previous game, this was the strangest of games. Lakers broadcaster Chick Hearn was so keyed up he opened his broadcast with: "From the Spectrum in Philadelphia, this is Keith Erickson."

All during the day there were reports from around the city of Abdul-Jabbar sightings, like UFO sightings. Cab drivers were calling TV stations; people reported seeing Abdul-Jabbar all over. The city was in near panic.

The 76ers were also skeptical. Were the Lakers going to spring a surprise? In regards to Abdul-Jabbar's absence, the 76ers adopted an attitude of . . . "We'll believe it when we don't see it."

No, Abdul-Jabbar was home, running in waist-deep water, preparing for either the seventh game or the Olympic 100-meter water run, both of which have been canceled.

His absence put the Lakers at something of a disadvantage. For the 76ers to lose this one would be the most embarrassing local development since the Liberty Bell turned up to be defective merchandise . . .

The most unbelievable part of the story has to be Magic.

Three years ago he was leading Everett High School in Lansing, Mich., to a state title. Last year, as a sophomore, he led Michigan State to an NCAA championship.

But that was all in the realm of plausibility. What happened with Magic this season, and especially Friday night, was not.

After the game, Magic was in tears.

"I'm just stunned, I can't even talk," he said.

"I feel good about it, it's unreal. It was just a great team effort."

Then he delivered another of his favorite lines.

"I strive under pressure."

He wouldn't take the credit—"Kareem brought us here. Without the Big Fella, we wouldn't be here. We won it for him and for ourselves."

Magic Johnson savors the 1980 championship with teammate Butch Lee. Johnson's 42-point, 15-rebound, seven-assist performance carried the Lakers to a Game 6 victory in the NBA Finals.

1980-81

They Also Serve Who Only Sit and Sit and Sit

Season Record

W54-L28 (.659)
Division: 2nd
First Round

Coach

Paul Westhead

Players

Kareem
Abdul-Jabbar

Jamaal Wilkes

Norm Nixon

Jim Chones

Magic Johnson

Michael Cooper

Mark Landsberger

Eddie Jordan

Butch Carter

Jim Brewer

Brad Holland

Alan Hardy

Myles Patrick

Tony Jackson

The Lakers' team is made up of the starters, the sixth man, and the Pine Brothers. Some Pine Brothers do so well they get to coach someday, as we learn from Scott Ostler's interview with the '79-80 Pines squad.

By Scott Ostler
January 24, 1980

Marty Byrnes, a reserve forward for the Lakers, played for the New Orleans Jazz last season. He also sat a lot. He remembers a game at Detroit when he was sitting, as usual, and the Jazz was losing big, as usual. Every Jazz player except Byrnes had been in the game.

"Hey, Byrnes!" yelled a fan behind the Jazz bench, "You gotta be better than somebody!"

Not exactly the type of quote you'd want inscribed on your tombstone, but when you sit on the bench in the NBA, you learn to cope with the insecurity, inactivity and cute little remarks from the customers.

The loneliness of a long-distance sitter. It's the hardest easy job in the world.

The Lakers' non-starters, who refer to themselves collectively as the Pine Brothers, were discussing the subject recently in an airport as they sat (what else?) and waited for a team flight.

"Sitting on the bench is tough to deal with," said Lakers rookie Brad Holland, who is averaging 46 minutes a game on the bench. "So you try to make it as fun as possible . . . We're kidding around, but it's not really funny."

We'll be the judge of that, Brad.

But first, a little historical background.

The team seating area in basketball used to be called the bench, until about 15 years ago when a frustrated second-string NBA center named Reggie Harding . . . declared: "I ain't ridin' the pines any more."

Pines. Technically incorrect. Courtside seats in the NBA are not constructed of pine, or any other wood. But backboards in the NBA aren't made from boards, either. And Harding, who had a feel for the language,

if not the game, knew it would sound silly to say, "I ain't gonna sit on no metal folding chairs any more."

So the bench became known as the pines (or pine), and ridin' the pines became the accepted term for exile on the bench.

The Lakers' non-starters adopted the name Pine Brothers [last] season. It's not original. The name was used by subs on rookie Ollie Mack's high school team.

The Pine Brothers: Don Ford (fifth season, UC Santa Barbara), Mike Cooper (second season, New Mexico), Byrnes (second season, Syracuse), Mack (rookie, East Carolina) and Holland (rookie, UCLA).

The interview went something like this:

Question: Is there a leader of the Pine Brothers?

Cooper: Prez (Don Ford) is our leader. He's my hero. He's President Pine.

Q: Do you have assigned seats on the bench?

Ford: No, but if the team's going good, no one will change up. That's protocol. If the team's going bad, we'll switch seats around. Sometimes the starters are perturbed when they come out of the game. They like to sit at the end of the bench, so we move. You don't want them to sweat on you, so you give up your seat. Especially if it's a long road trip. You don't want to get your uniform wet and dirty.

Q: Which is the best seat?

Ford: You like to go to the end, away from the coach . . .

Q: Who usually gets the end seat?

Cooper: Marty or Prez, usually. They leave the huddle early.

Q: Why is the end seat the best?

Byrnes: You don't have to ask for water or Gatorade, you can just reach it for yourself . . .

Ford: When you sit at the end, you can make comments without being censored. In fact, if the bench is long enough you can barely hear the coach when he calls you into the game.

Holland: The end seat in San Diego is the best because it's angled toward the court so you can see real well.

David Rivers, looking at the camera, has some good company on the Lakers' bench during the 1988-89 season, but he and those who rode the NBA's "pines" before him had what one columnist called "the hardest easy job in the world."

Ford: That seat is usually taken by Brad or the chicken (San Diego's mascot).

Q: During the game, do you try to notice things about strategy and plays?

Ford: If we knew anything about strategy and plays we'd be starting. We just try to give a little encouragement, like "Way to go."

Q: How are the fans who sit behind the benches?

Ford: You can establish a relationship with the fans. In Portland they talk to me a lot. Well, actually they yell at me a lot. It's kind of fun, really, as long as they don't throw anything. I've been hit with beer, ice, things like that.

Byrnes: Last year Rich Kelley (New Orleans center) was having a bad game and he sat down on the bench. A fan handed him a box of popcorn and said, "Here, eat this. You ain't going back in."

Q: Marty, how does this team's bench compare to New Orleans'?

Byrnes: This is a mild bench. At New Orleans they liked to play jokes. I was sitting on the end of the bench and a guy three seats up said (cupping his hands over his mouth to disguise his voice), "Byrnes! Byrnes!" I ran up to the coach, but of course he hadn't called me. That was my initiation.

Q: How are the actual seating accommodations?

Ford: Houston has excellent seats, real thick padding, but there's not enough seats, so you can't spread out. That's especially important on the road, when everyone's got smelly uniforms. Last night (Detroit) was poor. The seats are nice, they're well padded, but the floor is elevated, so you sit with your knees in your chin.

Byrnes: The worst thing is when you're up by 12 points with a minute and a half left and the other team's got three timeouts left. You have to keep getting up and down.

Q: Speaking of timeouts, where do the Pine Brothers stand during timeouts?

Byrnes: That depends on where the (TV) camera is. If you can, you lean down and try to get on TV.

Ford: We see the red light, that's when we pep up.

Byrnes: If at all possible, you try to show a bandaged hand or a knee brace, so they know why you're not playing. And you have to act like you're into the huddle. You do that for about 15 seconds, then you figure they're into the commercial.

Q: Do you spend a lot of time looking at girls?

Ford: The starters do when they're on the bench, because they don't have time to do that while they're playing. We have more time, so we can pick our spots.

Q: Do you get your uniforms cleaned even if you don't play?

Ford: Jack (trainer Jack Curran) will tell us we can get our uniforms washed, then he'll kind of giggle, like it's really necessary to wash 'em.

Q: Is there a Pine Brothers Hall of Fame?

Byrnes: My all-time great Pine Brother is Aaron James (at New Orleans). He knew what was going on at all times in the game, on the bench and in the stands. He was on every player and both officials simultaneously. He could be screaming at the ref and pointing out girls in the stands at the same time.

Ford: I used to idolize Pat (Riley, Lakers assistant coach and a former player—and nonplayer). He had a lot of style on the end of the bench.

Riley (eavesdropping): I remember after one game, Gail (Goodrich) was really upset. He said to me, "Can you believe I only played 42 minutes?" And here I hadn't played in 10 games. Wilt (Chamberlain) used to tell the coach, "I think you should put Pat in, he hasn't played in 30 games."

Q: When you're introduced in pregame ceremonies, is there anything special you try to do?

Ford: The main concern is to not trip over your warm-ups.

Stop the Music;
the Party's Over

Despite an injury that sidelined Magic Johnson for forty-five games, the team stayed on its feet, achieving a .659 winning percentage in the 1980-81 season. But when it came to the playoffs, the Lakers were dancing to a different drummer.

By SCOTT OSTLER
April 6, 1981

Disco Dad, the ancient peanut vendor who dances on center court at the Forum in what passes for timeout entertainment at Lakers games, trotted to center court and waited for his music.

The band, however, didn't take the cue. Disco Dad shuffled around awkwardly, then finally slinked off the court in danceless embarrassment.

And that's the way it was Sunday afternoon for the World Champion Los Angeles Lakers. The WCLA Lakers played without their music. They were like a ballet troupe with no accompaniment—out of sync, out of place and, finally, out of business.

They went out, not with a bang but with an airball. By Magic Johnson, of all people, firing up a four-foot jump shot—from 10 feet.

Moses Malone caught Magic's pop fly and the Houston Rockets—the Houston Rockets?—had eliminated the WCLA Lakers.

The Lakers' captain, Kareem Abdul-Jabbar had pulled the old backdoor play, fled the scene of the crime, by the time reporters were admitted to the losers' locker room. A few of the eyewitnesses remained, however.

"I tell you, to be quite frank," Jamaal Wilkes said, "I've gotta go home and think about it. I don't have any words of wisdom. It was Moses, and they played well. We seemed to struggle with our offense, I can't say why.

"I feel tired. I don't think I've quite absorbed what's happened. Tonight in bed, it'll probably hit me like a bolt of lightning."

Lakers owner Jerry Buss was outwardly calm, but his Coors can seemed to be shaking just a little.

"It's better to be a Laker and a loser than to be anything else in the world," Buss said.

He should have seen the scene in the Houston locker room, where Moses and Calvin Murphy and Mike Dunleavy battled over a champagne bottle like it was a rebound. If the Rockets go all the way (what am I saying?), they'll be hard-pressed to come up with a higher degree of happiness.

I asked Buss his reaction to some recent stories in The Times and the Herald Examiner where Norm Nixon, and then Magic Johnson, seemed to be saying that the Lakers have an internal problem or two. Nixon feels he is being asked to play out of position, and Magic feels some of his teammates resent him.

"I thought it was a cheap blow when they publish stories like that just before the series," Buss said.

A minute later, he elaborated.

"At least 200 people came up to me and said, 'Why is it the newspapers in L.A. try to create dissension? In every other city, they're supportive of the team.'

"I just think [the players] try as much as they can to be honest and straightforward with you, and by the direction of your questioning, you can control the answers.

"I think most people feel they would like to see the papers more supportive of a team entering the playoffs . . . I didn't see any articles on the fantastic love and camaraderie shared by the Lakers."

Buss, who holds doctorate degrees in physics and chemistry, flunked Journalism I on Sunday. The reporters who wrote the stories didn't use police interrogation techniques. The players involved are both very much experienced in dealing with the media, and in recognizing a reporter's notebook and pencil.

As for love and camaraderie, whatever happened to all that hand-slapping and hugging that seemed so vital to the Lakers' success last year?

Buss stopped short of blaming the media for the Lakers' stunning collapse.

"The only frustrating part," Mike Cooper said, "is that everyone on our team, we really looked forward to winning the championship again. I really wanted to win, to show people we're for real and it wasn't a fairy tale thing last year.

"I feel like I lost my best friend." . . .

Last May, when the Lakers won the Big Enchilada, who would have thought that a year later they would be cleaning out their lockers, the Houston Rockets would be swilling champagne, and Jim Chones would be saying things like:

"They just outplayed us . . . I don't know if it is frustration, or more just 'what the hell happened?' . . ."

Disco Dad was in the men's restroom, toweling off his head. "They just quit," he said, and he wasn't referring to the band. "Just too much Moses."

There was no music. Just the sound of Lakers dreams going down the drain.

1980-81 Season Highlights

Kareem Abdul-Jabbar is named to the All-NBA First Team.

Abdul-Jabbar leads the Lakers with an average of 26.2 points per game and 10.3 rebounds.

The Lakers record their second of 12 consecutive seasons with at least 50 victories.

Houston's Bill Willoughby (32), at 6 feet 8, reaches to Kareem Abdul-Jabbar's peak as the Rockets stop the defending champion Lakers in 1981, sending them out in the first round.

Norm Nixon (left) leads the Lakers in assists, averaging 8.8 per game.

Magic Johnson (right) misses 45 games after a knee injury but still leads the NBA in steals for the first of two consecutive seasons, with a club record of 3.43 per game.

1981-82

Buss Makes Westhead Disappear; Is It Magic?

Season Record

W57-L25 (.695)
Division: 1st
NBA Champion

Coach

Paul Westhead
(7-4),
and Pat Riley
(50-21)

Players

Kareem
Abdul-Jabbar

Jamaal Wilkes

Magic Johnson

Norm Nixon

Michael Cooper

Bob McAdoo

Mitch Kupchak

Mark Landsberger

Kurt Rambis

Eddie Jordan

Mike McGee

Jim Brewer

Kevin McKenna

Clay Johnson

In his first season as head coach of the Lakers, Paul Westhead led the team to an NBA championship. In his third, he was fired. At a press conference announcing the move, team owner Jerry Buss said Magic Johnson's unhappiness had nothing to do with Westhead's departure—the team just wasn't exciting enough.

By RANDY HARVEY
November 20, 1981

Saying he was reacting as a fan, Jerry Buss, owner of the Lakers, fired Coach Paul Westhead Thursday in a bizarre, sometimes-confusing press conference at the Forum.

Pat Riley, Westhead's assistant, is the new head coach, at least for the interim. Former Lakers coach Jerry West will assist Riley with the offense, at least temporarily...

Westhead came to the Lakers before the 1979-80 season as an assistant coach but took over the team after 14 games, when Coach Jack McKinney was seriously injured in a bicycle accident. When Westhead officially became head coach in May 1980, after the Lakers won the world championship, Buss called him "the best coach in the world."

Eighteen months later, although Westhead had the best winning percentage among active National Basketball Assn. coaches with 112 victories in less than two seasons, Buss no longer was enamored with him, not so much because of substance but because of style.

Buss insisted his decision had nothing to do with guard Magic Johnson's outburst after a game in Salt Lake City Wednesday night when Johnson said he wanted to be traded because of differences with Westhead.

Buss said he already had decided last Sunday... to fire Westhead but had been persuaded to postpone the action by General Manager Bill Sharman and West, who until Thursday was a special consultant to the team.

"It was obviously a difficult decision for us,"

Buss said. "It is in no way intended to criticize anybody whatsoever. However, after experiencing the excitement of the Lakers and the particular brand of basketball I have grown accustomed to, I have been very disappointed in not seeing that exciting team of two years ago. This decision started after the first or second game and reached these proportions sometime in the last few days.

"I feel I have a responsibility to give the fans of Los Angeles a very exciting brand of basketball ... I enjoyed 'Showtime,' as it used to be called, I want to see it again."

Westhead, 42, was in the second year of a four-year contract, which, including bonuses, was worth an estimated $1.1 million. He has been offered an executive position in one of Buss' other companies but has made no commitment. Westhead was unavailable for comment Thursday...

It had been apparent that Westhead's job was in jeopardy since last summer, when Buss told an Orange County reporter, "Now we'll find out if Westhead is a genius. He wanted the talent. Now he's got it. Now let's see what he does with it."

Less than three weeks into the season, Buss decided he had seen enough. Even though the Lakers rebounded from a 2-4 start with five straight victories, they were still struggling. Of their 11 games, nine were decided by four points or less.

Receiving most of the blame for the Lakers' slow start was a new offense, which Westhead installed during training camp. Whether it was because they couldn't or didn't want to, the Lakers never were comfortable with the offense.

"Everyone had come to the same conclusion," Buss said. "The offense was not working."...

The situation reached the point of no return Wednesday night when Johnson asked to be traded. "The timing was very unfortunate," said Buss, who said he would have fired Westhead within a week even if Johnson hadn't spoken out.

But when Johnson did speak out, Buss decided to make an announcement Thursday, even though he apparently had not made up his mind about a successor to Westhead. Buss invited Sharman and

Smiles are for October's preseason photo shoots, like the one endured by (from left) Michael Cooper, Norm Nixon, Kareem Abdul-Jabbar, Mitch Kupchak, Coach Paul Westhead, Jamaal Wilkes and Magic Johnson. By November, the view of some Lakers had turned decidedly less positive with the introduction of Westhead's new offense. Owner Jerry Buss' verdict? The coach had to go.

West to his home, Pickfair, Thursday morning to discuss his options before making a final decision.

There was still some confusion when the press conference began Thursday afternoon about who would be the new head coach. Buss wanted it to be West and thought he had a commitment from him to at least assume a role as a co-coach with Riley. When Buss made his announcement, he said West would be the offensive coach and Riley the coach.

But at his meeting with Sharman and West earlier Thursday, Buss had misunderstood the plan they presented. West, who was not happy during the three years he was the Lakers' head coach, clar-

ified the arrangement at the press conference.

"I'm going to be working with and for Pat Riley," West said. "He is the head coach. I hope my position will be short-lived."

Riley said he plans no major changes in the offense but will put more emphasis on the options that the Lakers ran the last two years.

After being informed of the announcement, Johnson said he no longer wants to be traded. "I'm just happy to be here in L.A.," he said. "I wasn't happy. Some of the other guys weren't happy. But I didn't make the changes. That was up to the head man, Dr. Buss. I just want to play. That's the bottom line."

A Memorable, Magical Title for Lakers

The Lakers had dispatched their Western Conference playoff rivals handily, beating Phoenix four games straight in the semifinals and doing the same against San Antonio in the conference finals. But when it came to the NBA Finals, Philadelphia proved more challenging. Up three games to two, the Lakers had their chance to put away the championship in Game 6 on their home court–and they did.

By RANDY HARVEY
June 9, 1982

For the second time in the last three years, the Lakers are on top of the National Basketball Assn. While that hardly constitutes a dynasty, this is a team that won't soon be forgotten.

Few will be writing epics about Game 6 of their best-of-seven final series against the Philadelphia 76ers. The Lakers simply did what they had to do Tuesday night at the Forum, beating the 76ers, 114-104.

But when it was over, and the Lakers had clinched the championship, four games to two, the moment was no less satisfying. To use one of Coach Pat Riley's favorite words, there was much to savor.

For Riley, 37, it was a triumphant conclusion to his most bizarre experience in professional basketball. He took over the team 11 games into the season from Coach Paul Westhead, who was fired, and, admittedly often directing by instinct, emerged with a championship.

"I wouldn't have believed it if somebody had told me this eight months ago," he said. "But it's here now, and I believe it."

For Magic Johnson, it was his second championship in three years since he left Michigan State, where he also won a championship, and the second time he has taken home the trophy as the most valuable player in the final series. Two years ago, against the 76ers, he won the MVP award for his 42-point, 15-rebound magical performance in the decisive Game 6. This time, he won it for his blue-collar consistency.

Against the 76ers, Johnson, 22, led the Lakers in rebounds (10.8) and was second in assists (8.0). He also averaged 16.2 points. Tuesday night, he had 13 points, 13 rebounds and 13 assists. Who says 13 is an unlucky number?

While on the subject of luck, how about Bob McAdoo? The only question is whether the Lakers were luckier to have him or he was luckier to have them. Three times the league's scoring champion early in his career, McAdoo, 30, now has his first championship ring. No one can say he didn't earn it. Even though he was coming off the bench, he finished as runner-up to Johnson for the series MVP award, voted on by writers and broadcasters...

McAdoo is known primarily as a scorer, a reputation he did nothing to damage in this series by averaging 16.3 points. In the last two games, he made 19 of 28 shots, including eight of 14 Tuesday night for 16 points. But the play that Riley singled out as the most significant of Game 6 was one by McAdoo on defense.

The 76ers, who fell behind, 9-0, at the beginning and played catch-up the rest of the way, almost caught up with five minutes remaining in the third quarter.

The Lakers were leading, 76-75, but Ju-

lius Erving was out front on the 76ers' fast-break and was ready to slam home a dunk when McAdoo caught him from behind, maneuvered between him and the basket and blocked the shot cleanly. It was one of three blocked shots for McAdoo, who also had nine rebounds...

To the credit of the 76ers, whose hearts have been questioned in the past, they never quit. Even when they fell behind by 11 in the fourth quarter, they fought back to within three, 103-100, with 3:52 remaining.

But on their next trip downcourt, the Lakers came down with four offensive rebounds before center Kareem Abdul-Jabbar finally got a shot to fall. He also was fouled and completed a three-point play to give the Lakers a 106-100 lead with 3:07 remaining.

Only 17 seconds later, McAdoo grabbed a rebound at the other end and passed downcourt to Jamaal Wilkes, who was all alone for a layup to give the Lakers an insurmountable 108-100 lead. It was only seconds later when Michael Cooper and Riley embraced in front of the bench, and the celebration began...

Abdul-Jabbar finished with 18 points, 11 rebounds and five blocked shots as he won his third championship in 13 years...

This game also was satisfying for Wilkes, who, after hitting only three outside shots in the previous five games, hit three in a row in the second quarter Tuesday night and finished with 27 points...

But it was difficult to point to one player's performance as the difference in this victory, as evidenced by six of the eight Lakers who played scoring in double figures.

It was that kind of game. It was that kind of season.

1981-82 Season Highlights

The Lakers sign Bob McAdoo (right) after Mitch Kupchak suffers a severe knee injury and is lost for the season.

The Lakers have a club record 51 assists vs. Denver (February 23, 1982), the third-highest in NBA history.

The Lakers' Norm Nixon (10) and the 76ers' Maurice Cheeks (10) may look as if they're in the same ballet, but on the court Los Angeles maintained the upper hand, dispatching the 76ers, four games to two, in the 1982 Finals.

Magic Johnson is named MVP of the regular season and of the NBA Finals.

Kareem Abdul-Jabbar, at age 34, leads the team in scoring with an average of 23.9 points per game, making 57.9% of his shots.

1982-83

A Wild-Mannered Laker in Disguise

Season Record

W58-L24 (.707)
Division: 1st
NBA Finals

Coach

Pat Riley

Players

Kareem
Abdul-Jabbar

Jamaal Wilkes

Magic Johnson

Norm Nixon

James Worthy

Bob McAdoo

Michael Cooper

Kurt Rambis

Dwight Jones

Mike McGee

Clay Johnson

Mark Landsberger

Eddie Jordan

Steve Mix

Billy Ray Bates

Joe Cooper

Fans loved Kurt Rambis' take-no-prisoners style of play during the '80s. After the 1988 season he signed with Charlotte, and the first time he reappeared in the Forum with the Hornets, the fans gave him a standing ovation as he was presented his '88 Lakers' NBA championship ring. He played for Phoenix and Sacramento and rejoined the Lakers in '93-94 as a player and later a coach. He was named head coach of the Minnesota Timberwolves in August of 2009.

By JIM MURRAY
May 16, 1982

The first look you get at Kurt Rambis coming downcourt in a basketball game, you figure he must own the ball. Or, his daddy owns the team. Either that or he's just a faculty member doing a shoot-around for a paper he's doing on the effect of intercollegiate athletics on the work ethic. Fully annotated and laced with allusions to the Freudian symbolism of the moving pick.

First of all, he's too white. But, on top of everything, it's those glasses. Nobody, repeat nobody, plays big-time basketball in horn-rimmed glasses. You got to have the peripheral vision of a walleyed pike to play this game. You got to have all these cute moves where you could go through a car wash without getting wet. Kurt Rambis would go through a car wash like a 1931 Nash. He should play the game in a helmet. He goes to the basket like a cop busting up a crap game or a guy on a motorcycle jumping cars.

There were people who couldn't bear to look when Kurt Rambis tried out for the Lakers at Palm Springs last summer. When someone asked what position he was trying out for, the answer came back, "I don't know, probably fullback." When Kurt got the ball, it was fourth and goal on the one . . .

Still, whenever a ball got loose, there was Kurt, glasses and all, elbows, knees and feet, surrounding the ball. It's not a good idea to drop a ball around Kurt Rambis. Unless you're insured. Kurt plays like he's an 18-wheeler on Interstate 95 with the lights out and the brakes shot . . . Rambis acts like the ball

owes him money. There are some people who think "Loose-Ball Foul" is his first name. That's because all you seem to hear all night long is "Loose ball foul, Rambis, fourth personal, fifth team foul, Julius Erving shooting two."

One thing about Kurt Rambis: He's not nonchalant about anything. He treats a basketball game like Hitler treated Poland. So, a lot of people thought Kurt Rambis trying to make the Lakers was just an interesting social experiment, like letting a family of gorillas live in a condo in Palm Beach for a summer. They just hoped he didn't hurt anybody . . .

Among those who had his doubts was Kurt Rambis. He had been something of a legend at Santa Clara where his horn-rimmed looks had gotten him the nickname Superman. He used to average 19 points and rebound everything but the hands on the scoreboard clock. The Knicks drafted him in the third round, but, when he showed up they thought he was from the Auto Club . . . When he got cut, he had no trouble finding another job. Athens, Greece, was putting a team together.

When the Lakers were putting a team together, they figured they'd have no trouble finding Kurt in Athens . . . But, Kurt didn't want to come to the NBA again. He'd been burned once . . . Paul Westhead was coach of the Lakers at the time and the Lakers had everything but someone to get a ball for them now and then. Westhead liked Rambis. He didn't care how he looked out there so long as he had the ball . . .

The Lakers, too, found out Kurt Rambis looked a lot better with the basketball. He pulled a job off the backboard, literally. "What you liked about Rambis," notes Westhead, "was that, if you dug an elbow in his ribs, you were gonna get it back a few plays later. He didn't initiate it. There's no room in basketball for guys who knock you over just to impress the coaches. But, Kurt impressed the older players because he didn't back off . . . Kurt went from No. 12 on the bubble in the lineup to No. 9 and No 8."

On Dec. 19, the Lakers' million-dollar power forward, Mitch Kupchak, broke a knee bone. When the Lakers bought Bob McAdoo, Rambis began wonder-

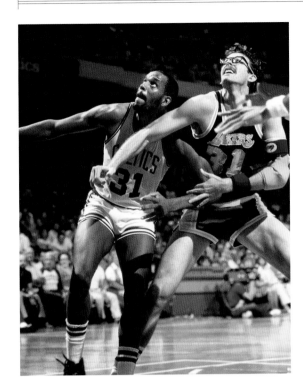

Kurt Rambis' energy, work ethic and signature eyeglasses made him a crowd favorite and a staple in the Lakers' lineup. As he told the *Los Angeles Times'* Scott Howard-Cooper: "The fans always appreciated all the little dirty stuff I did, all the things nobody else really liked to do . . . once they got over laughing at me the first time they saw me on the court."

ing if they played baseball and basketball in China, but in a game against Indiana he went out and grabbed 14 rebounds, shut down his man, who was only Herb Williams, and got the starting forward job.

No one ever called Rambis "Slick." The refs would blow two fouls on him before he got dressed He got one foul for every seven minutes of play. But he led the team in rebounds nine times, in blocked shots 18 times (only Kareem Abdul-Jabbar got more), and in steals six times . . .

The other night, in a crucial game in the NBA playoffs, he slapped around the San Antonio Spurs unmercifully—15 rebounds, eight points, one assist, and only five personals. Kurt has learned to remove basketballs from people rather than vice versa. Sometimes, of course, he's got to learn to wait till they get it though.

The moral of the story: If you don't look like a basketball player in Madison Square Garden, go to Greece where they don't know what a basketball player is supposed to look like, and the next thing you know, you'll be pounding the boards in the NBA playoffs, looking more like Mr. Basketball or Dr. K all the time.

Lakers Already Have Next Season in Mind

For fans, there's nothing so painful as the sting of defeat on the home turf. But for the Lakers' brass, there was the small solace that it gave them a jump on planning for success in the next season. After all, they had to worry about re-signing Kareem Abdul-Jabbar. And would James Worthy bounce back from a broken leg? One thing was sure: Coach Pat Riley had no interest in trading away any of his "Great Eight."

By RANDY HARVEY
June 2, 1983

On the whole, the Lakers were glad to be in Los Angeles Wednesday rather than Philadelphia.

As long as Philadelphia was going to win the National Basketball Assn. championship anyway, everyone agreed it was just as well that the 76ers did it in Game 4 at the Forum Tuesday night instead of delaying the inevitable until Game 5, which was scheduled for tonight at the Spectrum.

It saved the players from having to take another cross-country flight and enabled them to get on with business, which consisted primarily of dividing playoff earnings.

As far as the team's officials were concerned, it allowed them a head start toward regaining the championship.

Coach Pat Riley and his assistant, Bill Bertka, were in their offices at the Forum early Wednesday, as was club President Bill Sharman. General Manager Jerry West and scout Dave Wohl flew to Chicago for a tryout camp.

After losing in the Finals to the Lakers last season, Philadelphia traded its two centers—Darryl Dawkins and Caldwell Jones—and replaced them with Moses Malone, who was better than both combined.

Now it's the Lakers' move.

Their options are limited . . . Unlike last season when they were able to improve an already excellent team by acquiring James Worthy with the first selection in the draft, they don't have a draft choice this year until the third round . . .

According to the salary restrictions established by the new collective bargaining agreement, neither will the Lakers be able to enter the free-agent market unless something drastic happens.

Falling in that category would be the departure of Kareem Abdul-Jabbar, who as of Tuesday night officially became a free agent. Signing the 36-year-old center to a new contract is the Lakers' first priority this summer.

"We have to sign him, unless somebody knows something that I don't know," Riley said. "We'll be going into a rebuilding program if we don't. After seven years of being the fulcrum of our offense, we wouldn't be able to recover from the loss of him in one year either physically or psychologically.

"He and Moses are the best centers in the league. I don't care about his age. He carried us to the Finals this year. Against Portland and San Antonio, his scoring average increased from 20 points during the regular season to 29, and his minutes increased from 30 to 40. Without him, we wouldn't have gotten here.

"It's time for people to stop judging him for what he doesn't do for us but for what

he does do for us. He makes it possible for us to win 60 games and gets us to the Finals. He makes everybody better because teams we play have to guard him with three and four guys.

"Also, from a business standpoint, he's made this a very successful season. He and Magic are what makes the business go." . . .

Abdul-Jabbar's asking price is $2 million a year for the next two years, but that presumably is open to negotiation since he has insisted all season that he prefers to finish his career with the Lakers.

According to the league's collective bargaining agreement, if Abdul-Jabbar doesn't sign with the Lakers, the Lakers could take half of his $1.1-million salary and spend it on a free agent. Their first choice, like almost everyone else's, is Boston forward-center Kevin McHale . . .

But, unless Abdul-Jabbar leaves, the only way they can make a bid for McHale would be to decrease their current salary load by trading a couple of their first eight players. Guard Norm Nixon has been mentioned as a possibility, although Buss said this week he planned to continue negotiations with Nixon this summer for a lifetime contract. The talks haven't progressed smoothly to this point.

Riley is unalterably opposed to trades involving any of the Great Eight.

"When we're healthy we're still one of the best two teams—Philly and L.A.," he said. "The only restructuring we need to do is to get healthy. All of the pieces fit right now."

That is assuming that Worthy recovers from his broken leg. All indications are that he will . . .

1982-83 Season Highlights

The Lakers become the first NBA championship team to add the No. 1 draft pick—North Carolina's James Worthy—to the next season's roster.

Worthy shoots a club rookie record 57.9% from the field before suffering a broken leg in the final week of the regular season.

Magic Johnson (next page) leads the NBA in assists (10.5) and earns All-NBA First-Team honors for the first time.

Ready to move forward, Lakers Coach Pat Riley (left) congratulates 76ers Coach Billy Cunningham in the locker room after Philadelphia had swept Los Angeles in the 1983 Finals. The Lakers would reach the Finals again in five of the next six years.

Kareem Abdul-Jabbar and Magic Johnson are selected for the 1982 Western Conference All-Star Team.

1983-84

Abdul-Jabbar Hits Jackpot With Skyhook in Las Vegas

Season Record

W54-L28 (.659)
Division: 1st
NBA Finals

Coach

Pat Riley

Players

Kareem
Abdul-Jabbar

Jamaal Wilkes

James Worthy

Magic Johnson

Bob McAdoo

Byron Scott

Mike McGee

Michael Cooper

Swen Nater

Calvin Garrett

Kurt Rambis

Larry Spriggs

Mitch Kupchak

Eddie Jordan

It may have been a "home" game for the Utah Jazz, who played part time in Las Vegas, but on this night the crowd was there to see Kareem Abdul-Jabbar make history. In the fourth quarter, they got their wish when Abdul-Jabbar eclipsed Wilt Chamberlain's all-time NBA scoring record. Before he retired in 1989, Abdul-Jabbar added nearly 7,000 more points to raise the standard to 38,387.

By RANDY HARVEY
April 6, 1984

LAS VEGAS—In a city where everyone dreams of the big score, the Lakers' Kareem Abdul-Jabbar hit the biggest one in National Basketball Assn. history Thursday night.

It came, appropriately, on a right-handed skyhook—his ultimate weapon—from 15 feet with 8:53 remaining in the fourth quarter of a 129-115 victory over the Utah Jazz.

The points, his last of the night, gave him 22, one more than he needed to surpass the NBA's previous all-time regular-season scoring record of 31,419 held by Wilt Chamberlain.

Chamberlain, who retired in 1973 after playing the final five years of his 14-year NBA career for the Lakers, did not attend the game as it had been anticipated that he would.

But that detracted little, if anything from Abdul-Jabbar's moment.

Those who were here to see it included a crowd of 18,389. That was announced here as the largest crowd ever to see Utah play, as if it was Utah the crowd had come to see, and 139 more than capacity at the Thomas and Mack Arena, where the Jazz is playing 11 games this season.

It seemed as if everyone in the arena was standing each time the Lakers had the ball in the fourth quarter, which Abdul-Jabbar entered needing only two points to tie Chamberlain.

He did that on a dramatic dunk 65 seconds into the quarter.

Off the bench came Lakers guard Magic John-

son, who had asked for relief late in the third quarter after having to guard another celebrated scorer, Utah's Adrian Dantley. But with Abdul-Jabbar so close to history, Johnson wanted to be part of it.

He had to wait as the Utah defense, which tightened considerably around Abdul-Jabbar after he scored 16 first-half points, seemed determined not to go down in the record books as the other team. It was almost as if Wilt himself were guarding Abdul-Jabbar.

With two and three defenders surrounding Abdul-Jabbar, Johnson tried twice to force the ball inside to the 7-foot-2 center, but Rich Kelley, a 7-1 journeyman, knocked it away and into the hands of teammates both times.

When Johnson finally succeeded, it was Abdul-Jabbar's turn to force one. Fighting off three defenders, he shot a 12-foot skyhook that did not come close despite the crowd's coaxing.

But the next time the Lakers had the ball, the crowd on its feet again, Abdul-Jabbar took a pass in the low post position from Johnson, gave a head fake toward the basket to lose his shadows and then moved to a safe range to launch his skyhook.

The only Jazz player close to Abdul-Jabbar, 7-4 center and fellow UCLA alumnus Mark Eaton, could only watch as the ball sailed over his head and cleanly into the basket.

In his 15th NBA season and less than two weeks from his 37th birthday, Abdul-Jabbar had surpassed a record that once was believed to be unsurpassable . . .

Players from both teams congratulated Abdul-Jabbar at mid-court, where he also was greeted by his parents, Cora and Ferdinand Lewis Alcindor of New York City, and by NBA Commissioner David Stern.

Stern presented Abdul-Jabbar with the game ball and made a brief speech, followed by one even briefer by Abdul-Jabbar . . . Oscar winners should take note.

"As an individual, I can enjoy this," Abdul-Jabbar said later in a postgame press conference. "(But) it was like asking Hank Aaron what he remembered more, hitting his 715th home run or winning the World Series. It would be tough for him to answer.

"It's kind of hard not to have a sense of history

Kareem Abdul-Jabbar, the star with the ubiquitous goggles, dunks over Jeff Wilkins of the Utah Jazz on his record-setting night at Las Vegas' Thomas and Mack Arena. After becoming the NBA's all-time leading scorer, Abdul-Jabbar said, "It's kind of hard not to have a sense of history about this night."

about this night. Everyone was telling me the significance of breaking the record."

As for Chamberlain, one of Abdul-Jabbar's early idols, the Lakers center said: "I have a lot of respect for him. Whatever I did tonight. I could never eclipse him totally."

Abdul-Jabbar will have an opportunity to address Chamberlain personally tonight, when the Lakers honor their captain with a ceremony at the Forum before a game against Kansas City. In expressing his regrets Thursday for not attending the

game here, Chamberlain told Lakers officials he would be present at the Forum.

Abdul-Jabbar could have saved the record-breaking points for the Forum. When he tied Chamberlain, the Lakers had a 17-point lead, 110-93, and the game well in hand. Lakers Coach Pat Riley gave Abdul-Jabbar the option of watching the rest of the game from the bench.

"I called him over and asked him, 'Well, is it tonight or tomorrow?' "Riley said later. "And he said. 'Let's do it.'"

The Much Ado Wherever He Went Was Obviously About Nothing

As "Showtime" rose, so did the reserves. Michael Cooper matched up on defense against Larry Bird. Bob McAdoo matched up on offense against anyone. He started once in his four seasons in L.A. but was the team's fifth-leading scorer in 1983-84, averaging 13.1 points. As Lakers Coach Pat Riley told Jim Murray, in 1985: "Actually, we think of Mac as a starter."

By JIM MURRAY
April 23, 1985

Not too many years ago, he was considered the most devastating force to come into the National Basketball Assn. in his decade. Teams jockeyed to get draft rights to him. When Buffalo got him, the Braves figured it was a clear path to the title.

No one could contain him. Only Wilt Chamberlain ever threw in more points in a season. Only 16 players in history, only two of them active, threw in as many total points. He pulled down a thousand rebounds a year. One year, he scored 40 or more points in a game 19 times. He was Rookie of the Year one season, Most Valuable Player another.

He was averaging more than 30 points a game. And, then, all of a sudden, Bob McAdoo was being shopped around the league like a hot watch or a haunted house. He went to the New York Knicks for Tom McMillen and John Gianelli, who together didn't have half as many points and never would.

He continued to storm the basket, he averaged 26 points and 12 rebounds a game

for the Knicks. He put in 2,097 points and was third-best in the league when suddenly he found himself on the way to Boston for two pieces of paper and somebody named Tom Barker. He went from being an NBA legend to a vagabond . . . He went to Detroit and then to New Jersey and finally to Los Angeles.

No one could understand it. The touch was still there, the points were still there. He didn't slug baby seals over the head with baseball bats in the off-season . . . He was a basketball player, one of the game's best ever. And he couldn't keep a job.

The Lakers got him for a draft selection and a kind word in 1981 when Mitch Kupchak went down. They kept wondering when they'd find out what the catch was. Maybe McAdoo turned into a bat at midnight, or liked to set fire to orphanages.

They're still waiting to find out—two conference titles and one league championship later . . .

But, with the Lakers, Bob McAdoo went from being the franchise to being a face in the crowd. It was like the star being asked to play the butler. Not everyone can play the butler, and the betting around the league was that McAdoo was not one of them. McAdoo was no character actor . . . McAdoo played the guys who got the girl, not the horses. The whisper was that the Lakers would find they had got Bob McE-go.

As usual, McAdoo fooled the league. He reveled in the role. He proceeded to give an Academy Award performance as best supporting player . . . No one else

Bob McAdoo (11) reaches for another level above Celtics' Larry Bird in the 1984 NBA Finals.

in the league comes off the pines at crucial moments and fires in 22 points in 23 minutes or 18 points in 20 minutes the way McAdoo do. No one protects a lead as jealously.

Said McAdoo: "It's a perfect blend of roles for me."

1983-84 Season Highlights

Kareem Abdul-Jabbar is congratulated by Wilt Chamberlain at a Forum ceremony (right) a night after Abdul-Jabbar had eclipsed Chamberlain's career scoring record.

Magic's 1984 milestones: single-game NBA playoff assist record (24); club-record assist average (13.1 per game), leading the NBA; club-record assists for one quarter (12).

The 1984 NBA Finals were rough on the Lakers, who had two overtime defeats in the best-of-seven series loss to the Celtics. That was especially true for Kurt Rambis (above, right), who was clotheslined by Kevin McHale in a 129-126 overtime Game 4 loss at the Forum. Years later, Larry Bird said of the play: "We had to do what we could because we couldn't keep up with them. They were running us out of the building."

In Game 7, rookie Byron Scott (4) and James Worthy (left) have their moments as Magic Johnson boxes out Danny Ainge, but Boston prevailed, 111-102.

1984-85

Lakers Leave Boston Hanging in Rafters in Finals

Season Record

W62-L20 (.756)
Division: 1st
NBA Champion

Coach

Pat Riley

Players

Kareem
Abdul-Jabbar

James Worthy

Magic Johnson

Byron Scott

Mike McGee

Michael Cooper

Bob McAdoo

Larry Spriggs

Kurt Rambis

Jamaal Wilkes

Mitch Kupchak

Ronnie Lester

Chuck Nevitt

Earl Jones

Only one word was necessary after the Los Angeles Lakers won an NBA championship in Boston for the first time in franchise history: Redemption.

By THOMAS BONK
June 10, 1985

History, we know now, does not always repeat.

The Lakers, who have spent their entire existence on a collision course with Boston Celtics history, won the championship of a lifetime after a quarter of a century of trying.

They beat the Celtics, 111-100, Sunday on the parquet floor of ancient Boston Garden to win the National Basketball Assn. championship in six games, 4-2. Yes, it actually happened.

Of the 15 Celtics championship banners hanging from the rafters of Boston Garden, eight of them came from beating the Lakers in the championship series. The most recent one was from last season.

There would be no 16th, at least not this season. Not from this Lakers team, which was on a mission of redemption, and found it behind their 38-year-old center, the one with the goggles and the hook shot.

Kareem Abdul-Jabbar, the greatest scorer in the history of the NBA, rained 29 points down through the hoop to finish off a series of performances that won him the most-valuable-player award...

At the same time, the Lakers finished one of the longest streaks of pain and futility brought upon one team by another in the history of the NBA...

"We got the monkey off our backs at last," James Worthy said. "The hurt is gone."

Eight times the Lakers had played the Celtics for the NBA title and eight times they had lost. That's over now. And so is the Celtics' chance of becoming the first NBA team to repeat as champions since they last did so in 1969. Boston had

never before lost a deciding game in the championship series in Boston Garden, but that's over now, too...

"Somewhere along the way, it was bound to happen," Lakers Coach Pat Riley said. "Maybe it was meant to be. But if we were ever going to break the domination of the Celtics over the Laker franchise and get all those skeletons out of our closet, it's so much sweeter to do it here."...

The Celtics' stranglehold on the Lakers ended at 3:30 p.m. EST, when Michael Cooper dribbled out the clock, protecting a Lakers lead that didn't emerge until the third quarter.

At halftime, the game was tied, 55-55, but the Lakers made their first five shots of the second half, four of them by Abdul-Jabbar, and took a 65-61 lead. Suddenly, the Celtics were reeling.

Magic Johnson, widely identified as the main Laker in search of redemption after last season's loss to the Celtics, inspired the Lakers' attack with 14 assists, 14 points and 10 rebounds. It was Johnson who kept getting the ball to Abdul-Jabbar. It was Johnson who continued to push the ball upcourt to force the tempo and tire the Celtics...

"When I came out early to practice, I thought, 'We have our chance,'" Johnson said. "It was a long year living with defeat. This year, we didn't make mistakes."...

After Larry Bird, who had 28 points in defeat, sank a jumper to bring the Celtics to within 65-63, the Lakers quickly moved out to a 73-63 lead. Abdul-Jabbar scored on a drive, Worthy dunked off an assist by Johnson and then Byron Scott suddenly appeared for the first time in this series.

Scott dropped a jump shot from the baseline, then stole the ball from Kevin McHale, a play that led to Kurt Rambis tipping in a missed shot that gave the Lakers' their 10-point margin.

"From that point on, it was ours," Riley said.

Earlier, it was McHale's. The 6-foot-10 Celtic forward, for whom the Lakers were never really able to find a defense, scored 21 points in the first

half and finished with 32, but he fouled out with 5:21 remaining and the Lakers leading, 94-88 . . .

Boston Coach K.C. Jones used only seven players. Scott Wedman and Greg Kite, the two Celtics substitutes, totaled nine points in 26 minutes. [With the Lakers] daring the Celtics guards to shoot from the outside, Dennis Johnson and Danny Ainge were a combined six for 31 for 17 points.

"We made them tire," Magic Johnson said. "They were only playing a few guys. My job was to push the ball up the court until they broke. We made 'em lose it. I saw they were tired, so we ran them into the ground." . . .

Bird brought the Celtics to within five points, [when] McHale fouled out. The Lakers scored their next five points on free throws, and Magic's driving layup gave them a 99-90 lead with 4:24 to play.

After that, the end was in sight. The end of Celtics domination, the end of Lakers redemption, the end of the season . . .

"I feel like we just won the whole world," owner Jerry Buss said.

Neither the Celtics' banners, which hung barely visible above, nor the parquet floor below could keep Kareem Abdul-Jabbar and the Lakers from their championship destiny in 1985. Abdul-Jabbar, shown shooting over Boston's Larry Bird, took the Finals' MVP honors.

Finally, Players Past and Present Can Stand Tall

After decades of bad bounces in Boston Garden, Lakers players and fans knew exactly what it meant to clinch the title on the parquet floor in the 1985 Finals.

By SCOTT OSTLER
June 10, 1985

Hey, Frank Selvy. Hey, Jerry, Elgin, Wilt, Hot Rod, Rudy LaRusso, Ray Felix...

Wherever you guys are, find a quiet place, lift up a glass of your favorite drink and knock one down in honor of your Lakers.

They have squashed the leprechaun; they have taken the weed-eater to the patch of four-leaf clovers.

Jack Kent Cooke, blow up a balloon. Jack Nicholson, think back on all the lean seasons when you were sitting courtside but nobody noticed. Throw back your head and give us your best, nastiest Randall P. McMurphy laugh.

At 12:34 p.m. Sunday, L.A. time, of course, the organically grown, solar-powered, Malibu-Margueritaville-Hollywood Lakers put an end to the Celtics' domination.

They treated the hallowed Celtics championship banners hanging in the rafters of the Boston Garden with all the reverence of laundry on a clothesline.

In a sweatbox antique of an arena, where opposing teams come to die, where the only air circulation is courtesy of M.L. Carr's whirlybird towel, the Lakers outrunned, outgunned, outmuscled and out-Celticed the Celtics.

They did it for themselves and for all the Lakers who are no longer suited up.

"We played for everybody else, all the Laker teams of the past," Magic Johnson said. "It's better than a win, I tell you, because of what happened to all the other teams."

This one was also for Kareem the Elder, too old to rock and roll, too old for the heat, but still cookin' in the kitchen.

"Just think about it," said Abdul-Jabbar, who has a better perspective on sports history than anyone on the Lakers. "We'd never beaten Boston. Jerry lost to Boston [six] times, and Elgin never beat them. I feel for those guys. You look back at how great they played and you just want to do it."

So you do it. You do it despite the banners. "Kareem Elbow-Jabbar," "Kurt Igna-Rambis," "Can you say choke? Kiss it goodby, L.A."

You do it despite the tradition, the Celtics' hex, the green ghosts of Celtics past, the oppressive history of Celtics domination...

What time was it out there, Magic?

"It was winnin' time," Magic said.

... This one, this game, this series, was played above the rafters, above the banners and above the smoke from Red Auerbach's stinking victory cigar.

"You play against anybody else, you can't play this hard," Magic said. "We had to play on a higher level, past what we played the rest of the season and in the playoffs..."

Yea, this one's for you, too, Magic. The goat of the playoffs last season. And for Kurt Rambis, Lord of the Sewers. And for Doc Kerlan, the Lakers' team physician since they came to Los Angeles in 1960, who threw one of his crutches out on the court Sunday to protest a call in the fourth quarter.

And this one's for Riley, whose perfect hair and GQ wardrobe became a symbol of the prettiness of the Lakers...

Riley gave the team a Knute Rockne pregame talk. He invoked the series history, especially last season's finals, the pain and humiliation of losing to the Celtics. He reminded his team of the crowing and woofing the Celtics have been doing ever since.

"Our whole theme is that somewhere along the line, no matter what obstacles are in your path, you have to stand strong, plant your feet and make a stand," Riley said. "And we did. We're the best team in the world."

His players believed that going into the game. The Lakers didn't come to Boston this time to be intimidated, humiliated, beaten. Had they lost Sunday, they would have had a workout Monday, but most of the players didn't even bring their workout sweats.

Did Mitch Kupchak, for example, bring his workout gear to Boston?

"No, of course not," Kupchak said indignantly.

Cocky? Sure, the Lakers are cocky...

See, this one is special. It's not just another Super Bowl win, another World Series victory. This one is bigger.

This one is for a quarter-century of frustration at the hands of the dreaded Celtics, in one of the most heated of professional sports rivalries. This one is for Chick Hearn, Freddy Schaus, Tommy Hawkins, Jamaal Wilkes, Doris Day, and for all the players and fans, Minnesota and Los Angeles, who have choked on a quarter-century of Red's cigar smoke.

The air is clear. The sun is shining. Lift one to the rafters.

1984-85 Season Highlights

Magic Johnson averages an all-time NBA-record 17 assists in one playoff series (vs. Portland).

The 1985 NBA Champion Lakers meet with President Reagan at the White House.

The Lakers of 1985—the team that finally beat the Boston Celtics—never forgot the close-but-not-enough frustrations of the 1960s-era teams before them. Jerry West, left, whose role spanned both generations, and Pat Riley savor the moment, above, at the 1985 team's 20-year reunion at Staples Center.

Byron Scott (4) becomes the only Laker ever to lead the NBA in three-point field-goal percentage (43.3%).

Kareem Abdul-Jabbar, voted MVP of the 1985 NBA Finals, joins Jerry Buss and Bob McAdoo (right) in the trophy celebration.

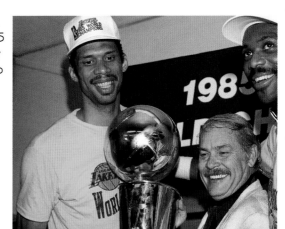

1985-86

Each Laker Has a Way of Facing Game Day

Season Record

W62-L20 (.756)
Division: 1st
West Finals

Coach

Pat Riley

Players

Kareem
Abdul-Jabbar

James Worthy

Magic Johnson

Byron Scott

Maurice Lucas

Michael Cooper

Mike McGee

A.C. Green

Kurt Rambis

Mitch Kupchak

Larry Spriggs

Ronnie Lester

Petur
Gudmundsson

Chuck Nevitt

Jerome
Henderson

When the season is on the line, it's time for "Gunsmoke," the "Rockford Files," and game film. But sometimes even tried and true routines can't help put enough points on the scoreboard. Despite their preparation, the Lakers couldn't fend off the Houston Rockets.

By SCOTT OSTLER
May 21, 1986

This is a game day, so game-day routines will be followed.

This might turn out to be the last game day of the season for the Lakers, since they trail the Houston Rockets, three games to one, in this Western Conference Finals, but you have to go with what got you here.

James Worthy will eat dinner about 2:30 this afternoon, then stretch out in bed to watch back-to-back reruns of "Gunsmoke." After Marshal Dillon has saved Dodge City twice, James will arise and get ready for work.

Kurt Rambis will feed his infant son, take the family dog for a walk, then fall asleep watching either "Kung Fu" or "Rockford Files."

Magic Johnson will listen to music, and, as he does before every game, receive a bouquet of balloons and a delivery of flowers. Balloons, tunes and roses.

Michael Cooper will take his pregame meal sitting in front of his television, watching videotapes. He'll study the game films intently—forward, reverse, slo-mo . . . Looking for something. What? Something the Rockets do that can be exploited. A step, a fake, a slight hesitation before a pass . . . Something that will make a difference.

Detective Cooper already will have read all the L.A. newspapers, looking for more clues. Indications of a psychological weakness somewhere. A cocky statement by a Rockets player that Cooper can use as motivation.

Before leaving for the Forum, Cooper will put on some music—maybe an old Earth, Wind and Fire album—take a shower, get ready. Wanda Coo-

per will screen the phone calls, but she'll let Michael talk with his uncle, Tom Butler, who calls before every game with words of encouragement and technical advice.

Tom's call is part of the routine, a routine that must be honored.

Chick Hearn will be, well, what's a stronger word for nervous? He'll take his dog for several walks this afternoon, then Chick will hose down the backyard several times. He'll start serious clock-watching around noon, then he'll lie down for a nap, which will turn out to be a half-hour fidget.

All morning he'll pepper his wife, Marge, with cosmic questions about the Lakers.

"But he's not really talking to me," Marge says. "He's talking to the air."

For the Lakers and their families, this is a crisis time. Within the space of a season, they have gone from World Champs to a struggling, desperate team on the verge of elimination from the playoffs . . .

"I think Kurt is pretty uptight," Linda Rambis said. "It's more frustration than anything else. It would be one thing if he could put his finger on what's going wrong, but you can't put your finger on it.

"He's been real edgy. We had a screaming match last night. Thank God we have the little guy to break up the tension. Oh, and Kurt had a nightmare, I just remembered. I forgot to ask him what it was about, but we were both asleep, and I shifted and bumped into him, and he jumped about 50 feet."

Rambis is assigned to guarding Akeem (the Dream) Olajuwon, the Rockets' inhuman human. You would think Rambis had paid his bad-dream dues during the games.

Each player deals with the crisis time in his own way. Worthy has been staying calm. Worthy is a calm guy.

"Around the house he hasn't been changing his demeanor or disposition," Angela Worthy says. "He does a very good job keeping basketball in perspective. He doesn't come home, rant and rave, throw things. He knows it's time to do or die, and he's been very calm about it."

"People were calling up after the [last] game, really bummed out. I want to win, but I also realize that a lot worse things could happen. There are people starving in this world."

The Houston Rockets, for instance. World's hungriest team.

Do the Rockets have a weakness? If so, Michael Cooper will find it.

"He's been real quiet, quieter than usual," Wanda Cooper says. "He hasn't even been playing with the kids. He's been thinking a lot. He'll just sit around and chew on his thumbnail . . . He's very introspective.

"He's been watching (game) films. I tape the games and edit out the commercials. Monday he

watched films for at least seven hours . . ."

The world, or that portion of it populated by Lakers fans, is searching desperately for solutions, answers, ways to win.

"I think it would be a great shot in the arm if the wives would come in at the end of practice and give a little pep rally," Angela Worthy said. "We could do a satire of the Laker Girls, some kind of boosting skit. They need something. Something is missing."

It's a nice idea. But there won't be a pep rally today. Nothing new, nothing different.

This is a game day, and game-day routines will be carried out.

Whether it was the 1980s or the 2000s, the Lakers have always taken an individual approach to preparing for big games. Before Game 4 of the 2001 Finals, Shaquille O'Neal found his own way to relax.

It's Lakers vs. Texas in Playoffs, and Fan vs. Kareem

The Lakers started the season with a 24-3 record, notched 62 regular-season wins and dispatched San Antonio in three straight games, then Dallas (4-2) before losing to Houston (4-1) in the Western Conference Finals. In Dallas, one fan took out his frustration on Kareem.

By THOMAS BONK
May 9, 1986

The Lakers finally got rid of the Dallas Mavericks Thursday night, 120-107, but not before one last taunt. Dick Motta didn't do it, and Pat Riley didn't do it, either. But guess who did?

If you said Kareem Abdul-Jabbar, then you can advance to the Western Conference Finals along with the Lakers, who will meet the Houston Rockets.

But first, Abdul-Jabbar had to say goodbye to the Mavericks, so he did it with uncharacteristic bravado. Maybe Abdul-Jabbar's manner explains what would happen to him later.

The whole thing began with only a couple of minutes left in the game and the Lakers safely ahead. Abdul-Jabbar walked to the first row of fans seated along the sideline of Reunion Arena and cupped one hand to his ear.

"I just wanted to hear what they had to say then," Abdul-Jabbar said later. "It got kind of quiet out there."

Then it got kind of wet out there.

As Abdul-Jabbar left the court after the victory . . . he was doused by two full cups of beer poured by one fan in the stands . . .

Abdul-Jabbar . . . took his second shower, the conventional kind, and disappeared

in an elevator—not more than five minutes after his impromptu first shower. But before the quick exit, Abdul-Jabbar made sure he was noticed. He scored 27 points in 38 minutes and singlehandedly took over the game when the Lakers went ahead to stay in the second quarter . . .

"Kareem wanted the ball," Laker guard Magic Johnson said. "When he gets the look in his eye like that, nothing can stop him."

. . . Extended to six games by the Mavericks, the Lakers believe they learned something from their experience.

"We learned that it's not going to be an easy road, that's for sure," forward Kurt Rambis said . . .

Referees Ed Rush and Joey Crawford were not calling a tight game, and that normally favors the more aggressive team . . .

Abdul-Jabbar, who had been somewhat passive during the series, changed all that in a hurry. He even got into a disagreement with Mark Aguirre.

When Aguirre scored inside to bring the Mavericks within 54-47, he apparently clipped Abdul-Jabbar on the chin.

"I got an elbow in the face," said Abdul-Jabbar, who conducted a very brief postgame interview just before the doors closed on the elevator.

After Aguirre's accidental blow landed, Abdul-Jabbar ran upcourt rubbing his chin and, on his way to his position, detoured slightly to place his left forearm beneath Aguirre's chin.

Aguirre said something to Abdul-Jabbar and then tried to shake the Lakers center's hand. But Abdul-Jabbar kept his hand on his hip, so Aguirre eventually just touched it and walked away.

Although the Mavericks managed to close the Lakers' lead to 91-89, Michael Cooper sank his fourth three-pointer of the game. Cooper's basket, perhaps more than anything else, with the possible exception of Aguirre's left ankle, doomed the Mavericks.

Aguirre, who scored 14 of his 28 points in the third quarter when the Mavericks rallied, twisted the ankle late in the quarter and had to leave the game . . .

Even without Aguirre, the Mavericks went down hard. Rolando Blackman, who scored 12 points in the fourth quarter, came back with a jumper after Cooper's three-pointer to bring the Mavericks within 94-91.

"We retained our composure," Cooper said. "We stick together, and Kareem is our glue."

James Worthy and Johnson figure in there too. Worthy immediately banked in a short jumper, and after Byron Scott rebounded a miss by Jay Vincent, who was playing for Aguirre, Johnson drove for a three-point play.

Johnson scored 13 points in the fourth quarter and finished with 21 points and 17 assists.

Blackman and Worthy scored, then Johnson and Vincent scored before Worthy and Scott gave the Lakers a safer lead, 105-98.

James Donaldson scored the last meaningful Dallas basket before Abdul-Jabbar got loose for consecutive baskets that finally silenced the boisterous Reunion Arena crowd.

Riley seemed relieved that his team was finally able to finish off the Mavericks.

"I knew we were going to be tested," the Lakers coach said. "I expected to be. I didn't expect a cakewalk. Maybe this six-game series opened up our minds that it's going to be tougher."

1985-86 Season Highlights

Kareem Abdul-Jabbar, James Worthy, and Magic Johnson all start for the Western Conference All-Star Team.

Johnson becomes the first player to receive more than one million votes in All-Star Game balloting.

The Lone Star State finally stopped Kareem Abdul-Jabbar (33) in 1986 when the Lakers center ran up against the Houston Rockets' Twin Towers—Ralph Sampson (50) and Akeem (who later changed his name to Hakeem) Olajuwon (34)—in the Western Conference Finals. Sampson made the last-second shot that finished off the Lakers' hopes in Game 5.

1986-87

Post Up and Pin It Down— Whatever That Means

A frustrating Game 5 loss wouldn't derail the Lakers in the 1987 Finals, but it did set the table for this sports columnist to let loose on the sport in his unique witty style.

By JIM MURRAY
June 14, 1987

Season Record

W65-L17 (.793)
Division: 1st
NBA Champion

Coach

Pat Riley

Players

Magic Johnson

James Worthy

Byron Scott

Kareem Abdul-Jabbar

Michael Cooper

A.C. Green

Kurt Rambis

Mychal Thompson

Billy Thompson

Wes Matthews

Frank Brickowski

Adrian Branch

Mike Smrek

When you shoot at a king, make sure you kill him.

When you get three aces, make sure you bet them.

When you get your man on the ropes in a title fight, throw the right.

When you hit the stretch in the Kentucky Derby with a lead, go to the whip.

When you get a lap lead at Indy, turn up the boost.

When you get a three-foot putt in the Open, make it.

When you get to set-and-match-point, go to the net.

And when you get the Boston Celtics down three games to one in the championship finals, go to the hoop, hit the backboards, trot out the three-pointers. Go for the jugular. Drive a stake into their chests.

Don't try to smuggle the thing into the hangar. Don't stand around waiting for the next guy. Don't be "patient." Patience is for guys who drive camels for a living.

When you got the Celtics in execution position, throw the switch. Get the ball to Magic. Don't sit Abdul-Jabbar down a whole quarter. Don't sit him down a whole minute while the Celtics are just hanging on, looking up at the clock, hoping for the bell.

I never thought I'd see a Celtics team that would seem to have its back to the wall with a 16-point lead. A Celtics team that would dread a fourth quarter. Yet, here they were, like a fighter who's built up a big lead but is running out of gas and trying not to get knocked out in the final minutes.

But the Lakers kept waiting for them to fall. The Celtics would disintegrate as usual in the fourth quarter. Those old bones would begin to creak, their mouths would fall open, they would begin to pant, limp, gasp. They kept waiting for their throats to rattle.

The fourth quarter has become such a haunted house for Boston in this series that even network announcers who should have known better reacted hysterically, as if the Celtics had blown their chances because they were leading only 96-77 going into the final 12 minutes.

Now, ordinarily, teams leading by 19 with only one quarter to play can put that thing in the hangar with subs. The fourth quarter used to belong to the Celtics. But, more than the Celtics have changed. The game has changed.

Basketball used to be played on the floor. Now, it's played in the air. It's played by competing identified flying objects. It's a dogfight. In the air over the trenches. They've taken the infantry out of this war. When Joe Fulks, or whoever, first unveiled the jump shot 40 years ago, he probably never envisioned a game that would take place 20 feet in the air from then on.

It's depressing for those of us old characters who remember when there was a center jump after every basket. I mean, we barely get used to "three to make two" and they take that out of the game.

We're forever saying in some dismay "But didn't he walk?" when some guy takes off at the top of the key—or even half court—and somehow gets that ball to the basket without once dribbling it . . .

What, pray tell, is a loose ball foul? You committed a foul in our day, somebody went to the line.

In a way, I was kind of hoping that the Lakers would win Thursday and take the game out of here. That's another thing I can't get used to. Basketball, and it's almost July.

But, that's not all. Someday, somebody's going to have to explain to me precisely what a high post is. I get a headache just thinking about it. I've put it off long enough. I try to look smart when someone says to me, "Kareem is posting up on him!" I

try not to look miserable. I nod and agree but it just looks to me as if Kareem is standing there, hands on knees, trying to catch his breath. But, hey! If he's posting up, somebody better do something about it, right? . . .

"Key" itself is a term I've finally gotten comfortable with. Except that, as soon as I did, they started to call it the paint. Would you believe they didn't have a three-second violation when I learned the game? You could take a chair in the paint if you wanted to.

What's a half-court game . . . what's a transition game? What's boxing out? I thought that was when you bet three or more horses nine ways in an exacta at the track . . .

What's the difference between a slam dunk and a jam . . . between a fastbreak and an ordinary se-

ries of passes and runs up court? . . . I'm glad to see the hook shot back. At least I can relate to it—even though I thought it went out with Hooks Houbregs.

Well, as you can see, the Lakers didn't let us off the hook Thursday. We're going to have to go through at least one more game with Magic posting up in the paint or Bird trying to box him out in the transition—or the half-court—game or maybe trying to get a board.

Whatever happened to the two-hand set shot, the simple layup, the travel call? When is the game going to come back to earth? Or call it a season?

If the Lakers get the Celtics in the coffin early today, I'll thank them to nail it shut so that we're well out of this strange game—for a few months at least.

Magic Johnson lets fly with his famous "junior-junior skyhook" that beat the Celtics in Game 4 of the 1987 NBA Finals. After giving Boston some life in Game 5, the Lakers closed the door on the best-of-seven series in Game 6.

Showtime Defense Saves Title Game

The Lakers won 10 consecutive playoff games at home in 1987, defeating Denver (3-0), Golden State (4-1) and Seattle (4-0) before facing the Celtics in the Finals. But that series wasn't the slam dunk fans expected. It wasn't until Game 6 that the Lakers sealed their fourth title of the 1980s with a 106-93 victory.

By JIM MURRAY
June 15, 1987

The Lakers lined the Boston Celtics up against the wall and shot them Sunday. Finally.

The battleship finally ran down the rowboat. Russia took Kabul. Four aces beat two pair. Joe Louis knocked out King Levinsky. The 1927 Yankees won the pennant. Magic Johnson can start to smile again. Kareem Abdul-Jabbar may play another 10 years. Pat Riley can take his tie off and let his hair dry. Larry Bird can go back to being white. Jack Nicholson can go back to playing whackos.

It's over. It wasn't a game, it was an execution. The Celtics should have been blindfolded. What took so long? It was such a messy application of capital punishment, any judge ... would have commuted the Celtics' sentence. The Celtics went out like the mad monk Rasputin. The Lakers had to try poison, shooting, choking and finally, so to speak, had to drown them in the Neva River.

Here was a team that could barely walk, led by a guy who was too white to be any good and sporting a backcourt that could fit in a Volkswagen, and the popular call before the series started was that the Lakers should win it in four games—or less—or

be ashamed of themselves. Some people thought the Humane Society should ban it. It was as one-sided as bullfighting. Vegas put the spread at infinity. The Celtics looked in poor light like Bonaparte's retreat.

The Lakers, who were supposed to run the Celtics right off the Seal Beach Pier, won the game and the championship on, of all things, defense.

The Boston Celtics didn't score a basket for the first 4 minutes 19 seconds of the third quarter and didn't score again until 7 minutes 47 seconds had elapsed.

The game ended for all intents and purposes at the half. The Celtics led by five, not nearly enough. The Celtics are like squirrels. They have to hoard points like nuts for the coming winter, otherwise known as the fourth quarter. They need a minimum of 15.

The turning point in Game 6's 106-93 victory came when the Celtics still had a one-point lead in the opening minutes of the third quarter and were driving for the basket.

James Worthy was part of a double-team operation on the Celtics' Kevin McHale with an option to sag off on Boston guard Dennis Johnson when some instinct told him McHale was going to pass ... When McHale let it go, Worthy materialized. "I reached out to deflect it." He had only semi-possession of it ...

While he was fighting to keep the ball in fair territory, he looked out of the corner of his eye and saw a familiar apparition—Magic Johnson on the way to the basket. He half-rolled, half-threw the ball to Magic who swooped on the hoop for the dunk shot that put the Lakers ahead, 57-56.

And that was the old ball game ...

The Celtics went quietly after that. The Lakers outscored the Celtics 18-2 nearly eight minutes into the period and 30-12 for the whole third period. After that, it wasn't a game, it was a procession, a clinic in free-flow basketball. The Celtics just became the instruments for the Lakers to give a symphony. The fourth quarter was a contest only if you consider Beethoven's Fifth a contest.

... But it might [not have gone so well] for L.A. if it were not for the remarkable talents of a Laker who may be the best ever to play his position in this league.

With Earvin Johnson, as with Bill Russell before him, you throw away a stat sheet in evaluating his effectiveness on a basketball court. Magic just does what has to be done. Steal, dribble, shoot, pass—he handles a basketball the way a riverboat gambler handles a deck of cards. Or a magician a silk hat ...

What you look at with Magic Johnson are championships. This is the fourth world title the team has won since Magic joined them. One of the years they didn't, he was injured most of the year ... Magic is a one-man theater. He adjusts. The Lakers, smelling a one-sided game, came out falling all over themselves Sunday. "We ... came out too ready," explained Magic after the game. ... "We had to spread out, loosen up," Magic perceived. And corrected.

... "This is the best team I ever played for," he said earnestly after the game ... "I never played on a team before that had everything ..."

This team has everything all right. Magic Johnson. Other teams have had Mr. Clutch—or Mr. Outside or Mr. Inside. This team has Mr. Everything. And he comes with the title.

1986-87 Season Highlights

Magic Johnson is voted MVP of the regular season and the NBA Finals and is selected to the All-NBA First Team.

Johnson averages a career-high 23.9 points per game and leads the league in assists with 12.2 per game, also the season high for the NBA.

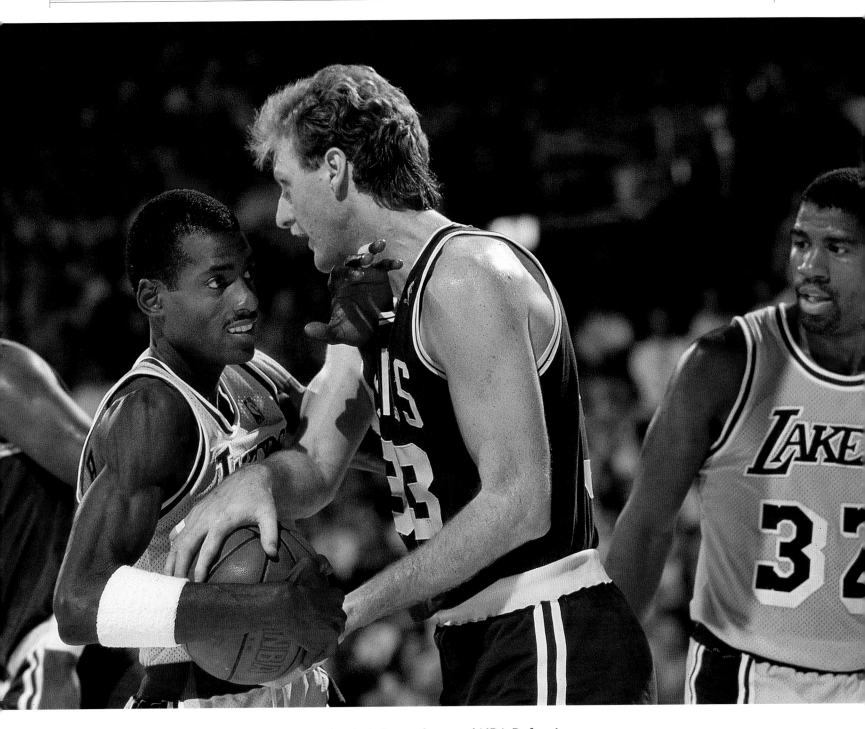

In 1987, Michael Cooper became the first and only Laker to be voted NBA Defensive Player of the Year. Larry Bird (33), who often praised Cooper's defensive skills, gets a personal reminder of Cooper's toughness as Magic Johnson looks on.

The '86-87 Lakers, later chosen as one of the top 10 teams in NBA history, snap the Boston Celtics' 48-game home winning streak on December 12, 1986.

Mitch Kupchak retires in September of 1986 and becomes the Lakers' assistant general manager.

Mychal Thompson, acquired in February of 1987, comes off the bench to average 10.1 points a game.

The Lakers race to a 29-0 lead against Sacramento on Feb. 4—40-4 after the first quarter—and do not allow the Kings a field goal the first period.

THE LAKERS • 139

1987-88

It's All Prime Time With Magic

Season Record

W62-L20 (.756)
Division: 1st
NBA Champion

Coach

Pat Riley

Players

Byron Scott

James Worthy

Magic Johnson

Kareem
Abdul-Jabbar

A.C. Green

Mychal Thompson

Michael Cooper

Wes Matthews

Kurt Rambis

Milt Wagner

Tony Campbell

Mike Smrek

Ray Tolbert

Billy Thompson

Jeff Lamp

Magic Johnson lifted his team and the spirits of Lakers fans, while lifting an entire league. In 1988, his clutch play let the Lakers squeak past the Dallas Mavericks, ensuring that at least one marquee team would be in the NBA Finals, where his exciting style of play could boost a TV network—and entertain a nation of viewers.

By JIM MURRAY
June 5, 1988

OK, Ms. B, think we can pull together a memo for CBS? Something they should know? Slug it "Attn. Network Sports." Ready?
Dear CBS,
Boy, did you guys dodge a bullet! A cannonball.

I bet you thought a week ago you had coming up in the NBA Finals, Dempsey-Tunney, Notre Dame-Army, Borg-McEnroe, Germany-Russia. I mean, you had the Celtics-Lakers, basketball's version of World War III, right?

Then, shockingly, you lost the Celtics to that funny little team in Detroit. The Cylinders, or something like that.

And, then it looked as if the Lakers were going to succumb to the same paralysis, the same malady—sudden old age. The Dallas Mavericks spotted them two games, then caught them and almost passed them.

All of a sudden, you didn't have Dempsey-Tunney, you had a club fight in Toledo—or Bonecrusher Smith against Tim Witherspoon.

I mean, you weren't going to get Magic Johnson, you were going to get Derek Harper. Forget Kareem Abdul-Jabbar, how does James Donaldson grab you? You want Dennis Johnson and you settle for Dennis Rodman. How many cars you think he's going to sell for you? He might bring back the Edsel.

You almost got Dallas-Detroit. Think about that for a minute. You think Jack Nicholson's going to go watch that?! You think Billy Crystal, Dyan Cannon, John McEnroe, Michael Jackson are going to fly in to be courtside to see how Rolando Blackman matches up with Joe Dumars, whoever they are? Gimme a break! They could have played in masks . . .

Well, you don't have Dempsey-Tunney, but you still have Dempsey. It'll play in Dubuque. It'll sell razor blades, fill the Silverdome, sell basketball.

You can send the check to Earvin Johnson. He saved your show for you. He usually does.

You see, Magic Johnson doesn't play a game, he orchestrates it. No one ever took charge of a basketball game the way Magic Johnson does, not Oscar Robertson, Walt Frazier, not even the great Bob Cousy . . .

When he first came to the Lakers nine years ago, the Lakers were an excellent team, given to a kind of mechanical perfection, disinterested efficiency. They played their game with a shrug, hurried into the shower, gave perfunctory, one-syllable answers to the press and disappeared into Hollywood . . .

Magic changed all that. He brought a smile as wide as a canyon, and he brought a joy to the game it hadn't seen. He woke up the stands, lit up the locker room. Hell, he lit up the league . . .

He could do whatever he wanted to with a basketball. You needed 40 points, you got 40 points. You needed 20 rebounds, you got those, too. But he was probably the most unselfish great player in the history of the game. Magic didn't play for the numbers, he played for the championships . . .

The great ones all have this game-day look about them. It's the faraway look of a lion who suddenly sees a movement in the bush. Ben Hogan used to get it when he came to the back nine of an Open only one shot behind.

"If you had any sense, it'd scare you," Lakers Coach Pat Riley said after Saturday's game in which Magic Johnson saved the title and your network ratings . . . "Earvin had this look when he showed up in the locker room in the morning." Magic, typically, showed up for a 12:30 game at a quarter to 9 and he had what Riley calls his "see through" look . . .

Magic Johnson, with a gift for inventive passes that would stop opponents in their tracks, didn't only help the Lakers win five titles in the 1980s, he made it fun.

In the third period, with the score seesawing, the Lakers went ahead, 67-65. Magic could see Kareem under the basket, too. He was a full length of the court away.

But Magic uncorked a pass like a guy throwing to home plate from center field. He hit Kareem where the captain was able to stuff the shot and draw the foul.

That was the old ballgame. That did it for Dallas. The score was suddenly 70-65, and the Lakers never looked back.

Magic sits in a locker room after a game, and he's got more ice around him than the Titanic, but he's saved more than L.A.'s season. He's saved your show for you. You're going to miss Larry Bird. But not much. If Magic gets that look, Detroit may start to wish it had lost. Or Dallas won. But Magic kept the show on Broadway.

Lakers Repeat Their Title Feat

After a convincing NBA championship victory in 1987, Coach Pat Riley had virtually promised a repeat the next year. It took everything the Lakers had, with grueling seven-game series in the Western Conference Semifinals, the Western Conference Finals and the NBA Finals. The team wouldn't win another championship until 2000.

By GORDON EDES
June 22, 1988

I t took both the suddenness of a sprinter and the heart of a marathoner, but the Lakers crossed the finish line of their two-year run Tuesday night at the Forum with history borne triumphantly on their shoulders and brazen guarantees safely tucked away in their memories.

With James Worthy carrying the baton in Game 7, the Lakers outdistanced the Detroit Pistons, 108-105, to become the first team since the Boston Celtics in 1969 to repeat as champions of the National Basketball Assn. Worthy, voted the most valuable player of the series, chose this night to have the first triple-double of his career—36 points, 16 rebounds and 10 assists—bringing the Lakers to what may be the end of their championship ring cycle—five rings in the '80s.

"I don't have any feelings left just now— I feel raw for them," said Lakers Coach Pat Riley, who had pledged the Lakers to another title within a half-hour of the team's championship victory over the Boston Celtics in 1987.

"At the end of the game, what were we doing? We were watching a great basketball team hold on. We were holding on, and we had a big enough lead to do so."

But barely. The Lakers, who had burst ahead of the Pistons by making their first 10 shots of a third quarter that began with Detroit ahead by five and ended with the Lakers up by 10, nearly had a 15-point lead expire in the last 7:27.

Detroit, which limped into the game with Isiah Thomas playing on one good leg, pulled within one point, 106-105, on Bill Laimbeer's three-point basket with six seconds left. But Magic Johnson, who had 19 points and 14 assists, spotted A.C. Green for the breakaway layup that finished off the Pistons and completed what Johnson called the most difficult season of his life . . .

For a time, the Pistons placed a heavy boot on the Lakers' necks, taking a 52-47 halftime lead as Kareem Abdul-Jabbar went scoreless, Byron Scott had just five points, Cooper was 0 for 4 from three-point land and Johnson had as many turnovers (three) as baskets (three).

Thomas, meantime, a doubtful starter who was still on crutches when he arrived at the Forum Tuesday afternoon, had 10 points and four steals by the intermission, having dribbled unchallenged down the floor for the basket that gave Detroit its five-point advantage.

"We wanted to stop throwing the ball away," Johnson said. "We had 11 turnovers in the first half—we'd been averaging 11 a game.

"We wanted to establish our game in the first three minutes [of the third quarter]. Let them know, 'We're here.' "

Scott was the first one to go calling, throwing down a thunderous dunk over Piston center Laimbeer on the break. That triggered a succession of Laker relays downcourt, with Worthy scoring seven straight points and Scott pouring in 11 . . . [giving] Los Angeles a 70-59 lead.

The Lakers didn't miss a shot in the period until Scott put up an airball with 5:05 left.

. . . But the Pistons made a last grab to get it back—with both Thomas and Adrian Dantley on the bench—in the last seven minutes.

"I don't even know what happened in the last minute, minute and a half," Riley said. "I was just holding on."

. . . In a four-minute span, Detroit sliced 13 points off its deficit, outscoring the Lakers, 17-4, to pull within two, 98-96 . . . [A series of plays] cut the Laker margin to 102-100 with 1:18 left . . . [and then] 105-102 with 16 seconds left. With 14 seconds to go, Worthy was fouled, but he made just one, and Laimbeer's three-pointer made it a one-point game with six seconds left.

Johnson, however, put a stop to the mounting hysteria right there with his court-length pass to Green.

Moments later, Commissioner David Stern was handing a trophy to Lakers owner Jerry Buss, and the Lakers were bathing in bubbly.

. . . For Johnson, this championship season had its bittersweet aspect, as well.

"This was the hardest championship season, not just because we went to seven games three times," Johnson said. "Playing against Isiah in a championship is probably the hardest thing I've ever had to do—trying to stay away from each other, trying not to be friends."

. . . While other Lakers were laughing and carrying on in the last half-minute, Johnson was still cold sober.

"With 20 seconds to go, we were celebrating like we were the champs. I said, 'Hey, don't celebrate.' I'm always scared. I'm scared until the final buzzer goes off . . ."

1987-88 Season Highlights

Michael Cooper (21) ends up hitting a jump shot with seven seconds left in Game 5 of the conference semifinals that helps the Lakers get past Utah.

The Lakers become the first team in NBA history to win three consecutive seven-game playoff series 4-3 (over Utah, Dallas, and Detroit).

The Lakers become the first team since the 1968-69 Celtics to win back-to-back NBA championships.

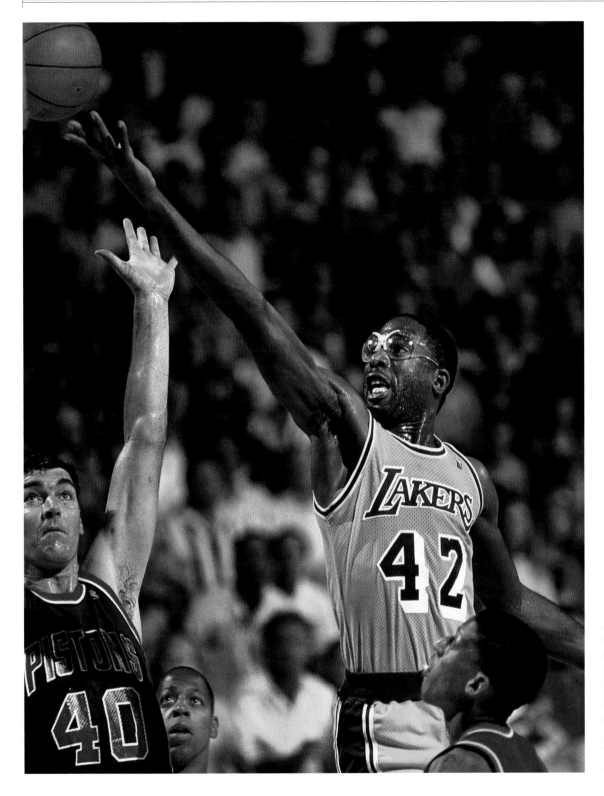

James Worthy shows a golden touch in the 1988 Finals, becoming the series' Most Valuable Player with the first triple-double of his career—36 points, 16 rebounds and 10 assists in Game 7.

Kareem Abdul-Jabbar's 787-game streak of scoring in double figures is snapped December 4, 1987, by Milwaukee.

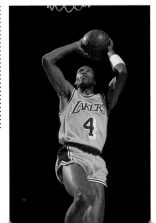

Byron Scott leads the team in scoring with an average of 21.7 points per game.

Friends off the court, Magic Johnson and Isiah Thomas kiss before the NBA Finals' tipoff.

1988-89

Retirement Party Reveals Another Side of Kareem

Season Record

W57-L25 (.695)
Division: 1st
NBA Finals

Coach

Pat Riley

Players

Magic Johnson

James Worthy

Byron Scott

A.C. Green

Kareem
Abdul-Jabbar

Mychal Thompson

Orlando
Woolridge

Michael Cooper

Tony Campbell

David Rivers

Mark McNamara

Jeff Lamp

The end of Kareem Abdul-Jabbar's career took him to every arena in the league, a farewell tour that brought countless accolades for one of the most accomplished players in NBA history. But the last stop was the most touching. He had come home to the Forum.

By SCOTT OSTLER
April 24, 1989

Due to coincidence rather than plan, the rocking-chair throne for Kareem Abdul-Jabbar's farewell ceremony Sunday was placed directly on the low post spot where Kareem could have his mail delivered.

A funny thing didn't happen when the honored guest settled into that Forum low post for the festivities. Nobody rammed an elbow into his kidneys and tried to bulldoze him off the court, or hung on his forearms like Spanish moss, or clawed at his goggles or wrapped a chokehold on his Adam's apple.

Big Fella was hit with none of the traditional defensive stratagems that have limited him to under 40,000 career points. That kind of stuff would come later, during the game against the Seattle SuperSonics. First it was time to honor Kareem on this, the last stop of his world farewell tour. The Forum farewell.

A fine tour it has been, incidentally. Already stashed away at Skyhook Manor in Bel-Air is an incredible array of gifts gathered from around the league, thoughtful and useful items. Kareem was given a hunk of the Boston Garden floor. The Celtics figured that because the man helped dismantle their dynasty, he might as well help dismantle their building.

That square o' parquet will go great at Kareem's mansion, something for guests to wipe their feet on. And his will be the only home in Bel-Air with Boston termites. He was given a surfboard, a sailboat and a fishing pole, which is nice, because even a 42-year-old fella needs bathtub toys . . .

Wonderful tokens of affection and respect, but what would the final farewell, the home-court party, be like? It was swell. Heartwarming. Kareem cried, and so did Magic Johnson, and the Forum fans sent Big Fella into his retirement—after the playoffs, of course—with a touching display of their affection and appreciation . . .

So many nice touches. Jack Nicholson showed up wearing a top hat and tails and T-shirt, trying as usual to blend in with the crowd. Jack probably was mowing his lawn Sunday morning, lost track of the time and didn't have a chance to change clothes before dashing to the Forum.

"Is that Nicholson?" Chick Hearn asked during a break in his broadcast. "Pretty nice. Looks like he's going to fly over the cuckoo's nest again."

Kareem's 8-year-old son, Amir, posted up his old man and sang the Star-Spangled Banner to kick off the party. Hearn, the emcee, read a tribute sent by George (Read My Telegram) Bush, saluting Kareem's career and his character, and absolving Big Fella of any blame for Irangate or the oil spill . . .

Chick has been a Kareem fan since the beginning. It's the old philosophical question: If a skyhook falls in the forest of players and Chick doesn't call it—"Fakes left, swings right, GOOD!"—does it count? Nobody knows, because Hearn has called 'em all, every last skyhook over the last 14 seasons . . .

There were gifts, of course. Lakers owner Jerry Buss will build a tennis court at Kareem's Hawaiian villa, so Big Kahuna can brush up on his forehand, backhand and skyhook serve. The Lakers' players, coaches and trainer chipped in to buy Kareem a Rolls-Royce, and one rumor is that if Big Fella helps them win another National Basketball Assn. title, they'll buy him the motor.

The most touching moment of Sunday's ceremony was the initial ovation for Kareem, bringing tears that he had to brush away. Where were the windshield-wiper goggles when he needed them? When Kareem spoke, when he thanked the fans for being fans, Magic Johnson cried.

"I started cryin' when he was talking," Magic said, "because I see it got to him. Was I surprised? Yeah, it was great to see . . . I saw another side of

Kareem Abdul-Jabbar signals his appreciation while astride his new Harley-Davidson, a gift from the Milwaukee Bucks. At his Forum tribute, the star center delights as his son Amir sings the national anthem, with Lakers broadcaster Chick Hearn standing by as master of ceremonies. Abdul-Jabbar later said he was so nervous for Amir he forgot to stand during the anthem.

him come out. I'll never forget this day."

. . . The first time I saw Abdul-Jabbar, he was a UCLA freshman named Lew. That was back in 1965, when gas was 10 cents a gallon, the earth was flat, and Lew had a barber, not a buffer. Alcindor opened that particular freshman game with a pounding slam-dunk, and the sold-out Pauley Pavilion crowd actually laughed.

It took L.A. fans, and the rest of the country's fans, a while to appreciate the man's talents, to realize that Kareem was more than tall. He could play, and he could win. The only thing freakish about him was his grace, and his uncanny knack of being on teams when world titles were won.

Sometimes now, on the bad days, we forget just how incredible this dude once played, and for how many years and for how many championship teams. Three National Collegiate Athletic Assn. titles at UCLA, five NBA championships with the Lakers. Eight titles over 22 seasons, interrupted by that six-year side-trip to Milwaukee.

No athlete ever gave more, for so long, to this city.

Sunday the fans said thanks, and this time they weren't laughing.

Before Injuries, Lakers Are Playoff Perfect

The Lakers had a great launch into the 1988-89 playoffs, shutting out Portland (3-0), Seattle (4-0), and Phoenix (4-0), even managing to beat the Suns when Magic fouled out in Game 1 of the Western Conference Finals, as Jim Murray recounts here. But hamstring injuries to Johnson and Byron Scott cost them in the NBA Finals, leaving Detroit to sweep the Lakers (4-0) and ending a chance for a third straight title.

By JIM MURRAY
May 21, 1989

OK, break up the Lakers. I've seen enough. Tell the Detroit Pistons or the Chicago Bulls to mail in the loss. Oh, sure, Phoenix was not so easy. Phoenix almost phooled them.

That's not the point. The point is, the Lakers win playoff games when they are down, 41-12. And, then, they win playoff games with Magic Johnson on the bench for the critical part of the game.

I mean, it's considered an act of faith the Lakers cannot win anything without Magic. Magic has to have the ball, not a seat, for the Lakers to be champions.

Giving Magic the basketball is like giving Hitler an army, Jesse James a gang, or Genghis Khan a horse. Devastation. Havoc. He's one of the more demoralizing forces in sports, Dempsey with a hook, an Unser with a car, Henry Aaron on a slow curve. Magic Johnson without a basketball is an offense against nature.

... You have to bear in mind Magic hasn't fouled out of a playoff game since Reagan's first term in office. In fact, the first year. He hasn't fouled out of any kind of game in five years. Magic is usually too smooth to draw a whistle. He has this guileless face of a kid playing an angel in a school play. He has practiced the art of looking incredulous till he's better at it than a New York pickpocket.

Magic's "Who me?!" look is as good as the rest of his game . . . Al Capone would have been freed if he could feign the reproachful, pained look Magic musters up right after he has knocked somebody out of bounds or charged to the basket like a runaway freight as he did twice in a little over a minute Saturday.

NBA protocol calls for the official to look for the nearest part-time player to deal off the foul call in these situations. Wilt Chamberlain, for example, never fouled out of a game in his life. In those days, they were afraid customers would call for their money back.

But Magic got too reckless in a 127-119 victory in Game 1 of the Western Conference Finals Saturday. He roughed up more guys on his way to the basket than a Mafia loan collector. Magic came through the key like a fullback on the one-yard line. They either had to give Phoenix a foul or the last rites.

Magic, of course, acted as if he couldn't believe it. It was a case of mistaken identity. Persecution. He grimaced, rolled his eyes heavenward, tried to look the way you imagined Joan of Arc or the prisoner of Shark Island looked.

It didn't work. Magic had to sit out almost the whole third quarter and there were only seven minutes left in the game when he came back in the fourth period.

The Lakers had squandered a 16-point lead in the course of the action. He soaked up his final, disqualifying foul with 2:23 to play, and the Lakers in front, 116-111 . . .

Phoenix did not go gentle into that good night. The Suns proved to be persistent, dogged and determined. They completely misunderstood their role. This wasn't supposed to be a game, it was supposed to be a festival . . . The Lakers were to give an exhibition of championship basketball, the Suns were props. It was supposed to be Tyson-Spinks. It turned out more Dempsey-Firpo.

The subs, in a sense, won it. While Magic was out, instead of just staging a delaying action, just trying to keep the game in sight till their leader returned, they carried the fight to Phoenix . . .

The Phoenix Suns are mystery guests in the tournament this year. A funny little team of anonymous nobodies, as unknown as a bunch of stagecoach robbers, they proved to be young, fast and not at all in awe of the two-time world champions. They were on the Lakers like a posse after a rustler . . .

But if the Lakers can win with Magic on the bench . . . if they can win spotting playoff opponents 29 points—they may have to get them their own league. If 31 minutes out of Magic Johnson is enough for the Lakers, they're not a team, they're a dynasty . . .

Of course, when Magic came back with five fouls Saturday, the team was behind, 99-100. When he finally left the game for good, five minutes later, the team was ahead, 116-111. As Phoenix Coach Cotton Fitzsimmons was to say after the game, "I'd a whole lot rather see Magic sitting than playing."

1988-89 Season Highlights

The Lakers record victories in their first 17 home games.

Magic Johnson, shown at the trophy presentation with NBA Commissioner David Stern, is named MVP of the league.

Lakers trainer Gary Vitti does what he can to keep Magic Johnson's hamstring ready for game action, but an injury in Game 2 of the 1989 NBA Finals kept the Lakers' star on the sidelines. Johnson tried to return for Game 3 but had to leave after five minutes. Making it worse was the absence of Byron Scott, who injured his hamstring during team practices before the Finals.

Johnson becomes the only player in Lakers' history to lead the NBA in free-throw percentage (91.1%).

A.C. Green (45), with Mychal Thompson looking on, leads the Lakers in rebounds with an average of 9.0 per game.

The Lakers average 114.7 points per game, higher than any Lakers team in the next 20 years.

1989-90

Curtain Down on Showtime?

Season Record

W63-L19 (.768)
Division: 1st
West Semis

Coach

Pat Riley

Players

Magic Johnson

James Worthy

Byron Scott

A.C. Green

Orlando
Woolridge

Mychal Thompson

Vlade Divac

Michael Cooper

Larry Drew

Mark McNamara

Jay Vincent

Steve Bucknall

Mel McCants

Jawann Oldham

Mike Higgins

With Kareem Abdul-Jabbar gone from the squad and the Lakers eliminated by Phoenix in Game 5 of the second round of the playoffs—the team's earliest exit from postseason play since 1981—many were wondering whether they were witnessing the end of Showtime.

By JIM MURRAY
May 20, 1990

In the locker room after Game 5, the night the bubble burst, the interviewer was blunt. "Is," he asked Lakers Coach Pat Riley, "the dynasty over?"

Riley's tie matched the striped shirt. The cuff links glittered in the TV lights. Pat Riley looked like a center spread in GQ. But it was not a question he wanted to hear.

"No," he said carefully, "it needs a little upgrading like any dynasty. But it's definitely not over. There's too much talent left."

Over in another area, The Dynasty itself was sitting, toweling off in front of a row of perspiring print and electronic reporters. Magic Johnson was almost whispering. His famous smile was present, his answers were polite, G-rated. But he sounded like a man rehearsing his farewell tour.

Johnson has always been the last man out of a locker room. So long as there's a question to be answered, airtime to fill, Magic is patiently available. He turns out the lights, leaves with the janitor.

But on this night, he appeared not to want the moment to end. In another corner of the dressing room, Arsenio Hall, no less, waited for his friend to get through, get dressed and go into the night. He finally gave up the vigil. Magic was going over his answers for each new set of people as soon as they arrived.

Is the dance over? Is Showtime as long gone as vaudeville? Does Magic want to spend his twilight years feeding the ball to a succession of players more suspect than prospect, a generation of hope-to-be's but never-will's, a team of fading stars and confused rookies?

Magic has been on the Yankees. Magic has lived on the top of the hill. Does he want to go back down into the pits? He has never known the agony of mediocrity. Where Magic goes, the lights shine, the cameras wink, the crowds cheer. Does he want to wind down his career now with the, so to speak, Atlanta Braves?

It takes two men to run a basketball team—one to bring the ball upcourt and the other to score with it or rebound it.

When those two men were Magic Johnson and Kareem Abdul-Jabbar, the surrounding cast didn't matter. A guy to suck up the fouls here. A guy to get the loose ball there. Magic and Kareem made them all look like all-stars.

It wasn't a league, it was a parade. The Lakers either won or were in the NBA's championship series every year—except for two fluke years when Houston got lucky in a prelim.

But this year, the Lakers were well beaten. They squandered leads, they threw the ball away, their tongues were out and they were gasping for breath, sneaking peeks at the clock. The Phoenix basketball expert, Joe Gilmartin, put it best. "The Lakers," he said sadly, "remind me of an old fighter who has gone to the ring once too often. His eyes are cut, his nose is bleeding, his legs are shot, his ears are ringing and he's fighting on pure instincts. It's painful to watch . . . "

Couldn't the league see this team had a hole in it? Kareem couldn't last forever, but when he left, was the team ready? When Babe Ruth left, the Yankees had Lou Gehrig and Joe DiMaggio. When Abdul-Jabbar left, the Lakers had Mychal Thompson and Vlade Divac. Any team that has Magic Johnson still has cards to play. Unfortunately, there are not enough aces. Not even Magic can hold off the league when the playoffs come and the blue chips are on the table.

The Lakers used to have this reproductive capacity. The Elgin Baylor-Jerry West mini-dynasty ebbed, and along came Wilt Chamberlain. When Wilt retired, owner Jack Kent Cooke went out and finagled Kareem Abdul-Jabbar.

This time, there are only banners in the dust. When the cry rings out, "The King is dead!" there's no answering echo, "Long live the King!" There isn't any.

There's nothing wrong with the Lakers that a Patrick Ewing, Akeem Olajuwon or David Robinson couldn't fix. But there's nothing wrong with the Sahara that a flood couldn't fix.

Even the coach is making noises like a man about to go over the wall. "I can't honestly say what I'm going to do," acknowledges Pat Riley, sounding like a guy who's got the bags packed and the motor running...

They tell you the game has changed. They talk grandly of "half-court games" or "transition games" and call double-teaming "trapping." Detroit wins by holding everybody to 86 points, they assure you. The other team never gets the ball.

The other team would get the ball if it were the 1980-87 Magic-Kareem Lakers. Detroit would be lucky to hold them under 86 for three quarters. But Magic can't pass the ball to himself. Michael Jordan is the only one who can.

The game hasn't changed, players have. They get old.

Vlade Divac shows a flair around the hoop, but the Lakers, without Kareem Abdul-Jabbar, were clearly a different team in 1990. The Phoenix Suns stopped them in the Western Conference Semifinals.

Even the Best NBA Coaches Don't Endure

After taking over as head coach eleven games into the 1981-82 season, Pat Riley amassed a 533-194 regular-season record over nine years along with a 102-47 record in the postseason, winning nine Pacific Division titles and four NBA championships. He left the Lakers after the 1990 playoffs and became co-host of NBC's "NBA Showtime" the next season. He later worked as coach of the New York Knicks and general manager and coach of the Miami Heat.

By SAM MCMANIS
June 11, 1990

Pat Riley coached the Lakers for nine seasons. These days, in the NBA, that's an eternity. Coaching tenures last about as long as car batteries—about four years.

Longer than that, and the act grows stale. Players tend to lose interest in the same motivational tactics over 82 games and, for some teams, six weeks of playoffs. As Larry Bird once said about Bill Fitch—or was it K.C. Jones or Jimmy Rodgers—"all coaches wear thin." . . .

The NBA is a players' league. Players and coaches say it all the time. Before submitting his resignation, Riley was the coach with the second-longest tenure with the same team. That Riley lasted nine seasons might be more impressive an accomplishment than his NBA-record 73.3% winning record or his 102 playoff coaching victories, also a record . . .

Two days after the Lakers were eliminated from the playoffs, Riley noted the irony that he once was applauded as a motivational wizard for times he raised his voice to players. "Now," he said, "it leads to player grumbling."

One of Riley's strengths has been motivation. A lot of coaches are capable tacticians, but Riley tried different ways to reach veterans such as Kareem Abdul-Jabbar, Magic Johnson and Michael Cooper.

He spliced together tape of game action with rock music. He sent late-summer letters to each player, detailing individual goals. He thought up seasonal themes, such as "no rebounds, no rings," "the guarantee," "the career best year." He gave his share of effective speeches . . . But the same script can grow tiresome. By this season, many Lakers players privately considered Riley's speeches, quarterly report cards, summer letters and catch-phrases predictable and ineffective . . .

Riley's relationship with Jerry West, the Lakers' general manager, also deteriorated. The two had coexisted for a good part of the '80s with differing philosophies about running the team . . . The last two seasons, the relationship had run its course and the two often clashed. Publicly, they maintained the appearance of solidarity.

Riley might have been too good for his own good. Or perhaps simply too popular. As a general rule, coaches do not have nearly the star value as players in the NBA. In college basketball, the opposite is true. On the Lakers' name-recognition list, Riley rated a close second to Johnson. And Riley's endorsement portfolio was as healthy as Johnson's . . .

Riley's practices were known for being rigorous but, again, not as taxing as some have portrayed. This season, Riley routinely gave Johnson, James Worthy and Mychal Thompson—veterans with nagging, lingering injuries—practices off the day after games. Byron Scott was held out of many practices to nurse his injured left hamstring.

But Riley reportedly lost what remained of his popularity among the players when he rode them hard in practices for three consecutive days before the start of the playoffs.

There is irony here too. During that same time, the Lakers were fined $25,000 by the league for Riley's decision to hold out Johnson, Worthy and Thompson from the final regular-season game in Portland.

Riley may have been guilty of not responding to the players' wants and needs. An example was Riley's decision to take the team to a Santa Barbara retreat during an eight-day break before the start of the last season's NBA Finals against Detroit. The players wanted to stay in Los Angeles with their families, but Riley wanted a "training camp" atmosphere away from most of the media so they could "bond" heading into the finals. Riley held rigorous practices daily, and even sneaked in an intra-squad game replete with referees and fans.

The result? First Scott, then Johnson suffered hamstring injuries . . .

But there was a bigger reason that Riley could no longer relate to the players. They had heard it all before. They had tuned him out. So, like a radio station that changes formats to attract listeners, the Lakers soon will have a new coach, Mike Dunleavy.

If Dunleavy can last nine seasons in the same job, as Riley did, he will be the exception to what has become the rule among NBA coaches. For all of his reported faults, Riley proved exceptional.

1989-90 Season Highlights

Magic Johnson is named the league's MVP for the second consecutive year and the third time in four years, and also MVP of the All-Star Game.

Johnson sets a team regular-season record with 24 assists (vs. Denver November 17, 1989).

Pat Riley didn't always appear to have the same joy in his role in the 1989-90 season, but his statistics were impressive. Riley was voted the NBA's Coach of the Year and gained his 500th career victory and his 100th playoff victory, at the time becoming the NBA's all-time leader in playoff coaching wins.

The Lakers post the league's best regular-season record (63-19), the fifth time in six seasons they win more than 60 games.

Kareem Abdul-Jabbar's jersey is retired in a ceremony at the Forum.

Vlade Divac (left) works his way up, becoming the team leader in blocks (1.4 average) after being the Lakers' first-round pick in 1989.

CHAPTER FIVE

Changing of the Guard

Seasons 1990-91 through 1998-99

IT MAY BE the only era in sports history that closed with a simple declarative statement. On November 7 of 1991, Earvin "Magic" Johnson addressed a large and somber gathering of media at the Forum. "Because of the HIV virus that I have attained," Magic said, "I will have to retire from the Lakers today."

Johnson was 32, still in his prime. He had been the league MVP two of the previous three seasons. Since the retirement of Kareem Abdul-Jabbar two years earlier, Johnson has been spreading his offensive wings. He would make three brief comebacks, but the Lakers had lost their leader, their Magic.

After reaching the NBA Finals in 1992, the Lakers spent seven seasons falling short. They reached the conference finals once and went through four coaches, including Magic Johnson for 16 games ('93-94), without finding a championship formula.

Since the beginning of the franchise, the Lakers have run on star power. Now Kareem and Magic were gone. James Worthy retired in '94, and '94-95 was the only season in Lakers history, to the present, in which the team did not suit up a future Hall of Fame player.

So it was that in '96 Jerry West went shopping for diamonds. The general manager signed free agent Shaquille O'Neal, considered by many an underachiever, and traded to draft 17-year-old Kobe Bryant. They were a mismatched pair in many ways, but as the team neared the new century, hope was in the air.

—Scott Ostler

1990-91

Lakers Win Right to Play Bulls

Season Record

W58-L24 (.707)
Division: 2nd
NBA Finals

Coach

Mike Dunleavy

Players

James Worthy

Magic Johnson

Byron Scott

Sam Perkins

Vlade Divac

Terry Teagle

A.C. Green

Mychal Thompson

Tony Smith

Elden Campbell

Larry Drew

Irving Thomas

Tony Brown

Cool Mike Dunleavy from Brooklyn overcame comparisons to Pat Riley in his first year as Lakers coach, breaking in five new players and a new system, wrote Mark Heisler. Then the playoffs hit and the team peaked in the Western Conference Finals against the Portland Trail Blazers.

By MARK HEISLER
May 31, 1991

Danny Ainge said the Lakers had already stolen the Trail Blazers' heart and Thursday night, the Lakers claimed the body and soul as well. Not that Portland gave them up easily.

They rallied from a 15-point deficit and had Terry Porter shooting an open 17-footer for the lead in the closing seconds.

Porter missed, and several adventures later, the Lakers won, 91-90, taking the Western Conference Finals, 4-2, returning to the NBA Finals for the ninth time in Magic Johnson's 12 seasons to face the Chicago Bulls and Michael Jordan, making his first trip.

"Unbelievable," said Mike Dunleavy, the first rookie coach in the Finals since Pat Riley. "The only reason I took this job a year ago was this team had a chance to win a championship. Here it is, May 30, and I'm still right."

"Unbelievable" was a word heard more than once Thursday. Porter's shot was rebounded by Johnson, who threw the ball the length of the court, trying to kill the last three seconds . . . But let him tell the story.

"I knew they were going to foul me, so I threw the ball out," Johnson said, "and the clock stopped!

"I looked up and it was stopped at 2.2 seconds left! I said, 'Where are we, Boston Garden?' This is unbelievable!

"Finally, when the ball got to half court, the clock started moving again."

The clock had one-tenth of a second left when the ball went out of bounds at the far baseline. The Trail Blazers got a last inbounds play, Buck Williams throwing it to the other end, where it was batted away, making the Lakers champions of the West . . .

This was the last act in a heart-stopping fourth quarter. If the Lakers look back, they may shudder.

If the Trail Blazers look back, they may weep.

With the Lakers ahead, 89-88, and less than a minute left, Portland ran a four-on-one fast break, but Cliff Robinson dropped Jerome Kersey's pass out of bounds.

"You design things," Coach Rick Adelman said, "but you get a four-on-one, you can't design anything better than that. That's a dunk, we take the lead and put the pressure on them."

Oh no you don't.

"I took my eyes off it for a second," Robinson said. "It was a little harder than I expected . . ."

. . . At the other end, Johnson drove the lane and zipped a pass under the basket to Vlade Divac, who was fouled. Divac made two free throws with 43 seconds left. The Lakers led, 91-88. Porter, whose outside shooting had pulled the Trail Blazers back in, scored his 23rd and 24th points with a little luck, banking in a 15-footer by accident.

With 35 seconds left, Portland was within 91-90. Johnson drove the lane again and zipped another pass to Divac. Divac pivoted left to right and put up a shot, but the 6-foot-7 Kersey blocked it. The 24-second clock ran out. Portland had the ball with 12.5 seconds remaining.

"I could have strangled him (Divac)," Johnson said, laughing. "He should just have gone and dunked it."

. . . The Trail Blazers put the ball in Clyde Drexler's hands, defended by James Worthy, bad left ankle and all. Other Lakers helped cut Drexler off. The ball swung to Porter, alone on the right wing.

Porter, 10 for 17 at that moment, three for four on three-pointers, shot and missed . . .

"It just didn't go down. It felt good leaving my hand. It was right on line. It was just a tad short."

So were the Trail Blazers . . .

"It's just sweet," Johnson said, beaming. "I just can't tell you how it feels. Considering everything—all you guys doubting us, picking us fifth and sixth in the West, writing us off when we were 2-5. And rightly so, because we looked like a bad team."

A.C. Green perseveres under the basket against the Portland Trail Blazers as the Lakers come out on top in the 1991 Western Conference Finals.

Lakers Wear Down Over Time in Finals

In 2009, Phil Jackson won his 10th NBA title as a coach—a record he would not have attained if his Chicago Bulls had not beaten the Lakers in the 1991 Finals. While their loss to Michael Jordan's Chicago Bulls was frustrating, the Lakers took heart at reaching the championship series after opening the season with a new coach and a 1-4 mark. The Magic vs. Michael Finals turned on Game 3.

By MARK HEISLER
June 8, 1991

The Lakers hit the Bulls with their best shot.

The bad news, Lakers fans, is that it wasn't good enough.

The Bulls erased a 13-point third-quarter deficit, tied the game on Michael Jordan's 14-foot jumper with 3.4 seconds left in regulation and then won it in overtime, 104-96, for a 2-1 lead in the NBA Finals.

"Now I know how they felt a little bit," Mike Dunleavy said, having just surrendered his recently won home-court advantage.

Now he knows how Buster Douglas' manager felt: The Lakers got flattened.

Having complained that his team was outhustled in its Game 2 loss, Dunleavy saw the Lakers outrebounded in Game 3, 46-29.

The beating on the offensive boards was worse—24-8...

"A lot of it is the fact that Jordan commands so much attention," Dunleavy said.

"When you come to him, you have to help and it leaves alleys open for other players to come to the boards." ...

Amazingly, this looked like their game. Bludgeoned 22-10 on the boards in the first half, but trailing only 48-47, the Lakers hit the Bulls with a haymaker in the third quarter, holding them without a field goal for 6:20 in an 18-2 spurt for a 67-54 lead. The Laker Girls were dancing, the crowd was singing "I love L.A." Once the fans stood and cheered nonstop during a two-minute timeout, an impressive performance for a Forum crowd.

The Bulls were clearly rattled, but youth and inexperience notwithstanding, they regained their poise.

John Paxson's baseline drive for a layup ended the drought.

By the end of the quarter, after Scottie Pippen beat James Worthy down the lane for a driving layup, the Lakers' lead was down to 72-66.

The Bulls kept up the surge in the fourth quarter. It was close to the end. Chicago was ahead, 90-89, when Vlade Divac made the play of his young career, grabbing a weak pass from a pressured Magic Johnson at the top of the key, wheeling past Horace Grant as Jordan tipped the ball away, regaining possession in the lane, going up as he was jostled by Pippen and making a tough layup.

Pippen was called for the foul, his sixth. Divac's free throw gave the Lakers a 92-90 lead with 10.9 seconds left.

All the Lakers had to do was contain Jordan at the end of the game, as they had in Game 1.

Jordan to that point had missed 16 of his 24 shots.

Bulls Coach Phil Jackson decided to go the length of the floor. Dunleavy saw the alignment and called time out to discuss it. Jackson stayed with it.

Jordan brought the ball up against Byron Scott, jumped over him for a 14-footer before Divac arrived and hit it. It's not nice to fool with Mother Nature or Michael Jordan.

"I told (Craig) Hodges and Paxson, 'Be ready to shoot the three,' " Jordan said later.

"I thought they'd double-team me. In that situation, I'm so used to teams sending someone at me.

"I went down, beat Byron Scott and hit the shot."

Said Dunleavy: "We were trying to send him to our help. They had some shooters in the game we had to be careful about. . . . I thought he made a shot with a defender all over him. You can't ask for much more than that. The other alternative was to go with somebody before it was time to go double-team him and maybe open up somebody under the basket for an easy shot.

"I wasn't displeased at the shot he got. I was displeased that he made it."

The Lakers couldn't get off a good shot. More displeasure awaited.

Dunleavy inserted rookie Elden Campbell at the start of the overtime, to try to win the tap—which Campbell did.

Dunleavy then audaciously ran a play, a Johnson lob, hoping for a dunk by Campbell that would have brought the house down. The play didn't work. Campbell wound up taking a short jump shot, which was blocked.

And the Lakers never could get the lead in overtime...

"It's going to be a long series, I'm not worried about that," Johnson said.

He may be the only one.

1990-91 Season Highlights

Mike Dunleavy is Jerry West's choice for the Lakers' new coach.

Vlade Divac (12), who got his share of encouragement from Magic Johnson, leads the Lakers in rebounds, averaging 8.1 per game.

Two NBA eras cross paths when Magic Johnson and Michael Jordan do battle in the 1991 Finals at the Forum.

The Lakers win 16 consecutive games between January 9 and February 5, the second-longest winning streak in team history at the time.

With 19 assists vs. Dallas April 15, Johnson breaks Oscar Robertson's NBA assist record with 9,888.

James Worthy (left) and Johnson (right) play in the All-Star Game.

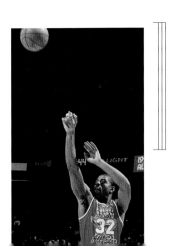

1991-92

Warning, HIV: No Hiding Now

Season Record

W43-L39 (.524)
Division: 6th
First Round

Coach

Mike Dunleavy

Players

Sedale Threatt

Byron Scott

A.C. Green

James Worthy

Sam Perkins

Terry Teagle

Elden Campbell

Vlade Divac

Tony Smith

Chucky Brown

Rory Sparrow

Jack Haley

Cliff Robinson

Keith Owens

Demetrius Calip

Magic Johnson's announcement that he had contracted HIV, the virus that causes AIDS, shocked the world. The infection effectively ended his playing career, though he did make an appearance in the All-Star Game, was part of the 1992 Olympic Dream Team and briefly coached the Lakers in 1994. Johnson made a short comeback with the Lakers in the 1995-96 season. Outside of basketball, he used his name recognition and enormous popularity to advocate for safe sex and HIV/AIDS awareness.

By JIM MURRAY
November 10, 1991

Never see Magic coming down the floor with the basketball again? Never see this little lopsided grin as he chivies the defender around like a yo-yo, then suddenly bursts with a behind-the-back, no-look pass to an open teammate for a baseline jumper? Never see that again?!

Magic, the most unselfish great player I have ever seen in any sport?

Magic, the superstar who actually liked us ink-stained wretches of the press, who stayed in the locker room until the last notebook was filled, the last microphone talked into, the last hand shook?

Wait a minute, God. Please! You can't do that to us! Not Magic. Tell us, it's not Magic...

You can't take away Showtime USA. Those happy nights at the Forum when Magic had the ball and everything was going to be all right and the audience was standing and cheering and laughing and it was good to be alive and at a Laker game and you went home and petted the dog and kissed the kids and reminded yourself to give at the office so the poor people could feel as good as you did.

Magic did that to the community. Shucks, he did that to the game... He brought a smile to L.A.'s face. He shouldn't be breaking our hearts now... Somebody up there goofed.

What's Jack Nicholson going to do? What are the Lakers going to do?... Magic turned them into the happiest band of troupers this side of the Seven Dwarfs.

And how he could play basketball! The game was invented for people like Magic. It was like watching Nureyev doing "Swan Lake," Astaire dancing down stairs. I always said Magic Johnson with the basketball was Babe Ruth with a bat, Willie Mays with a glove, Rocky Marciano with his nose cut, Caruso with a high C, Nicklaus with a one-iron, John Wayne with a horse...

He had this marvelous charisma on court. He is 6 feet 9, 225 pounds, and, if you were a defender, you wanted to call 911 when you saw him coming... but he managed to look like Bambi out there. All innocence and grace...

I remember the first time I saw Earvin Johnson. It was in 1979, the Lakers had just signed him and owner Jack Kent Cooke had arranged an interview for me. I was having catastrophic eye problems at the time and could hardly see across the table. But you could see Magic's smile anywhere...

You perceive a lot when you can't see, and what I heard in the voice of this new young recruit was kindness. Compassion. I realized this was not just some cocky young jock, this was something special...

He was the biggest star in L.A., but I would often chance upon him walking the shops of Century City by himself. No entourage. No flunkies clearing the way as if he were in a sedan chair. He parked his own car—a Jeep...

HIV may have picked on the wrong guy this time. There's a way to play HIV—go into seclusion, shut off your phone, cancel your mailing address, go into a cave of your own fears and hide...

If AIDS thinks it has a clear shot to the basket, it hasn't been paying attention. Magic is not about to put his hands up in the air and take this lying down...

HIV may have blown its cover this time. Plagues work best in darkness and silence. Embarrassment is its ally.

Magic is not going to let it get away with it. He

The day Lakers fans
will never forget:
Magic Johnson
announces he has HIV.

served notice by appearing forthrightly in public, baring his soul, knocking the chip off the enemy's shoulder. He's going to block this shot, too. A champion does not quit in his corner. A hero does not cower in the dark . . .

Nobody has things all its own way against Magic Johnson. Ask Bird, Isiah, Dominique, Jordan. Magic may be winning something far more important than a Final Four, an NBA championship, player of the year. Magic may be winning for a whole generation. Let's pray he can slam-dunk this one . . .

If he can, I want to see that smile!

From Beginning to End, It's Magic All-Star Game

After his All-Star MVP performance, Magic Johnson went on to win gold with the Olympic Dream Team in Barcelona but would not play another regular-season game for the Lakers until the 1995-96 season.

By MARK HEISLER
February 10, 1992

I f parting this was, it was such sweet sorrow.

If it turns out to be prelude instead, don't be surprised.

The master of any moment, Magic Johnson returned from a three-month absence Sunday, scored 25 points in the West's 153-113 romp and was named the Most Valuable Player of the NBA All-Star Game.

And this story is not winding down.

In four months, he will join the U.S. Olympic team . . .

That wasn't vintage Johnson, the player Sunday ("If you ask me how I played, I played OK"), but it was the vintage showman.

He made nine of 12 shots.

He sank three three-pointers in the fourth quarter, including a backing up 25-footer on the final attempt of the day.

He hit a 15-foot jump hook over Detroit's Dennis Rodman, who had never eased up before and wasn't about to start here.

"Dennis told me, 'I'm gonna guard you tough. You're not scoring on me,'" Johnson said.

"I couldn't wait to post him up."

The game, dominated by Johnson's appearance, which had become a national controversy, was more theater and less a contest.

The East players seemed to accept supporting roles and didn't even muster All-Star level intensity. The 40-point margin was an All-Star Game record.

It was more a collection of moments.

— Johnson and Isiah Thomas exchanging their usual pregame kiss on the cheek, standing at half court in a thicket of minicams and microphones.

— The crowd cheering 15 seconds before Johnson was introduced and for the next 1:40, until the Star-Spangled Banner.

— The East players breaking their line while the crowd applauded and crossing the floor to embrace Johnson: first Thomas, then Michael Jordan, Charles Barkley, Patrick Ewing and on down the line.

"First of all, I was shocked," Johnson said later. "But I enjoyed every hug, every high-five that I received.

"Those are the things that you take with you forever. You take this whole moment. You bottle it up and you never let it out.

It could not be said by game time that all doubts about the propriety of his appearance had disappeared . . .

In Sunday's New York Times, columnist George Vecsey wrote:

"It is not exaggerating to say that no athlete has ever felt so much support, so much love . . ."

Striking a different note, the Orlando Sentinel's Larry Guest wrote:

"Persistent rumors have emerged, suggesting a basketball game may intrude into the busy schedule of this weekend's Magic Johnson HIV/AIDS Workshop."

Johnson said he knew there were questions in the minds of his teammates, but Saturday's practice got everyone over the hump.

Golden State's Don Nelson, making his All-Star coaching debut, held a real practice rather than the usual walk-through, with players actually asked to run full court.

"I'm a dummy," Nelson said. "I didn't know.

" . . . I wanted them to run the fastbreak we were going to use and run our motion offense. Most of all, I wanted Magic to have a chance to scrimmage, to see where he was. I knew after that long away, he had to be wondering, 'Where's my game?' I thought that really calmed him down."

The West controlled the opening tip and the ball went to Johnson . . . whose pass was intercepted.

His first shot was a short hook, which he left short. He rebounded the miss and was fouled.

When he hit the first free throw a fan yelled: "MVP!"

Late in the game, Johnson was guarding Thomas . . . Johnson made him take a 20-footer, which Thomas missed. The crowd roared.

Then Johnson guarded Jordan, who settled for another jump shot and missed. The crowd roared louder.

Then Johnson hit his 25-footer.

"If this is going to be it for me, I wanted to go out this way," Johnson said . . .

"He stops two of our greatest players one-on-one without help," Nelson said. "He makes that shot. It was a storybook ending. It was Disneyland, and we're here."

They don't call him Magic because he does card tricks.

1991-92 Season Highlights

James Worthy (42) leads the Lakers in scoring, averaging 19.9 points per game.

Sedale Threatt (right photo) is ninth in the NBA in steals with a 2.05 per game average.

Magic Johnson, driving between East All-Stars Charles Barkley and Scottie Pippen, elevated the show at the 1992 All-Star Game.

On February 20, A.C. Green plays in his 456th consecutive game, setting a club record.

In November, the Lakers win a season–high nine consecutive games after Magic Johnson retires as Mike Dunleavy is selected NBA Coach of the Month.

Chick Hearn broadcasts his 2,500th consecutive game on March 13 at Cleveland.

1992-93

Scott Will Always Be a Laker

Season Record

W39-L43 (.476)
Division: 5th
First Round

Coach

Randy Pfund

Players

Sedale Threatt

James Worthy

A.C. Green

Vlade Divac

Anthony Peeler

Byron Scott

Sam Perkins

Elden Campbell

Tony Smith

James Edwards

Duane Cooper

Doug Christie

Benoit Benjamin

Alex Blackwell

After the 1992-93 season, Byron Scott went on to play for the Indiana Pacers and Vancouver Grizzlies before returning to the Lakers for one last season in 1996-97. Since then, he has gone on to coaching, taking over the reins for New Jersey Nets in 2000 and becoming NBA Coach of the Year in 2008 with the New Orleans Hornets.

By MIKE DOWNEY
July 25, 1993

On the dreaded but inevitable day that Byron Scott officially became an ex-Laker, the report in the next morning's newspaper bumped directly against an advertisement for Byron's summer basketball camps for kids.

The ad promised a once-in-a-lifetime experience and included, as one extra enticement: "Ride Share Available."

Let me tell you something.

Byron Scott can carpool with me any time.

He was our Los Angeles Laker. Jerry West came from West Virginia. Elgin Baylor was born in Washington, D.C. Kareem Abdul-Jabbar grew up in New York. Magic Johnson's home was Michigan. James Worthy flew in from North Carolina. But it was Byron Scott whose boyhood bedroom was 14 blocks from the Forum, who sneaked into the arena to watch the games, who broke the scoring record at Inglewood's Morningside High, who decorated his sneakers with Bob McAdoo's uniform number.

Byron was a literal chip off the old block.

That is why, when the time came for him to part company with the Lakers after spending nearly one-third of his life as one of them, Byron said see ya instead of farewell. That's why the player known to teammates simply as "B" said to his peers and to their fans, "I will see you in the Forum next season, not as a member of an opposing team, but simply as a long-time friend who now simply works out of town."

I hate the thought of Byron Scott's shots being counted on the side of the scoreboard reserved for VISITORS.

It won't be the same without 4 on the floor.

But he needn't worry.

Byron will always be one of us, never one of them ...

Lakers basketball meant a lot to Scott as a kid, which undoubtedly explains why he gave back so much as an adult. For several years, Byron has sponsored a "Challenge for Children" all-star game that benefits Orange County children's charities. When he recorded a song called "Give It Up for the Children," with Melvin Franklin of the Temptations and saxophonist Kenny G, all the proceeds went to Camp Ronald McDonald for kids fighting cancer. When I went to his house, the first thing Byron did was introduce me to his young sons. There was a miniature basketball hoop in the driveway, and I could picture them out there, even on days when Dad was exhausted from a long game and a longer trip home.

I have other pictures of Byron Scott in my mind.

I picture him reporting to the Lakers after an October 10, 1983, trade with the Clippers that cost the team the popular Norm Nixon ... He was frozen out and shunned for a while, forced to fight for respect from teammates and fans.

I picture him one season later, popping Scott shot after Scott shot, leading the league in three-point percentage, helping the Lakers win the division title by a league-record 20 games, getting champagne shampoos from teammates after beating Boston for the NBA championship.

I picture him two seasons later, playing Boston again for the title, playing poorly and sitting up all night with his wife, Anita, and Michael and Wanda Cooper, feeling as though he was being blamed for Lakers losses and being summoned for a pep talk by Pat Riley, who later described Byron's expression as being "like a face carved inside an Egyptian tomb."

I picture the anguish on Byron's face from a hamstring rip that kept him out of the 1989 Finals.

I picture the satisfaction on that face after accounting for 31 points against Orlando on Jan. 12,

1992, or when he scored the 11,000th point of his career three weeks later against Golden State.

I picture the concern on his face after the rioting that engulfed Los Angeles, and the painstaking effort he made to clarify what he meant when he said that he understood why it had happened.

I picture the joy in his eyes after the Lakers took two from Phoenix in the 1993 playoffs, and the exasperation he struggled to contain after missing the biggest shot of the season.

I picture everything Byron Scott did for the Lakers—his team, child and man.

Showtime's over, Byron, but we won't forget.

See ya.

Byron Scott left his mark in L.A. Only five players have been in more Lakers' playoffs.

1992-93 Season Highlights

Randy Pfund becomes the 10th head coach in Los Angeles Lakers history.

The Lakers become the first No. 8-seeded team to take a road series from a No. 1 team, defeating Phoenix twice, but lose in the first round.

Sedale Threatt leads the Lakers in scoring (15.1 points per game) and assists (6.9).

1993-94

Me-Me-Me-Me Turned Out to Be a Sour Note to Magic

In his brief incarnation as coach of the Lakers, Magic Johnson came away with a 5-11 record. But the performance was merely emblematic of the team's play. With a 33-49 record, the Lakers failed to make the playoffs for the first time in 18 years.

By SCOTT HOWARD-COOPER
April 17, 1994

It started as a slow burn, when Magic Johnson came into the Seattle Coliseum locker room late on March 31 and realized that the coaches were more upset after a tough three-point loss to the SuperSonics than the players. It escalated last week in Phoenix, when he criticized some starters for clocking out on the season seven games ahead of schedule.

Quickly, it had become apparent there were other factors making it difficult for Johnson to stay beyond this season as Lakers coach. His outside business interests . . . even the overseas basketball tours that he says bring in more money than an entire season of coaching. His family life, the option of being able to go to Hawaii on short notice for a vacation or to a boxing match.

There was one other factor that helped push him out. His players.

"It (the game) has changed a lot," Johnson said Friday night, after announcing he would not return for 1994-95. "Back when I was playing I used to love it. If you were late, those other 11 guys would just rag you until you couldn't be late any more. We understood how to help each other. If you had a baby, we all had a baby. Every guy was there. If you had a tragedy, every guy had a tragedy. It was just that family.

"Now you've got a lot of individuals. Everybody cares about me, I, I, I. 'Where's my minutes, where's my shots? What's wrong with my game? Why can't I get my game off?' So it's a lot of that now. And I don't like that."

It grew to bother him greatly. Ultimately, it was a factor in convincing him that 15 games were more than enough, at least with this team at this time.

Johnson's predecessor, Randy Pfund, and his assistant coaches used to get frustrated by the same thing. The difference was that Pfund wanted . . . to be an NBA head coach, so his only move was to lean into the wind and continue to try to mold. Johnson had another option. Leaving.

He took the job planning to stay no longer than the four weeks. He wanted to tighten the defense and, without any significant changes, get the offense to go more up-tempo. More than anything, though, he wanted to make a difference in attitude and approach.

His phrase was, "to teach the Lakers what it's like to be a Laker." . . . He never expected to hear players say they wanted a divorce from the championship-filled tradition. "They wanted that removed from them," Johnson said. "They didn't want to deal with that. They call themselves the '90s Lakers."

Is that good or bad?

"Look where we were and look where they are," he replied. "You can answer that yourself."

Said Larry Drew, an assistant coach and friend: "I won't say they drove him away. But what he wanted to accomplish and try to do just wasn't happening . . . Being focused. If we lost, he wanted them to understand why we lost. That didn't happen, and those are all the factors that snowballed."

Vlade Divac, asked if that criticism was fair, shrugged. Tough to say, he said. Doug Christie said he didn't know if Johnson's appraisal was totally true because he, for one, felt there was a lot to learn from the '80s. Nick Van Exel said it's going to be tough to start next season with another new system, but that "I'm going to try to milk him as much as I can."

George Lynch, one of handful of players who come early to practice . . . knew one thing for sure.

"If we would have had him from the beginning of the year, it would have made a difference," Lynch said. "But he came in too late to change some of the players."

Or change himself.

"When he was a player, he was in control," Kurt Rambis said. "As a coach, you don't have that kind of control and that frustration is something really hard to deal with. And he doesn't have to deal with it, so why should he?"

Magic Johnson's coaching stint in Los Angeles took its toll on the NBA legend,
who said he wanted to "teach the Lakers what it's like to be a Laker."

Sharman Ready to Step Up in Any Situation

Bill Sharman, inducted into the Hall of Fame as a player and a coach, was the Lakers' good-luck charm when it came to the NBA draft; As usual, he did OK for himself, and the team, in the 1994 draft lottery. The Lakers didn't get the first pick, but with the 10th they chose Eddie Jones, who played well enough on offense and defense to help the team improve its winning percentage to .585 in the 1994-95 season.

By JIM MURRAY
May 17, 1994

Bill Sharman with the basketball at the free-throw line was a sports work of art. Ruth with a fastball, Cobb with a base open. Dempsey with his man on the ropes. Hogan with a long par three. Jones with a short putt... Hope in a "Road" movie. Shoemaker on the favorite. Sinatra with Gershwin.

When it was Sharman at the line, the next sound you heard was swish! It was as foregone as the sun setting.

Before Sharman, a perfectly acceptable free-throw percentage was .700 or so...

In 1956-57, he threw in a .905 percentage. Two years later, it was .932. Two years after that, it was .921.

In the playoffs one year, it was .966. Sharman made 57 of 59 free throws. He once threw in 56 in a row.

... Bear in mind, this was a time when seven for 10 was All-Star stuff, a time when Wilt Chamberlain, for example, was deadlier from the floor than from the line. One year, Wilt shot .422 from the line and .649 from the floor, despite being double-teamed.

Sharman never shot worse than .800 from the line...

If that had been all he could do, his position would have been secure. But he was the first guard in the game to put up a field-goal percentage better than .400...

He was one of the keys of the great Celtics teams of the 1950s and '60s. With Bob Cousy, he formed one of the top backcourt duos of all time and they might even have unwittingly set the tone for the modern distinction of "point" guard and "shooting" guard. Cousy ran the floor, Sharman ran the basket...

As good as he was on court, Sharman was even more successful as a coach. He was coach of the year in three leagues. His style was the same as it had been on court—competent but unobtrusive. When he had a Laker team that included Chamberlain, Elgin Baylor, Jerry West and Gail Goodrich, Sharman didn't spend much time at the blackboard. That team won 33 consecutive games and won once by 69 points.

As skilled as he was and as hard as he worked, Sharman's career came to a close on an occupational hazard no one foresaw—he lost his voice.

For a guy who shouted as little as he did—Sharman's teams ran on their own adrenaline—it was incomprehensible. But you can't run a team by notepaper and sign language. His mysterious malady, which only lately, 20 years later, is permitting him to communicate, ended his coaching career.

But the Lakers were loath to lose a man with Sharman's depth of experience. He served first as general manager, then as president and now is a special consultant.

What they additionally wanted was his luck. Some guys go through life with a cloud over their head. Sharman goes through with a halo over his.

With the Boston Celtics, he arrived in the era when they were the New York Yankees of basketball. Bill Russell, the Jones boys (K.C. and Sam), Tom Heinsohn, Cousy, Jim Loscutoff, Satch Sanders. And Bill Sharman. He got used to winning right away.

So, the Lakers have a super-important assignment for their special consultant next week. They have found something their old coach also does well—call a coin flip. Win a draft lottery.

Sharman does everything well... But he is uncanny at calling coin flips.

Consider 1979. He had to win a flip to decide whether the Lakers got Magic Johnson or Sidney Moncrief or somebody.

Sharman called heads. On reflection, that may have been the most important call in the history of the franchise. Try to imagine the Lakers without Magic Johnson. Showtime would have been in Milwaukee...

We dissolve a few seasons to another flip of the coin, the one that decides whether the Lakers get James Worthy or Fat Lever or somebody.

Sharman wins that toss too. The Lakers need Sharman next week when the NBA's drafting procedures call for extracting a lucky ball from a tub full of them in order to determine the order of selection.

As usual, Sharman is the guy you want with the ball.

1993-94 Season Highlights

Vlade Divac leads the team in scoring (14.2 points per game) and rebounding (10.8).

Anthony Peeler, the 15th pick of the 1992 draft, develops into the Lakers' second-leading scorer with a 14.1-point average.

Bill Sharman was the Lakers' go-to coach in the early 1970s.

The high-flying contribution of Eddie Jones was one of the footnotes in the legacy of Sharman, the former Lakers coach, general manager, president, and unofficial good-luck charm.

The Lakers take Nick Van Exel with the 37th pick of the 1993 draft. He sets Lakers records for three-point field goals made (123) and attempted (364) in a season.

Van Exel plays in the Rookie Game during NBA All-Star weekend.

Sedale Threatt leads the Lakers in steals (1.36 per game) and free-throw percentage (.890).

1994-95

Worthy Hangs It Up, and So Will the Lakers

He was a seven-time NBA All-Star, a three-time Lakers champion, and one of the "50 Greatest Players in NBA History," who later would be inducted into the Basketball Hall of Fame. And, says former Boston Celtics player Kevin McHale, James Worthy was "a real warrior, but a very classy warrior."

By SCOTT HOWARD-COOPER
November 11, 1994

He was Thursday as he had been for his previous 12 years as a Laker, eloquent and graceful, soft-spoken about his accomplishments, an athlete relating the frustration of a once-great body wearing out and making it all seem so reasonable.

James Worthy said his knees had given out more than his will. The end, he insisted, came not after serious contemplation following the sudden death of his mother, or after struggling with a reduced role on a team whose other players talked of having watched him in the NBA Finals as junior high students, but after being struck with the achy joints of April and May in October. Two-a-days had hurt too much, he said, and he could imagine how he would be feeling by Game 63.

So he retired, making it official at a crowded Forum news conference and bringing the curtain down on an era in the process. Magic Johnson, Kareem Abdul-Jabbar and Michael Cooper, among others, were there to say goodbye to a friend—and the last link to Showtime.

"I'm happy that we can see James go out and we can all smile," said Abdul-Jabbar, the former captain. "We'll shed some tears later, but we can smile because he's walking out happy, the way he wants to leave."

He won't be entirely gone, either. Worthy said he might go into broadcasting and will probably stay close to the game . . . Owner Jerry Buss has decided to retire Worthy's No. 42 and hang it alongside those of the Laker immortals: Wilt Chamberlain, Elgin Baylor, Jerry West, Abdul-Jabbar, Johnson . . .

That isn't Buss' only tribute to the seven-time all-star. Retirement could have meant that Worthy was walking away from a contract that would pay $7.2 million this season and $5.15 million in 1995-96, or at least that he would have to settle for a percentage as a buyout. But he will be paid in full.

"You make a commitment to do something, so you do it," said Bob Steiner, Buss' spokesman. ". . . If you're not obligated to it legally, you certainly are morally from what James has meant to Jerry's happiness. Look at what the guy's done . . ."

Worthy, 33, alluded to the front office—primarily Buss, Executive Vice President West and General Manager Mitch Kupchak—during his remarks, noting that he played with legends and worked for legends. But the most insightful comments were saved for his decision to retire after 12 seasons and three championships.

"The thing that really wore on me was that I could only play one way," he said. "Some players, when they get older, they have a tendency to be able to adjust and find a way to continue. I just couldn't do it . . .

"I didn't feel good physically, and I knew I couldn't make the contribution that I needed and wanted to. So for the sake of the younger players that are really working hard, it was a mutual agreement with Dr. Buss and the Laker front office . . .

"I really feel relieved. I'm not looking back. I'm really just feeling very light, very happy that I was able to come to a decision and have it be the right one."

Thursday's proceedings were as much tribute as explanation, recollections of a spectacular small forward who probably never got his due from fans outside Los Angeles because he played with and was overshadowed by Johnson and Abdul-Jabbar . . .

Worthy scored 16,320 points and stands 52nd on the all-time NBA list. He spent more years as a Laker than anyone other than Abdul-Jabbar and West. He was at his best in the playoffs—thus the nickname "Big Game James"—averaging 3.5 more points than in the regular season and being named Finals MVP in 1988.

In the end, to the surprise of no one, Worthy was gracious.

"To be a Laker," he said, "was everything to me."

James Worthy, with Kareem Abdul-Jabbar and Magic Johnson beside him, announces his retirement on November 10, 1994.

'Baby Face' Pulling Magic's Old Tricks

Nick Van Exel played five seasons with the Lakers, beginning in 1993-94. He is credited with helping reverse the team's poor performance that season and helping spark a Lakers return to playoff competition.

By JIM MURRAY
March 16, 1995

T he first look you get at Nick Van Exel, you want to buy him an ice cream cone, sit him on the sergeant's desk, put a police hat on him and tell him to wait there, his mother will be along looking for him any minute.

Which is funny. Because, what you should really be doing when you spot Van Exel on a basketball court is assign two men to cover him at all times. "Go wherever he goes on the floor," you tell them. "Don't let that baby face fool you!"

There have been baby-faced killers before. Jack the Ripper probably looked like an altar boy.

So does Van Exel. But you shouldn't let those dimples, those big, soft eyes, smooth skin and shy smile fool you. Van Exel should be on the NBA's most-wanted list. Van Exel with a basketball is like Billy the Kid with a gun. You see him coming, you yell for help.

Nick is so quick, he could go in a revolving door behind you and come out ahead. Sometimes, at the top of the key, he seems to split in two like an amoeba. The guy guarding him doesn't know which Van Exel to cover, wants to call time and go to the bench and say, "How many Nick Van Exels are there?"

Nick Van Exel led the Lakers in assists in 1994-95, averaging 8.3 per game.

There's only one, but he has made an enormous difference to the Lakers this season.

No one ever called him "Air" or "Magic" or "Mr. Clutch." But he might be "St. Nick." Or "Mr. Quick."

That Nick the Quick wasn't drafted until 37th should be shocking—until you remember John Unitas wasn't drafted at all and Michael Jordan wasn't picked until third.

The Lakers couldn't believe their good luck finding Van Exel still in the window clear into the second round of the 1993 draft. They fell all over themselves to pick him up.

Van Exel had mixed feelings. "I had actually been hoping to go to Charlotte," he confessed the other night in the Lakers' locker room. "They were a young team on the verge. I thought that's where I belonged."

The Lakers are glad he didn't get the chance. The Lakers had been a rudderless team since the departure of Magic Johnson. The team had no one to go to, no one to rally around. No one was in charge on the floor.

Van Exel became the focal point. Of course, he isn't responsible for this season's success alone. Shrewd trades and drafts—notably Eddie Jones and Cedric Ceballos—beefed up the team. But Nick filled the big need. He was the point guard, what we used to call in this league playmaker.

"I like playmaker better," Van Exel says impishly. "It fits more what I do."

What he does is bring the ball upcourt for the Lakers. He's the ignition. The Lakers are not exactly a parked car without him, but they go into a higher gear with him. The Lakers have gone from a .476 team in 1992-93 to a .617 team since they gave him the ball. He's the quarterback on the court.

Does he see himself as taking over the role of Magic Johnson on this team? Van Exel smothers a grin. "Oh, no. I'm about a smile away from Magic," he giggles. "Magic smiled all the time. I pick my spots."

Magic, of course, was more than a smile. He was no worse than the second- or third-best all-time player. Magic had eight inches of height and 55 pounds on Van Exel. Magic scored 17,239 points almost by accident. What Magic was really about were the 9,921 career assists. Only one active player (John Stockton) has more than 7,000.

Van Exel leads the Lakers not only in assists (488), but in scoring (1,124 points) and free-throw shooting (209 points).

But it would be nice if he would (a) grow a beard; (b) growl and talk trash a lot; (c) smile more. It would be fair to the league, if he's going to take over games, if he looked the part. If he looked like 17.5 points and 10 assists a night and not some kid who showed up for the halftime win-a-trip contests.

1994-95 Season Highlights

Del Harris takes over the Lakers' reins and becomes NBA Coach of the Year after improving the Lakers' record by 15 wins over the previous season.

In a 108–95 win over Minnesota, Cedric Ceballos (23) becomes first L.A. player in nearly 20 years to score 50 points; he doesn't play in All-Star Game because of injuries.

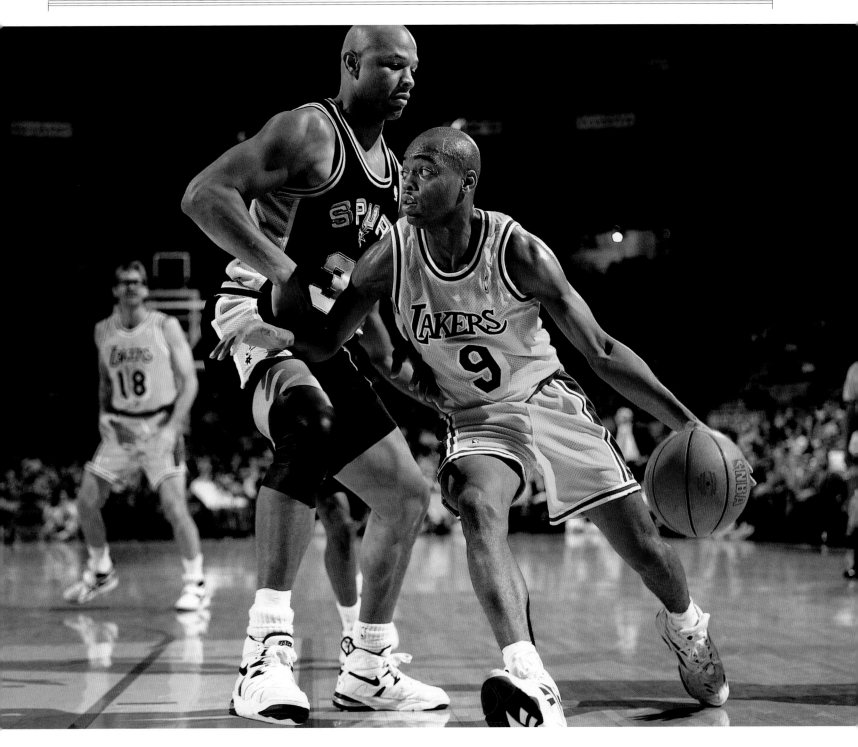

Nick Van Exel, looking for open teammates, gave the Lakers' offense a jolt after he was drafted in 1993. Van Exel was the Lakers' second-leading scorer in 1994-95, but he said, "I like playmaker better. It fits more what I do."

Jerry West is named the NBA executive of the year.

Eddie Jones is chosen most valuable player of the Rookie Game during All-Star Weekend as he scores 25 points.

Nick Van Exel makes a then-club-record eight three-point field goals on 16 attempts against Dallas on December 13, 1994.

1995-96

Magic on Retiring:
This Is for Good

Season Record

W53-L29 (.646)
Division: 2nd
First Round

Coach

Del Harris

Players

Cedric Ceballos

Elden Campbell

Nick Van Exel

Vlade Divac

Eddie Jones

Anthony Peeler

Sedale Threatt

Magic Johnson

George Lynch

Derek Strong

Corie Blount

Fred Roberts

Anthony Miller

Frankie King

After 4 1/2 seasons on the sidelines, Magic Johnson returned to the court on January 30, 1996, inspiring fans and his teammates with a near triple double—19 points, 10 assists, and eight rebounds in 27 minutes played. He went on to play 32 games, but the Lakers did not make it past the first round of the playoffs and he decided to re-retire. Still, he never really left the Lakers. A part owner, he is involved in marketing, public relations, and player issues. Outside of basketball, he is the chairman and CEO of Magic Johnson Enterprises, a business venture that, among other things, partners with Starbucks, fosters real estate development in underserved communities, and owns a chain of movie theaters.

By SCOTT HOWARD-COOPER
May 16, 1996

Once more for posterity:
"I'm retired," Magic Johnson said Wednesday. "It's over. It's done."
No, really.
"I did what I set out to do," he insisted, speaking at another news conference at the Forum to announce another retirement from the Lakers.

"I had a wonderful time. It was a great experience, a lot of fun. My son saw me play. I did it for myself as well, to prove that I could still do it. And I think I did it for everybody who has something, whether it's HIV or AIDS or anything else.

"This is not a sad day or a bad day. It's a good day. God blessed me to be able to come back, and God will continue to bless me after this is over. It's over now, and I'm happy about it. So there it is."

Well, sort of. There is also the rest of the explanation for the decision that was so sudden it even caught management by surprise when it came the day before.

Call it a preemptive strike, before dramatic confrontations could materialize. Before the Lakers may have made the decision for him and before his considerable latitude hindered the development of Nick Van Exel.

Both were strong possibilities. Johnson becomes a free agent July 1 and had said on several occasions he wanted to stay with the only pro home he has known, but his presence would take up as much as $3.75 million of the salary cap . . . To land one of the mega-stars, the Lakers might have had to renounce his rights, effectively cutting him loose . . . He preferred to retire now, as a Laker.

"If I would have come back, I knew I would probably have to come back somewhere else, and I am a Laker and I can't do that," he said. "I'm L.A. I'm an L.A. person. I love L.A. . . . "

The situation was just as delicate with Van Exel, the starting point guard but not the primary ballhandler whenever Johnson was on the court at point forward . . . Next season, Johnson wanted to play more in the backcourt, as much as 50% of his minutes.

"What? I'm whining and I'm doing this and that?" Johnson said, reacting to the criticism he received for those comments and others. "The whole thing about it is, Earvin Johnson is good with the ball in his hands . . . I'm a guy that needs the ball to be able to do something . . .

"It was never a confrontation between Nick and I. It never will be. Nick is like a little brother to me. It never was a situation with [Coach] Del Harris and myself or the players. It's just a situation that Earvin Johnson knows where he's good at and what he can do, and I've got to have the ball . . ."

Johnson did . . . concede there was some friction between himself and some players.

"The gap between the ages, it's a big difference," he said. "Maybe I couldn't adjust to them or maybe they couldn't adjust to me . . . It's not all their fault, it's not all my fault. Maybe I just came at a different time, that now it's changed and I can't adjust, because it's got to be some on me too."

There's always some regular season in the future. Even Michael Jordan said he wouldn't be surprised if Johnson played again.

"Me either," Magic responded.

Then he laughed that big laugh. He was joking . . . probably.

"It is over," he said. "Definitely. For sure."

After leaving the Lakers in 1991, Magic Johnson returns to the court on January 30, 1996. In his farewell at the end of the 1995-96 season, he said: "I had a wonderful time."

1995-96 Season Highlights

Cedric Ceballos scores a total of 1,656 points, averaging a team-high 21.2 points per game.

The Lakers exceed the 50-win mark for the 21st time in club history but fall in the first round to Houston despite having the home-court advantage.

Elden Campbell has a team-leading 212 blocks; his average of 2.59 blocks per game ranks sixth in the NBA.

1996-97

West's Keen Sense of Direction, Part I: Kobe Arrives

The summer of 1996 changed the Lakers' landscape: Vlade Divac out, Kobe Bryant in, Derek Fisher drafted, and finally Shaquille O'Neal arrived—all within a two-month span. A major piece was the draft-day trade in June of Divac, the lovable 7-foot-1 center from Serbia who had played all of his career with the Lakers and needed his wife to persuade him to go to Charlotte rather than retire. The deal, which was not official until July 11, wasn't extraordinary merely because it brought Bryant's exceptional talent to the Lakers. It was part of General Manager Jerry West's larger plan to free enough salary to acquire a prize that looked even bigger at the time.

By MARK HEISLER
June 30, 1996

East is east but West is still best: There aren't a lot of general managers who would have dared this one, trading one of the game's better centers for a 17-year-old high school guard, but he's Jerry West and they're not.

No one had drafted a high school guard before, much less traded a real player for one, but if the Charlotte Hornets can get Vlade Divac out of his bedroom (hint: try a two-year extension and some Serbian pastries), West will have.

West wasn't the only executive who saw greatness in Kobe Bryant. Several others did too. They just weren't willing to bet everything on it.

The new New Jersey Nets' boss, John Calipari, worked Bryant out late in the game, fell head over heels and seemed set to take him. "You have to understand," Calipari said the day before the draft, "we're building for two or three years from now."

On draft day, he let Kobe go by, making the safe pick at No. 8, Kerry Kittles, instead. Imagine if Calipari had needed to trade Shawn Bradley for Bryant? He wasn't even willing to trade Kittles.

This doesn't mean it's sure to work out for the Lakers, or even that it's the percentage play. This is blue sky territory. No one knows how it will work out because no one has ever done it.

It will be hard for Bryant, who has no idea what he's getting into, NBA father or no. He won't play as much as he wants (no one else does so it's asking a lot for him to understand) and he won't be able to dodge the spotlight.

On his first Christmas away from home, he'll be averaging about 3.4 points a game and people will be asking if he's disappointed with his progress, wishes he'd gone to school, etc. These days in the public mind, and that of many professionals, "long-term project" means "You've got 18 months to dazzle me." . . .

Bryant's upside, however, is greatness. Without a great player, the Lakers were merely respectable, which doesn't pay off here. They had last season's sixth-best record, but there wasn't going to be any sentiment for a parade or a rally unless fans could throw the players on the bonfire.

Respectability can be a hole. West has been trying to burrow out since Magic Johnson retired in 1991 and James Worthy's wheels burned out shortly thereafter, leaving the Lakers star-less.

They were a .500 team a year later when they traded Sam Perkins, their best player, for untested Doug Christie and notorious Benoit Benjamin. West thought Ben might be useful in a small way (he wasn't) and Christie might hit big (he didn't). By making the deal, however, West launched the Lakers into their future.

If it were easy, someone else would do it. Denial is preferred, illustrated most recently by the New York Knicks, riding soon-to-turn-34 Patrick Ewing to the end of his contract; and the Boston Celtics, bringing in their annual cap-eating veterans such as Dominique Wilkins and Dana Barros.

With a nod from Jerry Buss—he reportedly told his execs, "You know me, I'm a gambler"—West has just re-launched the Lakers in the highest-stakes roll of all.

They can now get $8.5 million under the cap but have only a chance, not an assurance, of getting Shaquille O'Neal.

Kobe Bryant, looking
all of 18 years old,
goes up for two points
in one of his first
games for the Lakers.

West's Keen Sense of Direction, Part II: The Price for Shaq

Even as Shaquille O'Neal prepared for the Atlanta Olympics, Jerry West toiled. He hated to lose Anthony Peeler, but both Peeler and George Lynch had to go in a trade to free more funds to acquire O'Neal. Meanwhile, O'Neal's price climbed from $110 million to a reported $115 million to the final $120 million in the Lakers-Orlando Magic duel for the 24-year-old, 7-foot-1 center. Scott Howard-Cooper wrote of West: "He is tired, but not only from the lack of sleep. Tired of setting up trades and then having the other team renege on the deal, which happened as the Lakers tried to clear salary-cap room. Tired of the media, which ran with unfounded speculation that they had tampered with O'Neal, based mostly on the notion that Vlade Divac wouldn't have been traded unless Shaq was in the bag, right? ... 'It's taken a horrible toll on me. A horrible toll,'" West said of the process. But in the end, he compared O'Neal's signing to the birth of his children.

By MARK HEISLER
July 19, 1996

ATLANTA—Winning the highest-stakes bidding war in American sports history, the Lakers signed Shaquille O'Neal away from the Orlando Magic on Thursday, giving him a $120-million, seven-year contract that tilted the balance of power in the NBA with the stroke of a pen.

The deal is thought to have an "out," a clause making O'Neal a free agent again in three years, enabling him to test the market anew if rising inflation or other stars' salaries eat into his deal.

On the hook for a fortune, which could look like a bargain compared to what they may have to give him in 1999, the Lakers were ecstatic.

"This is an incredibly exciting day for the Los Angeles Lakers," Executive Vice President Jerry West said. "I can't tell you how excited Southern California is today. I called our office a little while ago and the response from bringing Shaquille O'Neal to the Los Angeles Lakers has been one that's unprecedented in our history...

"Over the last number of days, I can't tell you how many highs and lows that I've gone through. ... About 2:15 in the morning, when we signed the contract, was probably the most relieved I've ever felt in my life.

"I really can't explain. I've often thought that the birth of my children was something I'll never forget and just the excitement of this, for us to sign him, really ranks right there with it."

West was midwife in this delivery, the baby measuring 7 feet 1 and weighing 320 pounds. It required a Herculean effort, the Lakers dumping three players to make enough room under the salary cap so they could continue bidding competitively.

"Keep in mind the word 'change,' " O'Neal said. "To me, change is for the good. I'm a military child; I'm used to relocating every three, four years. The Lakers, they have great tradition, great big-man tradition, George Mikan, Kareem [Abdul-Jabbar]..."

O'Neal entered the league at a rock-solid 300 pounds and now has begun lifting weights. A throwback to the days when centers stayed under the basket and beat each other up, he has developed a good, if under-appreciated, post game... In four seasons, he has averaged 23, 29, 29 and 27 points and has a career shooting mark of 58%...

"He has a personality to go with his enormous ability," West said, "and in Los Angeles, it's a town with personalities and it's a town that will embrace a person like this."

POSTSCRIPT

Three months after signing O'Neal, West reflected on the process. In a story by the Los Angeles Times' Howard-Cooper, West said he seriously considered quitting as executive vice president of the Lakers...

"I couldn't sleep, continued to lose weight, which was probably the best thing about it, but emotionally I was spent...

"There were times, even after it was over with, that I just didn't think I had this in me any more. But getting away from it, and with so many very, very encouraging letters from our fans and people, that makes you feel better about yourself. You're appreciative of those things. That somewhat has, I think, put that to rest, for a while anyway."

A vacation to his native West Virginia helped—also his devotion to the game.

"It's the only thing I really know," West said of the decision to return. "The one thing I know about myself, I need to be busy. Sometimes it's not physical but it's emotional. When you have those kinds of considerations, I'd be lost if I wasn't doing something that at least I'd been involved in for quite a while and maybe more importantly feel like I can make a contribution."

1996-97
Season
Highlights

Shaquille O'Neal and Elden Campbell (right) help Lakers finish off Portland (3-1) in the playoffs' first round before Utah stops L.A (4-1).

Kobe Bryant becomes the first player in Lakers history to win the All-Star weekend's slam-dunk contest.

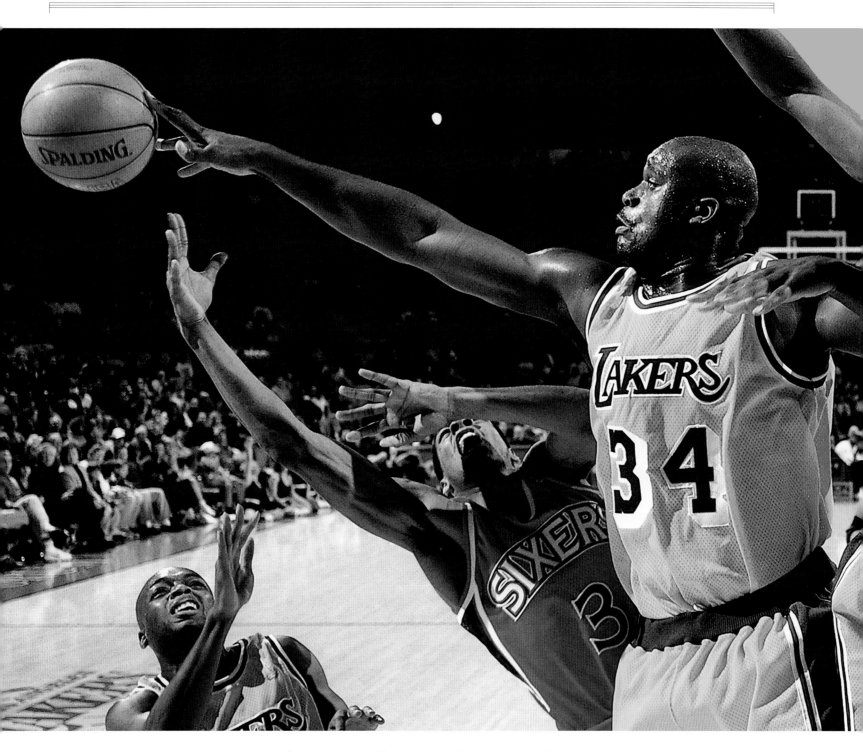

Shaquille O'Neal, blocking a shot by Philadelphia's Allen Iverson during the regular season, had a career playoff average of 27.7 points a game for the Lakers, second all-time on the team, behind only Jerry West.

O'Neal leads the team in scoring (26.2 points per game), rebounding (12.5), blocked shots (2.88), and field-goal percentage (.557).

Bryant, Travis Knight, and Derek Fisher all play in the Rookie Game during All-Star Weekend.

Eddie Jones plays in the All-Star Game. O'Neal is injured and does not play.

1997-98

A Star Is Born; His Name Is Kobe

Jim Murray reminds Lakers fans how it was when Kobe Bryant arrived on the scene.

By JIM MURRAY
February 15, 1998

Season Record

W61-L21 (.744)
Division: 2nd
West Finals

Coach

Del Harris

Players

Shaquille O'Neal

Eddie Jones

Kobe Bryant

Rick Fox

Nick Van Exel

Elden Campbell

Robert Horry

Derek Fisher

Corie Blount

Mario Bennett

Sean Rooks

Jon Barry

Shea Seals

You hear about Kobe Bryant, the Lakers' 19-year-old basketball whiz, and your first reaction is, the last time anyone this good appeared there was a star in the East. I mean, you want to say, "Come on, what are you trying to hand me? Nobody's this good!"

Oh, they don't claim he can heal the sick, raise the dead or make water into wine. They're not blasphemous. But they do insist that anything that can be done with a basketball, he can do it. Michael Jordan, my foot.

It gets to the point where, when you meet him the first time, you want to ask him what he did with the halo. Did he fly in—or just walk across Santa Monica Bay? You don't know whether to get his autograph or his blessing. Or just touch the hem of his warmup suit. You feel inadequate interviewing someone so perfect. It's a job for Matthew, Mark, Luke and John, not a mere sportswriter.

He's not 9 feet tall, as you might expect. He looks perfectly ordinary. Of course, he's single, lives with his parents. But he wasn't born in a stable. Or even a log cabin. He was raised partly in Italy, where his father played basketball. He speaks better Italian than the pope.

He has a nice sense of humor. He laughs a lot, keeps it light. Everyone likes him. He's not at all arrogant about his talent, just grateful for it. To a man, the New York media loved him at the recent All-Star Game there . . . They couldn't believe their good luck in finding a superstar this approachable. As for Kobe, he was having the time of his life. Bryant is no shrinking violet. If there's one attribute that sticks out all over him, it's confidence. Optimism. Accentuate the positive.

He eliminates the negative, all right. So, he missed the most crucial shot of the year last year, the one that would have beaten Utah and kept the Lakers in the playoffs had it gone in. Kobe didn't go home to perch on a ledge or go off to join the French Foreign Legion. He doesn't do sackcloth and ashes. He just shrugged and told himself that, the next time this happened, he wouldn't miss. "My time will come," he warns.

He didn't come cheap. The Lakers had to give up Vlade Divac to get him. And Divac was a 12-point-a-night, 800-rebounds-a-year, 7-foot-1 center.

Kobe's role on the Lakers? "My job is to spread havoc in the enemy, kind of a spark plug," he tells you. The idea is to get the other guys trying to look over both shoulders at once for him. He's a disrupter. "I figure out what the team needs and try to supply it," he tells you. "Get the ball to Nick (Van Exel), get open, set up, win." . . .

He plays to rave notices. Says Hall of Fame broadcaster Chick Hearn, who has been known to restrain his enthusiasm for the modern player on occasion: "Kobe is a 28-year-old in a 19-year-old body. The things he does with no college experience is beyond belief. He has total confidence. He'd walk up to a Michael Jordan or a backup guard with the same degree of skill and enthusiasm and expectations of success. He's a star on and off the court. I've seen lots of them come and go but none with the potential of Kobe Bryant. Someday, we'll be able to brag 'We knew him when!' "

You see what I mean? He comes into focus to the sound of organ music and the smell of incense.

You can see why you don't know whether to genuflect or buy him a lollipop when you first meet him . . .

He has his doubting Thomases. To the prediction he has a chance to become the next Michael Jordan, they retort, "In 10 years he has a chance to be the next Kobe Bryant." . . .

Any way you look at it, you may want to get his autograph before he ascends into golf heaven. He won't be hard to find. He'll be the one walking through doors without opening them. Michael may be Air Jordan but Kobe is Heir Jordan.

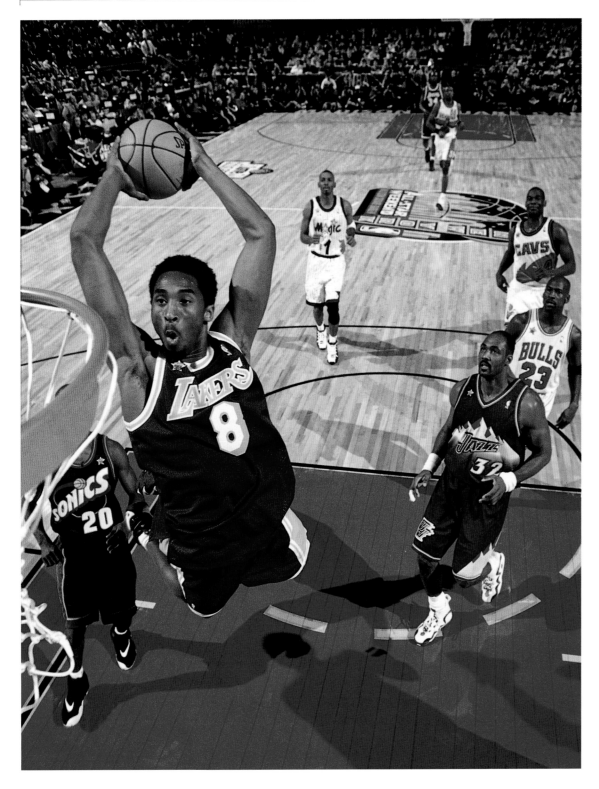

Kobe Bryant pumps up the West offense in his first All-Star appearance, scoring 18 points at Madison Square Garden in 1998.

Pages 180-81: Staples Center, the new home of the Lakers, provides a dramatic backdrop for the team in a March 2000 game against Indiana Pacers. The teams would meet again in the 2000 NBA Finals.

1997-98 Season Highlights

The Lakers lead the NBA in scoring, averaging 105.5 points per game but fall to Utah in West Finals, averaging 90.5 points.

Shaquille O'Neal scores 50 points on April 2 against New Jersey in a 117-106 Lakers win.

Kobe Bryant, Nick Van Exel, Eddie Jones, and O'Neal all play in the All-Star Game.

STAPLES Center Facts

- Opened October 17, 1999, with Bruce Springsteen; first regular-season Lakers game November 3, 1999.
- Anchor of LA LIVE, a $2.5-billion 4 million square-foot sports, entertainment, and residential district covering 27 acres, with the 7,100-seat Nokia Theater.
- Home of Los Angeles' Lakers, Kings, Clippers, and Sparks.
- Construction cost $407 million.
- $116 million paid by Staples, Inc., for naming rights in a 20-year deal.
- 950,000 square-foot arena, 150 feet high, on a 10-acre site.
- 18,997 seats for Lakers basketball; 18,118 seats for hockey.
- Changeover from hockey to basketball in less than two hours.
- 20,000 seats for concerts.
- 160 luxury suites leasing for up to $307,500 a year; 2,500 club seats.
- 1,200 TV monitors and 675 speakers outside seating area.
- Nine-foot-high shower heads in basketball locker room.
- More than 4 million visitors, about 250 events, annually.
- Events have included Barbra Streisand, U2, the Grammy Awards, 2000 Democratic National Convention.
- Owner/operator AEG and L.A. Arena Company; developers Philip Anschutz and Edward Roski, Jr., are co-owners of the Lakers.

1998-99

Zensational Day: Jackson Coming to LaLa Land

The Lakers played under three head coaches in the lockout-shortened 1998-99 season—Del Harris, Bill Bertka in an interim role, and former Laker Kurt Rambis, who launched his coaching career with a then-record-tying nine consecutive victories. Their 4-0 loss to the Spurs in the conference semifinals ended their playoff hopes. Lakers owner Jerry Buss later announced that Phil Jackson, who coached the Chicago Bulls to six NBA championships, would be the new head coach.

By J.A. ADANDE
June 17, 1999

Some scenes are hard to grasp, no matter how much we've been prepared.

Reports that the Lakers were going to sign Phil Jackson surfaced almost a week ago. Even after the word came on Tuesday that it was a done deal, it still didn't seem entirely real when Jackson stepped to a lectern at the Beverly Hills Hilton, after Jerry West introduced him as the newest coach of the Los Angeles Lakers.

Was this actually happening? Phil Jackson, with the Lakers? Phil Jackson, a California dude?

The two public images of Jackson are the long-haired playing days with the New York Knicks and the glasses, double-breasted suits and suspenders he wore as the coach of the Chicago Bulls. They are like parts of a slide show on the progression of the Baby Boomers.

Now the next step. The logical step. To move on, he had to complete his hat trick of the nation's largest markets and come to Los Angeles, to a city and a state poised at the vanguard of the new millennium.

This is a town for people with a notion, an idea, a lot of hope. If I can just get the right agent and he can get me the right audition it will all fall into place.

Jackson had a notion too. If he could just bring his coaching style and his system to the talent-rich Lakers, it would all fall into place.

And—get this—he doesn't want to be the producer, doesn't demand his name above the title in the credits. All he wants to do is direct. At a time when even college coaches can come in and demand general manager duties and final say, Jackson will stick to coaching.

"I had to look at who I am, what I can do," Jackson said. "I have enough energy to coach and to put my energy behind the team. And I don't need the excess energy wasted on agents, on being the guy that makes the last call. I trust people to do the best at their job. I like to use people for what they can do, my whole staff, assistant coaches. I don't really think I need all that power and whatever else goes with it, the money.

"I don't want to be on the job 24 hours a day, seven days a week. I want to be able to take three months off in the summertime."

Because he has done his job well, Jackson's summers tend to be short. He worked in the NBA's last game, usually about two months after the regular season ended, for six of the last eight years. But after the Bulls' dynasty came to a contentious end . . . Jackson had a chance for extended time off . . .

"It was very interesting for me just to be kind of a private citizen, so to speak. That was very good. It was very good for me, very good for my family, very good for the relationships that I've had with my family. It was very invigorating for me to feel like I can go back and come to this game with a lot more energy than I ever thought I could come back to . . ."

When asked if he is an L.A. guy, Jackson said: "I can practice singing 'I Love L.A.' Maybe that'll help. But I do like the beach, and I'm looking forward to warm weather . . ."

Jackson fits into just about every niche this city has to offer. You want diversity? He gives you Buddhism, Christianity and Native American folklore in one source. You want the local industry? He wrote a one-act play that was performed in Chicago; now that he's here he'll have to start selling the screen rights . . .

Phil Jackson, after playing in New York and coaching in Chicago, makes his way to Santa Monica beach in Los Angeles. In his first three seasons with the Lakers, he led the team to three consecutive championships, then added a fourth title in 2009.

1998-99 Season Highlights

Dennis Rodman (73) joins the team although he plays only 23 games.

Eddie Jones, Elden Campbell are traded for Glen Rice in a five-player deal.

Rick Fox makes all five of his three-point shots on February 28, tying for third best on the Lakers' all-time list.

Kobe Bryant, reshaping his game as he goes from No. 8 to No. 24, has the final word during the rebirth of Lakers' dominance.

CHAPTER SIX

A New Dynasty

Seasons 1999-2000 through 2008-09

THE LAKERS of the first decade of the century were a blend of forces physical, mental, and emotional, but not to be overlooked was the metaphysical. Seemingly incompatible egos found harmony, resulting in six trips to the NBA Finals and four championships.

The curtain rose in 1999 with Phil Jackson leaving retirement to become coach. Jackson brought to the Lakers Zen Buddhism, Native American mysticism, and the triangle offense. The first time Jackson beat a tom-tom in the locker room, Kobe Bryant snickered.

But Bryant and Shaquille O'Neal, who had spent the two previous seasons dancing awkwardly, their frustration growing, became partners in crime. They worked within the triangle, as taught by Jackson's right-hand man Tex Winter, and the Lakers christened the new Staples Center by beating the Indiana Pacers in the 2000 Finals, ending a 12-year title drought.

Jerry West soon resigned as general manager, after four decades at the core of the Lakers, but the machine he assembled kept purring, winning the next two championships.

Then, tragedy and decline. Chick Hearn, the team's voice and spirit since the first season in Los Angeles, died in the summer of 2002. After the Lakers lost the '04 Finals, O'Neal was traded. Jackson retired, his stormy relationship with Bryant having taken a toll on both men.

End of an era? A season later, Jackson returned, his Zen recharged, and he and Bryant began rebuilding. In 2009, sixty seasons removed from the team's NBA birth and first championship, the Lakers were back on top.

—Scott Ostler

1999-2000

Wow! The West Is Won

In 1991, the last time they went to the NBA Finals, the Lakers had been vanquished in five games. Now, on the verge of a chance to redeem themselves, the team had fallen behind in the last game of the Western Conference Finals. Things were dark. Then the dawn broke.

By TIM KAWAKAMI
June 5, 2000

The past tugged at them, and the Portland Trail Blazers tugged harder.

They looked weighed down and desperate, and tripped toward failure again.

Then, at the moment of truth, as darkness threatened, Kobe Bryant ran faster, Brian Shaw shot truer, and Shaquille O'Neal jumped higher than anyone could have dreamed . . .

In the fourth quarter of the seventh game of the third playoff series of the first season of Phil Jackson's Lakers coaching lifetime, the Lakers overcame a 15-point deficit, reeled in the Trail Blazers, and won a trip to the NBA Finals with a staggering 89-84 victory before 18,997 . . .

"Yeah, that was a daunting uphill battle that we had to face," Jackson said after it was over. "We made it back." . . .

The first three quarters, after which Portland led, 71-58, were the summation of . . . every significant victory [the Lakers] had failed to record during the last three seasons. O'Neal couldn't get the ball. The other Lakers couldn't get it into the basket. The Trail Blazers were whizzing into the lane, and throwing in three-point baskets. Jackson was calling timeouts to yell at his players.

After giving up a basket and two free throws to pump the Portland lead to 75-60 with 10:28 to play, the Lakers stopped Portland 10 consecutive times, began making shots of their own and soon panic turned to hope.

"You lose yourself in it," forward Glen Rice said of the explosion, which saw the Lakers outscore the Trail Blazers, 25-4, at one point.

Said Jackson: "[Game] 7s are interesting games, aren't they? I've never seen one quite like that before, or had a team that I thought had run out of gas as much as I thought they had in the third quarter . . . "

The Lakers tied the score for the first time in the fourth quarter at 75-75 on Shaw's second three-pointer of the quarter, with four minutes left, capping a 15-0 rocket-burst.

Earlier, Shaw banked in a three-point shot at the end of the third quarter, to narrow what had been a 16-point Portland lead, the largest of the game . . .

After Portland scored, O'Neal tied it again with two free throws (he was three for four in the final quarter). Then a few minutes later, Bryant drove into the lane and tossed the ball wildly toward the top of the backboard.

Only, about 15 feet in the air, O'Neal reached up with his right hand and intercepted the ball, as Bryant knew he would, and threw it down thunderously, to give the Lakers an 85-79 lead and nearly break Staples' roof to pieces . . .

"Heart and effort," said Bryant, who had 25 points, 11 rebounds, seven assists and four blocked shots, when asked how the Lakers pulled this off . . .

Said Rick Fox, of forcing Portland into 12 straight missed shots: "We did things defensively first, then we knocked down some shots.

And what does it feel like to pull off the greatest Game 7 comeback in NBA history?

"It's a spent feeling," said Fox, sprawled in front of his locker . . . Several players said the key moment came late in the third quarter, when Jackson called time out and told them to stop trying to force the ball inside to O'Neal . . .

"Phil said to us, 'Hey, there are four guys around Shaq, shoot the shot, just shoot it. Forget about Shaq,' " Fox said.

"They were daring us to make them. And we finally made them."

Said Ron Harper: "We did some bad things, but somehow we survived."

Kobe Bryant is head and shoulders above the crowd as he
blocks a shot in Game 7 of the Western Conference Finals.

First At Last; Lakers Win First Title in a Dozen Years

Indiana did not give up, but the Lakers would not give in. It had been a twelve-year drought, and it was up to the team's franchise players to slake L.A.'s thirst.

By TIM KAWAKAMI
June 20, 2000

All they had to do was follow the stars, who burned bright, burned long, and burned to be champions.

Two blazing stars, who guided the way, through darkness and desperation, failed hopes and renewed dreams.

It was not easy. It was not inevitable . . .

At times, it verged so close to heartbreak that it was difficult to separate the tears of joy from those of exhaustion, and collapse.

But, at the last moment, in the midst of the last battle, the last comeback, the last attack and the last summoning of collective will and breath, the Lakers turned to Shaquille O'Neal and Kobe Bryant, who did not fail them.

O'Neal, the biggest star, and Bryant, the shiniest, carried them to a 116-111 Game 6 victory over the Indiana Pacers on Monday before 18,997 at Staples Center, delivering an NBA championship to a franchise that had waited 12 years for this . . .

"We rode Shaq's back," guard Ron Harper said of O'Neal, who scored 41 points, grabbed 12 rebounds, blocked four shots and was the unanimous winner of the finals most-valuable-player award, following his MVP for the regular season . . .

Said Glen Rice of O'Neal and Bryant:

"I'll tell you, that's the best duo that I've seen in a long time. And they are going to be together, forever." . . .

Finally, inside a Lakers locker room drenched with champagne and overflowing emotion, O'Neal grabbed several of his teammates, and just started jumping, jumping, jumping . . . crashing against cameramen, bumping against walls, as if there was too much energy and happiness to contain any of it . . .

It was O'Neal who was the man the Lakers turned to all season, and it was, of course, O'Neal again who led the charges against the Pacers, who shot themselves to a lead and did not easily give it up.

"I've never seen anybody dominate like that, ever," Lakers owner Jerry Buss said as champagne sprayed all around him. "I mean, obviously, Wilt Chamberlain was something very special, but quite honestly, [O'Neal] played probably the best basketball any player has ever played." . . .

O'Neal's last surge put them ahead, 110-103, with 3:02 left, but that was not the end of it.

Reggie Miller, who scored 25 points, made a jumper, Austin Croshere a free throw and Dale Davis two, while O'Neal missed three out of four free throws when he was fouled intentionally.

After Croshere made two more free throws with 1:32 left, it was 110-109, and Staples rumbled with apprehension . . .

"You've seen this team step up to the challenges," said Rick Fox, who made a crucial three-point basket in the fourth quarter . . .

"This is the M.O. of this team—when people look back on this championship

team, they'll say we were able to wow you with exciting basketball and then force you to check your pacemakers."

Bryant made two free throws with 13 seconds left to give the Lakers a 114-109 lead, then two more to end the scoring, end the season, and start the party . . .

Bryant did not have a dominant game, but scored 26 points (on eight-for-27 shooting), grabbed 10 rebounds and had four assists . . .

"We just knew we had to survive some things," said Coach Phil Jackson, who won his seventh championship as a coach in his first season with the Lakers. "The excruciating moments of Shaq at the free-throw line . . .

"In the fourth quarter, we found a place where they couldn't stop us."

The Lakers took their first lead of the second half, 91-90 . . .

After three-pointers by Rick Fox and Robert Horry, suddenly the Lakers had a 97-92 lead; back-to-back O'Neal dunk putbacks jumped it to 101-94.

But Indiana kept grinding . . . and it was tied, 103-103 . . .

So one last Lakers revival was necessary.

In the celebratory locker room, John Salley splashed anyone in sight, Green sprinted around like a teenager and everyone else stood around, dazed and bleary-eyed . . .

"What a way to start the millennium," Jackson said at the trophy presentation.

Said O'Neal: "Phil was able to keep us poised. When you look at a guy like Phil, if you're a leader, he's not worried.

"I think we needed Phil to do it."

1999-2000 Season Highlights

The Lakers' record of 67–15 is the season's best in the NBA and the second–best in team history.

A.C. Green, acknowledging fans' applause, breaks the professional basketball record by playing in his 1,042nd consecutive game on November 26.

The Lakers make Devean George their first-round pick of the 1999 draft and sign Ron Harper, Brian Shaw, and John Salley.

Shaquille O'Neal owns the scene in 2000, becoming only the third player in history to be MVP of the All-Star Game, regular season, and NBA Finals.

2000-01

Baq to Baq: O'Neal Is MVP as Lakers Repeat Title Feat

Season Record

W56-L26 (.683)
Division: 1st
NBA Champion

Coach

Phil Jackson

Players

Shaquille O'Neal

Kobe Bryant

Rick Fox

Horace Grant

Isaiah Rider

Brian Shaw

Robert Horry

Ron Harper

Mike Penberthy

Derek Fisher

Devean George

Mark Madsen

Tyronn Lue

Greg Foster

Stanislav
Medvedenko

The fans sent a message, and the team heard it: Put the dissension, the jealousy aside. Eyes on the prize. The Lakers had to power past Portland, Sacramento, and San Antonio to get to the Philadelphia 76ers. They did, and with plenty left to spare.

By BILL PLASCHKE
June 16, 2001

A Hollywood axiom was dumped on its blow-dried head here Friday by a team more about scars than sunsets, with a spirit thick enough to be imprinted on a sidewalk.

Sequels never work?

This one did.

About midnight here, the final credits were dragged across the First Union Center floor by the rumbling, swaggering, champagne-soaked and howling Lakers.

The NBA Championship Returns.

The Lakers won a second consecutive NBA championship that, with the possible exception of zero confetti and 20,0000 congratulatory boos and curses, was better than the first.

Or, in the words of Ron Harper as he zeroed his liquor-soaked glare around a crowded locker room that once held only a couple of dozen believers:

"Y'all thought that we wouldn't be here now. But we found a way back."

The final statistics were a 108-96 victory over the Philadelphia 76ers for a four-games-to-one NBA Finals decision...

Fifteen wins in 16 playoff games, the best in NBA playoff history...

The team that once refused to behave like a team finished Friday's final game with four players scoring in double figures, with seven players getting assists, with Shaquille O'Neal plowing and Kobe Bryant flying and Derek Fisher coolly nailing it all together with three after three after three...

"This is better than last year because everybody wrote us off," said Rick Fox, bouncing on a locker room bench the way his team bounced

on everyone else. "Of course, they had reason to write us off."

O'Neal spent the first months of the season in a funk. He ended it by slapping his hand rhythmically on the championship trophy's gold ball, turning into a rap instrument...

Bryant spent much of the season criticized for acting like a kid. He ended it stalking down the hall with an adult glare, in an oversized leather Lakers jacket, swinging the trophy like a weapon.

"The first championship was like a honeymoon," Kobe said. "This time around, we went through so much adversity..."

Look at this franchise.

Eight championships in the last 30 years, or one every 3.75 years.

Seven of those belong to Jerry Buss, who must now be considered the best sports owner in Los Angeles history.

He spends what it takes, and he had the smarts to hire the now-retired best executive in the history of the NBA. Jerry West's fingerprints will be with this team as long as O'Neal, Bryant, and Fisher are part of it.

"I don't think anybody believed we could really defend the title," Buss said. "But we have the best fans, and the best faith."

It was the fans who pushed the pedal on this playoff sprint, way back on April 22, rattling Staples Center for the playoff opener against Portland in a Game 1 that felt like a Game 7...

O'Neal and Bryant understood exactly.

Their season-long feud over everything from shots to endorsements ended in that playoff opener with O'Neal's 20 rebounds and Bryant's seven assists.

The big guy wasn't going to pout. The kid was going to share. The rest of the NBA never had a chance...

A team known for its savvy suddenly showed its strength. And like the pesky runt that has finally realized the giants' wrath, the 76ers' jaws dropped and their will evaporated.

The Lakers won in a blowout in Game 4, setting

up the relatively easy win Friday.

"If you could see the look on my face, my eyes were like a deer in headlights," Fisher said of his feelings after hitting a three-pointer with 51 seconds left for a clinching 10-point lead . . .

Earlier in the quarter, when the 76ers had closed the gap to nine, Fisher nailed an equally dramatic three-pointer over Allen Iverson and Aaron McKie.

With the crowd roaring, he fell backward, watched the ball drop through the net, then carefully put his left index finger to his lips.

But Los Angeles? You can shout.

Shout about Phil Jackson becoming the best playoff coach in history and moving just one championship shy of equaling Red Auerbach's record nine titles.

Shout about Shaquille O'Neal officially becoming the next Wilt Chamberlain, matching Wilt with two titles.

Shout about Kobe Bryant getting better, and Derek Fisher breaking loose, and Robert Horry sticking around for another run.

. . . Just don't shout too loud, or too long. O'Neal is 29. Fisher is 26. Bryant is 22.

You may need your voice.

The long reach of Shaquille O'Neal rules in the 2001 Finals against the Philadelphia 76ers. He was again the Finals' MVP.

Perfectly Flawed Season Became Nearly Perfect

On the way to the championship, the Lakers won 11 consecutive postseason games. After losing the first game in overtime to Philadelphia in the NBA Finals, they won four straight.

By TIM BROWN
June 16, 2001

Kobe Bryant sat alone in a shower, the voices of his teammates echoing off the tiles. Exhausted, a little sad, utterly satisfied, he cradled a championship trophy in his arms.

Not far away, Shaquille O'Neal danced and sang in a 10-magnum champagne spray, presented by his teammates.

Theirs are the faces of another championship season for the Lakers, their second in a row . . . The Lakers defeated the Philadelphia 76ers, 108-96, at First Union Center to win the NBA title in five games.

"We were just out to prove that we can do it this time around," Bryant said, finally. "We just went through so much adversity, so much ups and downs. It was good to win it . . . But, as far as a dynasty, I don't know . . ."

Robert Horry observed his teammates from the doorway, and marveled at what they had done, and he along with them. Terribly flawed in the regular season, the Lakers grew and became the best postseason team in NBA history . . .

O'Neal, who averaged 33.0 points and 15.8 rebounds and had 17 blocks in five games, was the Finals' most valuable player for the second consecutive year. Indeed, he has changed . . . from the man who could not win to the man starting a collection of championship trophies.

"The first championship was to get the monkey off my back," O'Neal said. "Now, the ones that I get from now on will just be to try to stamp my name in history . . .

At 22, Bryant has won two titles, and he moved afterward with a glaze in his eyes, as though it weren't altogether real.

. . . Derek Fisher sat afterward with his

Kobe Bryant: A moment apart after title No. 2.

left arm around his mother. Both were soaked in champagne. Fisher's left cheek was smeared with pink lipstick, his mother's shade. He scored 18 points, all on six three-pointers in eight attempts . . .

Lakers Coach Phil Jackson had reminded them daily to stay in the moment, to play in the moment, and they did.

The moments piled up, into eight consecutive victories to end the regular season, and 23 wins in their final 24 games overall . . .

The eighth championship in Los Angeles Lakers history is the second under Jackson. He arrived two years ago today . . .

Ron Harper's championship is his fifth, "One for my thumb," he said of the ring that will arrive next fall. Horace Grant and

Horry have four each . . .

The 76ers came as hard as the Lakers assumed they would, and Allen Iverson, who scored 37 points, shot that side-saddle shot and kept shooting, as they figured he would. And Tyrone Hill returned to the series, particularly as a rebounder, just in time for the 76ers to get some second-chance points near the basket . . .

The Lakers didn't play their best game, only their last one . . .

The Lakers made 12 of 17 three-pointers. When Fisher made his fifth, when it fell through the basket through a hail of "Beat L.A.!" cries and pushed the Lakers' fourth-quarter lead to 96-84, Fisher raised a forefinger to his lips . . .

"It was an unbelievable run for us in the playoffs," Jackson said. "We played at a level in which we thought and visualized ourselves playing during the course of the year.

"Literally, their focus and concentration was incredible during this period of time. They were good. Hours spent in videotape, coaching energy that we spent on this team. They absorbed it and they absorbed the lessons learned from last year's playoffs very well."

Said Bryant: "I'll tell you what, right now it's a thing of the past. Next year, when people see us talking aggressively, it's not gonna be a thing of the past. Someone's going to blow it out of proportion until we win another championship, and it's gonna happen again. It's a cycle. It's gonna happen like that. We'll do our best to try to keep a team effort, keep a community. Hopefully, we won't have to go through what we went through this year. I don't think we will."

With a sweet assist, Kobe Bryant and Shaquille O'Neal show they're on the same page in the 2001 Finals.
Bryant averaged 24.6 points and 5.8 assists, and O'Neal averaged 33 points and 15.8 rebounds.

| 2000-01 Season Highlights | Jerry West leaves his position as Lakers' executive vice president of basketball operations and is replaced by Mitch Kupchak. | Ron Harper (right) and Robert Horry become the second and third players to win multiple championships as a member of two different teams. |  | Derek Fisher misses 62 games because of foot injury, then sets an NBA record with 15 three-pointers in a four-game series against San Antonio. |

2001-02

Horry Is Even Money; Last Shot a Rallying Cry for L.A.

Season Record

W58-L24 (.707)
Division: 2nd
NBA Champion

Coach

Phil Jackson

Players

Kobe Bryant

Shaquille O'Neal

Derek Fisher

Rick Fox

Devean George

Robert Horry

Lindsey Hunter

Samaki Walker

Stanislav Medvedenko

Mitch Richmond

Brian Shaw

Mark Madsen

Jelani McCoy

Joe Crispin

Mike Penberthy

Robert Horry's heart-stopping three-point shot in Game 4 of the Western Conference Finals didn't merely save the game. The Lakers went on to win two of the next three games, taking the series from Sacramento and moving on to the NBA Finals, where the team made history.

By TIM BROWN
May 27, 2002

After the buzzer ... the jump shot that left Robert Horry's hand with six-tenths of a second remaining, the shot that spellbound an arena and a series and two cities, fell.

It fell, and a budding NBA dynasty still had hope, and the Western Conference Finals still had purpose, and the Lakers let go of their fears on a taut, rigorous Sunday afternoon at Staples Center.

Horry gathered a loose ball 25 feet and straight on from the basket and swished a three-pointer that gave the Lakers a 100-99 victory over the Sacramento Kings, who only then lost the last of a 24-point lead. The series is tied at two games apiece ...

After a week of ... beating the Lakers in nearly every manner, the Kings made one critical error: They left the ball in Horry's grasp, with the game nearly over, when one shot could change the course of the series.

Less than a second from needing only one victory to eliminate the twice-defending champion Lakers, and leading, 99-97, the Kings watched Kobe Bryant miss a short runner with five seconds left, and Shaquille O'Neal miss a layup with three seconds left. Vlade Divac reflexively knocked the ball away from the rim, up the middle of the lane, one bounce to Horry, who took it with 1.5 seconds remaining ...

Horry stepped left, leaped, and let go, as Chris Webber floated past, his right hand inches beneath the ball. The buzzer sounded and, as a series held its breath, as Bryant held his fists to his shoulders and Rick Fox laid his head back to watch the ball

pass over him, the shot fell, exactly perfect.

"Oh," Horry said, "I knew it."

He knew, because of Philadelphia last year. Because of Portland last month. Because of all the other shots like it that have fallen for him ...

"He has a steel kind of will," Lakers Coach Phil Jackson said of Horry, whose shot gave the Lakers their first lead since 2-0 ...

The Lakers trailed by 20 after one quarter and by 24 in the second before they pushed back ...

Horry scored 16 points in the second half, 11 of them in the fourth quarter. O'Neal scored 27 points ... and took 18 rebounds. And Bryant, whose exhaustion required another liter of intravenous fluids after the game, scored 25 points. But ... it was Horry who carried them ...

"That's [a] lucky shot, that's all," Divac said. "You don't need skill in that situation. You throw it, it goes in, it goes in."

Typically he is subdued, but Horry was nearly aghast that Divac would suggest such a thing.

"If you go back and look at the shot, a luck shot is one of those guys who has no form," Horry said. "If you look at the shot, it was straight form. He shouldn't have tipped it out there. It wasn't a luck shot. I have been doing that for all my career. He should know. He should read the paper or something."

And Horry laughed ...

"He saved us today," O'Neal said.

The season was not yet doomed ... but the Lakers played on the brink of that ...

Jackson's cool demeanor often was gone, replaced by pointed shouts to play defense, to find the offensive rhythm within them, and scowls ...

Asked early what it would have been like had the Lakers lost, O'Neal said, "I don't believe in 'if.' If my father didn't meet my mother, and go on a date, I wouldn't be here. I don't believe in 'if,' but we just wanted to chop it down, just keep fighting and fighting."

Which, then, led him to Horry's shot.

"It was a great day," O'Neal said. "It was a blessed day for us. Thank God for Robert. Thank God his father met his mother too."

Robert Horry isn't about to call it luck as he lets a three-point shot fly over the reach of Chris Webber for one of the NBA's most dramatic buzzer-beating shots.

Threedom Rings: O'Neal is Three-Peat MVP

In Game 4 of the 2002 Finals, with the clock under four minutes and the lead at nine, Derek Fisher stood in the huddle and looked straight into Rick Fox's eyes and from three feet away screamed, "Three-peat!" Fox nodded... "We can see why the third time is the hardest," Fisher said. "But here we are."

By TIM BROWN
June 13, 2002

The third championship came as the others did, on the shoulders of Shaquille O'Neal, on the wings of Kobe Bryant, at the end of a season they were sure of, if sometimes they were among the few who were.

Late on Wednesday night, the Lakers ... pulled the joy of their NBA championship not from large green bottles, but from the teammates who sang with them in a locker room soaked in satisfaction.

The Lakers defeated the New Jersey Nets, 113-107, at Continental Airlines Arena, where O'Neal handed his Finals MVP trophy—his third in a row—to his teammates, and held his young daughter, Amirah, instead.

They won the best-of-seven series in four games, the first Finals sweep by the Lakers, the seventh in league history and the first in seven years, since O'Neal and his Orlando Magic were gone in four.

The Lakers have won 14 championships, two fewer than the Boston Celtics, and seem to be gaining momentum. O'Neal is 30. Bryant is 23. They pushed into a cinder-block room crowded by teammates, who chanted, "One, two, three! One, two, three!" And when

O'Neal was ready, corks banged off a tile ceiling, and he shouted hysterically when the champagne came.

Bryant, who a year ago slumped in a shower stall by himself, danced among them. Rick Fox held the game ball and a Bahamian flag. Derek Fisher turned his cap backward and shrieked for his third, as though it were his first ...

Phil Jackson won his ninth title as a coach in his ninth Finals appearance, tying Celtics legend Red Auerbach for the record. Afterward, Jackson lit a cigar, his own, and surrounded himself with his four children in a small room between locker rooms.

"It's my belief and my experience that the third victory in the three successive years is always the most unique and the most difficult one to fight your way through," he said. "This certainly was this year." ...

O'Neal limped terribly through the season, and could face off-season surgery to ease the pain from an arthritic toe. But he strode forcefully into a series he was expected to control, averaged 36.3 points and shot 59.5%. He scored 34 points and took 10 rebounds in Game 4 ...

He became the second player to win three consecutive Finals MVP awards. Mi-

chael Jordan did it twice last decade, also playing for Jackson, also as the game's most dominant force.

"It says we're a great team and ... everybody stuck to the script, everybody believed," O'Neal said. "Nobody ever got down, even, you know, when times were so-called hard."

Bryant scored 25 points, 11 while making four of six shots in the fourth quarter. Fisher scored 13 points, Robert Horry scored 12 and Devean George scored 11, including a three-pointer with just under eight minutes remaining that gave the Lakers a 92-89 lead they never gave back.

Nets forward Kenyon Martin scored 35 points, 13 in a taut fourth quarter. The Nets, however, lacked a consistent inside game ...

O'Neal set records for a four-game series for points (145), free throws made (45), free throws attempted (68) and blocks (11). As a result, the Lakers won their record eighth consecutive Finals game ...

Asked to consider the three, Bryant grinned.

"It's all the same, all the same," he said. "The first one is, it's all a novelty and it feels good. The first one will always be the best one. The second one, the adversity we went through throughout the course of the year made that one special.

"And this one, it's kind of making us step in as one of the great teams. It feels great. Having a seven-game series against Sacramento, being down, 3-2, it challenged us. We responded to it. It makes this one that much more special."

Before the opening tip, O'Neal looked into the crowd and found his stepfather, Phil Harrison. They made eye contact, O'Neal pointed and Harrison nodded.

Periodically, O'Neal would peer at Harrison, the man they call "Sarge," and he'd touch his chest with his right fist.

"Thank God for both of the Phils in my life," O'Neal said. "Phil Jackson, who always stayed on me. And Phil Harrison, who always stayed on me. I'm just so happy right now."

Shaquille O'Neal holds his daughter after winning title.

O'Neal, with his third consecutive MVP performance, has the 2002 Finals in his hands during a sweep of the New Jersey Nets.

Kobe Bryant, playing in his former hometown of Philadelphia, scores 31 points and is voted the All-Star Game's most valuable player.

Mark "Mad Dog" Madsen, a first-round pick in 2000, memorably dances at the Lakers' title celebration at Staples Center.

The Mouth That Scored for Lakers

When the Lakers moved to Los Angeles in 1960, they could not get a local radio station to broadcast their games. But when they made the '61 playoffs, team owner Bob Short appealed to an emerging radio and television sportscaster to fly to St. Louis to cover the Lakers' game for the Los Angeles audience. Thus began Chick Hearn's 42 years as the team's beloved play-by-play announcer, a career that continued until his death on August 5, 2002, at age 85.

By JIM MURRAY
January 11, 1998

When they refer to a player as a "sixth man" in basketball, they usually mean a guy who comes off the bench when the team is in retreat, takes the ball, picks the team up again, turns the game around and rights the situation . . .

But the best sixth man I ever saw never made a basket, drew a foul, blocked a shot, inbounded a pass or grabbed a rebound for his team.

You know, the Lakers over the years have had some pretty valuable individuals—Elgin Baylor, Jerry West, Wilt Chamberlain, Kareem Abdul-Jabbar, Magic Johnson . . . But the best backcourt man they ever had was Chick Hearn . . .

The Lakers picked up Chick Hearn for a song. He was no threat to any salary cap, but nobody with a basketball was any more valuable to the franchise than Chick with a microphone.

The Lakers had newly arrived from Minnesota, where they had been going broke, when Chick first joined them. Bob Short, the owner, was thinking of putting the team in a leaky boat in the Pacific at the time and cutting his losses when he approached Chick.

Chick knew basketball as few did. He had played in the AAU, the NBA of its time, and he had broadcast the frenetic high school tournaments in his native Illinois. Short persuaded Chick to do the play-by-play of a playoff game the Lakers and St. Louis Hawks were contesting. The result, I can sum up in one anecdote:

The week before, the Lakers and Hawks drew 2,800 fans to the Sports Arena for a playoff game. Chick did the next game at St. Louis on radio. When the teams came back to Los Angeles, there were 15,000 in the seats. They have more or less been there for every game since.

Before Chick, basketball broadcasts were just more interesting than test patterns. Basketball was a stepchild of sports at the time anyway. The old-time columnists referred to it as "whistle ball" or "bounce ball," a game for guys who didn't like to get their hair mussed in a real game like football.

Chick Hearn made it seem like World War III. He almost reinvented the game, gave it a whole new language. "Give and go," "turnaround jumper," "dribble-drive to the basket," "going for the hole" came into the lexicon of the game, maybe even "slam dunk."

Guys didn't just bring the ball upcourt, they were "yo-yoing the ball to the top of the key." Players didn't just get fooled, they got "faked into the popcorn machine." "Airball" might have been a Hearnism. "Skyhook" definitely was. Jerry West became "Mr. Clutch." The team of Johnson and Abdul-Jabbar became "Showtime." The game wasn't just iced when the lead got big, it was put "in the refrigerator."

Chick was no rah-rah boy, no cheerleader. "Why doesn't he sleep on his own time?" he would complain on the air about a local player who seemed to have lost interest in the game.

Chick and the Lakers were a match made in heaven. Romeo-meets-Juliet stuff. Laurel and Hardy. Before Chick Hearn, the Lakers played at junior college gyms, on stage at the Shrine Auditorium, wherever they could light. Then, Jack Kent Cooke bought the team and built the Forum. Chick filled it. Cooke signed him to an exclusive contract. He's still filling it. The game has gone through many changes, but the one constant was Francis Dayle Hearn . . .

On Jan. 19 at the Great Western Forum, he will be working his 3,000th consecutive game for the Lakers. You don't even want to know how many minutes that comes to. And that's only since 1965. He had done five years of sporadic games before then . . .

Of all the minutes of all the nights he has broadcast, Chick says he remembers best the night in 1970 when West threw in a basket from his own backcourt at the buzzer against the Knicks in an NBA Final. It only tied the game. Today, it would have been a three-point basket and won.

It was a fateful moment in Lakers history. But I would opt for a different one. I would put in there the night Short turned to assistant Lou Mohs and said, "How about if we try to get this fellow Chick Hearn to broadcast our games? I like his flair."

That was 10 years before the guys on the team now were even born. They should get a nickname for Chick too. "Mr. Clutch" still has a nice ring to it.

Chick Hearn started calling Lakers games in 1961.

Chick Hearn enjoys the moment as he introduces the Lakers during the championship rally at Staples Center in June of 2002.

Chick Hearn Facts

Was the Los Angeles Lakers' play-by-play announcer for 42 years.

Launched Lakers broadcasting career March 27, 1961, announcing Game 5 of the Western Division Finals in St. Louis. The Lakers won.

Broadcast a record 3,338 consecutive Lakers games starting November 21, 1965, and ending December 16, 2001.

Last called game was June 12, 2002. The Lakers defeated the New Jersey Nets, 113–107, in the NBA Finals to win the team's ninth championship since moving to Los Angeles.

Credited with coining such terms as "slam dunk, " "air ball," and "no harm, no foul."

Nicknamed Lakers Jerry "Mr. Clutch" West, Wilt "The Stilt" Chamberlain, Kobe "The Kid" Bryant, Shaquille "Big Fella" O'Neal, and Michael "Secretary of Defense" Cooper, among others.

Named National Sportscaster of the Year three times (1959, 1965, 1987).

Received the Curt Gowdy Media Award from the Basketball Hall of Fame in 1992.

Won an Emmy Award for Excellence in Basketball Coverage, 1965.

Received a star on the Hollywood Walk of Fame in 1986.

Inducted into the American Sportscasters Hall of Fame in 1995.

Inducted into the Basketball Hall of Fame as a "contributor" in 2003.

2002-03

Fourclosed! Spurs End Lakers' Run

The San Antonio Spurs were the last team to win the NBA title before the Lakers began their three-year run. L.A.'s attempt at a fourth consecutive title was crushed by the eventual champion Spurs in the 2003 Western Conference Semifinals, but in the 2004 playoffs the Lakers stopped San Antonio.

By TIM BROWN
May 16, 2003

Season Record

W50-L32 (.610)
Division: 2nd
West Semis

Coach

Phil Jackson

Players

Kobe Bryant

Shaquille O'Neal

Derek Fisher

Rick Fox

Robert Horry

Devean George

Samaki Walker

Stanislav Medvedenko

Brian Shaw

Kareem Rush

Mark Madsen

Jannero Pargo

Tracy Murray

Soumaila Samake

Then it was done.

After three years, three NBA championships and all that came with them, it was done, the Lakers worn too thin in the middle, grown too old on the edges, the rest of the league having come too fast.

The San Antonio Spurs . . . eliminated the Lakers in the sixth game of the Western Conference semifinals on Thursday night, 110-82, at Staples Center.

With just more than two minutes remaining, the people stood and cheered in a 25-point deficit, and Laker Girls cried, and Lakers players touched one another's hands. They thanked them for all of it, a three-peat that brought Shaquille O'Neal and Kobe Bryant and Phil Jackson together, from basketball worlds apart . . .

"We had a tough couple of years with these guys," said Spurs Coach Gregg Popovich, eliminated the last two postseasons by the Lakers. "To finally play well enough . . . is beyond comprehension."

Tim Duncan, the league's most valuable player, scored 37 points and took 16 rebounds in the Lakers' second-largest home playoff loss since Jackson arrived four years ago . . .

Bryant, whose voice shook an hour after he left the floor, said, "It's a foreign feeling. I don't like the feeling. I don't think anybody else likes the feeling . . . I don't ever want to feel it again."

. . . There are five free agents . . . and Lakers management expects to rebuild in places around Bryant and O'Neal. So, some said goodbye for four months, others for longer, and Bryant, tough on his team-

mates in a regular season that brought only 50 wins, frowned now at what he knew would be change.

"I can't even form the words," he said. "We had so many battles together."

Bryant scored 20 points against the Spurs, and O'Neal had 31 points and 10 rebounds on a sore knee, he said, that hurt, "a little bit." There, again, was not enough around them, and so they lost the game and the series . . .

O'Neal sat out 12 games because of surgery, then three due to injury, and therefore the Lakers rushed and grinded through the final months, first to qualify for the playoffs, then to qualify well. Forward Rick Fox was injured in the first round and was lost until training camp at the least, and his replacement, Devean George, sprained his ankle a week later.

Jackson took a weekend off in the middle of the series against the Spurs . . . for an angioplasty procedure, ending months of fatigue and allowing him to return next year . . .

"We are severely disappointed we couldn't make a run for the championship . . ." Jackson said. " . . . We've gotten a little bit older, we suffered some injuries, we had a difficult year, as I told them in the locker room about 40 minutes ago . . . We stumbled, we fell, we lacked some discipline as a basketball club, and we paid the price for it."

O'Neal will bear some of the burden, even as he

once promised the fourth championship would be "on me." "It's always on me." ...

O'Neal turned 31 this season. He has three years remaining on his Lakers contract, and the Lakers could choose to extend it by three more years in September. Bryant, 25, has left his three-year extension on the table for nearly a year, and seems content to play next season as a walk-year. He can opt out of his contract in a year ...

"It finally caught up to us," O'Neal said. "We can get some extra rest now, regroup, get some free agents, get some new guys and get some new blood, and hopefully we can start a new run next year."

From left, Brian Shaw, Kobe Bryant, Shaquille O'Neal, Robert Horry, and Derek Fisher watch Game 6 of the Western Conference Semifinals slip away.

Looking Back to Go Forward

After the Lakers' NBA championship in 2000, Shaquille O'Neal and Kobe Bryant led the team to victories in nine consecutive postseason series, achieving a 34-7 record. The 10th—the 2003 Western Conference Semifinals—proved the team's undoing and prompted memories of better times.

By **J.A. ADANDE**
May 16, 2003

It was the night of June 19, 2000, some 90 minutes after Kobe Bryant leaped into Shaquille O'Neal's arms at the conclusion of their NBA Finals victory over the Indiana Pacers and their first championship together.

They had addressed the Staples Center crowd, spoken to the media and then they walked into the Los Angeles Kings' training room at Staples Center, where longtime NBA photographer Andrew Bernstein fired off five or six quick shots of the duo together.

A print now hangs in the Lakers' training room, one of several framed memories of Lakers glory . . .

Bryant found himself staring at the three-year-old photograph as he tried to comprehend what happened Thursday night, when the Spurs halted the Lakers' string of championships at three with a 110-82 pasting in Game 6 of the Western Conference Semifinals.

O'Neal is on the right side of the picture, holding his NBA Finals most valuable player trophy in his left hand, with his right hand held out as if to say, "Ta-dah!"

Bryant is on the left side, a white championship cap sitting askew on his head. His left arm is draped around O'Neal's shoulder

and he's holding the Larry O'Brien championship trophy in his right hand.

"It was our first trophy," he said, as wistfully as if it were a picture of his baby's first steps.

"I was looking at it and I just had to smile, because it's amazing how fast time flies . . . I was 21, he was 28. Now he's 31, I'm going to be 25 and we have three championships.

"But it made me realize how much you have to take advantage of every opportunity you have, because careers go by so fast. I mean, I remember that picture like it was yesterday. [Thursday] was the first time I had a chance to reflect on what we accomplished."

It was time to reflect because it was over.

. . . In 2000, it felt like it could go on forever. Now the duo could split as soon as next year if Bryant decides to exercise the opt-out in his contract . . .

"I think every year you try to repeat," Bryant said. "But what you have to understand is that teams reload and they restock and they try to dethrone you. They reloaded with the right ammo, with what they needed to battle." . . .

Bernstein will need a wider lens for the next picture, because it must include more players . . .

Over the course of this six-game series, O'Neal and Bryant . . . didn't have enough help.

A three-point basket (one in particular) from Robert Horry would have been nice. Or someone who might keep Tony Parker or Speedy Claxton out of the lane or perhaps someone to keep Manu Ginobili from crashing the offensive boards.

Without the help, even a breakthrough season by Bryant, who averaged a career-

high 30 points, couldn't make up for a less-than-100% O'Neal.

O'Neal missed the first 12 games while recovering from surgery on his toe, and missed three more games in February with a sore knee. Knee problems flared up again in this series.

"I think a lot of things caught up," O'Neal said. "Injuries, playing hard. We kind of struggled to win 50 games . . .

"This is something that's going to hurt. It's reality, it's life. You have to suck it up and move on . . . "

Bryant had trouble getting through a television interview immediately after the game Thursday, and took a while to compose his thoughts later.

Bernstein, the photographer, said there have been only two times when he couldn't bring himself to push the shutter button . . .

The first was after the 1989 NBA Finals when the Lakers were swept by the Detroit Pistons. The quickest way between the two locker rooms was through the showers, and . . . he saw Magic Johnson and Michael Cooper sitting on the floor, heads slumped, the water pouring down on them.

And the second time was Thursday night, when Bryant sat by himself in the trainer's room.

"It's just tough to lose," Bryant said. "We haven't experienced this feeling in three seasons."

There will be no pictures to commemorate May 15, 2003. Only painful memories.

Page 203: Those were the days: Kobe Bryant and Shaquille O'Neal pose for a portrait by photographer Andrew Bernstein in 2001.

2002-03 Season Highlights

Kobe Bryant sinks 12 three-point field goals on January 7, 2003, against the Seattle SuperSonics, setting the all-time NBA record.

The Lakers get draft rights to Kareem Rush (left) and acquire Tracy Murray in a trade involving Lindsey Hunter.

Bryant joins Elgin Baylor and Jerry West in averaging 30 or more points in a single season, becoming the youngest NBA player to reach 10,000 career points.

2003-04

0.4: The Fisher Fling

Season Record

W56-L26 (.683)
Division: 1st
NBA Finals

Coach

Phil Jackson

Players

Kobe Bryant

Shaquille O'Neal

Gary Payton

Devean George

Derek Fisher

Stanislav
Medvedenko

Karl Malone

Kareem Rush

Bryon Russell

Horace Grant

Rick Fox

Luke Walton

Brian Cook

Jamal Sampson

Maurice Carter

Jannero Pargo

Ime Udoka

Tim Duncan's miracle shot in the last second seemingly saved the Game 5 of the Western Conference Semifinals for the San Antonio Spurs. But the Lakers weren't done. Improbably, another miracle was within reach with fourth-tenths of a second left.

By TIM BROWN
May 14, 2004

The basketball was out of his hand a few feet when Derek Fisher began to believe.

And so, to him, it was not entirely unexpected that this shot—caught, aimed and released in just under four-tenths of a second Thursday night—had delivered the victory that never came for the Lakers last season and now brought them to the brink of the Western Conference Finals.

At the end of some of the most remarkable three minutes the NBA playoffs had ever seen, Fisher made a turnaround 18-footer with Manu Ginobili and the final horn coming fast, and the Lakers defeated the San Antonio Spurs, 74-73, in Game 5 of the Western Conference Semifinals at SBC Center . . .

A role player in a lineup of superstars, Fisher had answered two earlier shots by Spurs forward Tim Duncan.

Not far from where Robert Horry's three-point try rimmed out a year ago in the same fifth game, and with Horry on the floor for the Spurs, Fisher caught an inbounds pass from Gary Payton, turned and launched the shot. The arena grew quiet, and the players stood and watched . . .

The horn sounded as the ball cleared his fingertips. He stumbled backward . . .

"As it got closer," he said, "I knew the ball was going in."

Before, these moments were for other people. For Kobe Bryant, who'd made a 21-footer with 11.5 seconds to play to give the Lakers a 72-71 lead. But Bryant, his legs and body fading anyway as he made only four of 13 shots in the second half, was covered

on the last play. Shaquille O'Neal, who broke to the basket, was defended as well. Karl Malone screened Ginobili, for just a moment.

Payton went through his teammates, one at a time, and chose Fisher, Ginobili not far behind.

"He hit it," Payton said.

He hit it.

"The biggest shot of his life," said Fisher's brother, Duane Washington, fighting tears and a raspy throat 30 minutes later.

Less than a second after Duncan had put the Spurs ahead, 73-72, on an off-balance, in-O'Neal's-chest, fling-it-up 18-foot shot, Fisher made it. Less than three minutes after Duncan double-pumped and accidentally banked in another 18-foot shot from the top of the key, also over O'Neal, Fisher made it.

As memorable a shot in this Lakers generation, at least with Horry's in Game 4 of the 2002 Western Conference Finals, Fisher on the road, in a place the Lakers had not won a playoff game, surrounded by future Hall of Famers, he made it. The loss was the Spurs' first at home since March 1, 18 games ago . . .

As Lakers leaped into the air, chasing him, Fisher dashed the length of the court, pointing his right hand toward . . . Los Angeles? Surrounded by emergency medical personnel at the end of an entry tunnel, leaning over their television, he watched the replay and celebrated again when referees confirmed to an aching crowd the shot had left his hand on time . . .

Even then, Spurs Coach Gregg Popovich wasn't sure. The clock, he said, did not react to the catch. "I think it definitely started late," he said.

In fact, according to a league official, all three referees and an NBA-employed timekeeper have the

capability to start the clock. The first one starts it.

The Lakers could hardly be troubled by the Spurs' suspicions. They had played to a 16-point lead, then lost it over the final 15 minutes. Dynamic well into the third quarter, and having been carried by Bryant and Devean George offensively, by O'Neal and Malone defensively, they stumbled into the final minutes.

Tony Parker and Duncan began to score and their own offense became scattered, overly reliant on a tiring Bryant. So the Spurs drew back, went to Duncan and were ahead, 73-72, after Duncan made

his fall-away 18-foot shot with four-tenths of a second left. Duncan lifted himself from the court after his shot and was mobbed by thrilled Spurs, sure four-tenths would pass without harm.

But, as O'Neal noted, "One lucky shot deserves another. They got one on their end."

Fisher wouldn't call it that. He'd call it his due.

"That's a tribute to his focus and dedication to the team and putting the team first," said Rick Fox, who didn't play. "He's had to sacrifice for the betterment of the team, the addition of Gary. Tonight was a remarkable payback for his sacrifice."

Derek Fisher's famous "0.4" shot is safely in flight as the game clock above the backboard reads 0.0, as in the game's over.

In Malone's Final Season, Lakers Close West Title With a Rush

Karl Malone and Gary Payton joined the Lakers in July 2003 in search of a title. Their tour of duty included a surprise training-camp trip to play "Paintball" with their new teammates and later spend time with Air Force personnel who had returned from Iraq and Afghanistan. The players welcomed the team-building experience, especially at a time when Kobe Bryant also was under the glare of a legal action, but not all the rest of the season worked out as planned. Still, Malone, in what would be the last of his 19 NBA seasons, got to enjoy one more Western Conference championship. In the NBA Finals, the team gained just one win against Detroit.

By TIM BROWN
June 1, 2004

Before there would be much of a celebration Monday night, Karl Malone stared up at the people of Staples Center, pulled his cap down tight, lowered his head and jogged from the floor.

As Kareem Rush cradled the Western Conference championship trophy, won finally, 96-90, and in six games against the Minnesota Timberwolves, Shaquille O'Neal met Malone in the locker room.

The people chanted and Kobe Bryant shouted at them gleefully over the public-address system and Gary Payton watched from the back of a crowd of Lakers. Phil Jackson headed for his 10th NBA Finals, the Lakers to their fourth in five years as his team, and Malone would have none of it. Not yet.

The Finals start Sunday, in Los Angeles against the Detroit Pistons or in Indianap-olis against the Indiana Pacers. Malone had won conference championships before. He'd had these parties, seen this optimism, and twice been disappointed by Jackson's Chicago Bulls.

"I haven't done anything," he said. "I got back healthy. I was able to bring something to the team. But I haven't been able to bring the full package to this team. That's to win the title."

The arena floor filled with players and security guards and media and league officials who would be booed, all in the minutes after Rush had made six three-pointers, three in the fourth quarter, and O'Neal had scored 25 points and Kobe Bryant scored 20 and they'd all survived 22 points and 17 rebounds from Kevin Garnett.

In a quiet locker room, Malone, 40 years old and at the end of his 19th NBA season, pulled O'Neal close.

"I gave him a hug," he said. "I kissed him on the jaw. I told him I loved him. He told me, 'Thank you.'"

Twenty minutes later, O'Neal stood in a hallway, his baby daughter in his arms. He ordered her, "Kiss," and she left a damp circle on his cheek.

"I'm just glad," he said, "because of what happened this year. I feel like I'm a man of my word. I told him last summer I was going to get him to this point. That we were going to get him to this point. I feel good for him."

They were to be the best team ever assembled, when Malone and Payton arrived as free agents. But . . . Malone was struck down by the first serious injury of his career, Payton only put up with the system he volunteered for, and Bryant's legal en-tanglement seeped into nearly everything they did.

Now, they'll settle for being the best team this season, or the best team in springtime. Or, simply, the team holding the trophy in June, however it comes . . .

Malone had 10 points, 10 rebounds and seven assists and played Garnett, the league MVP, for everything he had. The Timber-wolves had hoped to wear out Malone . . .

Without Sam Cassell or Troy Hudson, their injured point guards, they handed the ball to Garnett, and he ran at Malone, and they pushed each other and leaned on each other.

With 19.4 seconds left, Garnett fouled out, leaving Malone and the Lakers victorious.

"I actually thought about retiring a couple times" in previous seasons, Malone said. "What if I would have? I would have missed out on this." On their way to their 22nd NBA Finals appearance since moving to Los Angeles in 1960 . . . the Lakers forced the Timberwolves into 19 turnovers and scored 33 points from them . . .

Rush, the second-year guard who'd made 10 threes in the postseason until Monday, was three for four from the arc in the final quarter, his first giving them a 71-68 lead. Slava Medvedenko came off the bench, made all three of his shots and scored six points in the fourth quarter. And the Lakers did not trail again . . .

By the end, his feet in a tub of ice water, the smile faded only some, Malone said it's been almost all he'd hoped it to be. Almost.

"It is kind of amazing," he said. "You just play hard and do the things you are capable of doing and we were able to do that. What a great effort. It is unbelievable."

2003-04 Season Highlights

Gary Payton (right) signs, along with Karl Malone, in July of 2003 and leads the Lakers in assists with an average of 5.5 per game.

Kobe Bryant and Shaquille O'Neal are selected to the All-NBA First Team for the third year in a row.

Karl Malone beats Michael Olowokandi (left) and Kevin Garnett as the Lakers clinch the Western Conference Finals' title in 2004.

Phil Jackson reaches 800 victories (800-301) faster than any coach in NBA history.

Karl Malone, at 40, records a triple-double November 28 against San Antonio, becoming the oldest player to achieve this in NBA history.

A statue honoring Earvin "Magic" Johnson is dedicated in February of 2004 at Staples Center.

2004-05

Lakers Agree to Deal O'Neal to Miami Heat

Season Record

W34-L48 (.415)
Division: 4th
Missed Playoff

Coach

Rudy Tomjanovich
(22-19),
Frank Hamblen
(12-29)

Players

Kobe Bryant

Caron Butler

Chucky Atkins

Lamar Odom

Chris Mihm

Jumaine Jones

Brian Cook

Tierre Brown

Brian Grant

Luke Walton

Stanislav
Medvedenko

Devean George

Sasha Vujacic

Vlade Divac

Kareem Rush

Tony Bobbitt

After the Lakers traded him, Shaquille O'Neal played 3 ½ seasons with the Miami Heat, where he won a title, and later went to Phoenix. In the summer of 2009, another trade sent him to Cleveland. Bryant remained with the Lakers, winning his fourth NBA championship in 2009.

By TIM BROWN
July 11, 2004

The Lakers have agreed in principle to trade Shaquille O'Neal to the Miami Heat, apparently ending a triumphant and tumultuous eight-year run in which the team won three NBA championships, team and league sources said Saturday.

In exchange for O'Neal, one of the greatest players of his era, the Lakers will receive forwards Lamar Odom and Caron Butler, center Brian Grant and a future first-round draft pick, the sources said . . .

O'Neal arrived as a free agent from the Orlando Magic in 1996, heralding the beginning of what many envisioned as a long-running championship dynasty, one pairing the game's most imposing big man with another new arrival, teenage rookie guard Kobe Bryant. Their dominance took hold in the 1999-2000 season with the arrival of Coach Phil Jackson and the first of three consecutive titles . . . But it all fell apart last season amid open rancor between the two and felony rape charges against Bryant . . . [The charges he faced in Eagle, Colo., were dismissed after his accuser declined to testify. Her civil suit was settled out of court.]

The agreement to trade O'Neal was reached on the day the Lakers introduced Rudy Tomjanovich to replace Jackson, who departed three weeks ago after Lakers owner Jerry Buss declined to offer him a new contract. The trade—as with Jackson's exit— is widely seen as a move to placate Bryant, who is a free agent after opting out of the final year of his contract . . .

O'Neal had intimated weeks ago that Buss had chosen Bryant over the good of the team, hoping to lure him away from other free-agent offers . . .

The Lakers could start the 6-foot-9 Grant at center, Odom at power forward, Butler at small forward and Gary Payton at point guard, with Bryant . . . perhaps at shooting guard. Karl Malone and Derek Fisher remain free agents with some interest in returning . . .

"If it really is a done deal, it's something that didn't have to happen," Fisher said . . .

"I don't think that when the season was over Shaq was really that adamant about leaving . . . But that changed when the line was clearly drawn that it wasn't his team and it was all about Kobe and that he'll have to take a back seat . . .

O'Neal met Saturday with Heat President Pat Riley and General Manager Randy Pfund in Orlando, Fla. . . .

Those close to Buss say he had become disenchanted with O'Neal, who sat out 15 games in each of the last three seasons, pouted about his contract and refused to stay in shape. At the end of the 2002-03 season, O'Neal weighed 358 pounds and had about 20% body fat . . .

In what appears to have been his final year as a Laker, O'Neal averaged 21.5 points—a career low— and 11.5 rebounds in the regular season . . .

Riley, who came to Los Angeles three weeks ago to interview for Jackson's job, now has O'Neal, the one-time league most valuable player, the three-time MVP in the NBA Finals and, at 32, still one of the game's most powerful players . . .

What then-General Manager Jerry West built eight years ago when he signed O'Neal with a $120-million contract and traded for the rights to Bryant appears to have run its course. O'Neal is on the verge of returning to Florida and Bryant, according to Lakers sources, has given the Lakers no indication that trading O'Neal would guarantee his return . . .

Along with Bryant, O'Neal had become the face of the Lakers and, in large part, the face of the league . . . While he at times seemed unchallenged during the regular season, O'Neal made his reputation in the playoffs, where he averaged 28.1 points and 12.9 rebounds before falling off somewhat this postseason.

Lamar Odom, driving in 2005 against Orlando's Hedo Turkoglu, became a linchpin of the Lakers' trade that sent Shaquille O'Neal to the Miami Heat.

2004-05 Season Highlights

Frank Hamblen (left) becomes the 17th head coach of the Los Angeles Lakers after Rudy Tomjanovich (right) steps down on February 2.

Sasha Vujacic is chosen by the Lakers with the 27th pick of the 2004 draft.

THE LAKERS • 209

2005-06

Lakers Get a Re-Phil

After Phil Jackson's return, the rebuilding Lakers lost in the first round of the 2006 and 2007 playoffs. In 2008, they won the Western Conference Finals. And in 2009, Jackson's team took the NBA championship after a 65-17 record in the regular season.

By TIM BROWN
June 15, 2005

Season Record

W45-L37 (.549)
Division: 3rd
First Round

Coach

Phil Jackson

Players

Sasha Vujacic

Kobe Bryant

Von Wafer

William "Smush" Parker

Devin Green

Aaron McKie

Laron Profit

Luke Walton

Devean George

Lamar Odom

Brian Cook

Stanislav Medvedenko

Kwame Brown

Andrew Bynum

Chris Mihm

Laron Profit

Jim Jackson

Ronny Turiaf

I f it looked like Phil Jackson, talked like Phil Jackson and walked like a wounded buck, then that must have been the past-present-future Lakers coach who stood in front of Los Angeles mid-afternoon Tuesday, adjusted his glasses and said something along the lines of, "I'm back," only longer and without the Jordanian flair.

He was gone a year, out experiencing life away from the game, on beaches in Australia and New Zealand, on a lake in Montana, on a veranda in Playa del Rey. He returned in a charcoal suit and sandals, T-shirt and beads, soul patch and poise, still the man who pushed and prodded and rankled the Lakers for five sometimes glorious seasons.

If something had changed in the disposition of the coach who'd come in with dexterity and gone out with a flame-thrower, it was evident in neither his words nor his gestures. After all, he'd already embraced Zen, already divorced, already found Jeanie, already won and, ultimately, already lost. He had already been cast from a franchise he helped deliver, already molded superstars into champions, already balanced unwieldy egos atop colossal expectations. Twice.

What he'd never done was return to the scene and smudge the fingerprints. He'd not taken a job in an organization that spurned him, in a building whose halls he walked, hand in hand, with the owner's daughter. Indeed, he'd been run out at the wrong end of a shotgun, only to return in time for dinner, in possession of the same thin grin and the same strategic designs on love, happiness and triumph.

So, the questions arrived for the coach whose face fell from the city's billboards but remained in souls of Lakers fans: How've you been? Where've you been?

"More than anything, the lessons were about stress," he said, "in particular the stress that you get and how the release from that changes personalities. My kids, who have all weighed in on this, all wanted to talk about why I wanted to come back to this stressful job."

He assured them, he said, "I can manage the stress that comes along with this game."

Once, Jackson's heart nearly gave out from it . . . His energy lagged and he once coached a playoff game with his cardiologist sitting across the floor, an ambulance backed to the tunnel that led to the gym. The Lakers lost twice when they were supposed to win. Shaquille O'Neal and Kobe Bryant could hardly look at each other anymore. Karl Malone and Gary Payton came and went without a championship. The media circled, the Detroit Pistons won, the parts scattered, some, like Jackson, to distant continents.

Not two weeks ago, Jackson called his agent, Todd Musburger, and told him, "I won't coach again."

"For the next 48 hours, I can't tell you how gloomy he was," Musburger said. "Then he called back and said, 'Maybe this is the job for me. That's how I'm thinking now.'"

Musburger chuckled . . .

Jackson required that period . . . before he was sure he could return to what he was. It is not as he left it, of course. But his old lessons will find new ears . . .

Horace Grant, retired . . . and living near Santa Maria, could hardly believe the news. He thought it best for the franchise, however, and hoped it would be best for the coach.

"Phil, it's that mystery thing again," he said. "He does a lot of things unconventionally. I think this is one of the most unconventional that I've seen him do . . .

Phil Jackson, after his "sabbatical" from the game, still has fire for the Lakers.

Grant paused and laughed again.

"Maybe there wasn't much trout fishing in Montana," he concluded.

Yeah, he just walked back in as if none of it had ever happened. He'll hang that old Indian feather off the sprinkler nozzle in his office, gather that familiar coaching staff, push that offense Jerry Buss came to despise...

It began in the days after Buss asked him to leave. Jackson rebuilt his body, groped for his own pulse, and found he had energy again...

A year later, he said it's about "reconciliation, redemption and resiliency," the three Rs of his return...

Yeah, he's back. Who else would be wearing the sandals?

81 for the Books

Just how good was Kobe Bryant's team-record scoring performance? He made 60.9% of his field-goal attempts (28 of 46) and 18 of 20 free throws. At that point in the season, entire NBA teams had scored fewer than 81 points on 88 occasions.

By MIKE BRESNAHAN
January 23, 2006

Michael Jordan never did it. Neither did Kareem Abdul-Jabbar, the league's all-time leading scorer. Wilt Chamberlain did it ... once.

Kobe Bryant carved out a piece of NBA history by scoring 81 points Sunday against the Toronto Raptors, the second-highest total ever and more than enough to lead the Lakers past the Raptors, 122-104, in front of an energized, if not disbelieving, sellout crowd of 18,997 at Staples Center ...

After Bryant blew past the 60-point mark, and then breezed by the 70-point plateau, fans stood for the final part of the fourth quarter, taking photos and chanting his name again and again.

Bryant, taken out of the game with 4.2 seconds to play, went to the bench and hugged Lakers Coach Phil Jackson.

Public-address announcer Lawrence Tanter implored fans to save their ticket stubs from the "historic night at Staples Center."

Teammates and staff members asked Bryant to sign copies of the box score. Lakers owner Jerry Buss said it was "like watching a miracle unfold." Magic Johnson called Bryant to congratulate him.

Bryant, who had 62 points before leaving the game after three quarters Dec. 20 against the Dallas Mavericks, beat Elgin Baylor's franchise record of 71 points, set in November 1960 against New York.

Bryant's 55 second-half points also set a franchise record for points in a half, topping the 42 he had against Washington in March 2003.

The Lakers, who finished 34-48 last season, reached the midpoint of this season's schedule with a 22-19 record.

"We are going from the bottom to the top all together, so it's important for us to enjoy the journey ..." Bryant said. "We are on a journey, and to put on a show like this for the fans here in L.A. is truly something special. I grew up in front of these people, and now they are seeing me as an older young man."

Bryant was 19 points shy of the record set by Chamberlain on March 2, 1962, in a sparsely attended game in Hershey, Pa.

"That's unthinkable," Bryant said of Chamberlain's mark. "It's pretty exhausting to think about it."

Bryant, hampered in recent weeks by a sore ankle, a balky wrist and sore hips, had 27 points in the third quarter, making 11 of 15 shots as the Lakers came screaming back from an 18-point deficit to take a 91-85 lead.

He had 28 in the fourth quarter, passing Baylor's franchise record with a 14-footer from the right side with 4:25 to play.

He then vaulted past Chamberlain's second-highest individual effort, 78 points, and into second place all-time after making the third of three free throws with 1:47 to play.

Chamberlain scored 78 for Philadelphia against the Lakers in a triple-overtime game in December 1961 ...

"I wasn't keeping track on what he had, and when I turned to [assistant Frank Hamblen] and said, 'I think I better take him out now,' ... he said, 'I don't think you can. He has 77 points,'" Jackson said. "So we stayed with it until he hit 80."

But Jackson was also true to his team-first approach.

"It's not exactly the way you want to have a team win a game," he said. "But when you have to win a game, it's great to have that weapon to be able to do it. I've seen some remarkable games, but I've never seen anything like that before."

The Lakers ... were ... lethargic for part of Sunday's game.

The Lakers' defense was soft and compliant, allowing the Raptors to make 24 of 39 shots (61.5%) in the first half. The Lakers' offense, on the other hand, struggled against the Raptors' zone defense, making only 20 of 50 shots (40%) in the first half ...

The Lakers trailed at halftime, 63-49.

Matt Bonner's three-pointer gave the Raptors a 69-51 lead with 9:55 left in the third quarter, but then the Lakers began extending their defense, bothering the Raptors with half-court traps.

Bryant was also a bother.

"We have four days off coming up here, and I would have been sick as a dog if we would have lost this game," Bryant said. "I just wanted to step up and inspire us to play well, and it turned into something special."

The Staples Center billboard tells the story.

Kobe Bryant had 55 of his 81 points in the second half of the Lakers' victory over the Toronto Raptors.

2005-06
Season
Highlights

The Lakers select 7-foot Andrew Bynum (age 17) with their first lottery pick since 1994; he becomes the youngest player to be selected in the history of the draft.

Kobe Bryant, voted to the All-NBA First Team, sets a Lakers record with 62 consecutive free throws over six games.

Lamar Odom records back-to-back triple-doubles against Golden State and Portland, becoming the seventh Laker all-time to post a triple-double.

2006-07

Kobe Still Has 50 Sense

Kobe Bryant's memorable 50-point-or-better scoring streak ended at four games. On the fifth day, he accounted for a mere 43 points in a 115-113 Lakers victory over the Golden State Warriors.

By MIKE BRESNAHAN
March 24, 2007

Several hours before he dipped another toe into historic waters, Kobe Bryant looked up sleepily while getting a pregame therapeutic massage.

He'd just heard someone in the Lakers' locker room say he needed 118 points Friday against the New Orleans Hornets to tie Wilt Chamberlain for most points ever in a four-game span. He weighed the comment with a slight smile, shook his head, and buried his face back under a towel.

He didn't get 118, but continued his spree with another 50, becoming the first player since Chamberlain in 1962 to accrue four consecutive games of at least 50 points.

He pushed and prodded the Lakers to a fourth consecutive victory, a 111-105 decision over the Hornets that tied their season-high winning streak. They are now two games ahead of the Denver Nuggets for sixth place in the Western Conference.

Bryant's outside shot was again almost infallible—16-for-29 shooting—and he played all but 1 minute 8 seconds.

Afterward, Coach Phil Jackson revealed the possible incentive for Bryant's recent binge.

"Do you remember there was a suspension about two weeks ago?" Jackson asked. "I think there's some motivation behind that.

"I don't know if we'd like to have that suspension all the time to have to work through, but I think there's some things there that motivate him in a certain sense. He's got that kind of passion."

Bryant was livid when the NBA threw a second one-game suspension at him two weeks ago

for striking another player after taking a shot. His tone that day was overcast, his sentences clipped and edgy when talking with reporters.

Fast-forward to Friday at New Orleans Arena, after Bryant's fourth game in a scoring string that now reads 65-50-60-50.

"The thing that was frustrating for me is that people were talking about me as a dirty player, which to me was pretty insulting," Bryant said.

"That's something I don't need to do. From that aspect, to have people talking about something else besides that is a much better feeling."

Indeed, people are talking.

He is now only the second player in league history to score 50 or more points in four consecutive games. Chamberlain had five consecutive 50-plus games in 1962, including his famous 100-point game.

Chamberlain also had seven consecutive games of 50 or more points, the longest streak in NBA history, in December 1961. Bryant spoke reverently after Friday's game, saying he initially associated Chamberlain with an acting role in the 1980s movie "Conan the Destroyer."

"When I was 6, I just knew him as Bombaata . . . I didn't know him as Wilt Chamberlain," Bryant said. "Then as I got older, I started understanding what he was all about as a basketball player."

Jackson also joined in the nostalgic mood when asked to compare Bryant to Michael Jordan, who had a three-game streak of 50 or more points in April 1987.

"It's phenomenal. It's incredible," Jackson said. "He's shooting [outside] more than Michael was. Michael was probably doing more post-up, more penetration, more at-the-basket kind of stuff.

"But Kobe's doing a whole range of things. I

Heels up during his streak of 50-plus games, Kobe Bryant goes up for a score while all five Memphis Grizzlies, including Pau Gasol (right), look on.

think his shooting has just been remarkable, the way he is raising up over people and knocking the ball down."

Bryant and Jackson tugged at each other throughout the game, Jackson asking if he need- ed a breather and Bryant declining the offer . . . Said Bryant: "I told Phil during the game . . . 'I can go 48 [minutes] tonight.' I just feel really, really good." The Lakers were thankful. The streak con- tinues.

Bryant Puts Pressure on the Front Office

The Lakers hadn't won a playoff series since beating Minnesota in the 2004 Western Conference Finals and they were just coming off a first round drubbing in five games at the hands of the Phoenix Suns. Kobe Bryant had seen enough and he made it clear—it was time for change. The pressure and trade requests continued through the off-season to the point that Bryant later acknowledged, "I thought I'd be in Chicago." But he stayed and the pieces, including Andrew Bynum, a player Bryant would have traded, began to come together.

By MIKE BRESNAHAN
May 5, 2007

The Lakers rolled uneasily through their final day of exit meetings, as Kobe Bryant reiterated his increasing frustration and General Manger Mitch Kupchak suggested that only one player was considered untouchable for off-season trade talks—the same player prodding upper management to improve the team.

Still simmering after the Lakers' first-round loss to Phoenix, Bryant voiced another degree of dissatisfaction during meetings Friday with Kupchak and Coach Phil Jackson, an unhappiness he later repeated publicly with such firmness that it made his blunt postgame appeal Wednesday ("Do something, and do it now") look like a minor request.

"I just told [Kupchak] this summer's about getting us to an elite level, doing whatever it takes to make it happen," Bryant said. "This is a competitive city. We're used to winning titles, not just winning games and being in the first round. We want to win championships. Now's the time.

"That's one of the things when I re-signed here, they promised they would build a contender and build a contender now. I don't want to have to wait any more than I already have." ...

Bryant, who will turn 29 in August, has a no-trade clause in his contract for at least one more season and remains the franchise's cornerstone, which means the Lakers will try to surround him with more talented pieces. He has four years and $88.6 million left on his contract but can terminate his deal after the 2008-09 season and leave two years and $47.8 million on the table, an unlikely event.

Kupchak, asked if every Laker was available in trade talks this off-season, singled out the one obvious selection and left others unmentioned.

"We're going to build the team around Kobe," Kupchak said.

That left 19-year-old center Andrew Bynum and oft-injured but productive forward Lamar Odom on the unprotected list.

It won't be easy to change the look of the Lakers, even though Bryant said his patience was currently "about as short as my 1-year-old daughter."

If the yet-to-be-determined salary cap is placed at $55 million next season, the Lakers would already be $3.4 million over it, meaning the only notable free-agent tool at their disposal would again be the mid-level exception, worth about $30 million over five years and offered to all teams that are over the salary cap. (The Lakers can sign free agent Luke Walton without affecting their cap status.)

In other words, the Lakers can make drastic steps only via trades, which means Kupchak could have a busy off-season.

"We understand there's no magic wand you can wave and make things happen," Kupchak said. "But we're going to be as aggressive as we've always been to get this team back to championship-level basketball."

Kupchak also acknowledged Bryant's frustration.

"I don't think anybody who's been with this organization—the Buss family, myself, Phil—feels any different," Kupchak said. "We feel the exact same way. Being in the first round or losing in the first round is not what we want to accomplish. We feel that we owe and want to provide more to the city than that."

Adding to the tension is the fact that Bryant isn't getting any younger.

"Obviously there's a window," Bryant said. "I feel fine physically. The important thing to me is winning now. It's not waiting, this, that and the other ...

"I don't play for anything but a championship. I want to get into the pocket with this city, where we, going into the season, believe that we have a shot at winning this whole thing."

Bryant couldn't predict whether big-name players such as Jermaine O'Neal or Kevin Garnett could be acquired by the Lakers during the off-season.

"I don't know," he said. "I just voiced my opinion. Now it's on them to do their job and go out there and try to make something happen."

2006-07 Season Highlights

Andrew Bynum becomes the all-time youngest Laker (19 years, 11 days) to get a double-double, with 20 points and 14 rebounds on November 17, 2006.

Ronny Turiaf, who had open heart surgery the year before, lifts the Lakers (23 points, nine rebounds) to victory over Golden State on November 1.

The Lakers defeat the Celtics on January 31, as Kobe Bryant gets 43 points, eight rebounds, and eight assists as fans in Boston chant "Kobe" and "MVP."

Andrew Bynum (left, in 2006) was an early target of concern from Kobe Bryant, the Lakers' 2007 All-Star MVP who urged management to improve the roster. But Bynum stayed and responded well before being injured.

The Lakers defeat the Dallas Mavericks on January 7 (101-98), ending Dallas' 13-game win streak, and giving Phil Jackson his 900th career win.

The Lakers sign first-round draft pick Jordan Farmar (left) and free agent Vladimir Radmanovic (right).

The Lakers' Luke Walton starts 60 games, averaging 11.4 points a game.

2007-08

Kupchak Broke Ice, Got a Gem

Pau Gasol took no time to fit in with the Lakers, contributing 24 points and 12 rebounds in his debut, a 105-90 victory over the New Jersey Nets. The team went on to finish the regular season 22-5 with Gasol in the lineup and reach the 2008 NBA Finals.

By MIKE BRESNAHAN
February 3, 2008

WASHINGTON—Tracked down at home late Friday night, Mitch Kupchak sounded relaxed and hopeful after pulling off the biggest NBA trade so far this season. A few hours after the landscape of the Western Conference shifted and shook, the Lakers' general manager discussed the inner workings of the Pau Gasol trade and what he expected from the newest acquisition...

The Lakers acquired Gasol and a second-round pick in 2010 from the Memphis Grizzlies for Kwame Brown, rookie guard Javaris Crittenton, first-round picks in 2008 and 2010, the draft rights to 2007 second-round pick Marc Gasol and retired guard Aaron McKie.

The desire to make a trade began when the Lakers struggled in the aftermath of Andrew Bynum's knee injury.

"Three weeks ago, we would not have made a deal," Kupchak said by phone. "But when Andrew went down, we didn't want to give away eight weeks. Lo and behold, Pau was available ..."

"It's hard trying to make a deal," Kupchak said. "It's like moving a glacier. As late as [Thursday] afternoon, it was dead, and then it came around quickly that night and we were able to finish the deal Friday morning."

Gasol, 27, arrived in Washington late Saturday after passing a physical earlier in the day in Los An-

geles. He probably won't play today after missing three of his last four games with the Grizzlies because of a sore back. "He'd be totally uninitiated," Coach Phil Jackson said.

Gasol, who was averaging 18.9 points, 8.8 rebounds and three assists a game for Memphis, said his Lakers debut probably would be Tuesday at New Jersey.

"I think he's going to fit because he knows how to play and he's a very good passer," Kupchak said. "I'm not sure I have to elaborate on his ability to score and rebound. He's unselfish and he has a presence that he knows how to play the game."

The move was decisive, and it signaled the end of the Brown experiment, a herky-jerky experience for the team since his arrival from Washington in August 2005 for Caron Butler and Chucky Atkins.

Mitch Kupchak

Brown averaged 7.4 points and 6.2 rebounds in 136 games with the Lakers and was booed at a home game against Phoenix last month after a series of turnovers and missed shots...

As with many big transactions, there's often buyer's remorse, which Kupchak acknowledged. It may not look like the Lakers gave up a lot to get Gasol, but they were cognizant of the unknown future—the loss of Crittenton and the first-round picks.

Kupchak said team officials were "concerned we gave up future talent, but we want to win today."

Assuming the Lakers continue an upward trajectory over the next few seasons, the draft picks they traded will be toward the end of the first round, making the loss of Crittenton the foremost thing on their minds.

"I think he has a chance to be a really, really good player," Kupchak said...

There were other notable reactions to the trade. From Lamar Odom: "We felt like we could compete for a championship with the team we had. With this addition, hopefully that dream comes true."

The addition of Pau Gasol in 2008 gave the Lakers a force in the middle.
He averaged 18.8 points a game in his first season for L.A.

Ronny Turiaf, sandwiched between Sasha Vujacic (left) and Luke Walton, is the center of the fun on the Lakers' 2008 Western Conference championship team that kept things light.

West Champions Stay Loose

"A gift," is what Los Angeles Times columnist Bill Plaschke called the Lakers' 2008 run to a Western Conference Finals' title. "An unexpected present slowly unwrapped to reveal constant surprises . . ." Plaschke recounted Ronny Turiaf's handshakes and dances from the bench, "Sasha Vujacic's stalk, Pau Gasol's stork, Jordan Farmar's cockiness, Derek Fisher's calm," and each of the players' attention to Lamar Odom's focus. Coach Phil Jackson summed up: "In past years, there was a certain sense that they weren't playing up to their potential. This team, they're trying to play up to their potential, and they're doing it, and that makes it much more of a joy."

By MIKE BRESNAHAN
May 30, 2008

The odyssey began on the shores of Honolulu, the Lakers convening for training camp without knowing what awaited them, other than a slew of grim possibilities.

Maybe Kobe Bryant would stay with the Lakers. Maybe he wouldn't. Maybe the Lakers would make the playoffs. Maybe they wouldn't.

But the purple and gold confetti fell again Thursday, this time with particular meaning.

The Lakers became the Western Conference champions, completing an implausible seven-month run with a 100-92 victory Thursday over the San Antonio Spurs at Staples Center.

After pushing through the tightest regular-season race in league history, the Lakers finished off the defending NBA champions, outscoring them by 21 points over the final three quarters and winning the West finals, four games to one . . .

A year ago today, Bryant publicly asked to be traded, but on Thursday, he had 39 points on 16-for-30 shooting, driving daggers into the Spurs again and again with 17 fourth-quarter points . . .

Jerry West, who put together more than his share of Lakers champions, presented the conference trophy to General Manager Mitch Kupchak, a symbolic gesture that was more than just the passing of a silver ball.

It was a reminder of all the franchise had been through over the past year.

And what was still ahead.

"As I told the players, there's nothing like losing the Finals for a negative feeling after you've played as well as you've played, not to finish the job up," Phil Jackson said . . .

Not that the Lakers didn't have fun when the West officially became theirs.

There was excitement in the locker room. Even joy. Players ribbed Sasha Vujacic for drilling a meaningless three-pointer at the buzzer. They soaked in the concept of being four victories away from the franchise's 15th title.

"We're a bunch of kids, so we enjoyed it," Bryant said. "We laughed, joked around, clowned around. . . . We are kind of a goofy bunch." . . .

At first, it looked like the Lakers were playing themselves into another trip to San Antonio, for Game 6.

They made only seven of 24 shots (29.2%) in the first quarter and trailed, 28-15. The Spurs led by as many as 17 points in the second quarter before the Lakers cut it to six at halftime, 48-42.

They kept chipping away until Luke Walton's three-pointer with 9:38 to play gave them the lead for good, 70-68, on the way to their 29th NBA Finals appearance.

"Never a dull moment with these boys," Jackson said.

Kobe Bryant couldn't leave soon enough as the 2008 Finals' celebration starts early for Celtics Coach Doc Rivers and two of his stars, Paul Pierce (left) and Kevin Garnett.

Buried in the Garden

Anticipating the Lakers-Celtics matchup in the 2008 Finals, the Los Angeles Times' *Mark Heisler, in a June 4 column, took readers through the history of the NBA's greatest rivalry, "encompassing all human emotions, starting, of course, with hate."... Yet, Heisler wrote: "Happily, the fear and loathing ran second to respect that grew into reverence among the participants, or at least some of them... After the Celtics' Game 7 victory in 1969, John Havlicek hugged [Jerry] West, who played for the Lakers with a sore hamstring wrapped like the leg of a mummy, telling him, 'I love you.'... Bill Russell flew out for West's farewell ceremony, announcing, 'If I could have one wish in life granted, it would be that you would always be happy.'... When Larry Bird retired, [Magic] Johnson flew East and donned a Celtics jersey for his retirement ceremony, whereupon Bird told him, 'Magic, get out of my dreams!' Bird presented Johnson at his Hall of Fame induction, noting, 'I was going to speak from my heart but, man, he broke my heart so many times, do I have anything left?' Sentiment ended at the tipoff. After the Celtics' Game 4 win in the Forum in the 1984 Finals, Bird, on the bus, saw Johnson*

slouch past, looking devastated. Said Bird later: 'I thought, Suffer.' "... And in 2008, the Lakers did.

By MIKE BRESNAHAN
June 18, 2008

BOSTON—Beaten L.A.

The Lakers came to their final resting place in the frenzied home of their most hated historical rival, drifting far from victory in a 131-92 Game 6 loss to the Boston Celtics that was every bit as uneven as the score indicated.

Looking nothing like the team that ripped through the Western Conference, the Lakers were yanked apart at the seams... in one of the most decisive games in NBA Finals history.

The Celtics won the series, 4-2, and took their 17th NBA championship, three more than the Lakers, in front of a jubilant crowd Tuesday at TD Banknorth Garden. The most one-sided game in Finals history remained a 42-point victory by Chicago over Utah (96-54) in 1998.

Game 4 will be the one that bothers the Lakers over the next 3½ months, a lost

24-point lead... but Tuesday night will also sting, the Celtics leading by as many as 43 in the final minutes...

Bryant spoke in short, clipped sentences after the game, frustration evident in his words and posture: "Just upset more than anything... But I'm proud of the way that we performed all year... At the same time, understand that second place just means you're the first loser."

Bryant... again shot poorly in Game 6—22 points on seven-for-22 shooting... For the series, he averaged 25.7 points and shot only 40.5%.

"Kobe started off that game with a hot hand and then I think his legs, you could see his shot was flat," Lakers Coach Phil Jackson said...

How bad was it? The "Hey, Hey, Hey, Goodbye" chant began with five minutes left.

Jackson tried to be positive afterward, recapping a season that included the Western Conference championship and Bryant's first MVP trophy. "We suffered injuries and survived a season and rebuilt our team and came back and had a great playoff run until the Celtics were able to extinguish that hope," Jackson said.

2008-09

Lakers Finally Get a Taste of Redemption

Season Record

W65-L17 (.793)
Division: 1st
NBA Champion

Coach

Phil Jackson

Players

Jordan Farmar

Derek Fisher

Sun Yue

Shannon Brown

Kobe Bryant

Sasha Vujacic

Trevor Ariza

Adam Morrison

Luke Walton

Lamar Odom

Pau Gasol

Josh Powell

Andrew Bynum

Didier Ilunga-
Mbenga

Vladimir
Radmanovic

Chris Mihm

The Lakers needed only five games against Orlando, but two went into overtime and one required a historic, frozen-in-time shot. "This wasn't just about one year," said Luke Walton. "This was about a lot of years."

By BILL PLASCHKE
June 15, 2009

Kobe Bryant scratched at it until it bled. Derek Fisher clawed at it until it hurt. The rest of them dug and dug until it finally, willfully, wonderfully disappeared.

The Lakers' seven-year itch is gone.

Awash in relief and redemption, Los Angeles' cornerstone sports franchise is once again champion of the NBA.

For the 15th time in franchise history, the fourth time this decade and the first time since 2002, the Lakers celebrated Sunday night with a title that was a tribute to reinvention and resilience.

Not to mention calisthenics, with Kobe Bryant leaping and pumping his right arm . . . before being mobbed by teammates after his team's clinching 99-86 victory over the Orlando Magic in the NBA Finals.

"This feels like a dream," said Bryant . . . "This doesn't feel real."

The four-games-to-one victory dripped not only of champagne, but history.

Phil Jackson becomes the greatest championship coach in NBA history, his 10th title surpassing the nine titles won by the Boston Celtics' Red Auerbach . . .

Bryant, the Finals MVP, becomes possibly the most unburdened player in NBA history as he finally wins a title without former teammate and nemesis Shaquille O'Neal, who had earlier won one without Bryant.

"I just don't have to hear that criticism, that idiotic criticism, anymore," said Bryant . . .

Sitting with a Moet-soaked T-shirt in the interview room underneath Amway Arena, Bryant shook his head, grinning and chuckling, the taut and tough leader finally admitting that the Shaq rap ripped him.

"It was . . . just annoying . . . I would cringe every time," he said . . .

There was also a milestone of sorts reached by owner Jerry Buss, who becomes the best sports owner of the 21st century.

The Lakers' fourth title since 2000 is more during that span than any other franchise in any other major sport, with this latest occurring after a reinvention that only Hollywood could love.

Since their last title in 2002, the Lakers have lived through the trading of one superstar, the trial of another superstar, three coaching changes, a historically blown first-round playoff series against Phoenix, a completely choked Finals against Boston and general daily turmoil . . .

Last year, the Lakers were outscored 34-15 in the second quarter before being run out of the Finals in a 39-point loss.

This year, the Lakers outscored the Magic 30-18 in the second quarter before cruising to the crown . . .

In that second quarter, we learned exactly who the Lakers were, as at one point they outscored the Magic 16-0 . . .

Fisher hit a three-pointer. Bryant stole the ball and found Trevor Ariza for another three-pointer . . . Bryant scored on a running jump shot, grabbed another defensive rebound, found Ariza for another three-pointer.

A twisting steal by Lamar Odom led to a Fisher layup. A diving steal by Ariza led to an Ariza free throw.

Yet another steal by Ariza led to a fastbreak in which the ball pinged from Laker to Laker to Laker until Odom scored on a scooping layup . . .

The road began in the summer of 2004 when Buss, angry at O'Neal's contract demands, traded the legendary center . . .

Weary of the hassles and feeling unloved by ownership, Phil Jackson also left the team . . . The results were madness, and in 2004-05 the Lakers didn't even make the playoffs . . .

General Manager Mitch Kupchak . . . remained steady in his vision and Bryant slowly grew up.

The first piece arrived from Miami in the deal for Shaquille O'Neal: career underachiever Odom. Then . . . Buss . . . paid Jackson $10 million a season to return.

Then . . . Bryant blasted the organization and said if the team wasn't improved, he wanted to be traded . . .

But again the general manager remained steady, answering Bryant's pleas by reacquiring Fisher while trading for Ariza and Pau Gasol.

"Got a new point guard, got a new wing, got a Spaniard, and then it was all good," Bryant said. "I had a bunch of Christmas presents that came early."

All those presents were finally opened Sunday night, Odom screaming, Gasol waving, wonder everywhere, the itch scratched, the . . . the journey complete.

Sasha Vujacic (18) gets no resistance from Orlando's Dwight Howard under the basket as the Lakers rout the Magic, 99-86, in Game 5 of the 2009 Finals to take the franchise's 15th title, including 10 in L.A.

Derek Fisher Cements Status in Lakers Lore

At 34, Derek Fisher delivered two of the biggest moments of the 2009 Finals.

By BILL PLASCHKE
June 12, 2009

Typical Fish.

At the end of the most indelible game of his enduring Lakers career, Derek Fisher disappeared.

He was swallowed by the long limbs of Lamar Odom, the long embrace of Andrew Bynum, the long hair of Sasha Vujacic.

His bald head was hidden in somebody's warmup jacket. His short arms were wrapped in somebody's giant ones.

After both tying and winning a game that will propel his team to an NBA championship, he was immediately enveloped not by camera lights but teammates, lost not in glamour but love, the most unassuming Laker never even having a chance to pump a fist.

Typical Fish.

Don't worry, after what happened Thursday night in front of a crowd that was stunned into silence, you'll see him again.

After his two jaw-flooring three-pointers led the Lakers to a 99-91 overtime victory against the Orlando Magic in Game 4 of the NBA Finals, you'll now officially be seeing him forever.

You'll see him on the firetruck at what is almost certain to be a championship parade after the Lakers took a 3-1 lead in the series . . .

You'll see him in constant video replays celebrating two shots that were even bigger than his famous 0.4 bucket in the 2004 conference semifinals in San Antonio.

His first shot, with 4.6 seconds remaining in regulation, tied the score. His second shot, with 31.3 seconds left in overtime, essentially won the game.

Only on the second shot did he crack a smile. Not once did he do a victory dance. After both shots he applauded not himself, but his teammates.

Typical Fish.

You also might see him in some sort of Lakers historical display outside Staples Center one day, although if it was a proper representation, his likeness wouldn't be in the front with Magic Johnson, it will be back by the loading dock with the rest of the working folk . . .

"It's not just about talent, it's about character, and he's a person of high character . . . not only in just his gamesmanship but also his intestinal fortitude," said Coach Phil Jackson.

He was all those things Thursday on a night when, after stomping all over the Magic, he showed up at his news conference in a pin-striped suit with white designer tennis shoes and no socks.

Typical Fish.

When asked where he would rank these shots in his career—13 years total, 10 with the Lakers—he laughed.

"Maybe 100, 101, something like that?" he said. "No, I mean, obviously . . . it's at the top."

It's at the top because, as the Lakers walked on to the court with the ball and a three-point deficit in the final seconds of regulation, Fisher was at rock bottom.

During the game, he had missed his previous five three-point attempts.

Yet he wasn't going to stop shooting.

"You know, I have a responsibility to my team that if I'm going to be on the floor, then I have to make a difference," he said.

A couple of facts.

During the postseason, he had been ripped by fans and media alike for being too old and slow, his most noticeable moment being a cheap shot of Houston's Luis Scola.

Yet he wasn't going to stop shooting.

"Now it's age, before it was other things in terms of not being able to shoot or not tall enough," he said. "I've always used those things as motivation to work even harder."

That hard work showed in his score-tying shot . . . when he saw that Jameer Nelson was backing away.

Incidentally, nice strategy Orlando, backing away when you could have fouled to prevent a three-point shot . . .

The ball swished through . . . and the game went into overtime.

"That's what it's about," said Bryant. "That's what the journey is about."

Ah, but the journey was just starting, completed by Fisher winning it near the end of overtime with a Kobe-like three-pointer . . . to give the Lakers a 94-91 lead . . .

And, yes, he smiled.

"I just sensed that was the dagger," he said . . .

Even Robert Horry never hit consecutive shots this big.

"No, I definitely don't compare myself to Robert Horry," said the unwitting hero, laughing. "I'm quite a few rings shy of where he stands."

Never about starring, always about winning.

Typical Fish.

2008-09 Season Highlights

Kobe Bryant is named All-NBA First Team, NBA All-Defensive First Team, and All-Star Game MVP.

Pau Gasol leads the Lakers in rebounds, averaging 9.6 per game.

The Lakers beat the Boston Celtics on December 25, ending their franchise-record 19-game winning streak.

Derek Fisher gets some space and makes Jameer Nelson (14) and Orlando pay. Fisher's game-tying three-point shot with 4.6 seconds left in regulation sent the game into overtime, where he hit another big three-pointer.

The Lakers defeat the Utah Jazz with 22 points from Andrew Bynum and 20 from Pau Gasol, getting their 65th victory to tie the 1986-87 season for the third best in franchise history.

Trevor Ariza's three-point shooting improves to 47.6% in playoffs, and he breaks open Game 5 of the NBA Finals with 11 points in the second quarter.

What next for the Lakers? Even after winning the title, Lakers officials take no break, reaching an agreement with Ron Artest while Ariza leaves for Houston.

THE LAKERS • 225

Kobe Arrives, but He's Always Been Here

With the Lakers' 2009 championship, Kobe Bryant left no doubt that he's one of the shining stars of the basketball universe.

By MARK HEISLER
June 16, 2009

Remember Shaq and Kobe? Now it's Kobe and Shaq. Actually, they're tied with four NBA titles apiece, but there's no doubt whose time this is ... finally ... with Kobe Bryant, who's 30 to Shaquille O'Neal's 37, on a young powerhouse, as opposed to being shopped around the league.

The Lakers won more than a title Sunday, which ranked with such watershed moments as the first one they won in Los Angeles in 1972; their first with Magic Johnson in 1980; and their first over the Boston Celtics in 1985.

This marks their return from a post-Shaq fall, and raises Phil Jackson above all coaches. Of course, it was only seven seasons between titles, however agonizing, and Jackson wasn't worried about his standing among coaches.

Above all, it marks the arrival of Bryant as a universally acknowledged all-time great, conferring a legitimacy that was withheld all his career.

Nakedly ambitious, oblivious to others' sensibilities, learning every lesson the hardest possible way, Bryant was, until recently, the most scorned NBA superstar since Wilt Chamberlain—in a much harder era to be scorned.

Now it's as if Kobe just went from zero titles to four—this one and the three he got with Shaq, which nobody mentioned before.

Making it as official as it gets, Hannah Storm of ESPN's "SportsCenter" announced Monday: "Kobe Bryant can now be placed on the list of the greatest players of all time." ...

Here's a news flash: Bryant has been this good for a long time.

He had this determination everyone is oohing and ahhing about as a rookie.

As far as making teammates better, he got over that hump while Shaq was still here, averaging a then-career-high 5.9 assists in 2002-03.

Winning was always everything and second place the same as last, but it's especially true on the level Bryant functions on, the quest to be the best ever.

Now, incredibly, after all he has been through, someone just lowered a stairway from heaven ...

Kobe and Shaq—then Shaq and Kobe—had a budding dynasty, but the operative word turned out to be budding, not dynasty.

In eight seasons, with what Boston General Manager Danny Ainge called the modern Wilt Chamberlain playing with the modern Michael Jordan, they won three titles.

Actually, by the time it was over, it seemed remarkable that they stayed together long enough to win any ...

With the Lakers supposedly on a mission after last spring's loss to the Celtics, this postseason started off as an awfully casual mission.

Lakers co-owner Magic Johnson watched their Game 4 humiliation by the Houston Rockets with the ABC studio crew in Bristol, Conn., smoke coming out of his ears.

"It's a new era," Johnson said last week, laughing. "This is their time. For me, I was embarrassed for them, to get blown out without Tracy McGrady, without Yao Ming. I would have gone into my room and not come out for two or three days."

These Lakers bristled at any suggestion they were embarrassed, with the blithe self-assurance they had shown all season.

Everywhere else, a sense of urgency was assumed, but there they were, still learning lessons and getting wake-up calls, until they finally felt what everyone else had all along: fear.

At that point Bryant, who had been oddly tranquil as counseled by Jackson, began baring his teeth—or, in other words, turned

back into Kobe Bryant.

The Houston debacle turned out to be their version of the 1985 Memorial Day Massacre in Boston, when the Lakers were embarrassed—er, taught a lesson they never forgot—and turned their entire history around ...

"It's just a special group," Derek Fisher said. "I think that's why you saw the emo-

tion that you saw tonight. We didn't act like we expected this to happen. I mean, we really celebrated like we didn't know this was coming."

The Lakers are a reflection of Jackson, but even more, Bryant. If they all had their own reasons for joy, Kobe's liberation was up there for everyone . . .

No one ever lived a life like Bryant's—

investing himself so completely, aiming for such heights, taking such falls, fighting back from such ignominy.

He's 30, and his career is finally what he thought it would be, at a time he can finally appreciate it—as opposed to the three titles he won by the time he was 23, when he couldn't imagine it being any other way.

The look tells all as 2009 NBA Finals' MVP Kobe Bryant rings up his fourth NBA title with 30 points, six rebounds, and five assists in the deciding game.

Pages 228-229: Bryant has Denver ducking in Game 6 of the West Finals.

ELGIN BAYLOR

LAKERS CAREER: 1958-1972
NUMBER RETIRED: November 9, 1983

All-time leading rebounder for the Lakers with 11,463.

Scored 23,149 points for the Lakers, the fourth-best all-time.

Seventh all-time on the Lakers with 3,650 assists.

Averaged 27.4 points and 13.5 rebounds per game for his career.

Named to the NBA All-Star Team 11 times.

Member of the All-NBA First Team 10 times.

Named one of the 50 greatest players in NBA history during the league's 50th anniversary season in 1996-97.

Led the Lakers in scoring in six different seasons.

NBA player for 14 years, all with the Lakers' franchise.

Averaged a then-club record 34.8 points a game in the Lakers' first season in Los Angeles. It remains second-best in team history.

Scored 71 points against the New York Knicks on November 15, 1960. At the time it was an L.A. franchise record. He was first NBA player to score more than 70 points in a game.

Recorded three of the top 10 single-game scoring efforts in team history, with 71, 64, and 63-point outings.

Scored a then-record 61 points in Game 5 of the 1962 NBA Finals against the Boston Celtics. He also had 22 rebounds in that game.

Scored 50 or more points in a game 17 times.

Grabbed 30 rebounds on Nov. 14, 1961, against Cincinnati.

Inducted into the Basketball Hall of Fame in 1977.

Named to the NBA 35th anniversary team, honoring the 11 best players during that span, including Lakers teammates Wilt Chamberlain and Jerry West.

WILT CHAMBERLAIN

LAKERS CAREER: 1968-1973
NUMBER RETIRED: November 9, 1983

Ranks first overall on the Lakers for career field-goal percentage at 60.5%.

Led the NBA in scoring and rebounding in the same season five times.

Averaged more than 18 rebounds a season four times for the Lakers.

Holds the Lakers' record for most rebounds in game with 42 against Boston on March 7, 1969.

Averaged a Los Angeles franchise-record 21.1 rebounds during the 1968–69 season.

Appeared in 13 NBA All-Star Games.

Named Most Valuable Player of the 1972 NBA Finals, averaging 14.7 points and 21 rebounds.

Member of the Lakers' 1971-72 championship team that won a record 33 consecutive games and a then-record 69 games overall.

Averaged 14.8 points and 19.2 rebounds in the 1971-72 championship season.

Led the NBA in rebounding 11 seasons, including four seasons with the Lakers.

Named NBA Most Valuable Player four times.

Member of All-NBA First Team seven times.

Member of the All-Defense First Team twice.

Scored 50-plus points in 118 games in his NBA career.

Inducted into the Basketball Hall of Fame in 1978.

Named one of the 50 greatest players in NBA history during the league's 50th anniversary season in 1996-97.

JERRY WEST

LAKERS CAREER: 1960-1974
NUMBER RETIRED: November 9, 1983

Career scoring average (27.0) ranks fourth all-time in NBA history.*

Playoff scoring average (29.1) ranks second all-time in NBA history, trailing only Michael Jordan.*

Lakers' all-time leading scorer (25,192).

Member of the All-NBA first team on 10 occasions.

Led the Lakers in scoring seven different seasons, highlighted by a career-best 31.3 during the 1965-66 campaign.

Member of the NBA's All-Defensive first team four times.

14-time NBA All-Star (All-Star Game MVP in 1972).

Member of the Lakers' 1972 NBA championship team.

Named MVP of the 1969 NBA Finals.

Established an NBA record by scoring 20-plus points in 25 consecutive NBA Finals games (since broken by Michael Jordan).

Holds the NBA record for most free throws made in a single season (840 in 1965-66).

Holds the NBA record for highest scoring average in a single playoff series (46.3 in 1965 six-game series vs. Baltimore).

Was the first draft choice in Los Angeles Lakers history (second pick overall in the 1960 NBA draft).

Led the NBA in assists during the 1971-72 season (9.7).

Inducted into the Basketball Hall of Fame in 1979.

14-year NBA veteran (all with the Lakers).

Was named one of the 50 greatest players in NBA history during the league's 50th anniversary season in 1996-97.

* All-time rankings apply to players who have completed their careers

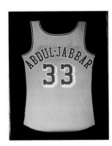

KAREEM ABDUL-JABBAR

LAKERS CAREER: 1975-1989
NUMBER RETIRED: March 20, 1989

All-time leading scorer in the NBA with 38,387 points, including 24,176 scored playing for the Lakers. He is second all-time in Los Angeles Lakers scoring.

Led the Lakers in scoring a club-record 11 consecutive seasons (1975-76 through 1985-86).

Averaged double-figures scoring in every season he played in the NBA.

Among the NBA all-time leaders in numerous categories, including minutes played (first, 57,446), blocked shots (third, 3,189) rebounds (third, 17,440), and free throws made (eighth, 6,712).

Set an NBA single-game record with 29 defensive rebounds on December 16, 1975, against the Detroit Pistons.

Selected to play in 19 NBA All-Star Games.

Led the NBA in blocked shots four times.

Sixth on the Lakers' all-time assists chart with 3,652 and sixth in steals with 983.

Played on five Lakers NBA championship teams.

Named NBA Most Valuable Player a record six times, including three with the Lakers (1976, 1977 and 1980).

Scored in double figures in an NBA record 787 consecutive games from December 4, 1977, through December 2, 1987.

All-NBA First Team 10 times, including six times with the Lakers; named to Second Team five times, including four times with the Lakers.

Played for the Lakers for 14 years in a 20-year NBA career.

Selected to the NBA's All-Defensive First Team on five occasions, including three times with the Lakers; and six times to the Second Team, including four with the Lakers.

Inducted into the Basketball Hall of Fame in 1995.

Named one of the 50 greatest players in NBA history during the league's 50th anniversary season in 1996-97.

EARVIN "MAGIC" JOHNSON

LAKERS CAREER: 1979-1991, 1995-1996
NUMBER RETIRED: February 16, 1992

Fourth on the NBA's career assists list with 10,141.

Led the NBA in assists four seasons.

Set a single-season club record of 13.1 assists per game during the 1983-84 season.

Led the NBA in steals in 1981 and 1982, and led the Lakers in steals nine times.

Shares the NBA playoff single-game record of 24 assists (May 15, 1984, against the Phoenix Suns; John Stockton did it in May 17, 1988, against the Lakers). Johnson also had 24 assists twice more in regular-season games. Twenty-four assists in a single game is the Lakers' record.

Led the Lakers in scoring for three seasons (1986-87, 1988-87, 1989-90).

Led the NBA in free-throw percentage (91.1%) in 1988-89.

Selected first overall by the Lakers in the 1979 NBA draft.

Three-time NBA Most Valuable Player (1987, 1989, 1990).

Twelve-time NBA All-Star (All-Star Game Most Valuable Player in 1990 and 1992).

Nine-time All-NBA First-Team selection (1983-91).

Played in nine NBA championship games.

Member of five NBA championship teams with the Lakers (1980, 1982, 1985, 1987, 1988).

First rookie to win NBA Finals' MVP award (1980).

Had 138 career triple-doubles.

Lakers averaged 59 victories per season during his career.

Named one of the 50 greatest players in NBA history during the league's 50th anniversary season in 1996-97.

JAMES WORTHY

LAKERS CAREER: 1982-1994
NUMBER RETIRED: December 10, 1995

First overall pick in the 1982 NBA draft.

Led the Lakers in scoring two consecutive seasons—1990-91 and 1991-92.

Played on three NBA championship teams with the Lakers (1985, 1987, 1988).

Twelve-year veteran of the NBA, all with the Los Angeles Lakers.

Most Valuable Player of the 1988 NBA Finals, when he averaged 22 points, 7.4 rebounds, and 4.4 assists. The Lakers beat the Detroit Pistons in a series that went seven games.

Posted a triple-double in the Lakers' Game 7 victory in 1988 with 36 points, 16 rebounds, and 10 assists.

Seven-time NBA All-Star from 1986-92.

Named to the NBA All-Rookie team in 1983.

Selected to the All-NBA Third Team twice, in 1990 and 1991.

Averaged 21.1 points and 5.2 rebounds per game in his post-season career (143 games).

Led the team in minutes played for three consecutive seasons (1988-89 through 1990-91).

Led the Lakers in field-goal percentage in 1985-86 and 1988-99.

Named one of the 50 greatest players in NBA history during the league's 50th anniversary season in 1996-97.

Ranks among all-time Los Angeles franchise leaders in several categories, including scoring (sixth, 16,320), steals (third, 1,041), field goals made (fifth, 6,878), and games played (ninth, 926).

Inducted into the Basketball Hall of Fame in 2003.

GAIL GOODRICH

LAKERS CAREER: 1965-1968, 1970-1976
NUMBER RETIRED: November 20, 1996

Ranks eighth all-time on the Lakers' scoring list with 13,044 points.

Ranks eighth all-time in assists in Lakers' history with 2,863.

Ranks seventh all-time among Los Angeles Lakers in free throws made with 2,830.

Led the Lakers in scoring for four consecutive seasons, 1971-72 through 1974-75.

Scored 53 points against Kansas City-Omaha on March 28, 1975.

Twice had streaks of 40 consecutive free throws without a miss.

Eight steals against Seattle on February 15, 1974.

Led the league in free throws made in the 1973-74 seasons with 508.

Ninth in the NBA in assists in the 1974-75 and 1975-76 seasons.

NBA All-Star selection in four consecutive seasons with the Lakers from 1972-1975.

Member of the 1971-72 championship team that won an NBA-record 33 consecutive games and had a regular season record of 69-13.

Named to the All-NBA First Team in 1973-74.

Inducted into the Basketball Hall of Fame in 1996.

Naismith Hall of Fame Has Strong Lakers Presence

Seven Los Angeles Lakers players, two coaches, one general manager, and one broadcaster have been inducted into the Naismith Memorial Basketball Hall of Fame in Springfield, Mass.

Elgin Baylor

He is considered one of the greatest forwards in NBA history. He averaged 27.4 points and 13.5 rebounds per game in his 14-year career with the Lakers. He led the Lakers to the NBA Finals eight times and was selected to the All-NBA First Team 10 times. Inducted in 1977.

Wilt Chamberlain

He was the dominating center on the Lakers' 1971-72 title team that won 69 regular-season games. He is the NBA's all-time rebounding leader with 23,924 and scored a record 100 points on March 2, 1962, for the Philadelphia Warriors against the New York Knicks. Inducted in 1979.

Jerry West

One of the greatest guards in NBA history, he was selected for the All-Star Game in each of his 14 years with the Lakers. He was the Lakers' first draft pick after the franchise moved to Los Angeles and is the team's all-time scoring leader with 25,192 points. Inducted in 1980.

Kareem Abdul-Jabbar

As a center, he was a nearly unstoppable force throughout his 20-year career in the NBA. Among his accomplishments were six NBA championships, six league MVP awards, 19 All-Star Game selections and two scoring titles. He is third all-time in blocked shots with 3,189. Inducted in 1995.

Gail Goodrich

The left-handed guard averaged 18.6 points for his career and was selected to the NBA All-Star Game five times. He led the Lakers in scoring with an average of 25.9 points per game in their 1971-72 championship season, when the team went 69-13 in the regular season. Inducted in 1996.

Earvin Johnson

The 6-foot-9 point guard was a member of five NBA championship teams, a league MVP three times, the NBA Finals' MVP three times, a nine-time member of the All-NBA First Team and a 12-time All-Star Game selection. He was also an Olympic gold medalist. Inducted in 2002.

James Worthy

The forward starred on three NBA title teams with the Lakers and was MVP of the 1988 Finals when he averaged 22 points, 7.4 rebounds, and 4.4 assists—including 36 points, 16 rebounds, and 10 assists in Game 7. He was a seven-time NBA All-Star and MVP of the 1982 NCAA Final Four. Inducted in 2003.

Bill Sharman

He was inducted into the Hall of Fame as both a player and as a coach. He coached the Lakers for five seasons, including the 1971-72 championship season. He won four NBA titles while playing guard for the Boston Celtics. Inducted as a player in 1975, as a coach in 2004.

Phil Jackson

After guiding the Lakers to three NBA championships from 1999 to 2004, he left for one year, returning in 2005. With the Lakers' 2009 championship, he has 10 NBA titles as head coach, the most ever, including six championships as head coach of the Chicago Bulls. Inducted in 2007.

Pete Newell

Inducted as a contributor, Newell was Lakers General Manager from 1972 to '76 and made the trade that brought Kareem Abdul-Jabbar from the Milwaukee Bucks in 1975. He coached Cal to the 1959 NCAA title and won a 1960 Olympic gold medal with a U.S. roster that included Jerry West. Inducted in 1979.

Chick Hearn

The broadcast voice of the Lakers from their arrival in Los Angeles until his death in 2002, he broadcast a record 3,338 games from November 21, 1965, to December 16, 2001. He coined the terms: "air-ball," "slam dunk," "ticky-tacky" and "dribble-drive." Inducted in 2003.

Los Angeles Lakers Championships

20

**PACIFIC DIVISION
CHAMPIONSHIPS**

1970-71	1982-83	1989-90
1971-72	1983-84	1999-00
1972-73	1984-85	2000-01
1973-74	1985-86	2003-04
1976-77	1986-87	2007-08
1979-80	1987-88	2008-09
1981-82	1988-89	

24

**WESTERN CONFERENCE
CHAMPIONSHIPS**

1961-62*	1972-73	1988-89
1962-63*	1979-80	1990-91
1964-65*	1981-82	1999-00
1965-66*	1982-83	2000-01
1967-68*	1983-84	2001-02
1968-69*	1984-85	2003-04
1969-70*	1986-87	2007-08
1971-72	1987-88	2008-09

*Western Division ... Above also represents NBA
Finals appearances

10

**NBA
CHAMPIONSHIPS**

1972	1988
1980	2000
1982	2001
1985	2002
1987	2009

Statistics do
not include the
Lakers' years in
Minneapolis.

Coaching Summary

L.A. LAKERS WIN/LOSS RECORD

Regular Season	2513-1459	(.633)
Playoffs	348-233	(.599)

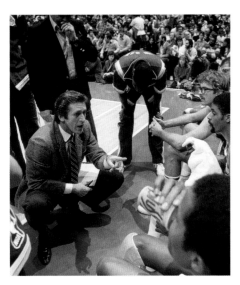

Pat Riley

L.A. LAKERS ALL-TIME COACHING SUMMARY

		REGULAR SEASON		PLAYOFFS		TOTAL	
	TITLES	W-L	PCT.	W-L	PCT.	W-L	PCT.
Fred Schaus	0	315-245	.563	33-38	.465	348-283	.552
Bill van Breda Kolff	0	107-57	.652	21-12	.636	128-69	.650
Joe Mullaney	0	94-70	.573	16-14	.533	110-84	.567
Bill Sharman	1	246-164	.600	22-15	.595	268-179	.600
Jerry West	0	145-101	.589	8-14	.364	153-115	.571
Jack McKinney	0	9-4	.692		—	9-4	.714
Paul Westhead	1	112-50	.691	13-6	.684	125-56	.691
Pat Riley	4	533-194	.733	102-47	.685	635-241	.725
Mike Dunleavy	0	101-63	.616	13-10	.565	114-73	.610
Randy Pfund	0	66-80	.452	2-3	.400	68-83	.450
Bill Bertka	0	2-1	.667		—	2-1	.667
Earvin Johnson	0	5-11	.313		—	5-11	.313
Del Harris	0	224-116	.659	17-19	.472	241-135	.641
Kurt Rambis	0	24-13	.658	3-5	.375	28-18	.609
Phil Jackson	4	496-242	.672	98-50	.662	594-292	.670
Rudy Tomjanovich	0	22-19	.537		—	22-19	.537
Frank Hamblen	0	12-29	.293		—	12-29	.293

Honor Roll*

LAKERS ALL-STARS/ TIMES SELECTED

Jerry West	14
Kareem Abdul-Jabbar	13
Earvin "Magic" Johnson	12
Kobe Bryant	11
Elgin Baylor	9
Shaquille O'Neal	7
James Worthy	7
Wilt Chamberlain	4
Gail Goodrich	4
Rudy LaRusso	3
Eddie Jones	2
Jamaal Wilkes	2
Cedric Ceballos	1
Archie Clark	1
A.C. Green	1
Rod Hundley	1
Darrall Imhoff	1
Norm Nixon	1
Nick Van Exel	1
Pau Gasol	1

ALL-STAR GAME HEAD COACHES

Pat Riley	(8)	1982, 1983, 1985, 1986, 1987, 1988, 1989, 1990
Fred Schaus	(4)	1963, 1964, 1966, 1967
Bill Sharman	(2)	1972, 1973
Phil Jackson	(2)	2000, 2009

ALL-NBA FIRST TEAM

Jerry West	(10)	1962, 1963, 1964, 1965, 1966, 1967, 1970, 1971, 1972, 1973
Elgin Baylor	(8)	1961, 1962, 1963, 1964, 1965, 1967, 1968, 1969
Earvin Johnson	(9)	1983, 1984, 1985, 1986, 1987 1988, 1989, 1990, 1991
Kobe Bryant	(7)	2002, 2003, 2004, 2006, 2007, 2008, 2009
Kareem Abdul-Jabbar	(6)	1976, 1977, 1980, 1981,1984, 1986
Shaquille O'Neal	(6)	1998, 2000, 2001, 2002, 2003, 2004
Gail Goodrich	(1)	1974

ALL-NBA SECOND TEAM

Kareem Abdul-Jabbar	(4)	1978, 1979, 1983, 1985
Kobe Bryant	(2)	2000, 2001
Jerry West	(2)	1968, 1969
Wilt Chamberlain	(1)	1972
Earvin Johnson	(1)	1982
Shaquille O'Neal	(1)	1999

ALL-NBA THIRD TEAM

Kobe Bryant	(2)	1999, 2005
James Worthy	(2)	1990, 1991
Shaquille O'Neal	(1)	1997
Pau Gasol	(1)	2009

Jerry West

BASKETBALL HALL OF FAME

	(Year of Induction)
Bill Sharman	1975
Elgin Baylor	1977
Wilt Chamberlain	1979
Pete Newell (contributor)	1979
Jerry West	1980
Kareem Abdul-Jabbar	1995
Gail Goodrich	1996
Earvin Johnson	2002
Chick Hearn (contributor)	2003
James Worthy	2003
Bill Sharman (coach)	2004
Phil Jackson (coach)	2007

Byron Scott

NBA MOST VALUABLE PLAYER

Kareem Abdul-Jabbar	(3)	1976, 1977, 1980
Earvin Johnson	(3)	1987, 1989, 1990
Kobe Bryant	(1)	2008
Shaquille O'Neal	(1)	2000

NBA FINALS MOST VALUABLE PLAYER

Earvin Johnson	(3)	1980, 1982, 1987
Shaquille O'Neal	(3)	2000, 2001, 2002
Jerry West	(1)	1969
Wilt Chamberlain	(1)	1972
Kareem Abdul-Jabbar	(1)	1985
James Worthy	(1)	1988
Kobe Bryant	(1)	2009

NBA COACH OF THE YEAR

Bill Sharman	(1)	1971-72
Pat Riley	(1)	1989-90
Del Harris	(1)	1994-95

NBA ALL-ROOKIE TEAM

Bill Hewitt	1968-69
Dick Garrett	1969-70
Jim Price	1972-73
Brian Winters	1974-75
Norm Nixon	1977-78
Earvin Johnson	1979-80
James Worthy	1982-83
Byron Scott	1983-84
Vlade Divac	1989-90
Nick Van Exel (second team)	1993-94
Eddie Jones	1994-95
Kobe Bryant (second team)	1996-97
Travis Knight (second team)	1996-97

NBA EXECUTIVE OF THE YEAR

Jerry West	1994-95

J. WALTER KENNEDY CITIZENSHIP AWARD

Michael Cooper	1985-86
Earvin Johnson	1991-92

NBA DEFENSIVE PLAYER OF THE YEAR

Michael Cooper	1986-87

NBA ALL-DEFENSIVE FIRST TEAM

Kobe Bryant	(7)	2000, 2003, 2004, 2006, 2007, 2008, 2009
Michael Cooper	(5)	1982, 1984, 1985, 1987, 1988
Jerry West	(4)	1970, 1971, 1972, 1973
Kareem Abdul-Jabbar	(3)	1979, 1980, 1981
Wilt Chamberlain	(2)	1972, 1973

NBA ALL-DEFENSIVE SECOND TEAM

Kareem Abdul-Jabbar	(4)	1976, 1977, 1978, 1984
Michael Cooper	(3)	1981, 1983, 1986
Shaquille O'Neal	(3)	2000, 2001, 2003
Kobe Bryant	(2)	2001, 2002
Eddie Jones	(2)	1998, 1999
A.C. Green	(1)	1989
Jim Price	(1)	1974
Jerry West	(1)	1969

* While with Lakers

All statistics are from the Los Angeles Lakers Media Guide and do not include the Minneapolis Lakers numbers. Special thanks to Josh Rupprecht of the Los Angeles Lakers.

Winning / Losing Streaks

ALL-TIME LONGEST REGULAR-SEASON WIN STREAKS U.S. PROFESSIONAL SPORTS HISTORY

33
1971-72
Los Angeles Lakers

26
1916
New York Giants

21
2006-08
New England Patriots

17
1992-93
Pittsburgh Penguins

LAKERS OWN PROFESSIONAL SPORTS ALL-TIME WINNING STREAK

The 1971-72 Los Angeles Lakers, who posted the second-best regular season record in NBA history (69-13), won a still-standing professional sports record 33 consecutive games from November 5, 1971, through January 7, 1972. The following is a game-by-game list of each victory:

Nov. 5	Baltimore	110-106
Nov. 6	@ Golden State	105-89
Nov. 7	New York	103-96
Nov. 9	@ Chicago	122-109
Nov. 10	@ Philadelphia	143-103
Nov. 12	Seattle	115-107
Nov. 13	@ Portland	130-108
Nov. 14	Boston	128-115
Nov. 16	Cleveland	108-90
Nov. 19	Houston	106-99
Nov. 21	Milwaukee	112-105
Nov. 25	@ Seattle	139-115
Nov. 26	Detroit	132-113
Nov. 28	Seattle	138-121
Dec. 1	@ Boston	124-111
Dec. 3	@ Philadelphia	131-116
Dec. 5	Portland	123-107

Dec. 8	@ Houston	125-120
Dec. 9	@ Golden State	124-111
Dec. 10	Phoenix	126-117
Dec. 12	Atlanta	105-95
Dec. 14	@ Portland	129-114
Dec. 17	Golden State	129-99
Dec. 18	@ Phoenix	132-106
Dec. 19	Philadelphia	154-132
Dec. 21	@ Buffalo	117-103
Dec. 22	@ Baltimore	127-120
Dec. 26	Houston	137-115
Dec. 28	Buffalo	105-87
Dec. 30	@ Seattle	122-106
Jan. 2	Boston	122-113
Jan. 5	@ Cleveland	113-103
Jan. 7	@ Atlanta	134-90
Jan. 9	@ Milwaukee	104-120 (L)

LONGEST WIN STREAK

(SINGLE SEASON)

33*	1971-72	16	1990-91
19	1999-00	15	1987-88
16	1999-00	14	1978-79

LONGEST HOME WIN STREAK

(SINGLE SEASON)

21	1976-77	17	1984-85
18	1979-80	17	1971-72
17	1988-89		

LONGEST HOME WIN STREAK

(COMBINED SEASONS)

27	2002-03	-	2003-04
24	1987-88	-	1988-89

LONGEST ROAD WIN STREAK

(SINGLE SEASON)

16*	1971-72
13	1972-73

* Denotes NBA Record

LONGEST LOSING STREAK

(SINGLE SEASON)

10	1993-94	6	1992-93
8	2004-05	6	1977-78
7	2006-07	6	1974-75
7	1991-92	6	1963-64
6	2004-05		

LONGEST HOME LOSING STREAK

(SINGLE SEASON)

6	1992-93	4	1983-84
5	2006-07	4	1969-70
5	2004-05	4	1991-92
5	1993-94 (TWICE)		

LONGEST ROAD LOSING STREAK

(SINGLE SEASON)

10	1963-64	9	1960-61
9	2004-05	8	1988-89
9	2003-04		

Jerry West

Season-By-Season Records

YEAR	COACH	LOS ANGELES REGULAR SEASON					PLAYOFFS	
		W-L	PCT	HOME	AWAY	NEUTRAL	W-L	ACHIEVEMENT
1960-61	Fred Schaus	36-43	.456	16-12	8-20	12-11	6-6	
1961-62	Fred Schaus	54-26	.675	26-5	18-13	10-8	7-6	West Champions
1962-63	Fred Schaus	53-27	.663	27-7	20-17	6-3	6-7	West Champions
1963-64	Fred Schaus	42-38	.525	24-12	15-21	3-5	2-3	
1964-65	Fred Schaus	49-31	.613	25-13	21-16	3-2	5-6	West Champions
1965-66	Fred Schaus	45-35	.563	27-11	13-21	4-3	7-7	West Champions
1966-67	Fred Schaus	36-45	.450	21-18	12-20	3-7	0-3	
1967-68	Bill van Breda Kolff	52-30	.634	30-11	18-19	4-0	10-5	West Champions
1968-69	Bill van Breda Kolff	55-27	.670	32-9	21-18	2-0	11-7	West Champions
1969-70	Joe Mullaney	46-36	.561	27-14	17-21	2-1	11-7	West Champions
1970-71	Joe Mullaney	48-34	.585	30-11	17-22	1-1	5-7	
1971-72	Bill Sharman	**69-13**	.841	36-5	31-7	2-1	12-3	NBA Champions
1972-73	Bill Sharman	60-22	.732	30-11	28-11	2-0	9-8	West Champions
1973-74	Bill Sharman	47-35	.573	30-11	17-24	--	1-4	
1974-75	Bill Sharman	30-52	.366	21-20	9-32	--	--	
1975-76	Bill Sharman	40-42	.488	31-10	9-32	--	--	
1976-77	Jerry West	**53-29**	.646	37-4	16-25	--	4-7	
1977-78	Jerry West	45-37	.549	29-12	16-25	--	1-2	
1978-79	Jerry West	47-35	.573	31-10	16-25	--	3-5	
1979-80	Jack McKinney (9-4) Paul Westhead (51-8)	60-22	.732	37-4	23-18	--	12-4	NBA Champions
1980-81	Paul Westhead	54-28	.659	30-11	24-17	--	1-2	
1981-82	Paul Westhead (7-4) Pat Riley (50-21)	57-25	.695	30-11	27-14	--	12-2	NBA Champions
1982-83	Pat Riley	58-24	.707	33-8	25-16	--	8-7	West Champions
1983-84	Pat Riley	54-28	.659	28-13	26-15	--	14-7	West Champions
1984-85	Pat Riley	62-20	.756	36-5	26-15	--	15-4	NBA Champions
1985-86	Pat Riley	62-20	.756	35-6	27-14	--	8-6	
1986-87	Pat Riley	**65-17**	.793	37-4	28-13	--	15-3	NBA Champions
1987-88	Pat Riley	**62-20**	.756	36-5	26-15	--	15-9	NBA Champions
1988-89	Pat Riley	57-25	.695	35-6	22-19	--	11-4	West Champions
1989-90	Pat Riley	**63-19**	.768	37-4	26-15	--	4-5	
1990-91	Mike Dunleavy	58-24	.707	33-8	25-16	--	12-7	West Champions
1991-92	Mike Dunleavy	43-39	.524	24-17	19-22	--	1-3	
1992-93	Randy Pfund	39-43	.476	20-21	19-22	--	2-3	
1993-94	Randy Pfund (27-37) Bill Bertka (1-1) Earvin Johnson (5-11)	33-49	.402	21-20	12-29	--	--	
1994-95	Del Harris	48-34	.585	29-12	19-22	--	5-5	
1995-96	Del Harris	53-29	.646	30-11	23-18	--	1-3	
1996-97	Del Harris	56-26	.683	31-10	25-16	--	4-5	
1997-98	Del Harris	61-21	.744	33-8	28-13	--	7-6	
1998-99	Del Harris (6-6) Bill Bertka (1-0) Kurt Rambis (24-13)	31-19	.620	18-7	13-12	--	3-5	
1999-00	Phil Jackson	**67-15**	.817	36-5	31-10	--	15-8	NBA Champions
2000-01	Phil Jackson	56-26	.683	31-10	25-16	--	15-1	NBA Champions
2001-02	Phil Jackson	58-24	.707	34-7	24-17	--	15-4	NBA Champions
2002-03	Phil Jackson	50-32	.610	31-10	19-22	--	6-6	
2003-04	Phil Jackson	56-26	.683	34-7	22-19	--	13-9	West Champions
2004-05	Rudy Tomjanovich (22-19) Frank Hamblen (12-29)	34-48	.415	22-19	12-29	--	--	
2005-06	Phil Jackson	45-37	.549	27-14	18-23	--	3-4	
2006-07	Phil Jackson	42-40	.512	25-16	17-24	--	1-4	
2007-08	Phil Jackson	57-25	.695	30-11	27-14	--	14-7	West Champions
2008-09	Phil Jackson	**65-17**	.793	36-5	29-12	--	16-7	NBA Champions

Bold denotes NBA's best regular-season record.

General Managers

LOUIS MOHS (1960-67)

Mohs moved with the team from Minneapolis. During his tenure as general manager, the Lakers made the playoffs every year and the NBA Finals four times. **Among notable players drafted:** Jerry West (1960), Leroy Ellis (1962), Gene Wiley (1962), Jim King (1963), Walt Hazzard (1964), Gail Goodrich (1965), Jerry Chambers (1966), John Block (1966), Archie Clark (1966).

FRED SCHAUS (1967-72)

Schaus was elevated to general manager in 1967. He is credited with building the 1971-72 team that gave the Los Angeles Lakers their first NBA title and made history with a 33-consecutive-game winning streak that same season. Wilt Chamberlain (1968) was his biggest acquisition. **Among notable players drafted:** Dick Garrett (1969), Willie McCarter (1969), Jim McMillian (1970).

PETE NEWELL (1972-76)

Newell served as the Lakers' general manager for four seasons after Schaus' departure for Purdue University. He helped engineer the trade that brought Kareem Abdul-Jabbar from Milwaukee to Los Angeles in 1975. **Among notable players drafted:** Kermit Washington (1973), Jim Chones (1973), Don Ford (1975).

BILL SHARMAN (1976-82; President, 1982-88)

Sharman became the team's general manager after Newell stepped down. Sharman built the foundation for the 1980s Showtime era with the first-round drafts of future Hall of Famers Magic Johnson in 1979 and James Worthy in 1982. **Among other notable players drafted:** Norm Nixon (1977), Michael Cooper (1978), Brad Holland (1979), Butch Carter (1980), Mike McGee (1981).

JERRY WEST (General Manager, 1982-94; Executive Vice President of Basketball Operations, 1994-2000)

West became general manager of the Lakers in 1982, when Worthy was drafted, after serving as head coach from 1976 to 1979 and as a special consultant from 1979 to 1982. West rebuilt and retooled the team's Showtime era that earned five NBA titles in the 1980s as well as bringing in Shaquille O'Neal and Kobe Bryant in 1996 and hiring Phil Jackson as head coach in 1999. **Among other notable players drafted:** A.C. Green (1985), Vlade Divac (1989), Elden Campbell (1990), Anthony Peeler (1992), Nick Van Exel (1993), Eddie Jones (1994), Derek Fisher (1996), Devean George (1999), Mark Madsen (2000).

MITCH KUPCHAK (General Manager, 1994-present)

Since Kupchak joined the front office in 1986, the Lakers have won six NBA titles. In February 2008, Kupchak pulled off one of his biggest trades, acquiring Pau Gasol from Memphis. **Among notable players drafted:** Brian Cook (2003), Luke Walton (2003), Sasha Vujacic (2004), Andrew Bynum (2005), Ronny Turiaf (2005), Jordan Farmar (2006).

Regular-Season Individual Records

MOST POINTS

Game	81	Kobe Bryant	vs. TOR	1/22/06
Half	55	Kobe Bryant	vs. TOR	1/22/06
Quarter	30	Kobe Bryant	vs. Utah	11/30/06
	30	Kobe Bryant	vs. DAL	12/20/05
Season	2,832	Kobe Bryant		2005-06
Career	25,192	Jerry West		1961-74

MOST FG MADE

Game	29	Wilt Chamberlain	vs. PHO	2/9/69
Half	18	Kobe Bryant	vs. TOR	1/22/06
Quarter	11	Kobe Bryant	vs. TOR	1/22/06
	11	Kobe Bryant	at SEA	2/2/99
Season	1,029	Elgin Baylor		1962-63
Career	9,935	Kareem Abdul-Jabbar		1976-89

MOST FG ATTEMPTED

Game	55	Elgin Baylor	vs. PHI	12/2/61
Half	28	Kobe Bryant	at BOS	11/17/02
	28	Elgin Baylor	at NY	11/15/60
Quarter	18	Elgin Baylor	at NY	11/15/60
Season	2,273	Elgin Baylor		1962-63
Career	20,173	Elgin Baylor		1959-72

HIGHEST FG PERCENTAGE

Game	1.000	Wilt Chamberlain (14-14)	vs. DET	3/11/69
Season	.727*	Wilt Chamberlain (min. 400 att.)		1972-73
Career	.605	Wilt Chamberlain (min. 2000 fgm)		1969-73

MOST FREE THROWS MADE

Game	23	Kobe Bryant	at NY	1/31/06
	23	Kobe Bryant	at CLE	1/30/01
Half	17	Kobe Bryant	at CLE	1/30/01
Quarter	14	Kobe Bryant	at Utah	2/26/07
Consecutive	62	Kobe Bryant		2005-06
Season	840*	Jerry West		1965-66
Career	7,160	Jerry West		1961-74

MOST FREE THROWS ATTEMPTED

Game	31	Shaquille O'Neal	vs. CHI	11/19/99
Half	20	Shaquille O'Neal	at GS	3/14/02
Quarter	15	Shaquille O'Neal	vs. LAC	11/5/00
Season	977	Jerry West		1965-66
Career	8,801	Jerry West		1961-74

FREE-THROW PERCENTAGE

Highest Game	1.000	Kobe Bryant (20-20)	at NY	2/2/09
Lowest Game (min. 10 att)	.000	Shaquille O'Neal (0-11)*	vs. SA	12/8/00
Season	.911	Earvin Johnson (min. 100 att.)	1988-89	
Career	.848	Earvin Johnson (min. 500 ftm)	1979-91,96	

MOST 3-PT FG MADE

Game	12*	Kobe Bryant	vs. SEA	1/7/03
Half	8*	Kobe Bryant	vs. WAS	3/28/03
Quarter	n/a	—	—	
Season	183	Nick Van Exel		1994-95
Career	1,204	Kobe Bryant		1996-present

* Denotes NBA Record

MOST 3-PT FG ATTEMPTED

Game	18	Kobe Bryant	vs. SEA	1/7/03
Half	n/a	—	-	
Quarter	n/a	—	-	
Season	518	Kobe Bryant		2005-06
Career	3,528	Kobe Bryant		1996-present

3-PT FIELD GOAL PERCENTAGE (MIN. 6 ATT.)

Game	1.000	Kobe Bryant (7-7)	vs. PHI	1/6/06
	1.000	Nick Van Exel (6-6)	vs. VAN	11/16/91
Season	.437	Sasha Vujacic (min. 100 att.)	2007-08	
Career	.378	Eddie Jones (min. 250 3fgm)	1994-99	

MOST REBOUNDS

Game	42	Wilt Chamberlain	vs. BOS	3/7/69
Half	27	Wilt Chamberlain	vs. BOS	3/7/69
Quarter	14	Happy Hairston	vs. PHI	11/15/74
	14	Wilt Chamberlain	vs. BOS	3/7/69
	14	Gene Wiley	vs. NY	11/5/62
Season	1,712	Wilt Chamberlain		1968-69
Career	11,463	Elgin Baylor		1959-72

MOST OFFENSIVE REBOUNDS (SINCE 1973-74)

Game	14	Shaquille O'Neal	at MEM	4/4/03
Half	9	Lamar Odom	vs. PHO	1/17/08
	9	Shaquille O'Neal	at MEM	4/4/03
	9	Happy Hairston	at CHI	2/16/75
Quarter	n/a	—	-	
Season	355	Happy Hairston		1973-74
Career	2,494	Kareem Abdul-Jabbar		1975-89

MOST DEFENSIVE REBOUNDS (SINCE 1973-74)

Game	29*	Kareem Abdul-Jabbar	vs. DET	12/14/75
Half	n/a	—	-	
Quarter	13*	Happy Hairston	vs. PHI	11/15/74
Season	1,111*	Kareem Abdul-Jabbar		1975-76
Career	7,785	Kareem Abdul-Jabbar		1975-89

MOST ASSISTS

Game	24	Earvin Johnson	vs. DEN	11/17/89
	24	Earvin Johnson	at PHO	1/9/90
Half	18	Earvin Johnson	vs. SEA	2/21/84
Quarter	12	Earvin Johnson	vs. SEA	2/21/84
Season	989	Earvin Johnson		1990-91
Career	10,141	Earvin Johnson		1979-91,96

MOST STEALS

Game	10	Jerry West	vs. SEA	12/7/73
Half	6	Kobe Bryant	vs. UTAH	2/13/06
	6	Eddie Jones	at PHI	11/26/96
	6	Eddie Jones	vs. BOS	12/26/95
	6	Sedale Threatt	at POR	3/3/92
	6	Jerry West	vs. SEA	12/7/73
Quarter	n/a	—	-	
Season	208	Earvin Johnson		1981-82
Career	1,724	Earvin Johnson		1979-91,96

MOST BLOCKED SHOTS

Game	17*	Elmore Smith	vs. POR	10/28/73
Half	11*	Elmore Smith	vs. POR	10/28/73
Quarter	6	Elmore Smith	vs. POR	10/28/73
Season	393	Elmore Smith		1973-74
Career	2,694	Kareem Abdul-Jabbar		1975-89

Season-By-Season Leaders

SCORING

		G	PTS	AVG
1960-61	Baylor	73	2538	34.8
1961-62	West	75	2310	30.8
1962-63	Baylor	80	2719	34.0
1963-64	West	72	2064	28.7
1964-65	West	74	2292	31.0
1965-66	West	79	2476	31.3
1966-67	West	66	1892	28.7
1967-68	Baylor	77	2002	26.0
1968-69	Baylor	76	1881	24.8
1969-70	West	74	2309	31.2*
1970-71	West	69	1859	26.9
1971-72	Goodrich	82	2127	25.9
1972-73	Goodrich	76	1814	23.9
1973-74	Goodrich	82	2076	25.3
1974-75	Goodrich	72	1630	22.6
1975-76	Abdul-Jabbar	82	2275	27.7
1976-77	Abdul-Jabbar	82	2152	26.2
1977-78	Abdul-Jabbar	62	1600	25.8
1978-79	Abdul-Jabbar	80	1903	23.8
1979-80	Abdul-Jabbar	82	2034	24.8
1980-81	Abdul-Jabbar	80	2095	26.2
1981-82	Abdul-Jabbar	76	1818	23.9
1982-83	Abdul-Jabbar	80	1717	21.5
1983-84	Abdul-Jabbar	80	1717	21.5
1984-85	Abdul-Jabbar	79	1735	22.0
1985-86	Abdul-Jabbar	79	1846	23.4
1986-87	Johnson	80	1909	23.9
1987-88	Scott	81	1754	21.7
1988-89	Johnson	77	1730	22.5
1989-90	Johnson	79	1765	22.3
1990-91	Worthy	78	1670	21.4
1991-92	Worthy	54	1075	19.9
1992-93	Threatt	82	1235	15.1
1993-94	Divac	79	1123	14.2
1994-95	Ceballos	58	1261	21.7
1995-96	Ceballos	78	1656	21.2
1996-97	O'Neal	51	1336	26.2
1997-98	O'Neal	60	1699	28.3
1998-99	O'Neal	49	1289*	26.3
1999-00	O'Neal	79	2344*	29.7*
2000-01	O'Neal	74	2125	28.7
2001-02	O'Neal	67	1822	27.2
2002-03	Bryant	82	2461*	30.0
2003-04	Bryant	65	1557	24.0
2004-05	Bryant	66	1819	27.6
2005-06	Bryant	80	2832*	35.4*
2006-07	Bryant	77	2430*	31.6*
2007-08	Bryant	82	2323*	28.3
2008-09	Bryant	82	2201	26.8

ASSISTS

		G	AST	AVG
1960-61	Baylor	73	371	5.1
1961-62	West	75	402	5.4
1962-63	Baylor	80	386	4.8
1963-64	West	72	403	5.6
1964-65	West	74	364	4.9
1965-66	West	79	480	6.1
1966-67	West	66	447	6.8
1967-68	Baylor	77	355	4.6
1968-69	West	61	423	6.9
1969-70	West	74	554	7.5
1970-71	West	69	655	9.5
1971-72	West	77	747	9.7*
1972-73	West	69	607	8.8
1973-74	Goodrich	82	427	5.2
1974-75	Goodrich	72	420	5.8
1975-76	Goodrich	75	421	5.6
1976-77	Allen	78	405	5.2
1977-78	Nixon	81	553	6.8
1978-79	Nixon	82	737	9.0
1979-80	Nixon	80	642	8.0
1980-81	Nixon	79	696	8.8
1981-82	Nixon	78	743	9.5
1982-83	Johnson	79	829*	10.5*
1983-84	Johnson	67	875	13.1*
1984-85	Johnson	77	968	12.6
1985-86	Johnson	72	907*	12.6*
1986-87	Johnson	80	977*	12.2*
1987-88	Johnson	72	858	11.9
1988-89	Johnson	77	988	12.8
1989-90	Johnson	79	907	11.5
1990-91	Johnson	79	989	12.5
1991-92	Threatt	82	593	7.2
1992-93	Threatt	82	564	6.9
1993-94	Van Exel	81	466	5.8
1994-95	Van Exel	80	660	8.3
1995-96	Van Exel	74	509	6.9
1996-97	Van Exel	79	672	8.5
1997-98	Van Exel	64	442	6.9
1998-99	D. Harper	45	187	4.2
1999-00	Bryant	66	323	4.9
2000-01	Bryant	68	338	5.0
2001-02	Bryant	80	438	5.5
2002-03	Bryant	82	481	5.9
2003-04	Payton	82	449	5.5
2004-05	Bryant	66	398	6.0
2005-06	Odom	80	443	5.5
2006-07	Bryant	77	413	5.4
2007-08	Bryant	82	441	5.4
2008-09	Bryant	82	399	4.9

REBOUNDS

		G	REB	AVG
1960-61	Baylor	73	1447	19.8
1961-62	Baylor	58	892	18.6
1962-63	Baylor	80	1146	14.3
1963-64	Baylor	78	936	12.0
1964-65	Baylor	74	950	12.8
1965-66	Ellis	80	735	9.2
1966-67	Imhoff	81	1080	13.3
1967-68	Baylor	81	1080	13.3
1968-69	Chamberlain	81	1712*	21.1*
1969-70	Hairston	56	687	12.3
1970-71	Chamberlain	82	1493*	18.2*
1971-72	Chamberlain	82	1572*	19.2*
1972-73	Chamberlain	82	1526*	18.6*
1973-74	Hairston	77	1040	13.5
1974-75	Hairston	74	1040	13.5
1975-76	Abdul-Jabbar	82	1383*	16.9*
1976-77	Abdul-Jabbar	82	1090*	13.3
1977-78	Abdul-Jabbar	62	801	12.9
1978-79	Abdul-Jabbar	80	1025	12.8
1979-80	Abdul-Jabbar	82	886	10.8
1980-81	Abdul-Jabbar	80	821	10.3
1981-82	Johnson	78	751	9.6
1982-83	Johnson	79	683	8.6
1983-84	Abdul-Jabbar	80	587	7.3
1984-85	Abdul-Jabbar	79	622	7.9
1985-86	Lucas	77	566	7.4
1986-87	Green	79	615	7.8
1987-88	Green	82	710	8.7
1988-89	Green	82	739	9.0
1989-90	Green	82	712	8.7
1990-91	Divac	82	666	8.1
1991-92	Green	82	762	9.3
1992-93	Divac	82	729	8.9
1993-94	Divac	79	851	10.8
1994-95	Divac	80	829	10.4
1995-96	Divac	79	679	8.6
1996-97	O'Neal	51	640	12.5
1997-98	O'Neal	60	681	11.4
1998-99	O'Neal	49	525	10.7
1999-00	O'Neal	79	1078	13.6
2000-01	O'Neal	74	940	12.7
2001-02	O'Neal	67	715	10.7
2002-03	O'Neal	67	742	11.1
2003-04	O'Neal	67	769	11.5
2004-05	Odom	64	653	10.2
2005-06	Odom	80	738	9.2
2006-07	Odom	56	547	9.8
2007-08	Odom	77	819	10.6
2008-09	Gasol	81	780	9.6

* Denotes NBA Leader

**Kobe
Bryant**

**Jerry
West**

**Elgin
Baylor**

**Magic
Johnson**

**Kareem
Abdul-Jabbar**

Season-By-Season Leaders

BLOCKED SHOTS

		G	BS	AVG
1973-74	Smith	81	393*	4.85*
1974-75	Smith	74	216	2.92
1975-76	Abdul-Jabbar	82	338*	4.12*
1976-77	Abdul-Jabbar	82	261*	3.18
1977-78	Abdul-Jabbar	62	185	2.98
1978-79	Abdul-Jabbar	80	316*	3.95*
1979-80	Abdul-Jabbar	82	280*	3.41*
1980-81	Abdul-Jabbar	80	228	2.85
1981-82	Abdul-Jabbar	76	207	2.72
1982-83	Abdul-Jabbar	79	170	2.15
1983-84	Abdul-Jabbar	80	143	1.79
1984-85	Abdul-Jabbar	79	162	2.05
1985-86	Abdul-Jabbar	79	130	1.65
1986-87	Abdul-Jabbar	78	97	1.24
1987-88	Abdul-Jabbar	80	92	1.15
1988-89	Abdul-Jabbar	74	85	1.15
1989-90	Divac	82	113	1.38
1990-91	Divac	82	127	1.55
1991-92	Campbell	81	159	1.96
1992-93	Divac	82	140	1.71
1993-94	Campbell	76	146	1.92
1994-95	Divac	80	174	2.18
1995-96	Campbell	82	212	2.59
1996-97	O'Neal	51	147	2.88
1997-98	O'Neal	60	144	2.40
1998-99	O'Neal	49	82	1.67
1999-00	O'Neal	79	239	3.03
2000-01	O'Neal	74	204	2.76
2001-02	O'Neal	67	137	2.04
2002-03	O'Neal	67	159	2.37
2003-04	O'Neal	67	166	2.48
2004-05	Mihm	75	108	1.44
2005-06	Mihm	59	73	1.24
2006-07	Bynum	82	128	1.20
2007-08	Bynum	35	72	2.06
2008-09	Odom	78	98	1.26

STEALS

		G	STL	AVG
1973-74	Price	82	157	1.91
1974-75	Allen	56	122	2.17
1975-76	Goodrich	75	123	1.64
1976-77	Chaney	81	140	1.73
1977-78	Nixon	81	140	1.73
1978-79	Nixon	82	201*	2.45
1979-80	Johnson	77	187	2.43
1980-81	Johnson	37	127	3.43*
1981-82	Johnson	78	208	2.67*
1983-84	Johnson	67	150	2.24
1984-85	Johnson	77	113	1.47
1985-86	Johnson	72	113	1.57
1986-87	Johnson	80	138	1.73
1987-88	Scott	81	155	1.91
1988-89	Johnson	77	138	1.79
1989-90	Johnson	79	132	1.67
1990-91	Worthy	78	104	1.33
1991-92	Threatt	82	168	2.05
1992-93	Threatt	82	142	1.73
1993-94	Threatt	81	110	1.36
1994-95	Jones	64	131	2.05
1995-96	Jones	70	129	1.84
1996-97	Jones	80	189	2.36
1997-98	Jones	80	160	2.00
1998-99	Jones	20	35	1.75
1999-00	Bryant	66	106	1.61
2000-01	Bryant	68	114	1.68
2001-02	Bryant	80	118	1.48
2002-03	Bryant	82	181	2.21
2003-04	Bryant	65	112	1.72
2004-05	Butler	77	110	1.43
2005-06	Bryant	80	147	1.84
2006-07	Parker	82	119	1.45
2007-08	Bryant	82	151	1.84
2008-09	Ariza	82	137	1.67

FIELD GOAL %

		FG	FGA	PCT
1960-61	Hawkins	310	719	.431
1961-62	LaRusso	516	1108	.466
1962-63	Barnett	547	1162	.471
1963-64	West	740	1529	.484
1964-65	West	822	1655	.497
1965-66	Boozer	365	754	.484
1966-67	Hawkins	275	572	.481
1967-68	West	476	926	.514
1968-69	Chamberlain	641	1099	.583*
1969-70	West	831	1673	.497
1970-71	Chamberlain	668	1226	.545
1971-72	Chamberlain	496	764	.649*
1972-73	Chamberlain	426	586	.727
1973-74	Hairston	385	759	.507
1974-75	Hairston	271	536	.506
1975-76	Abdul-Jabbar	914	1728	.529
1976-77	Abdul-Jabbar	888	1533	.579*
1977-78	Abdul-Jabbar	663	1205	.550
1978-79	Abdul-Jabbar	777	1347	.577
1979-80	Abdul-Jabbar	835	1383	.604
1980-81	Abdul-Jabbar	836	1457	.573
1981-82	Abdul-Jabbar	753	1301	.579
1982-83	Abdul-Jabbar	722	1228	.558
1983-84	McGee	347	584	.594
1984-85	Abdul-Jabbar	723	1207	.599
1985-86	Worthy	629	1086	.579
1986-87	Abdul-Jabbar	560	993	.564
1987-88	Abdul-Jabbar	480	903	.532
1988-89	Worthy	702	1282	.548
1989-90	Woolridge	306	550	.556
1990-91	Divac	360	637	.565
1991-92	Threatt	509	1041	.489
1992-93	Green	379	706	.537
1993-94	Lynch	291	573	.508
1994-95	Ceballos	497	977	.509
1995-96	Ceballos	638	1203	.530
1996-97	O'Neal	552	991	.557
1997-98	O'Neal	670	1147	.584*
1998-99	O'Neal	510	885	.576*
1999-00	O'Neal	956	1665	.574*
2000-01	O'Neal	813	1422	.572*
2001-02	O'Neal	712	1229	.579*
2002-03	O'Neal	695	1211	.574
2003-04	O'Neal	554	948	.584*
2004-05	Mihm	280	552	.507
2005-06	Cook	261	511	.511
2006-07	Bynum	247	443	.558
2007-08	Odom	417	795	.525
2008-09	Gasol	592	1045	.567

(Minimum 400 FGA)

FREE THROW %

		FG	FGA	PCT
1960-61	LaRusso	323	409	.790
1961-62	West	712	926	.769
1962-63	Baylor	661	790	.837
1963-64	West	584	702	.832
1964-65	West	648	789	.821
1965-66	West	840*	977	.860
1966-67	West	602	686	.878
1967-68	West	391	482	.811
1968-69	Egan	204	240	.850
1969-70	West	647	785	.824
1970-71	West	525	631	.832
1971-72	Goodrich	475	559	.850
1972-73	McMillian	223	264	.845
1973-74	Goodrich	508	588	.864
1975-75	Goodrich	318	378	.841
1975-76	Russell	132	148	.892
1976-77	Russell	188	218	.862
1977-78	Dantley	334	417	.801
1978-79	Dantley	292	342	.854
1979-80	Johnson	374	462	.810
1980-81	Cooper	117	149	.785
1981-82	Cooper	139	171	.813
1982-83	Johnson	304	380	.800
1983-84	Cooper	155	185	.838
1984-85	Cooper	115	133	.865
1985-86	Johnson	378	434	.871
1986-87	Scott	224	251	.892
1987-88	Scott	272	317	.858
1988-89	Johnson	513	563	.911*
1989-90	Johnson	567	637	.890
1990-91	Johnson	519	573	.906
1991-92	Scott	244	291	.838
1992-93	Scott	156	184	.848
1993-94	Threatt	138	155	.890
1994-95	Peeler	102	128	.797
1995-96	Johnson	172	201	.856
1996-97	Scott	127	151	.841
1997-98	Bryant	363	457	.794
1998-99	Rice	77	90	.856
1999-00	Rice	346	396	.874
2000-01	Bryant	475	557	.853
2001-02	Fox	94	111	.847
2002-03	Bryant	601	713	.843
2003-04	Bryant	454	533	.852
2004-05	Butler	275	319	.862
2005-06	Bryant	696*	819	.850
2006-07	Bryant	667*	768*	.868
2007-08	Fisher	166	188	.883
2008-09	Bryant	483	564	.856

(Minimum 100 FTA)
(w/ exception of '98-99 shortened season)
* Denotes NBA Leader

Season-By-Season Leaders

MINUTES PLAYED

		MIN	AVG
1960-61	Baylor	3133	42.9
1961-62	West	3087	41.2
1962-63	Baylor	3370	42.1
1963-64	Baylor	3164	40.6
1964-65	West	3066	41.4
1965-66	West	3218	40.7
1966-67	Imhoff	2725	33.6
1967-68	Clark	3039	37.5
1968-69	Chamberlain	3669	45.3
1969-70	West	3106	42.0
1970-71	Chamberlain	3630	44.3
1971-72	Chamberlain	3469	42.3
1972-73	Chamberlain	3542	43.2
1973-74	Goodrich	3061	37.3
1974-75	Goodrich	2668	37.1
1975-76	Abdul-Jabbar	3379*	41.2
1976-77	Abdul-Jabbar	3016	36.8
1977-78	Nixon	2779	34.3
1978-79	Abdul-Jabbar	3157	39.5
1979-80	Nixon	3231*	39.4
1980-81	Wilkes	3208	37.3
1981-82	Wilkes	3024	38.7
1982-83	Johnson	2907	36.8
1983-84	Abdul-Jabbar	2622	32.8
1984-85	Johnson	2781	36.1
1985-86	Abdul-Jabbar	2629	33.3
1986-87	Johnson	2904	36.3
1987-88	Scott	3048	37.6
1988-89	Worthy	2960	36.5
1989-90	Worthy	2960	37.0
1990-91	Worthy	3008	28.6
1991-92	Threatt	3070	37.4
1992-93	Threatt	2893	35.3
1993-94	Van Exel	2700	33.3
1994-95	Van Exel	2944	36.8
1995-96	Campbell	2699	32.9
1996-97	Jones	2998	37.5
1997-98	Jones	2910	36.4
1998-99	Bryant	1896	37.9
1999-00	O'Neal	3163	40.0
2000-01	O'Neal	2924	39.5
2001-02	Bryant	3063	38.3
2002-03	Bryant	3401	41.5
2003-04	Bryant	2447	37.6
2004-05	Bryant	2689	40.7
2005-06	Bryant	3277	41.0
2006-07	Bryant	3140	40.8
2007-08	Bryant	3192	38.9
2008-09	Gasol	2999	37.0

3-POINT FIELD GOALS MADE

		3FG	3FGA	PCT
1979-80	Johnson	7	31	.226
1980-81	Cooper	4	19	.211
1981-82	Johnson	6	29	.207
1982-83	Cooper	5	21	.238
1983-84	Cooper	38	121	.314
1984-85	Cooper	35	123	.285
1985-86	Cooper	63	163	.387
1986-87	Cooper	89	231	.385
1987-88	Scott	62	179	.346
1988-89	Cooper	80	210	.381
1989-90	Johnson	106	276	.384
1990-91	Johnson	80	250	.320
1991-92	Scott	54	157	.344
1992-93	Peeler	46	118	.390
1993-94	Van Exel	123	364	.338
1994-95	Van Exel	183	511	.358
1995-96	Van Exel	144	403	.357
1996-97	Van Exel	177	468	.378
1997-98	Jones	143	368	.389
1998-99	Bryant	53	135	.393
1999-00	Rice	84	229	.367
2000-01	Fox	118	300	.393
2001-02	Fisher	144	349	.413
2002-03	Bryant	124	324	.383
2003-04	Bryant	71	217	.327
2004-05	Atkins	176	455	.387
2005-06	Bryant	180	518	.347
2006-07	Bryant	137	398	.344
2007-08	Bryant	150	415	.361
2008-09	Fisher	120	302	.397

3-POINT FIELD GOAL %

		3FG	3FGA	PCT
1979-80	Cooper	5	20	.250^
1980-81	Holland	1	3	.333^
1981-82	M.Johnson	6	29	.207^
1982-83	M.Cooper	5	21	.238^
1983-84	Cooper	38	121	.314
1984-85	Scott	26	60	.433*^
1985-86	Cooper	63	163	.387
1986-87	Scott	65	149	.436
1987-88	Scott	62	179	.346
1988-89	Scott	77	193	.399
1989-90	Scott	93	220	.423
1990-91	Scott	71	219	.324
1991-92	Scott	54	157	.344
1992-93	Peeler	46	118	.390
1993-94	Van Exel	123	364	.338
1994-95	Peeler	84	216	.389
1995-96	Peeler	105	254	.413
1996-97	Jones	152	389	.391
1997-98	Jones	143	368	.389
	Van Exel	123	316	.389
1998-99	Rice	53	135	.393
1999-00	Rice	84	229	.367
2000-01	Penberthy	55	139	.396
2001-02	Fisher	144	349	.413
2002-03	Fisher	85	212	.401
2003-04	Russell	43	112	.384
2004-05	Jones	102	261	.391
2005-06	Odom	80	215	.372
2006-07	Cook	46	115	.400
2007-08	Vujacic	118	270	.437
2008-09	Fisher	120	302	.397

(^Min. 100 3FGA not met by any player)
* Denotes NBA Leader

NBA Team Leaders

TEAM SCORING

1997-98	105.5
1985-86	117.3
1971-72	121.0
1965-66	119.5
1948-49	84.0

TEAM REBOUNDING

2008-09	43.9
1999-00	47.0
1972-73	55.6
1971-72	56.4

TEAM ASSISTS

1979-80	29.4
1971-72	27.2
1965-66	24.2

TEAM BLOCKED SHOTS

1996-97	7.01
1975-76	6.44
1973-74	7.96

TEAM STEALS

Have never led NBA

TEAM FIELD GOAL %

1998-99	.468
1988-89	.502
1985-86	.522
1984-85	.545
1983-84	.532
1982-83	.528
1979-80	.529
1978-79	.517
1977-78	.487
1968-69	.467
1967-68	.477

TEAM FREE THROW %

1965-66	.773
1964-65	.763
1963-64	.766
1953-54	.731
1955-56	.786

FEWEST TURNOVERS

Have never led NBA

Year-By-Year Playoff Results

Year	1ST ROUND Opponent	W-L	2ND ROUND Opponent	W-L	3RD ROUND Opponent	W-L	NBA FINALS Opponent	W-L
1961	Detroit	3-2	St. Louis	3-4	—		—	
1962	—		Detroit	4-2	—		Boston	3-4
1963	—		St. Louis	4-3	—		Boston	2-4
1964	St. Louis	2-3	—		—		—	
1965	—		Baltimore	4-2	—		Boston	1-4
1966	—		St. Louis	4-3	—		Boston	3-4
1967	San Francisco	0-3	—		—		—	
1968	Chicago	4-1	San Francisco	4-0	—		Boston	2-4
1969	San Francisco	4-2	Atlanta	4-1	—		Boston	3-4
1970	Phoenix	4-3	Atlanta	4-0	—		New York	3-4
1971	Chicago	4-3	Milwaukee	1-4	—		—	
1972	Chicago	4-0	Milwaukee	4-2	—		New York	4-1
1973	Chicago	4-3	Golden State	4-1	—		New York	1-4
1974	Milwaukee	1-4	—		—		—	
1975	—		—		—		—	
1976	—		—		—		—	
1977	Golden State	4-3	Portland	0-4	—		—	
1978	Seattle	1-2	—		—		—	
1979	Denver	2-1	Seattle	1-4	—		—	
1980	—		Phoenix	4-1	Seattle	4-1	Philadelphia	4-2
1981	Houston	1-2	—		—		—	
1982	—		Phoenix	4-0	San Antonio	4-0	Philadelphia	4-2
1983	—		Portland	4-1	San Antonio	4-2	Philadelphia	0-4
1984	Kansas City	3-0	Dallas	4-1	Phoenix	4-2	Boston	3-4
1985	Phoenix	3-0	Portland	4-1	Denver	4-1	Boston	4-2
1986	San Antonio	3-0	Dallas	4-2	Houston	1-4	—	
1987	Denver	3-0	Golden State	4-1	Seattle	4-0	Boston	4-2
1988	San Antonio	3-0	Utah	4-3	Dallas	4-3	Detroit	4-3
1989	Portland	3-0	Seattle	4-0	Phoenix	4-0	Detroit	0-4
1990	Houston	3-1	Phoenix	1-4	—		—	
1991	Houston	3-0	Golden State	4-1	Portland	4-2	Chicago	1-4
1992	Portland	1-3	—		—		—	
1993	Phoenix	2-3	—		—		—	
1994	—		—		—		—	
1995	Seattle	3-1	San Antonio	2-4	—		—	
1996	Houston	1-3	—		—		—	
1997	Portland	3-1	Utah	1-4				
1998	Portland	3-1	Seattle	4-1	Utah	0-4	—	
1999	Houston	3-1	San Antonio	0-4	—		—	
2000	Sacramento	3-2	Phoenix	4-1	Portland	4-3	Indiana	4-2
2001	Portland	3-0	Sacramento	4-0	San Antonio	4-0	Philadelphia	4-1
2002	Portland	3-0	San Antonio	4-1	Sacramento	4-3	New Jersey	4-0
2003	Minnesota	4-2	San Antonio	2-4	—		—	
2004	Houston	4-1	San Antonio	4-2	Minnesota	4-2	Detroit	1-4
2005	—		—		—		—	
2006	Phoenix	3-4	—		—		—	
2007	Phoenix	1-4	—		—		—	
2008	Denver	4-0	Utah	4-2	San Antonio	4-1	Boston	2-4
2009	Utah	4-1	Houston	4-3	Denver	4-2	Orlando	4-1
Totals		107-60		115-71		61-30		65-72
(LA Only)		(.641)		(.618)		(.670)		(.474)

Shaquille O'Neal

Lakers Individual Playoff Records

POINTS

Game	61	Elgin Baylor	@ BOS	4/14/62
Half	33	Elgin Baylor	@ BOS	4/14/62
Quarter	22	Elgin Baylor	vs. DET	3/15/61

FIELD GOAL PERCENTAGE

Game	1.000	Wilt Chamberlain	vs. ATL (9-9)	4/17/69
	.917	James Worthy	@ BOS (11-12)	5/31/84
Half	n/a	--	--	--
Quarter	n/a	--	--	--

FIELD GOALS MADE

Game	22	Elgin Baylor	@ BOS	4/14/62
Half	12	Elgin Baylor	@ BOS	4/14/62
	12	Kobe Bryant	@ MIN	4/20/03
Quarter	10	Gail Goodrich	vs. GS	4/25/73

FIELD GOALS ATTEMPTED

Game	46	Elgin Baylor	@ BOS	4/14/62
Half	25	Elgin Baylor	@ BOS*	4/14/62
Quarter	13	Elgin Baylor	@ BOS	4/14/62
	13	Gail Goodrich	vs. GS	4/25/73
	13	Mike McGee	vs. DEN	5/22/85
	13	Kobe Bryant	@ SA	5/13/03

3-PT FIELD GOALS MADE

Game	7	Nick Van Exel	vs. SEA	5/4/95
	7	Robert Horry	@ UTAH	5/6/97
Half	n/a	--	--	--
Quarter	n/a	--	--	--

3-PT FIELD GOALS ATTEMPTED

Game	13	Nick Van Exel	vs. SEA	5/4/95
Half	n/a	--	--	--
Quarter	n/a	--	--	--

3-PT FG MADE WITHOUT A MISS

Game	7	Robert Horry	@ UTAH	5/6/97

FT MADE WITHOUT A MISS

Game	17	Gail Goodrich	@ CHI	3/28/72
Half	14	Jerry West	vs. BAL	4/5/65
Quarter	11	Larry Spriggs	vs. DAL	4/28/84

FREE THROWS MADE

Game	21	Kobe Bryant	vs. UTAH	5/4/08
Half	19	Earvin Johnson	vs. GS*	5/891
Quarter	11	Larry Spriggs	vs. DAL	4/28/94
	11	Earvin Johnson	vs. GS	5/8/91
	11	Kobe Bryant	vs. UTAH	5/8/97

FREE THROWS ATTEMPTED

Game	39	Shaquille O'Neal	vs. IND*	6/9/00
Half	22	Shaquille O'Neal	vs. IND*	6/9/00
Quarter	16	Shaquille O'Neal	vs. IND	6/9/00
	16	Shaquille O'Neal	vs. NJ	6/5/02

REBOUNDS

Game	33	Wilt Chamberlain	vs. CHI	4/4/71
Half	19	Wilt Chamberlain	vs. CHI	4/19/71
Quarter	n/a	--	--	--

* Denotes Record

OFFENSIVE REBOUNDS

Game	11	Shaquille O'Neal	vs. SAC	5/6/01

DEFENSIVE REBOUNDS

Game	18	Kareem Abdul-Jabbar	@ GS	5/4/97

ASSISTS

Game	24	Earvin Johnson	vs. PHO*	5/15/94
Half	15	Earvin Johnson	@ POR*	5/3/85
Quarter	10	Earvin Johnson	vs. DEN	5/22/85
	10	Earvin Johnson	vs. HOU	4/27/91
	10	Earvin Johnson	@ POR	5/18/91

STEALS

Game	7	Earvin Johnson	vs. POR	4/24/83
	7	Byron Scott	@ GS	5/10/91
Half	6	Byron Scott	@ GS	5/10/91
Quarter	3	Kobe Bryant	vs. BOS	6/15/08
	3	Kobe Bryant	vs. BOS	6/12/08
	3	Derek Fisher	vs. UTAH	5/14/08
	3	Luke Walton	@ PHO	4/24/07
	3	Derek Fisher	vs. MIN	5/25/04
	3	Kareem Rush	vs. HOU	4/28/04
	3	Kobe Bryant	@ HOU	4/23/04
	3	Kobe Bryant	vs. HOU	4/17/04
	3	Robert Horry	vs. NJ	6/7/02
	3	Tyronn Lue	vs. PHI	6/6/01
	3	Rick Fox	vs. POR	4/26/01
	3	Kobe Bryant	@ SA	5/17/99
	3	Cedric Ceballos	@ SA	5/16/95
	3	Sedale Threatt	@ PHO	5/9/93
	3	Byron Scott	@ GS	5/10/91

BLOCKED SHOTS

Game	9	Kareem Abdul-Jabbar	vs. GS	4/22/77
Half	n/a	--	--	--
Quarter	n/a	--	--	--

Wilt Chamberlain

Pau Gasol serves young fans at the Lakers Thanksgiving Celebration in 2008.

Lamar Odom teaches a youngster dribbling skills at a basketball clinic in 2008.

The Lakers Reach Out to Youth

The Los Angeles Lakers Youth Foundation provides educational, athletic, and recreational opportunities for Los Angeles area youth and supports non-profit youth and community organizations. Much of the support comes from team owner Dr. Jerry Buss, who donates money as well as tickets, merchandise, and autographed items, which help many non-profit charities as well as schools, libraries, and churches.

Some of the programs supported by the foundation include Read to Achieve, Student and Teacher of the Month, the "Freedom Through My Eyes" Art/Essay Contest, Junior Lakers, A Season of Giving, Fit for Life, and Lakers Eco-All Stars. Read to Achieve consists of an annual reading challenge, book drives, Reading Time Outs, and development of Lakers Reading and Learning Centers throughout Los Angeles and Hawaii. Since 2001, Read to Achieve has encouraged more than 160,000 students to read, created 14 Lakers Reading and Learning Centers and collected nearly 6,500 books to benefit those centers.

In the Student and Teacher of the Month program, honorees are nominated by their peers and recognized at a Lakers game for their outstanding academic and extracurricular achievements. "Freedom Through My Eyes" Art/Essay Contest encourages students to express their views on freedom for a chance to win an all-expense paid trip to Washington, D.C. The winning students are honored at a Lakers game, where their essays and artwork are displayed on the main concourse.

The Junior Lakers initiative uses basketball to encourage healthy living and teach young athletes teamwork, sportsmanship, and respect. The program includes an annual summer basketball camp, youth and coaches clinics, and the renovation of basketball courts throughout the city of Los Angeles. In addition, the Lakers Youth Foundation is a longtime and proud supporter of the Fast Breakin' Lakers wheelchair basketball team.

"A Season of Giving" spreads joy during the holidays. Events have included serving a traditional Thanksgiving meal to local children and families, groceries and turkey giveaways, hospital visits, holiday parties for kids, an on-court gift exchange program between players and children, and shopping sprees for children.

The Lakers' Fit for Life program tackles childhood obesity and encourages children to embrace regular exercise, develop healthy eating habits, and lead active lifestyles. The Lakers' Eco-All Stars program focuses on raising awareness about environmental issues and educating fans on how to reduce their carbon footprint. One element of the program is the monthly "My Better Lifestyle Award," which recognizes a fan for his or her efforts to live a more eco-friendly lifestyle.

The Lakers Youth Foundation uses its resources to raise funds to support community initiatives. Two of the main fundraisers are the annual Celebrity Golf Invitational Tournament and the In-Arena Auction. The auction is held at every Lakers home game and fans can bid on one-of-a-kind autographed memorabilia from the Lakers and other sports teams. Over the past ten seasons, nearly $2 million has been raised to provide life-enriching opportunities for Los Angeles youth.

To learn more about the Lakers community outreach programs and the Lakers Youth Foundation, visit www.lakers.com.

—Eugenia Chow,
Community Relations Director, L.A. Lakers

CREDITS

Photography

Front Book Cover: Left to right: (Abdul-Jabbar) ©1986 NBA Entertainment. Photo by Andrew D. Bernstein/NBAE/Getty Images; (Chamberlain)1973. Photo by George Long/Sports Illustrated/Getty Images; (West) 1970. Photo by James Drake/Sports Illustrated/Getty Images; (Johnson) ©1988 NBA Entertainment. Photo by Andrew D. Bernstein/NBAE/Getty Images; (Bryant) ©2009 NBA Entertainment. Photo by Andrew D. Bernstein/NBAE/Getty Images.

Page 1: Top ©2000 NBA Entertainment. Photo by Andrew D. Bernstein/NBAE/Getty Images. Bottom ©2002 NBA Entertainment. Photo by Andrew D. Bernstein/NBAE/Getty Images.wPage 2 ©2006 NBA Entertainment. Photo by Noah Graham/NBAE/Getty Images.

Page 5: ©2002 NBA Entertainment. Photo by Scott Quintard/NBAE/Getty Images.

Pages 6 and 7: Photo illustration. ©2009 NBA Entertainment. Photo by Andrew D. Bernstein.

Page 8: ©2009 NBA Entertainment. Photo by Andrew D. Bernstein/NBAE/Getty Images.

Page 10: 1980. UCLA Charles E. Young Research Library Department of Special Collections, Los Angeles Times Photographic Archives, copyright ©Regents of the University of California, UCLA Library.

Page 11: 1980. UCLA Charles E. Young Research Library Department of Special Collections, Los Angeles Times Photographic Archives, copyright ©Regents of the University of California, UCLA Library.

Page 12: 1982. UCLA Charles E. Young Research Library Department of Special Collections, Los Angeles Times Photographic Archives, copyright ©Regents of the University of California, UCLA Library.

Page 13: Left 1985. UCLA Charles E. Young Research Library Department of Special Collections, Los Angeles Times Photographic Archives, copyright ©Regents of the University of California, UCLA Library. Right 1987. UCLA Charles E. Young Research Library Department of Special Collections, Los Angeles Times Photographic Archives, copyright ©Regents of the University of California, UCLA Library.

Page 14: ©2001 NBA Entertainment. Photo by Robert Mora/NBAE/Getty Images.

Page 15: Left ©1988 NBA Entertainment. Photo by Nathaniel S. Butler/NBAE/Getty Images. Right ©2009 NBA Entertainment. Photo by Nathaniel S. Butler/NBAE/Getty Images.

Page 16-17: ©2000. Photo by Donald Miralle/Allsport/Getty Images.

Page 18: Top ©1949 NBA Entertainment. Photo by NBA Photos/NBAE/Getty Images. Bottom ©1955 NBA Entertainment. Photo by NBA Photos/NBAE/Getty Images.

Page 20: 1966. Photo by Walter Iooss Jr./Sports Illustrated/Getty Images.

Page 21: Left 1966. Photo by George Long/Sports Illustrated/Getty Images. Center 1965. Photo by George Long/Sports Illustrated/Getty Images. Right 1961. Photo by Darryl Norenberg/WireImage/Getty Images.

Page 25: 1961. Photo by Darryl Norenberg/WireImage/Getty Images.

Page 26: Top ©1960 NBA Entertainment. Photo by NBA Photos/NBAE/Getty Images. Bottom 1950s. Photo by Hulton Archive/Getty Images.

Page 27: Top 1960. Associated Press Photo/Matty Zimmermann. Bottom 1966. Photo by James Drake/Sports Illustrated/Getty Images.

Page 29: 1984. Photo by Richard Mackson/Sports Illustrated/Getty Images.

Page 30: 1961. Photo by John G. Zimmerman/Sports Illustrated/Getty Images.

Page 31: Top 1962. Photo by Herb Scharfman/Sports Illustrated/Getty Images. Bottom left 1960s. Photo by Focus on Sport/Getty Images. Bottom right 1984. Photo by George Tiedemann/Sports Illustrated/Getty Images.

Page 33: ©1963. NBA Entertainment. Photo by NBA Photo Library/NBAE/Getty Images.

Page 34: 1963. Photo by Fred Kaplan/Sports Illustrated/Getty Images.

Page 35: 1963. Photo by Russ Halford/Sports Illustrated/Getty Images.

Page 37: 1963. Photo by Darryl Norenberg/WireImage/Getty Images.

Page 38: Left 1963. Photo by Marvin E. Newman/Sports Illustrated/Getty Images. Right 1963. Photo by Darryl Norenberg/WireImage/Getty Images.

Page 39: Top 1963. Photo by Darryl Norenberg/WireImage/Getty Images. Bottom left ©1964 NBA Entertainment. Photo by Wen Roberts/NBAE/Getty Images. Bottom right 1963. Photo by Russ Halford/Sports Illustrated/Getty Images.

Page 41: 1965. Photo by George Long/Sports Illustrated/Getty Images.

Page 42: Left 1965. Photo by Focus On Sport/Getty Images. Right 1965. Photo by Focus On Sport/Getty Images.

Page 43: Top 1966. Photo by George Long/Sports Illustrated/Getty Images. Bottom left 1960s. Photo by Pictorial Parade/Hulton Archive/Getty Images. Bottom right 1965. Photo by George Long/Sports Illustrated/Getty Images.

Page 45: 1966. Photo by Rich Clarkson/Sports Illustrated/Getty Images.

Page 46: Left 1964. Photo by Rich Clarkson/Sports Illustrated/Getty Images. Right 1966. Photo by Walter Iooss Jr./Sports Illustrated/Getty Images

Page 47: Top 1966. Photo by Walter Iooss Jr./Sports Illustrated/Getty Images. Bottom left ©1970 NBA Entertainment. Photo by Walter Iooss Jr./NBAE/Getty Images. Bottom right ©1965 NBA Entertainment. Photo by NBA Photos/NBAE/Getty Images.

Page 48: 1972. Photo by Heinz Kluetmeier/Sports Illustrated/Getty Images.

Page 49: Top left 1972. Photo by Vernon Biever/WireImage/Getty Images. Center 1973. Photo by George Long/Sports Illustrated/Getty Images. Right 1968. Photo by George Long/Sports Illustrated/Getty Images.

Page 51: 1967. Photo by Darryl Norenberg/WireImage/Getty Images.

Page 52: Left 1966. Photo by Walter Iooss Jr./Sports Illustrated/Getty Images. Right 1963. Photo by Darryl Norenberg/WireImage/Getty Images.

Page 53: Top 1972. UCLA Charles E. Young Research Library Department of Special Collections, Los Angeles Times Photographic Archives, copyright ©Regents of the University of California, UCLA Library. Bottom left ©1967 NBA Entertainment. Photo by Ken Regan/NBAE/Getty Images. Bottom right 1968. Photo by Walter Iooss Jr./Sports Illustrated/Getty Images.

Page 55: 1968. Photo by George Long/Sports Illustrated/Getty Images.

Page 56: Left 1968. Photo by George Long/Sports Illustrated/Getty Images. Right 1968. Photo by George Long/Sports Illustrated/Getty Images.

Page 57: Top 1972. Photo by Stephen Green-Armytage/Sports Illustrated/Getty Images. Bottom left ©1966 NBA Entertainment. Photo by Wen Roberts/NBAE/Getty Images. Bottom right 1967. Photo by George Long/Sports Illustrated/Getty Images.

Page 59: ©1966. NBA Entertainment. Photo by Ken Regan/NBAE/Getty Images.

Page 60: 1971. UCLA Charles E. Young Research Library Department of Special Collections, Los Angeles Times Photographic Archives, Copyright ©Regents of the University of California, UCLA Library.

Page 61: Top 1969. Photo by George Long/Sports Illustrated/Getty Images.

Page 63: 1968. Photo by George Long/Sports Illustrated/Getty Images.

Page 64: Left 1970. Photo by George Long/Sports Illustrated/Getty Images. Right 1970. Photo by George Long/Sports Illustrated/Getty Images.

Page 65: Top 1970. Photo by James Drake/Sports Illustrated/Getty Images. Bottom left 1970. Photo by George Long/WireImage/Getty Images. Bottom right 1968. Photo by George Long/Sports Illustrated/Getty Images.

Page 67: Top 1971. UCLA Charles E. Young Research Library Department of Special Collections, Los Angeles Times Photographic Archives, Copyright ©Regents of the University of California, UCLA Library. Bottom left © 1969 NBA Entertainment. Photo by Dick Raphael/NBAE/Getty Images. Bottom right 1973. Photo by George Long/Sports Illustrated/Getty Images.

Page 69: Top 1966. Photo by Walter Iooss Jr./Sports Illustrated/Getty Images.

Page 70: Left ©1972 NBA Entertainment. Photo by Wen Roberts/NBAE/Getty Images. Right 1972. Photo by George Long/Sports Illustrated/Getty Images.

Page 71: Top 1972. Photo by Vernon Biever/WireImage/Getty Images. Bottom left 1972. Photo by George Long/WireImage/Getty Images. Bottom right 1972. Photo by George Long/Sports Illustrated/Getty Images.

Page 72: 1972. Photo by George Long/Sports Illustrated/Getty Images.

Page 73: 1972. Photo by George Long/Sports Illustrated/Getty Images.

Page 75: 1973. Photo by George Long/Sports Illustrated/Getty Images.

Page 77: 1970s. Photo by Focus on Sport/Getty Images.

Page 78: Left 1974. Photo by Vernon Biever/WireImage/Getty Images. Right ©1974 NBA Entertainment. Photo by Dick Raphael/NBAE/Getty Images.

Page 79: Top ©1974 NBA Entertainment. Photo by Dick Raphael/NBAE/Getty Images. Bottom left 1974. Photo by Vernon Biever/WireImage/Getty Images. Bottom right ©1973 NBA Entertainment. Photo by Dick Raphael/NBAE/Getty Images.

Page 80: 1978. Photo by Focus on Sport/Getty Images.

Page 81: Left 1974. UCLA Charles E. Young Research Library Department of Special Collections, Los Angeles Times Photographic Archives, Copyright ©Regents of the University of California, UCLA Library. Center 1975. UCLA Charles E. Young Research Library Department of Special Collections, Los Angeles Times Photographic Archives, Copyright ©Regents of the University of California, UCLA Library. Right ©1978 NBA Entertainment. Photo by NBA Photos/NBAE/Getty Images.

Page 83: 1974. UCLA Charles E. Young Research Library Department of Special Collections, Los Angeles Times Photographic Archives, Copyright ©Regents of the University of California, UCLA Library.

Page 84: Left 1970s. Photo by Focus on Sport/Getty Images. Right 1977. Photo by Rogers Photo Archive/Getty Images.

Page 85: Top 1975. Photo by George Long/Sports Illustrated/Getty Images. Bottom left 1975. Photo by Rogers Photo Archive/Getty Images. Bottom right 1974. Photo by Ron Kuntz Collection/Diamond Images/Getty Images.

Page 87: 1975. UCLA Charles E. Young Research Library Department of Special Collections, Los Angeles Times Photographic Archives, Copyright ©Regents of the University of California, UCLA Library

Page 88: Left ©1976 NBA Entertainment. Photo by Wen Roberts/NBAE/Getty Images. Right 1975. Photo by John G. Zimmerman/Sports Illustrated/Getty Images.

Page 89: Top ©1977 NBA Entertainment. Photo by Dick Raphael/NBAE/Getty Images. Bottom ©1976 NBA Entertainment. Photo by Robert Lewis/NBAE/Getty Images.

Page 91: 1978. Photo by George Gojkovich/Getty Images.

Page 92: Left 1976. Los Angeles Lakers, Inc. Right ©1977 NBA Entertainment. Photo by Robert Lewis/NBAE/Getty Images.

Page 93: Top 1977. Photo by Hank Delespinasse/Sports Illustrated/Getty Images. Bottom 1978. Photo by Rogers Photo Archive/Getty Images.

Page 95: ©2005 NBA Entertainment. Photo by Joe Murphy/NBAE/Getty Images.

Page 96: Left 1978. Photo by Rogers Photo Archive/Getty Images. Right 1970s. Photo by Focus on Sport/Getty Images.

Page 97: Top 1978. Photo by Rogers Photo Archive/Getty Images. Bottom 1978. Photo by Rogers Photo Archive/Getty Images.

Page 99: ©1978 NBA Entertainment. Photo by NBA Photos/NBAE/Getty Images.

Page 100: Left ©1979 NBA Entertainment. Photo by Tony Neste/NBAE/Getty Images. Right 1978. Photo by Rogers Photo Archive/Getty Images.

Page 101: Top 1970s. Photo by Focus on Sport/Getty Images. Bottom ©1979 NBA Entertainment. Photo by NBA Photos/NBAE/Getty Images.

Page 102: ©1983 NBA Entertainment. Photo by Andrew D. Bernstein/NBAE/Getty Images.

Page 103: Left 1980. Photo by Peter Read Miller/Sports Illustrated/Getty Images. Center ©1984 NBA Entertainment. Photo by Andrew D. Bernstein/NBAE/Getty Images. Right 1987. Photo by Peter Read Miller/Sports Illustrated/Getty Images.

Page 104: ©2009 NBA Entertainment. Photo by Jesse D. Garrabrant/NBAE/Getty Images.

Page 105: (Please refer to photo key on Page 251 for corresponding number) 1. 1987. Photo by Peter Read Miller/Sports Illustrated/Getty Images. 2. 1987. Photo by Peter Read Miller/Sports Illustrated/Getty Images. 3. 2009. Photo by Noel Vasquez/Getty Images. 4. 2009. Photo by Noel Vasquez/Getty Images. 5. 2009. Photo by Noel Vasquez/Getty Images. 6. 2009. Photo by Noel Vasquez/Getty Images. 7. 2008. Photo by Noel Vasquez/Getty Images. 8. 2008. Photo by Noel Vasquez/Getty Images. 9. 2009. Photo by Noel Vasquez/Getty Images. 10. 2009. Photo by Noel Vasquez/Getty Images. 11. 2007. Photo by John W. McDonough/Sports Illustrated/Getty Images. 12. 2008. Photo by Noel Vasquez/Getty Images. 13. 2004. Photo by Vince Bucci/Getty Images. 14. 2009. Photo by Noel Vasquez/Getty Images. 15. 2009. Photo by Noel Vasquez/Getty Images. 16. 2008. Photo by Noel Vasquez/Getty Images. 17. 2009. Photo by Noel Vasquez/Getty Images. 18. 2008. Photo by John W. McDonough/Sports Illustrated/Getty Images. 19. 2004. Photo by Vince Bucci/Getty Images. 20. ©1988 NBA Entertainment. Photo by Andrew D. Bernstein/NBAE/Getty Images. 21. 2009. Photo by Noel Vasquez/Getty Images. 22. 2009. Photo by Noel Vasquez/Getty Images. 23. ©2009 NBA Entertainment. Photo by Andrew D. Bernstein/NBAE/Getty Images. 24. ©2008 NBA Entertainment. Photo by Andrew D. Bernstein/NBAE/Getty Images. 25. 2009. Photo by Noel Vasquez/Getty Images. 26. 2009. Photo by Noel Vasquez/Getty Images. 27. 2009. Photo by Noel Vasquez/Getty Images. 28. 1986. Photo by Brian Lanker/Sports Illustrated/Getty Images.

Page 107: ©1980 NBA Entertainment. Photo by Rich Pilling/NBAE/Getty Images.

Page 108: Left 1979. Photo by Lane

CREDITS

Stewart/Sports Illustrated/Getty Images. Right ©1980 NBA Entertainment. Photo by Scott Cunningham/NBAE/Getty Images.
Page 109: 1980. Photo by Peter Read Miller/Sports Illustrated/Getty Images.
Page 111: 1980. Photo by Peter Read Miller/Sports Illustrated/Getty Images.
Page 113: 1988. Photo by Tim Defrisco/Getty Images.
Page 114: 1981. Photo by Peter Read Miller/Sports Illustrated/Getty Images.
Page 115: Top 1981. Photo by Richard Mackson/Sports Illustrated/Getty Images. Bottom left 1980. Photo by Rogers Photo Archive/Getty Images. Bottom right 1980s. Photo by Focus on Sport/Getty Images.
Page 117: 1981. Photo by Lane Stewart/Sports Illustrated/Getty Images.
Page 118: 1980s. Photo by Focus on Sport/Getty Images.
Page 119: Top 1982. Photo by Richard Mackson/Sports Illustrated/Getty Images. Bottom 1982. Photo by Manny Millan/Sports Illustrated/Getty Images.
Page 121: Left ©1984 NBA Entertainment. Photo by Andrew D. Bernstein/NBAE/Getty Images. Right ©1985 NBA Entertainment. Photo by Andrew D. Bernstein/NBAE/Getty Images.
Page 122: 1982. Photo by Heinz Kluetmeier/Sports Illustrated/Getty Images.
Page 123: Top ©1983 NBA Entertainment. Photo by Andrew D. Bernstein/NBAE/Getty Images. Bottom left 1982. Photo by Richard Mackson/Sports Illustrated/Getty Images. Bottom right ©1982 NBA Entertainment. Photo by Andrew D. Bernstein/NBAE/Getty Images.
Page 125: Left 1984. Photo by John W. McDonough/Sports Illustrated/Getty Images. Right 1984. Photo by John W. McDonough/Sports Illustrated/Getty Images.
Page 126: Top ©1984 NBA Entertainment. Photo by Dick Raphael/NBAE/Getty Images. Bottom ©1984 NBA Entertainment. Photo by Andrew D. Bernstein/NBAE/Getty Images.
Page 127: Left ©1984 NBA Entertainment. Photo by Dick Raphael/NBAE/Getty Images. Right 1984. Photo by Peter Read Miller/Sports Illustrated/Getty Images.
Page 129: 1985. Photo by Manny Millan/Sports Illustrated/Getty Images.
Page 130: ©1985 NBA Entertainment. Photo by Andrew D. Bernstein/NBAE/Getty Images.
Page 131: Top ©2005 NBA Entertainment. Photo by Noah Graham/NBAE/Getty Images. Bottom left ©1985 NBA Entertainment. Photo by Andrew D. Bernstein/NBAE/Getty Images. Bottom right ©1985 NBA Entertainment. Photo by Andrew D. Bernstein/NBAE/Getty Images.
Page 133: ©2001 NBA Entertainment. Photo by Andrew D. Bernstein/NBAE/Getty Images.
Page 134: ©1987 NBA Entertainment. Photo by Andrew D. Bernstein/NBAE/Getty Images.
Page 135: 1986. Photo by Richard Mackson/Sports Illustrated/Getty Images.
Page 137: 1987. Photo by Manny Millan/Sports Illustrated/Getty Images.
Page 138: 1987. Photo by Getty Images.
Page 139: Top 1987. Photo by Peter Read Miller/Sports Illustrated/Getty Images. Bottom 1987. Photo by Mike Powell/Getty Images.
Page 141: 1988. Photo by John W. McDonough/Sports Illustrated/Getty Images.
Page 142: ©1988 NBA Entertainment. Photo by Peter Read Miller/NBAE/Getty Images.
Page 143: Top 1988. Photo by John W. McDonough/Sports Illustrated/Getty Images. Bottom left 1987. Photo by Mike Powell/Allsport/Getty Images. Bottom right ©1989 NBA Entertainment. Photo by Andrew D. Bernstein/NBAE/Getty Images.
Page 145: Top 1988. Photo by John Biever/Sports Illustrated/Getty Images. Bottom 1990. Photo by Stephen Dunn/Getty Images.
Page 146: ©1989 NBA Entertainment. Photo by Andrew D. Bernstein/NBAE/Getty Images.
Page 147: Top 1989. Photo by Mike Powell/Getty Images. Bottom left 1988. Photo by Tim Defrisco/Getty Images. Bottom right 1989. Photo by Ken Levine/Allsport/Getty Images.
Page 149: 1990. Photo by Peter Read Miller/Sports Illustrated/Getty Images.
Page 150: ©1990 NBA Entertainment. Photo by Jon SooHoo/NBAE/Getty Images.
Page 151: Top 1989. Photo by Ken Levine/Allsport/Getty Images. Bottom left 1989. Photo by Stephen Dunn/Allsport/Getty Images. Bottom right 1989. Photo by Mike Powell/Getty Images.
Page 152: ©1998 NBA Entertainment. Photo by Andrew D. Bernstein/NBAE/Getty Images.
Page 153: Left 1991. Photo by Kevin Levine/Getty Images. Center 1999. Photo by Walter Iooss Jr./Sports Illustrated/Getty Images. Right ©1998 NBA Entertainment. Photo by Andrew D. Bernstein/NBAE/Getty Images.
Page 155: 1991. Photo by Stephen Dunn/Allsport/Getty Images.
Page 156: Left 1990. Photo by Stephen Dunn/Allsport/Getty Images. Right 1991. Photo by Peter Read Miller/Sports Illustrated/Getty Images.
Page 157: Top ©1991 NBA Entertainment. Photo by Andrew D. Bernstein/NBAE/Getty Images. Bottom left ©1991 NBA Entertainment. Photo by Nathaniel S. Butler/NBAE/Getty Images. Bottom right ©1991 NBA Entertainment. Photo by Nathaniel S. Butler/NBAE/Getty Images.
Page 159: 1991. Photo by Kevin Levine/Getty Images.
Page 160: Left ©1993 NBA Entertainment. Photo by Nathaniel S. Butler/NBAE/Getty Images. Right 1992. Photo by Richard Mackson/Sports Illustrated/Getty Images.
Page 161: Top 1992. Photo by Damian Strohmeyer/Sports Illustrated/Getty Images. Bottom left 1992. Photo by John W. McDonough/Sports Illustrated/Getty Images. Bottom right 1992. Photo by Tim DeFrisco/Sports Illustrated/Getty Images.
Page 163: Top 1992. Photo by John W. McDonough/Sports Illustrated/Getty Images. Bottom 1992. Photo by Layne Murdoch/Allsport/Getty Images.
Page 165: 1994. Photo by J.D. Cuban/Allsport/Getty Images.
Page 166: Left 1994. Photo by John W. McDonough/Sports Illustrated/Getty Images. Right 1993. Photo by Stephen Dunn/Getty Images.
Page 167: Top left ©1995 NBA Entertainment. Photo by Andy Hayt/NBAE/Getty Images. Top right 1970. Photo by George Long/WireImage/Getty Images. Bottom left ©1994 NBA Entertainment. Photo by Jon SooHoo/NBAE/Getty Images. Bottom right 1994. Photo by J.D. Cuban/Allsport/Getty Images.
Page 169: 1994. Photo by Al Bello/Getty Images.
Page 170: Top 1994. Photo by Mitchell Layton/Getty Images. Bottom left 1995. Photo by Mitchell Layton/Getty Images. Bottom right 1994. Photo by Vince Bucci/AFP/Getty Images.
Page 171: Top ©1995 NBA Entertainment. Photo by Andy Hayt/NBAE/Getty Images. Bottom left ©1993 NBA Entertainment. Photo by Andrew D. Bernstein/NBAE/Getty Images. Bottom right ©1995 NBA Entertainment. Photo by Andrew D. Bernstein/NBAE/Getty Images.
Page 173: Top 1996. Photo by Richard Mackson/Sports Illustrated/Getty Images. Bottom 1996. Photo by Vincent Laforet/AFP/Getty Images.
Page 175: 1996. Photo by Elsa Hasch/Allsport/Getty Images.
Page 176: Left 1997. Photo by Jed Jacobsohn/Getty Images. Right ©1997 NBA Entertainment. Photo by Nathaniel S. Butler/NBAE/Getty Images.
Page 177: Top ©1996 NBA Entertainment. Photo by Jon SooHoo/NBAE/Getty Images. Bottom left ©1997 NBA Entertainment. Photo by Andy Hayt/NBAE/Getty Images. Bottom right ©1997 NBA Entertainment. Photo by Nathaniel S. Butler/NBAE/Getty Images.
Page 179: Top ©1998 NBA Entertainment. Photo by Andrew D. Bernstein/NBAE/Getty Images. Bottom 1998. Photo by Dan Levine/AFP/Getty Images.
Pages 180 and 181: 2000. Photo by Stephen Dunn/Allsport/Getty Images.
Page 181: Top Right 1999. Photo by Tom Hauck/Allsport/Getty Images.
Page 183: 1999. Photo by Walter Iooss Jr./Sports Illustrated/Getty Images. Bottom left 1999. Photo by Mike Fiala/AFP/Getty Images. Bottom right 1999. Photo by Vincent Laforet/Getty Images.
Page 184: ©1998 NBA Entertainment. Photo by Andrew D. Bernstein/NBAE/Getty Images.
Page 185: Top left ©2002 NBA Entertainment. Photo by Andrew D. Bernstein/NBAE/Getty Images. Center ©2004 NBA Entertainment. Photo by Andrew D. Bernstein/NBAE/Getty Images. Right 2009. Photo by Ronald Martinez/Getty Images.
Page 187: ©2000 NBA Entertainment. Photo by Andrew D. Bernstein/NBAE/Getty Images.
Page 188: 1999 Photo by Jim Ruymen/AFP/Getty Images.
Page 189: ©2000 NBA Entertainment. Photo by Nathaniel S. Butler/NBAE/Getty Images.
Page 191: 2001 Photo by Manny Millan/Sports Illustrated/Getty Images.
Page 192: ©2001 NBA Entertainment. Photo by Robert Mora/NBAE/Getty Images.
Page 193: Top ©2001 NBA Entertainment. Photo by Andrew D. Bernstein/NBAE/Getty Images. Bottom 2001 Photo by Harry How/Allsport/Getty Images.
Page 195: 2002. Photo by Hector Amezcua/Sacramento Bee/ZUMA Press
Page 196: 2002. Photo by Ezra Shaw/Getty Images.
Page 197: Top ©2002 NBA Entertainment. Photo by Nathaniel S. Butler/NBAE/Getty Images. Bottom left 2001. Photo by Andy Lyons/Getty Images. Bottom right ©2002 NBA Entertainment. Photo by Noah Graham/NBAE/Getty Images.
Page 198: University of Southern California.
Page 199: ©2002 NBA Entertainment. Photo by Andrew D. Bernstein/NBAE/Getty Images.
Page 201: 2003. Photo by Jeff Gross/Getty Images.
Page 202: 2002. Photo by Lisa Blumenfeld/Getty Images.
Page 203: ©2002 NBA Entertainment. Photo by Andrew D. Bernstein/NBAE/Getty Images.
Page 205: ©2004 NBA Entertainment. Photo by Andrew D. Bernstein/NBAE/Getty Images.
Page 206: Left 2003. Photo by Lisa Blumenfeld/Getty Images. Right 2001. Photo by Lucy Nicholson/AFP/Getty Images.
Page 207: Top ©2004 NBA Entertainment. Photo by Andrew D. Bernstein/NBAE/Getty Images. Bottom left ©2003 NBA Entertainment. Photo by Rocky Widner/NBAE/Getty Images. Bottom right ©2004 NBA Entertainment. Photo by Kent Smith/NBAE/Getty Images.
Page 209: Top ©2005 NBA Entertainment. Photo by Fernando Medina/NBAE/Getty Images. Bottom left ©2005 NBA Entertainment. Photo by Juan Ocampo/NBAE/Getty Images. Bottom right ©2005 NBA Entertainment. Photo by Juan Ocampo/NBAE/Getty Images.
Page 211: ©2005 NBA Entertainment. Photo by Fernando Medina/NBAE/Getty Images.
Page 212: ©2006 NBA Entertainment. Photo by Jeffrey Bottari/NBAE/Getty Images.
Page 213: Top ©2006 NBA Entertainment. Photo by Noah Graham/NBAE/Getty Images. Bottom ©2005 NBA Entertainment. Photo by Andrew D. Bernstein/NBAE/Getty Images.
Page 215: ©2007 NBA Entertainment. Photo by Joe Murphy/NBAE/Getty Images.
Page 216: ©2006 NBA Entertainment. Photo by Rocky Widner/NBAE/Getty Images.
Page 217: Top 2006. Photo by Lisa Blumenfeld/Getty Images. Bottom left ©2006 NBA Entertainment. Photo by Andrew D. Bernstein/NBAE/Getty Images. Bottom right ©2006 NBA Entertainment. Photo by Fernando Medina/NBAE/Getty Images.
Page 218: 2008. Photo by John W. McDonough/Sports Illustrated/Getty Images.
Page 219: ©2008 NBA Entertainment. Photo by Sam Forencich/NBAE/Getty Images.
Page 220: ©2008 NBA Entertainment. Photo by Evan Gole/NBAE/Getty Images.
Page 221: ©2008 NBA Entertainment. Photo by Jesse D. Garrabrant/NBAE/Getty Images.
Page 223: ©2009 NBA Entertainment. Photo by Andrew D. Bernstein/NBAE/Getty Images.
Page 224: ©2009 NBA Entertainment. Photo by Noah Graham/NBAE/Getty Images.
Page 225: Top 2009. Photo by Chris Graythen/Getty Images. Bottom left ©2007 NBA Entertainment. Photo by David Sherman/NBAE/Getty Images. Bottom right ©2009 NBA Entertainment. Photo by Andrew D. Bernstein/NBAE/Getty Images.
Page 227: 2009. Photo by Ronald Martinez/Getty Images.
Pages 228 and 229: ©2009 NBA Entertainment. Photo by Andrew D. Bernstein/NBAE/Getty Images.
Page 230: Top 1969. Photo by George Long/WireImage/Getty Images. Bottom ©2000 NBA Entertainment. Photo by Andrew D. Bernstein/NBAE/Getty Images.
Page 231: Top 1968. Photo by George Long/Sports Illustrated/Getty Images. Bottom ©2000 NBA Entertainment. Photo by Andrew D. Bernstein/NBAE/Getty Images.
Page 232: Top 1970. Photo by James Drake/Sports Illustrated/Getty Images. Bottom ©2000 NBA Entertainment. Photo by Andrew D. Bernstein/NBAE/Getty Images.
Page 233: Top ©1983 NBA Entertainment. Photo by Andrew D. Bernstein/NBAE/Getty Images. Bottom ©2000 NBA Entertainment. Photo by Andrew D. Bernstein/NBAE/Getty Images.
Page 234: Top 1980. Photo by Manny Millan/Sports Illustrated/Getty Images. Bottom ©2000 NBA Entertainment. Photo by Andrew D. Bernstein/NBAE/Getty Images.
Page 235: Top 1986. Photo by Dick Raphael/Sports Illustrated/Getty Images. Bottom ©2000 NBA Entertainment. Photo by Andrew D. Bernstein/NBAE/Getty Images.
Page 236: Top 1972. Photo by Walter Iooss Jr./Sports Illustrated/Getty Images. Bottom ©2000 NBA Entertainment. Photo by Andrew D. Bernstein/NBAE/Getty Images.
Page 237: Top row (Baylor)1966. Photo by James Drake/Sports Illustrated/Getty Images. (Chamberlain) 1972. Walter Iooss Jr./Sports Illustrated/Getty Images. (West) 1972. Photo by Darryl Norenberg/WireImage/Getty Images. Middle row (Abdul-Jabbar) 1984. Photo by John W. McDonough/Sports Illustrated/Getty Images. (Goodrich) 1973. Photo by Walter Iooss Jr./Sports Illustrated/Getty Images. (Johnson) ©1990 NBA Entertainment. Photo by Jon SooHoo/NBAE/Getty Images. (Worthy) 1993. Photo by Al Bello/Getty Images. Bottom row (Sharman) ©1972 NBA Entertainment. Photo by Wen Roberts/NBAE/Getty Images. (Jackson) 2009. Photo by John W. McDonough/Sports Illustrated/Getty Images. (Newell) ©2002 NBA

Entertainment. Photo by Jennifer Pottheiser/NBAE/Getty Images. (Hearn) ©2002 NBA Entertainment. Photo By Andrew D. Bernstein/NBAE/Getty Images.

Page 238: 1982. Photo by Paul Kennedy/Sports Illustrated/Getty Images.

Page 239: Top right ©1990 NBA Entertainment. Photo by Andrew D. Bernstein/NBAE/Getty Images. Bottom left 1986. Photo by Stephen Dunn/Allsport/Getty Images.

Page 240: ©1971 NBA Entertainment. Photo by Wen Roberts/NBAE/Getty Images.

Page 243: Left to right (Bryant) 2000. Photo by Donald Miralle/Allsport/Getty Images. (West) 1968. Photo by George Long/Sports Illustrated/Getty Images. (Baylor) 1966. Photo by James Drake/Sports Illustrated/Getty Images. (Johnson) ©1990 NBA Entertainment. Photo by Jon SooHoo/NBAE/Getty Images. (Abdul-Jabbar) 1970s. Photo by Focus on Sport/Getty Images.

Page 246: ©2001 NBA Entertainment. Photo by Andrew Bernstein/NBAE/Getty Images.

Page 247: 1973. Photo by Walter Iooss Jr./Sports Illustrated/Getty Images.

Page 248: Left and right ©2008 NBA Entertainment. Photos by Juan O'Campo/NBAE/Getty Images.

Page 256: Left 1963. Photo by Marvin E. Newman/Sports Illustrated/Getty Images. Right 2009. Associated Press Photo/Reed Saxon.

Back Book Cover: Left to right (Worthy)1986. Photo by Dick Raphael/Sports Illustrated/Getty Images. (Baylor) 1969. Photo by George Long/WireImage/Getty Images. (Goodrich) 1972. Photo by Walter Iooss Jr./Sports Illustrated/Getty Images. (O'Neal) ©1997 NBA Entertainment. Photo by John SooHoo/NBAE/Getty Images. Photo of Phil Jackson ©2008 NBA Entertainment. Photo by Andrew D. Bernstein/NBAE/Getty Images.

Key to Celebrity Fans
Appearing on page 105

1. Johnny Carson
2. Dyan Cannon
3. Eddie Murphy
4. Diane Keaton
5. Jennifer Finnigan; Jonathan Silverman
6. Adrien Brody
7. Zac Efron; Vanessa Hudgens
8. Denzel Washington; DJ AM
9. Jessica Biel; Justin Timberlake
10. Leonardo DiCaprio
11. Ashton Kutcher; Demi Moore
12. Will Ferrell
13. Garry Shandling; David Duchovny
14. Drew Barrymore
15. LL Cool J
16. David Beckham
17. Dr. Dre with daughter Truly
18. Arnold Schwarzenegger
19. Dennis Hopper
20. Bill Murray; Magic Johnson
21. Maria Shriver with children Christina, Patrick, and Christopher
22. Steven Spielberg
23. Dustin Hoffman; Kobe Bryant
24. Kevin James; Adam Sandler
25. Neil Patrick Harris
26. Kelsey Grammer
27. Seal; Heidi Klum
28. Jack Nicholson; Magic Johnson

Los Angeles Times Writers

The work of these current and former Los Angeles Times *reporters and columnists whose stories appear in this book can be found in the newspaper's archives at* latimes.com *along with Lakers coverage by other* Times *staff members over the past fifty years.*

J.A. Adande was a *Times* sportswriter and columnist whose Lakers coverage included the arrival of Phil Jackson in 1999. He now works for ESPN.

Thomas Bonk was a *Times* beat writer who covered the Lakers for three seasons in the splendor of Showtime. He now works for *golfdigest.com*.

Mike Bresnahan is *The Times'* Lakers' beat writer whose most recent work included the 2009 NBA playoffs and Finals.

Tim Brown was a *Times* beat writer who covered the Lakers' "Three-Peat" championship teams. He now covers baseball for *Yahoo! Sports*.

Dwight Chapin was a Times sportswriter in the 1960s onward. He later worked for the *San Francisco Chronicle*.

Mike Downey was a *Times* columnist who wrote about the Lakers in the 1990s before becoming a Metro columnist. He returned to sports writing for the *Chicago Tribune*.

Bill Dwyre was *The Times'* sports editor before becoming a columnist. He covers all sports.

Gordon Edes was a *Times* beat writer who covered the Lakers' championship series against the Detroit Pistons in 1988. He now writes about baseball for *Yahoo! Sports*.

Mal Florence was a *Times* beat writer who covered the Wilt Chamberlain era, including the 1972 NBA championship season.

Ted Green was a *Times* beat reporter covering the Lakers pre-Showtime and into the 1980s. He is now a sports television producer in Los Angeles.

Dan Hafner was a *Times* beat writer who covered the Lakers in the 1960s.

Randy Harvey was a *Times* beat writer and columnist who covered the heyday of Showtime in the mid-1980s. He later became sports editor at the *Baltimore Sun* and *Los Angeles Times* and is associate editor of *The Times*.

Mark Heisler is *The Times'* national NBA columnist and a former beat writer. Selected for Basketball Hall of Fame's Curt Gowdy Media Award in 2006, he has written extensively about the Lakers since the 1980s.

Scott Howard-Cooper was a *Times* basketball writer who covered Magic Johnson and James Worthy, among others. He later worked at the *Sacramento Bee* and now writes about the NBA for *SI.com*.

Tim Kawakami was a *Times* beat writer whose coverage included the 1999–2000 championship season. Kawakami later became a columnist for the *San Jose Mercury News*.

Charles Maher was a *Times* columnist who wrote about the Lakers in the 1970s.

Sam McManis was a *Times* beat writer who wrote about Lakers Coach Pat Riley in the 1990 season. McManis is a columnist for the *Sacramento Bee*.

Jim Murray, *The Times'* late Pulitzer Prize-winning columnist, wrote about the Lakers from their arrival in L.A. to the dawn of the Kobe Bryant era.

Scott Ostler was a *Times* beat writer and columnist who covered the blossoming of Showtime in the early 1980s. He is a columnist for the *San Francisco Chronicle*.

Bill Plaschke is an award-winning *Times* columnist whose coverage of the Lakers has included player profiles, game stories, and the team's run to the championship in 2009.

Mel Zikes was a *Times* beat writer whose coverage of the Lakers began with their first exhibition game on October 9, 1960, in Los Angeles.

Several books about the Lakers have been written by L.A. Times staff writers including: **Steve Springer**, a chronicler of Lakers history, and Magic Johnson, *Chick: His Unpublished Memoirs and the Memories of Those Who Loved Him; The Los Angeles Times' Encyclopedia of the Lakers*; and **Scott Ostler** and **Springer**, *Winnin' Times: The Magical Journey of the Los Angeles Lakers*; **Mark Heisler**, *Kobe and the New Lakers Dynasty; Madmen's Ball: The Continuing Saga of Kobe, Phil, and the Los Angeles Lakers*; and *The Lives of Riley*; and **Tim Kawakami** and **Scott Howard-Cooper**, *Laker Glory: The 2000 NBA Champions.*

EPILOGUE

The challenge, when the Lakers moved to Los Angeles in 1960, was not to tap into the area's love for pro basketball, but to create it. Mediocrity would be fatal to the struggling franchise; the Lakers would have to electrify. Central Casting delivered Elgin Baylor and Jerry West. To teammates, they were Motormouth and Zeke From Cabin Creek. To opponents, they were unstoppable. To their fans, they were dazzling. Baylor and West, joined at the heart, defined Lakers basketball for a half century. In 2009, Los Angeles honored them with a plaque at the Coliseum, only yards away from where it all started, a million thrills ago, and just down the road from where it continues today. —Scott Ostler

Long Before Showtime, They Were the Lakers' Show

By BILL DWYRE
February 5, 2009

Playing the game of basketball, in a city that didn't notice or care at first, they were joined at the hip. Still are.

Elgin Baylor and Jerry West were the basement cement blocks on the ritzy high-rise building now known as the Los Angeles Lakers. Long before much of the ga-ga masses who now worship the Purple and Gold were even born, Baylor and West were piling bricks and spreading plaster.

Before Kobe, before Shaq, even before Magic, the seed of professional basketball in the West was planted by Baylor and West. They were the pied pipers, the water on the sapling.

On Wednesday they stood in the peristyle end of the Los Angeles Memorial Coliseum, two 70-somethings, shoulder-to-shoulder in front of a bronze plaque, with photographers clicking away. They were there for recognition, both fitting and overdue. So were the words that began the first two paragraphs on the plaque:

"Jerry West was fire."

"Elgin Baylor was ice."

Until a few years ago, these Coliseum ceremonies honored only the dead, and only those who had accomplished a measure of their excellence in the Coliseum. But Coliseum Commissioners David Israel and Zev Yaroslavsky led a movement to extend those honors to the living, and to the entire complex, which includes the Sports Arena.

Baylor and West were obvious choices. Baylor and West together even more so . . .

The master of ceremonies was Tommy Hawkins, for five years a teammate of Baylor and West after the Lakers moved . . . to the

Sports Arena in 1960 . . . The laughs came easily.

"We got here a few years after the Dodgers," Hawkins said. "They arrived on airplanes, greeted by a crowd of thousands, and they had a parade. We drove in through San Bernardino at midnight. Nobody knew and nobody cared."

Both Hawkins and Baylor joked about that first year in the Sports Arena.

"We'd come back from a two-week trip," Hawkins said, "and we'd get off the plane and they put us in vans and trucks with speakers on the top and they'd give us a script and we'd drive around the city, reading: 'Hi there. I'm Tommy Hawkins of the Lakers. We're back in town after a two-week trip and we'll have five games at home. First up, the Knicks on Tuesday night.'"

[Mitch] Kupchak, [the Lakers' general manager], speaking later, said, "I'm having trouble visualizing Kobe and Pau Gasol, riding through the streets with a speaker system . . ."

There was much banter about Kobe's recent 61-point game against the Knicks in the current Madison Square Garden. Baylor once had 71 in the old building . . .

[Former Laker Keith] Erickson said that West was the only player he has ever seen who could score 40 points in a game in which his hamstring was torn and he couldn't run. He said Baylor once "averaged a couple of ticks under 20 rebounds a game for the entire season, and now, one of these guys gets 15 one night and they hold a parade . . ."

Baylor said he was honored to have West as a friend, and West, four years younger than Baylor at 70, said Baylor had been a mentor and he had never told him that . . .

In the end, even though they had worked for other teams . . . they were both Lakers, together, through and through.

Nobody can ever question that. It is there, in bronze.

Bill Plaschke
Big Ben Is Ready for Prime Time

In Seattle, 12th Man Sounds Off

l Night for Lakers

For McAdoo, Proof Is All in the Winning

San Diego May Get Lakers (on TV)
A Cable Deal Could Soothe Bucks in Move of Clippers to L.A.

LAKERS BEAT CELTICS AS BAYLOR G...

L.A. Takes 3-2 Lead in Playoff

Jim Murray
Bullpens and Broz

Los Angeles Times
Sports

Dodgers Nip Braves Before 48,486

Walls' Hit Decide It in 9th, 5-4 — RODGERS HERO OF 12.5 ANGEL ROMP

Traffic Jam Turns Fans Away From Ball Game

Giant Homers Crush Errant Cincy, 13-6

Oxy Captures Mile Relay to Nip UCLA, 66½-64½; Yang Gets 18

Chamberlain Reportedly Traded to Lakers

Laver Chops Up Roche in Final at Wimbledon
Over Fellow Aussie Pro in Duel of Southpaws

Rigney Criticizes Bullpen Following Angel's 5-1 Loss

Reds Whip Dodgers in 12th, 2-0

Trevino Shoots 4-Under 68, Leads Boros by One in Buick

BASEBALL STANDINGS

It Rains Base Hits for Orioles at Three (Four?) Rivers
8-4 Win Puts Baltimore 1 Up; Garcia 4 for 4

Jim Murray
They Call This Genius?

Sports

Jabbar's Hook at Buzzer Beats Clippers, 103-102
Lakers Rally to Win in Final Minute Despite 46 Points by Free; Magic Scores 26 in Debut

It's the Stanford Arms Against the USC Legs

WEAVER'S CHANGES PAY OFF BIG

SPORTS

Abdul-Jabbar Hits Jackpot With Sky Hook in Las Vegas

New Record-Holder Is a New Man

Dodgers Start Anderson, Finish Cardinals on Homer by Marshall in the 12th, 5-2

Still Shining

This Time, Angels Turn Tie in Ninth Into a 7-4 Defeat

SPORTS

F LAKERS

Boston Recovers in Time to Hand Yankees 9-7 Loss

It's MAGIC!
'How else can I explain those rainbows when there is no rain?'

The New Starting Center Puts Lakers Over the Top, 123-107

PARTY TIME
Magic Tells the Captain: Let's Dance

Sports

76ers' Fondest Dream Winds Up a Nightmare

THE MAGIC NUMBERS

Reuss Gives the Dodgers a Start and an 8-6 Win

FILLY VS. NEW FACES IN PREAKNESS

Los Angeles Times
NBA FINALS
99 GAME 5 86
PLAYER OF THE GAME

RING IT UP!

Lakers finish off Magic for 15th NBA title, their 10th in L.A. Jackson's record 10th as a coach and Kobe's fourth — and his first without Shaq

It didn't exactly go as planned, but the result was expected and we even learned a thing or two

Bryant, the Finals MVP, says 'I don't have to hear that idiotic criticism anymore' after decisive Game 5 win

Inside: Blake powers Dodgers past Texas; Weaver sharp again as Angels blank Padres. Section C

SPORTS

L.A. GOES WILD! LAKERS WORLD CHAMPS
Wilt Shrugs Off Injury, Leads 114-100 Win Over Knicks

Sports

he Beginning to the End, It's Magic

West Finally Plays on an NBA Winner

THE CHAMPIONS!

Austrian Is King of Hill

Los Angeles Times
NBA CHAMPS
15 TITLES AND COUNTING

Los Angeles Times
NBA FINALS
GAME 5 • LAKERS 108, PHILADELPHIA 96

Baq to Baq

O'Neal Is MVP Again as Lakers Repeat Title Feat by Holding Off 76ers for the Fourth Game in a Ro

Bill Plaschke
Part I Was a Huge Hit but the Sequel Is an Epic

Perfectly Flawed, Became Nearly